Praise for *My Name Is Not Harry*

As he has done throughout his career as one of Canada's most distinguished journalists, Haroon has written a book which challenges us to aspire to build a more inclusive country. He does so with a critical but optimistic eye. Haroon personifies the motto of the Order of Canada: "They desire a better country."

— Michael Goldbloom, principal and vice-chancellor, Bishop's University, and former publisher, *Toronto Star* and *Montreal Gazette*

From the moment he arrived in his adopted country, Haroon Siddiqui taught us that sometimes it's the adopted country that must adapt to the newcomer, and not the other way around. Drawing on his family's deep tradition of Islamic scholarship and critical thinking, Siddiqui brought objective, equitable, post-colonial thinking to cozy, monarchist, Wonder Bread Canada of the late 1960s. In doing so, he was at least two decades ahead of his time.

— Michael Dan, neurosurgeon-turned advocate for human rights and social justice

Haroon Siddiqui's memoir is located in a dynamic and liminal place. He speaks to us from the spaces in between East and West, North and South, Muslims and non-Muslims. Siddiqui is a leading voice of Canadian cosmopolitanism. His witty, informative, and unapologetic book is a vital record of the time when large-scale immigration and war transformed this country.

— Karim H. Karim, chancellor's professor, journalism and communication, Carleton University

Haroon Siddiqui has written a beautiful memoir. It is, of course, his story and a rich, fascinating one at that. But as always with Haroon, when he writes, we learn about ourselves as human beings and as Canadians. Brilliant.

— Kathleen Wynne, former premier, Ontario

Wow, just wow. An absolutely incredible book. If ever there has been a mind ready to explore the untold side of a story, a voice ready to speak about hard truths, and a man with an unwavering commitment to rights and justice, that is Haroon. This sweeping memoir shows us why. We are a richer nation for his insights and his words.

— ALEX NEVE, former secretary general, Amnesty International Canada

This is a love letter to the new Canada that allows its citizens, whether a Harry or a Haroon, to be what they are and what they want to be. An extraordinary memoir. Of his youth in India, his enduring fascination with cricket and with food — yes, foods of India and elsewhere.

— JOHN ENGLISH, chair, Canadian International Council

Haroon Siddiqui is a brilliant writer, with a wit as sharp as his insight. This memoir takes us from British India to post-9/11 Canada through the voice of a true pioneer. Before there was a Naheed Nenshi or an Omar Sachedina or a Farrah Nasser, there was Haroon Siddiqui. When I was growing up, he was often the only person of colour and the only Muslim with a strong journalistic voice on the national stage. He continues to open our eyes and build our nation.

— NAHEED NENSHI, former mayor, Calgary

An outstanding memoir, beautifully written. Tells the fascinating story of Siddiqui's life, from his early years in India during and after Independence to his nearly fifty years as a nationally respected journalist in Canada. He chronicles the multicultural evolution of Canada in the same well researched, highly readable, and candid manner that we have come to expect. As always, his passion for social justice shines through.

— DENNIS O'CONNOR, former associate chief justice of Ontario and head of the Maher Arar Commission of Inquiry

Canada is an oasis of multicultural harmony in an increasingly fractious world where the liberal order is in disarray, and isolationism and majoritarianism are ascendant. This book shows how and why Canada is so splendidly different. Haroon Siddiqui is a uniquely Canadian talent. He's at home in different milieus, and he bridges disparate worlds and finds common ground. He personifies the new confident Canada.

— SIR CHRISTOPHER ONDAATJE, former Bay St. banker and bob-sledding Olympian, adventurer, and author

There's massive Islamophobia in the Western world, and anybody who pretends that's not the case is either unconcerned with the truth or hasn't been paying attention. Haroon Siddiqui offers a distinctive and insightful perspective on being Muslim in the post-9/11 world.

— CHARLES TAYLOR, professor emeritus, McGill University

The gift of honesty is precious: it radiates through this book. A rich and wonderful read.

His words call us to intellectual honesty. We do need this reminder.

— NATHALIE DES ROSIERS, principal, Massey College, University of Toronto

What a great read. A thoroughly engaging, frank, and insightful memoir by one of the major international journalists of our time.

— JOHN L. ESPOSITO, distinguished professor, Walsh School of Foreign Service, Georgetown University

Haroon Siddiqui is among our keenest observers of world politics, not only because of his critical acumen and searing honesty but because he is a global thinker with a cosmopolitan vision, in contrast to so many merely provincial North American journalists. His memoirs show why.

— JUAN COLE, Richard P. Mitchell Collegiate professor of history, and director, Arab and Muslim American Studies, University of Michigan

Praise for the Author

Haroon Siddiqui is a trailblazer of astonishing vision and compassionate decency. Nuanced and brilliant, he is unique in the pantheon of great Canadian journalists.

— Right Honourable Adrienne Clarkson,
26th governor general of Canada

[Siddiqui] opened the eyes and ears of Canadians to the world around them.

— Jean Chrétien, 20th prime minister of Canada

He is one of Canada's most outstanding journalists.

— Roy McMurtry, former Ontario chief justice

Haroon attacks sacred cows. He's not afraid to be unpopular. He has made a real difference, and that's a real tribute to a journalist.

— John Honderich, former publisher, *Toronto Star*

We wanted to light candles, we were so happy [when he was named editorial page editor of the *Toronto Star* in 1990].

— Carol Tator, York University academic,
co-author of *The Colour of Democracy*

He doesn't speak with the same voice as the majority media voice. He doesn't write from the perspective of the old generation of Canadian journalists.

— John Fraser, former master, Massey College, University of Toronto

Before most everyone else, there was Haroon Siddiqui. At a time when too much of our thinking was inward, Haroon reminded us of Canada's important role in the world, and the potential for progressive and enlightened global engagement. We've been fortunate that Haroon's unique lifetime journalistic experience has been at the service of all Canadians over several decades.

— Tony Burman, former editor-in-chief, *CBC News*,
former managing director, Al Jazeera English

He is an extraordinary man of real distinction whose contribution to this country has been of far-reaching influence. He spreads a message that goes far deeper than the concepts of tolerance, which used to be our goal. He consistently has sought to walk the often-besieged middle way.

— JUNE CALLWOOD, author, activist

Haroon and I did not always agree, sometimes passionately so. Yet our disagreements were always anchored on understanding and civility. On the battle against racism, xenophobia, anti-Semitism, and Islamophobia, we were as one.

— BERNIE FARBER, former head, Canadian Jewish Congress

He provided a moral compass and created an atmosphere of open discussion, vigorous debate, and a mandate to push the causes of social justice.

— ROYSON JAMES, former *Toronto Star* columnist

He is an exemplary illustration of the fact that some of the best Canadians are those who chose this country, as compared to those of us who had the good fortune to be born here.

— FIL FRASER, former president and CEO, Vision TV

Throughout his career, Haroon has quietly effected change, and it has been a change for the better. Canada is a much stronger nation for the many accomplishments of Haroon Siddiqui.

— MICHAEL MARZOLINI, founder and chair, Pollara Strategic Insights

His unwavering commitment to the basic principle of fairness remains an inspiration to a generation of Canadian journalists and their readers.

— KATHY ENGLISH, chair, Canadian Journalism Foundation

Haroon Siddiqui brings three key components to his work: new research, original thoughts, and rich, incisive writing. Never preaching, he seeks to persuade his readers to reflect upon issues.

— NATIONAL NEWSPAPER AWARDS

My Name Is Not Harry

My Name Is Not Harry

Haroon Siddiqui A Memoir

DUNDURN PRESS

Copyright © Haroon Siddiqui, 2023

All rights reserved. No part of this publication may be reproduced, stored in a retrieval system, or transmitted in any form or by any means, electronic, mechanical, photocopying, recording, or otherwise (except for brief passages for purpose of review) without the prior permission of Dundurn Press. Permission to photocopy should be requested from Access Copyright.

Publisher: Kwame Scott Fraser | Acquiring editor: Russell Smith | Editor: Michael Carroll
Cover designer: Laura Boyle, based on concept by Faisal Siddiqui

Library and Archives Canada Cataloguing in Publication

Title: My name is not Harry : a memoir / Haroon Siddiqui.
Names: Siddiqui, Haroon, author.
Description: Includes bibliographical references and index.
Identifiers: Canadiana (print) 20230467776 | Canadiana (ebook) 20230467814 | ISBN 9781459748903 (softcover) | ISBN 9781459748910 (PDF) | ISBN 9781459748927 (EPUB)
Subjects: LCSH: Siddiqui, Haroon. | LCSH: Muslims—Canada—Biography. | LCSH: Muslims—Canada—Social conditions. | LCSH: Muslims—India—Social conditions. | LCSH: Islamophobia—Canada. | LCSH: Islamophobia—India. | LCSH: Newspaper editors—Canada—Biography. | LCGFT: Autobiographies.
Classification: LCC FC106.M9 Z7 2023 | DDC 305.6/970971092—dc23

We acknowledge the support of the Canada Council for the Arts and the Ontario Arts Council for our publishing program. We also acknowledge the financial support of the Government of Ontario, through the Ontario Book Publishing Tax Credit and Ontario Creates, and the Government of Canada.

Care has been taken to trace the ownership of copyright material used in this book. The author and the publisher welcome any information enabling them to rectify any references or credits in subsequent editions.

The publisher is not responsible for websites or their content unless they are owned by the publisher.

Printed and bound in Canada.

Dundurn Press
1382 Queen Street East
Toronto, Ontario, Canada M4L 1C9
dundurn.com, @dundurnpress

Dedication

Many people shaped my life and thus this memoir.

In India, parents Hafiz Mohammed Moosa and Hafiza Amtul Baseer blessed me and my siblings with a gloriously happy childhood. They excused my early failures — at pre-med, pre-engineering, even cricket — and my meanderings through a science degree and English literature.

T.G. Vaidyanathan, my dear English prof and mentor, nudged me into journalism. S.A. Govindarjan, journalism prof, inculcated reportorial discipline and got me started with an internship at the *Hindu*, an outstanding secular newspaper, headquartered in Chennai.

Uncle Hafiz Syed Sarwar Hussain taught me the Qur'an and Islam — "Smile, you're a Muslim."

Roland Michener, high commissioner to India, said, "Young men like you should go to Canada."

In Canada, Clark Davey, managing editor of the *Globe and Mail*, offered no job but opened the door to the *Brandon Sun* in Manitoba.

Lew Whitehead, owner-publisher there, a gem of a man, let me spread my wings for a decade.

Ray Timson, managing editor of the mighty *Toronto Star*, hired me. Beland Honderich and son John, publishers both, gave free rein to my mostly dissident views for 38 years. And let me promote diversity of content and personnel, not only at the paper but across Canada.

Brothers Suleman and Yousuf helped maintain family bonds across the oceans, especially after the premature deaths of our dear sisters, Amina, Maryam, and Syeda.

At home, wife Yasmeen and sons Fahad and Faisal, and their wives Fatema and Elizabeth, each highly successful in their own right, form a loving family that also serves as an emotional and intellectual anchor.

And, finally, Canada — our home and native and adopted land — that made my journey possible without compromising my self-esteem or my conscience.

Contents

1	Expo 67	1
2	Ram and Rumi	13
3	The Milieu That Made Me	29
4	The End of Colonialism	43
5	The Fall of Hyderabad	53
6	Happy Childhood	67
7	The Making of a Journalist	89
8	End of the Good Life	113
9	An "Indian" on the Prairies	125
10	Good to Go at a Moment's Notice	151
11	In the Trenches	171
12	The Browning of Canada	185
13	The Editorial Perch	199
14	Multicultiphobia	219
15	Becoming a Columnist	239
16	Post-9/11 Canada	257
17	Afghanistan and Iraq Wars	275
18	Cultural Warfare on Muslims	297
19	Harper and Muslims	317
20	Media and Muslims	335
21	Rushdie and Muslims	359
22	An Incurably Optimistic Canadian	381
	Acknowledgements	401
	Notes	403
	Image Credits	415
	Index	417
	About the Author	451

Retirement send-off by *Toronto Star* cartoonist Patrick Corrigan, 2015.

1

Expo 67

LANDING IN MONTREAL DAYS BEFORE THE CLOSING OF EXPO 67, I WAS asked by the immigration officer the rote question: What are you bringing into Canada? Not much. Clothes, books, and $150 — or was it $200? — the maximum foreign exchange allowed out of India in those days.

That, however, wasn't the whole truth, now that I think about it five decades later. I was also bringing my cross-cultural Indian genes and my family DNA. Both were to prove decisive in Canada, especially after 9/11 when I was turned overnight from a columnist who happened to be Muslim into a Muslim columnist whose only job was to apologize for my faith and condemn fellow Muslims. Being an Uncle Tom wasn't part of the family ethos — several ancestors had stood up to the sultans of their day. My second column after 9/11, "It's the U.S. Foreign Policy, Stupid," evinced much abuse, as would dozens of others in the following months and years, including the ones opposing the war on Iraq under false pretences and the endless war on terror.

I was labelled an apologist for terrorism, Saddam Hussein, and the Third World. Any terrorist incident anywhere and I'd be asked: "What do *you* have to say about this?" I was deemed personally responsible. Dinner invitations dried up. Those who used to woo me because of my position stopped calling. Acquaintances avoided eye contact. There was social media bullying. Poison oozed out of the nearly 40,000 emails and other responses to my columns, even as a majority of respondents by far remained quintessentially Canadian

— polite, fair, open-minded, and committed to the idea that Canada became a light unto nations not by imitating the United States or Europe but by setting its own high standards.

Having never faced outright racism in Canada, this hatred seemed un-Canadian. Perhaps it wasn't. Japanese Canadians, like Japanese Americans, were interned during the Second World War. Post-9/11, Canadian and American Muslims were similarly burdened with collective guilt and made to feel psychologically interned.

With Islamophobia being the new anti-Semitism, old anti-Jewish tropes have been applied to Muslims: Islam is incompatible with secularism, just as Judaism was said to be; Muslims can't be trusted, just as Jews couldn't be; Muslims harbour dual loyalty, just as Jews did and ostensibly still do; Muslims wield too much influence, as did the Jews and still do; and sharia is seditious, just as Jewish religious law was alleged to be. Sure enough, polls confirmed that religious antipathy toward Jews ran not that far behind hostility toward Muslims, especially in Quebec.

For columnists, criticism and excoriation come with the turf. We develop thick hides. Still, the post-9/11 hysteria was potent, combining religious bigotry with racism. Internet bullying was in its infancy, and I was accorded the dubious distinction of being among its early victims. Yet I didn't lose sleep over it.

What sustained me was not some grand ideology or a heroic act of courage but simply the "baggage from back home," an ethos of rolling with the punches and a reflexive recoiling from the American imperial proclivity of pulverizing weaker nations and the Western habit of abandoning minorities exactly when they most need protection. Those instincts helped make me a more useful Canadian, as they also did during such reporting stints as the Soviet invasion of Afghanistan and the Islamic Revolution in Iran.

So there's something to be said about immigrants who are well anchored and arrive brimming with self-confidence, a sense of self-worth, and a view of the world different than that of the native-born. They resist admonitions to "do in Rome as the Romans do." They follow the law, of course, our common holy parchment. Anything beyond that is subjective, often a tool to lord over newcomers. Immigrants are delighted to come, having chosen this land. But they

1 Expo 67

don't necessarily feel "grateful" for being given immigration — a contract of mutual benefit. They feel little or no need to apologize for their racial, religious, cultural, ethnic, and linguistic identity in deference to majoritarian mores. They don't pretend to develop amnesia the moment they arrive in Canada. Nor do they want to reinvent themselves, as did those who escaped the Iron Curtain and other hellholes and did very much want to forget what they left behind.

We, on the other hand, want to retain as much of our pasts as possible. In my case, a strong sense of self-identity born of an indulgent upbringing of unconditional love, and as an inheritor of thousands of years of Indian civilization as well as 1,500 years of Islamic religious, cultural, and literary heritage, I didn't feel inferior to anyone. I could go anywhere, knock on any door, walk into any room, meet anybody. My past was my pride and part of my present and my future.

Yet this valuable commodity counts for little on the point system by which Canada chooses immigrants based on education, skills, and proficiency in English or French. Nor is it properly acknowledged in the narratives of those who tell tales of having come with $5 in their pockets and made themselves billionaires by their own brilliance.

* * *

I hadn't heard of Toronto until I got to college where an eclectic English lecturer had us read a book published by the University of Toronto Press in 1945 — *Some Tasks for Education* by Sir Richard Livingstone. How and why he chose that book, we had no idea. Canada wouldn't loom large for me until a few years later when I worked at the Press Trust of India, the national news agency in Bombay (since renamed Mumbai).

To break the monotony of the midnight copy-editing shift, the chief editor, a crusty yet kind old man, agreed to let a colleague and me get some reporting assignments. There were diplomatic and trade events galore that the agency didn't bother to cover, but we could and did file a few paragraphs. That appealed particularly to my old classmate and roommate, Syed Sajjad Hyder, who was always looking for a free drink. We'd turn up at various consulates, no matter their insignificance or geopolitical affiliation. India was a non-aligned nation and so were we. It was for one such get-together at the plush Taj Hotel at India Gate by the Arabian Sea that Roland Michener, the Canadian high commissioner, flew in from Delhi. That proved to be a fateful encounter. In the chitter-chatter of the reception, he said, "Young men like you should go to Canada."

With youthful irreverence, I responded, "Why would anyone want to go to Canada. It's so cold there, isn't it?"

Not long after that I had to quit my job and go home to Hyderabad when my father, *abba* in Urdu, had a heart attack. As the older son, I was soon looking after Abba, his business, and the family.

* * *

A Canadian immigration officer was coming to Hyderabad to interview candidates. I got in on his roster at the last minute. He intimated that I'd make the cut. The bar to qualifying was low then. The offer lay dormant for a year — I had responsibilities — but I was granted an extension to enter Canada by the end of October 1967. I was caught between staying or leaving India: for Syracuse University where I had admission for graduate work in journalism; England where some college mates had gone on an easily obtainable work voucher; Australia where some cricketing friends, Christians mostly, had migrated; or act on the lucky accident of Mr. Michener's advice.

Staying a few days in London en route to Canada, I had the rude shock of having to get up in the middle of the night to feed shillings into a heat meter. This was the centre of the empire? But Westminster Bridge, Big Ben, and the parliamentary precincts seemed familiar, so etched had the landmarks been in our heads even in post-colonial India.

Montreal was exhilarating. People were swept up by the spirit of the Canadian centennial and Expo 67. Buckminster Fuller's geodesic dome was more dramatic than the geometric onion domes of great mosques and Sufi shrines. Moshe Safdie's Habitat housing complex came across as a dramatic, cleaner, multi-storied update of the dense shantytowns of Bombay.

The icing on the cake, though, was the homemade Indian food served by my host, a fellow Hyderabadi, Ali Hussain. He had come to study at McGill

1 Expo 67

University, stayed, and established himself as a chartered accountant. In the best Indian tradition, he had received the new arrival at the airport. Similarly, in Toronto, another fellow Hyderabadi, Siddiq Burney, was waiting at the bottom of the staircase at Union Station. He lived in a Thorncliffe Park high-rise that had an indoor swimming pool, a novelty for those of us from the tropics.

At the immigrant settlement centre downtown, the officials were helpful and generous — offering money for rent, winter clothing, and groceries unasked. Embarrassed, I wanted to find work quickly. I made my way to the *Globe and Mail* to meet Clark Davey, the managing editor. Cherubic, cheerful, chatty, welcoming. But he was emphatic in saying no to a job: "Go get some Canadian experience elsewhere first."

"But I already have experience," I replied.

He wasn't persuaded. "I had a bad experience with two fellows from India who couldn't write English."

"Are you penalizing me for your own bad hiring?"

"Yes," he said unapologetically. "But I can phone the owner of the *Brandon Sun* in Manitoba. It's a good paper."

"Why would anyone want to go to Manitoba? Isn't it even colder there than here?"

I emerged onto cold King Street determined to prove him wrong but at the same time with a vibe of warmth from him — a gruff uncle dishing out tough love.

The quickest available job was in sales at the Simpsons department store at Yonge and Queen Streets. I promptly applied and just as promptly got rejected. A fellow Hyderabadi, Desh Bandhu, working there couldn't believe it. "No one gets rejected around here," he told me. "You must've been awful in the interview." He soon got to the bottom of it. "Why the hell did you say you have two degrees? That makes you overqualified, you idiot! Go back, apply again, and say you only have matriculation."

"How can I do that?"

"Didn't you matriculate?" He then counselled me to wait a day or two before reapplying and to "make sure the lady who rejected you isn't there."

Selling men's clothing in the basement of the store was a good gig at around $85 per week plus commissions. Soon we were among the best dressed, thanks to our supervisor, Mr. Thomson, an early exponent of clearing out the inventory once enough profits had been made. He'd frequently discount leftover overcoats, suits, pants, whatever. If the items still didn't move, he'd let the staff buy at $20, $10, even $5.

He was an easy boss as long as we stayed on our toes and adhered to his two ironclad edicts: "Answer the damn phone" and "Customer is king, customer is never wrong," mottos that have long since been systematically set aside by both the private and public sectors. I've thought often of Mr. Thomson and also of the shoppers at Simpsons who were friendly, talkative, and inquisitive, especially about India — an invaluable orientation to Canadians for a new immigrant.

The only complaint about our Indian-ness that I overheard was by a gentleman in an apartment building where some friends lived. He wondered why Indians visiting each other lingered so very long in the corridors, elevators, and lobby: "Why can't they say their damn goodbyes inside the apartment and just leave?" Because they're Indian — relaxed about rules, exuberant yackety-yacks whose old-world protocol dictates they escort guests back to their cars.

Across from Simpsons, the lunch counter at Woolworths served hot pea soup. That lasted only until the revelation that it contained bits of bacon. Hot dogs not being our cup of tea, it was down to grilled cheese on white bread with fries and ketchup, bland and sweet, unlike the salty Indian variety with the zing of red chilies.

There were plenty of cuisine challenges. No lamb, no goat, only beef that I didn't grow up consuming. No yogurt, only something called sour cream, a blob that bloated the tummy. Very few fruits, vegetables, and spices. No guava, no mango, no papaya. No brinjal, no okra, no gourd. No coriander, no cloves, no cumin, no cardamom, no saffron, purportedly procurable only in some Ukrainian neighbourhoods around Easter. No basmati rice, only the short, stubby, parboiled kind that took forever to soften and came out clumpy, no doubt because we didn't know how to cook it.

Apprised of the sad state of affairs, my mother (*amma* in Urdu) in India said, "In that case, son, you'd better come back home."

There were other drawbacks.

No cricket. Nor any news about it, even in sports page statistics — this former dominion had failed to pick up the very best of England. Evenings were dull, barren of visible human activity except for people going pubbing, an alien concept for us. Sundays were deader — shops shut, roads deserted. Silent streets *sans* human beings took some getting used to.

A culture shock of another sort was to hear some men routinely refer to women as "bitches" — vulgarity I associated with the uncouth back home. Another was to see cheer girls in skimpy clothes perform for mostly men at televised football games. But one woman commanded reverence, the queen, whom we in India had gotten rid of long ago along with the maharajahs. One man who evinced frequent homages from Canadians was Winston Churchill, the racist. He who had labelled Indians "a barbarous people," "a beastly people with a beastly religion" (Hinduism), "the beastliest people in the world next to Germans." He had exacerbated the 1943 Bengal famine that had killed millions by insisting that Indian rice exports for the Allied war effort not be interrupted. He who had called Gandhi "a naked fakir" whom he wanted "bound hand and foot at the gates of Delhi and then trampled by an enormous elephant with the new [British] viceroy seated on its back."

The Orange parade on Yonge Street reminded me of the annual Shia Muslim mourning processions back home that raised sectarian Sunni-Shia passions, especially when one side took perverse pride in needling the other. I was told Toronto was the Belfast of Canada.

Yet I didn't feel out of place in Canada, perhaps because of the still-prevalent British accents — Ron Collister of the Canadian Broadcasting Corporation (CBC) sounded comforting. Politics seemed thrilling. A former prime minister, John Diefenbaker, was toppled just like that in a vote at a party convention in 1967. A year later, the Liberals elected an exciting leader, Pierre Elliott Trudeau. His rally at Nathan Phillips Square not far from Simpsons was more fun than the ones of Jawaharlal Nehru. I recall attending one with Abba. Tens of thousands turned up not so much to hear him but rather for *darshan*, viewing the great man. His speeches in Hindi mostly went over their heads in our part of the country. But it didn't matter.

Canadians were working their way out of a parochial, prejudiced past and learning to let immigrants, including non-white, non-Christian ones, keep their identity and dignity. They let me be. No one violated the core of my being. This Muslim from polyglot India could be at home in Canada.

A job in journalism remained elusive. The rejections piled up from the CBC, the *Toronto Star*, Toronto's *Telegram*, the *Hamilton Spectator*, and all the way down to the *Perth Courier*. No Canadian experience, which couldn't be acquired without a job, which couldn't be obtained without Canadian experience. A rigmarole that didn't apply to arrivals from Fleet Street who were welcomed by newspapers the way colonial outposts ushered in those from the head office.

The public relations department of Toronto Hydro said no, too. Just as well in retrospect.

It was time to swallow my pride and go back to Clark Davey. He was gracious. He called Brandon.

* * *

Arriving close to midnight at the isolated, dimly lit train station way north of Brandon, the four disembarked passengers were driven in a battered limo into darkness. No light in sight for kilometres. Then, a faint glow in the distance — ah, the town did have electricity! I felt stupid for having thought otherwise.

The next day, walking into the deserted weekend newsroom, I found a stout, bald, bespectacled gentleman who thrust his hand out. "I'm Garth Stouffer, news editor." He was quick to come to the point. "Do you know what frontage foot is?"

"No idea. Never heard of it."

"You better learn. You'll be covering City Council starting Monday."

"I will, but please, no chasing ambulances and cops."

"Okay," he said, and showed me to a metal desk.

Covering City Hall wasn't like covering cricket matches that were full of *tamasha*, the circus-like atmosphere of tens of thousands clapping and screaming. At Brabourne Stadium in Bombay, Garfield Sobers, the great West Indian cricketer from Barbados, had instantly fallen in love with a budding Bollywood actress, gotten engaged, and just as quickly called it off.

1 Expo 67

A stylish Indian batter, the handsome Abbas Ali Baig, a fellow Hyderabadi, inspired a young woman to bustle down from an elite stand and run onto the ground to plant a kiss, leaving him flushed and the stadium stunned. Now I was at a near-empty Brandon City Council chamber late at night, taking notes on a debate about the mill rate.

But soon there was the thrill of covering the 1969 Manitoba provincial election that brought about a revolution, a first-ever New Democratic Party (NDP) win under the dynamic leadership of Ed Schreyer. That was followed by a battle royal over the introduction of public auto insurance. It triggered the biggest-ever demonstration at the Legislative Assembly in Winnipeg, with dire warnings of socialists killing capitalism. Its noisy intensity and passion unnerved many a Manitoban. To me, it felt lively, very Indian. Schreyer faced a more mundane challenge: anti-monarchist Dippers were needling him about hosting Queen Elizabeth II for the 1970 Manitoba centennial. At his sprawling suburban bungalow, Cabbage Patch, he explained that Her Majesty's visit had been in the works for years and that he couldn't un-invite her. Making no headway, he snapped, "Look, my mother loves the queen, and that's good enough for me." He wasn't going to waste any political capital on the issue.

I was less prudent on the protocol with the queen. During that trip, I got too close to her at Canadian Forces Base Shilo as she signed the guest book "Elizabeth R"; I was shooed away by crusty Prince Philip. A few years later, I was in my office when the phone rang, with owner Lewis D. Whitehead summoning me to his office upstairs. He looked unusually grim. "I hear you didn't get up yesterday at the singing of 'God Save the Queen.'"

It had been at a Rotary lunch or perhaps the Lions Club. "Yes," I said sheepishly, "but you know, I'm not a monarchist and you're a skeptic yourself."

It didn't matter. "As long as she's the queen, you get up for the royal anthem."

"Yes, sir."

Mercifully, I hadn't had to publicly pronounce allegiance to the queen to become a Canadian. Those coming from a Commonwealth country didn't have to. We could sign a silent pledge on the citizenship application form, which I did and mailed the papers and received confirmation that I was a certified Canadian. Since then, the requirement has been standardized for all immigrants.

I had gone to Brandon with the intention of getting a year or two of experience but stayed 10 glorious years. The minus 35 cold was conquered after one or two debilitating experiences that made me cry — an immigrant's rite of passage to Canada. My yogurt supply had been engineered — Kala Gopinath, a friend, had gone to India and brought back a few spoons of culture, and once her first batch turned out well, the dozen or so Indian families were all set.

I might have been the first Muslim in Brandon in the contemporary era, though the Muslim presence in the Wheat City dated back to a Syrian-Lebanese family in the early 20th century. They were part of the first wave of Muslims to the Maritimes in the late 19th century from the Levant. There was no *jum'ah*, the Friday congregation, which like the Jewish *minyan*, requires a quorum — not 10 but at least three. No *halal* meat, which could only be found in Winnipeg, a two-hour drive. However, there was a Qur'anic alternative: "The food of those given the Scripture is lawful for you and your food is lawful for them" (Qur'an 5:5).

Ramadan in summer meant that the dawn-to-dusk fasting lasted 16 to 17 hours — the lunar calendar being 11 days shorter, Ramadan rotates through the seasons. Muslims in the Yukon and the Northwest Territories faced even longer fasting days. Guidance was sought from back home. One fatwa suggested that we follow the clock in the holy cities of Mecca and Medina. Another was more pragmatic: divide the day in half and fast for 12 hours — God having commanded the believers to make religion easy, not difficult. "Allah intends for you ease, not hardship" (Qur'an 2:185).

The *Brandon Sun* had a custom of distributing free turkeys for Christmas. In India, such freebies were given to the poor. I was quickly straightened out. I took mine and quietly passed it on to a neighbour, having never tasted the bird and not wanting to. No sooner had that awkward moment been dexterously managed than office colleague John Mayhew, a kindly Englishman, insisted on serving a leftover dinner on Boxing Day. I avoided the rubber, ate the alien trimmings.

After two promotions at the newspaper, I went to my first Canadian Managing Editors Conference, in St. John's, Newfoundland. That was 1974. At the opening reception, there was Clark Davey of the *Globe*. He beamed with pleasure — my presence told him that I'd made it.

"Now you can come to the *Globe* any time you want," he told me.

What a guy! "But I've just been promoted," I replied.

"Call me when you're ready," he insisted.

I did four years later in 1978. He offered me a job as his assistant, starting in the fall. A few weeks later, he phoned to let me know ahead of the news breaking that he was leaving the *Globe* to be publisher of the *Vancouver Sun*. But my job offer stood; he had arranged for me to be an editorial factotum for none other than the great Richard Doyle, editor-in-chief. But with Davey gone, I ended up taking an offer from the *Toronto Star*, courtesy of managing editor Ray Timson.

That year, Schreyer lost the election to Sterling Lyon. A stern fellow, he had been elected Conservative Party leader two years earlier, yet wouldn't learn to say my name. So one day I told him, "Premier, my name is not Harry. I don't want to be Harry. I am Haroon — that's my name."

2

Ram and Rumi

THE MOSQUE SHARES A WALL WITH THE HINDU TEMPLE. IT'S THE ONLY such neighbourly arrangement I know of in India, home to past Hindu-Muslim pogroms and a nasty sectarian present. On the Jama Masjid side of the wall is the courtyard where Muslims pray. On the other side are the deities of the Laxmi Narayana Mandir.

The twin places of worship are in my ancestral town of Kandhla, 89 kilometres northeast of Delhi. The mosque dates to the 14th century. The stone structure needed repairs in 1842, and the congregants proposed expanding it to the empty portion of the adjacent plot that had a small temple. The Hindus objected. The case went to court. Neither side had proper documentation. The British colonial judge suggested the parties bring reliable witnesses — a Muslim on behalf of Hindus and a Hindu to vouch for Muslims. The Hindus chose Maulana Shah Mahmud Baksh, a Sufi scholar respected for his integrity. My great-great-great-grand uncle, however, didn't want to appear before an English judge, given the family's increasing antipathy to British rule. The judge arranged to absent himself for Baksh's testimony. Baksh asserted that since the land belonged to the Hindus, it was entirely up to them what was or wasn't built on it.

The mosque and the mandir have existed ever since, the temple even expanding in the 1940s. In the early 20th century, the mosque is where *Dada* (my grandfather), Hafiz Mohammad Ismail, started a madrasah, a school for Islamic education — not the kind the Central Intelligence Agency (CIA) helped build in northern Pakistan in the 1980s to train and arm mujahideen guerrillas. Their job? Help end the Soviet occupation of Afghanistan.

Dada's madrasah is still there. It has about 50 students. They not only memorize the Qur'an and study Islamic history and ethics but also acquire computer skills and learn Hindi, the national language, as well as English. Dada Ismail, buried not too far away, might not approve — he and his contemporaries having actively boycotted English as part of India's struggle for independence.

Near the mosque is Durga Sweets, run by Sandeep Namdev Kumar, a Hindu. He's famous for his *gajar halwa* — grated carrots cooked in whole milk and sugar, laced with pure *ghee* (clarified butter), *khoya* (evaporated milk solids), and garnished with slivered pistachios and almonds. By the time we get to the shop during a 2017 trip, a box has already been deposited in our car for the return journey to Delhi. That's courtesy of our host, my cousin, Faizul Islam, whose property the shop is on.

I hadn't visited Kandhla for decades until 2015 to start retracing the lives of ancestors. In 2017, I returned with my younger brother, Suleman, and again, in 2019, with Suleman and our youngest brother, Yousuf.

Next door to Durga Sweets is Faizul Islam's ancestral house, a heritage property. No sooner do we arrive than a team of helpers serves a sumptuous lunch of chicken korma, daal, rice, and freshly cooked rotis, flatbread puffed up on a hot skillet and rushed to the dining table in a steady stream. When it's time to depart for Delhi, Faizul Islam locks the house, stands in the outer courtyard, presses his palms against the whitewashed wall, and intones the prayer for the safety of property and possessions, an insurance policy for the believers:

بِسْمِ اللّٰهِ، تَوَكَّلْتُ عَلَى اللّٰهِ، وَلَا حَوْلَ وَلَا قُوَّةَ إِلَّا بِاللّٰهِ

In the name of Allah, I place my trust in Allah and there is no might nor power except with Allah.

As we're slowly driven out of the street, Faizul Islam is greeted by shop-keepers, Muslim and Hindu alike: *"Namaste," "Salam Alaikum."* Some touch his extended hand, others hand him little paper bags, samples of their products — dry fruit, roasted peas, sweetmeat — which he accepts with the practised grace of a respected elder.

On the outskirts of the village, we stop at his farmhouse, surrounded by mango, guava, and lychee groves. They remind me of other family orchards I'd seen here on a visit in the 1940s, properties that were lost or confiscated during and after Partition in 1947 at the end of British colonial rule.

The First Siddiquis

Nearly two-thirds of Kandhla's current population of nearly 50,000 is Muslim. Their presence in the region goes back to the 12th century. That was when my first ancestor came from Iraq. Abu Sayeed Qadri was a native of Ray, near Tehran, long part of the Abbasid Empire, centred in Baghdad, the birthplace of Sufism. He came via Makran, the badlands between Iran and the northern outposts of old India, but now part of Pakistan. Settling in Kairana, 10 kilometres north of Kandhla, he traced his paternal lineage to Abu-Bakr Siddiq, the first caliph and successor to the Prophet Muhammad in 632 CE, and maternal lineage to the second caliph, Umar al-Khattab al-Faruq.

We are thus both Siddiquis and Faruqis.

Given Mufti Qadri's reputation as an Islamic jurist, the sultan of the day in Delhi bestowed on him the title of *Shaikhul Islam* (Shaykh of Islam). Kandhla is in a fertile area known as Do Aab, "Two Rivers," between the Ganges and the Jumuna. Besides its agricultural abundance, Kandhla was famous as a cradle of theologians, scholars, poets, and calligraphers.

A disproportionate number of the *ulama* (Islamic scholars) were from our family, who authored 90 percent of the nearly 750 books written by Kandhlavis. Of the nine notables listed by Wikipedia, six were family members. A 1963 Urdu book, *Mashaekh-e-Kandhla* (The Shaykhs of Kandhla), says:

> The Siddiquis were among the distinguished families of India
> who were the cradle of knowledge, intelligence, and purity.

…

The family's greatest treasure was its thirst for knowledge and scholarship, and its courage. These characteristics distinguished this family in every age. For centuries, the family produced *ulama* [religious scholars], *fuzala*, [virtuous persons], *ahl-e qalam* [wielders of the pen — authors], *sha-er* [poets], *muftis* [Islamic jurists], experts in both *maqul* [rational] and *manqul* [traditional] sciences, as well as physicians.

…

The sterling example the family has set in propagating knowledge and *islah* [reform, personal upliftment] is difficult to find anywhere else in the Muslim world in this age.

…

Despite their own hereditary scholarship, piety, and spirituality, one special characteristic of this family was its willingness to maintain relations with and attain knowledge from other scholars and Sufis of high merit.

The author was Abul Hasan Ali Nadvi, one of the most distinguished scholars of the 20th century on the Indian subcontinent. He added this about the Siddiqui women:

This family's women also ranked high in knowledge of Islam, in their Islamic rituals, and the reading and memorizing of the Qur'an.

…

The women of this family would regularly recite the Qur'an in *salah* [prayers] or listen to men reciting in *taraweeh* [night prayers in the month of Ramadan]. During that holy month, their households would be ringing with

Qur'anic recitations. The women were so knowledgeable
that they'd discuss the contents of what had been recited.

This was at a time when being a *hafiz*, someone who has memorized the entire 86,000-word Qur'an, was a male avocation. It largely still is. Yet several women of my family did the *hifz*, the memorization, including Amma, my mother, Amtul Baseer.

In Kandhla, the pious and the learned lived in a neighbourhood known as Mohalla Maulviyan, the locality of *maulvis*, the religious class. To this day, it retains its character — narrow, winding lanes with two- or three-storey row houses, some of them interconnected via a labyrinth of steep staircases. Faizul Islam, short and wiry, climbed those like a gazelle, while I struggled up slowly. The houses of my grandfather and father are very much still there, not much different than what I remember from my visits as a child.

Cousins married cousins or ventured outside the family for betrothal only among a tight circle of friends and acquaintances who shared their piety, *adaab* (etiquette) and *akhlaaq* (manners, behaviour, ethics).

Faizul Islam told me a most revealing story about his own marriage, reflecting the social mores of that time. "I did not know on the day of my wedding that I was getting married," he recalled. That fateful day his father and his future father-in-law were chatting with two highly respected shaykhs of the family, who suggested that "our two families, mine and my wife's, be joined. My father and the girl's father both thought it was a good idea. With the girl's consent obtained, my *nikah* [nuptial] was performed." Six people were present.

"Also decided was that there was no need for festivities or even a dinner — the money was donated for a *chabootra* [platform] at our mosque to accommodate the bigger Friday congregation. It was not uncommon in those days to forgo festivities and donate the cost to some worthy cause." And there was no worthier cause than a mosque courtyard, given the legacy of *Ahl-e-suffa*, "people of the platform," who spread Islamic knowledge during the Prophet Muhammad's time.

"Following the *nikah,* the bride joined the groom's house," Faizul Islam continued. "She and I have had a most loving relationship ever since."

"She may not think so," I teased.

"Go and ask her," he said.

I couldn't during that trip because she'd been ill, and she has died since. So has Faizul Islam, of Covid-19 in 2021. I knew him only since 2019, but it was as if we'd known each other forever, a tribute to his generosity and our family connections.

The historic norm of arranged marriages endures among Hindus, Muslims, and Sikhs.

* * *

When venturing out, the women of Kandhla wrapped themselves in a chador, which was also the custom for middle-class Hindu and Sikh women. Lipstick wasn't known, certainly not in Kandhla. Women wore the *kurta*, a tunic that hangs to the knees; a *shalwar*, pleated pantaloons; and a *duputta*, a wraparound cloth worn over the head and shoulders, like that of Benazir Bhutto, the slain former prime minister of Pakistan, and now of Malala Yousafzai, the 2014 Nobel Peace Prize laureate.

For men, no rings, no bling. They wore the male version of the *kurta* and pyjama, white or in some muted colour. And a vest and cap of various types: the *kufi* skullcap that is fuller than a *kippa*; or the fez, taken from the Ottoman Turks; or a cloth turban. On special occasions, such as the festivals of Eid, or for weddings, men wore the more formal *sherwani*, the long coat buttoned to the neck and flowing to the knees, covering up the *kurta*, as did Prime Minister Jawaharlal Nehru started wearing after his return from studies in England in 1912.

Women were mostly homemakers, with little or no political or economic power. But they were highly respected in our family, often revered. "Paradise lies under the feet of your mother" — that famous saying of the Prophet was invoked often. Women were usually the first teachers of the children of the family, both boys and girl, as well as the children of the less educated and the poor in the neighbourhood who, in turn, helped around the house. Child labour, we might be tempted to call it. It was a common arrangement — free schooling at a time when there were few or no schools, especially for girls.

The children were also taught etiquette and basic skills: cooking and sewing for the girls, household chores and shopping for the boys.

The notion of *haya,* modesty, applied to both men and women, as per a Qur'anic injunction: "Tell the believing men to lower their gaze and to be mindful of their chastity.... And tell the believing women to lower their gaze and to be mindful of their chastity" (Qur'an 24:31).

Up to this day, I resist shorts — the three I've had for years I only take out of the drawer when flying off to some tropical beach where I rarely use them. Many Muslims never get naked when showering at a health club or a public place and avert their gazes from those who do. Those in France who insist that Muslim women exchange their burqinis for bikinis know not how deeply they scrape into the Muslim soul. Or perhaps they do. The Americans certainly did at Abu Ghraib, Guantanamo Bay, and the CIA "black sites" where they subjected Muslim detainees to forced nudity and had female guards watch over them. The parallels aren't the same, but there's no doubting the ensuing humiliation and hurt.

In Kandhla, people lived close to a mosque within hearing distance of the *muezzin's* calls five times a day. Many Muslims still do all over the world. The arrangement particularly suits the old, especially in the West — they get their daily walks and an antidote to loneliness.

Women didn't go to mosques, still don't in many Muslim lands, especially in the Arab world. But they increasingly do in the West, a welcome development for two reasons: it revives an Islamic tradition and does so in secular liberal democracies. During the Prophet Muhammad's time, women not only attended his mosque but also asked him questions. And during the annual *hajj* pilgrimage, women perform the nearly weeklong ritual with men and pray in the holy precincts of Mecca with them. Yet for centuries, women have been frozen out of the daily prayers in their local mosques for cultural reasons.

There was no drinking, of course, it being *haram,* "not permissible." No divorces or scandals, either. If there were, they aren't part of any written records or oral history I know of.

All this steadfast staidness makes the family come across as boring by today's standards. Far from it. That they don't fit contemporary clichés, in fact, makes them that much more interesting. Orthodox but not radical, conservative but not communal, fundamentalists but not Wahhabi, social conservatives but never bemoaning the birth of daughters — girls are as much a gift from God as boys. In our household, the boys were spanked for disciplinary purposes, but I don't recall either Abba or Amma ever raising their voices at my sisters — Abbi, Maryam, and Syeda.

That was the pecking order, fully absorbed and accepted. One service assigned to the brothers, mostly me, was to iron the clothes of Amma and especially the sisters for parties and special occasions such as the two Eids. The regular laundry came washed and folded, but the special clothes needed ironing. There being no closets to hang them in, they were folded and put away after the last use and came out crinkled. Maryam, my middle sister, was the fussiest. Every wrinkle had to be ironed out, and the front and back flap of her *kurta* had to fall just so.

Knowledge as Treasure

In Kandhla, life revolved around religion, especially the pursuit and propagation of Islamic knowledge through extensive reading, writing, and teaching.

Abba, circa 1960.

2 Ram and Rumi

The modest lifestyle that ensued wasn't regretted but rather celebrated as the most *halal*, Islamically permissible, way of earning a living. When my father started a construction company, some senior family members regularly bemoaned his worldliness. *"Miya Moosa, kya kar rahe ho?"* ("What are you doing, dear Moosa?"), meaning, "Why aren't you doing something more spiritually and intellectually uplifting?"

As Professor Ebrahim Moosa (no relation) of the University of Notre Dame notes in *What Is a Madrasah?*, a travelogue about the seminary in Deoband and other ones in India he'd gone to from his native South Africa to study:

> To take compensation for anything related to knowledge is not permissible. To serve the faith-tradition in the sphere of knowledge therefore requires sacrifice. Poverty is the ideal. One should adopt a lifestyle of frugality, self-effacing modesty, and reliance on God and shun materialism if one is to become a devout servant of the faith…. Knowledge is an *end* in itself, not a *means* to a career.[1]

The virtue of staying aloof from material pursuits didn't square with some family members accepting lands and other gifts from the Sultanate of Delhi. The yin-yang between asceticism and worldly gain, rejecting and accepting royal favours, standing up to the sultan of the age or being obeisant to him, seeking or resisting favours from the rich and powerful played out across generations, including mine. Happily, dissidents and truth-tellers generally prevailed. Saluting the sultan was for court poets and other hangers-on, not the intellectual class. Parroting the received wisdom of the age was the avocation of opportunists. Receiving gifts from the rich was to compromise oneself.

Cousin Faizul Islam offered an example. A family elder Shaykh Muhammad Zakariyya spurned an offer of hefty cash by a rich admirer who came bearing 200,000 rupees, a princely sum at a time when average salaries hovered around 100 or 200 rupees per month.

"I don't need it," said the shaykh. "I've enough for my basic needs."

The merchant insisted. Zakariyya rebuffed him.

After the third go-around, the shaykh relented and invited the visitor to join him for a meal, at the end of which, he said, "You persuaded me to accept your gift, for which I'm grateful. But since it is now mine, I gift it to your children."

The Rumi Connection

I grew up with Rumi, the great 13th-century Persian poet, now omnipresent in the West. Elders recited a Rumi verse to praise or admonish us, even knowing we were too ignorant to understand. They must have thought that dropping Rumi's words in our ears would do us some good. Rumi ran in the family — ancestors had translated him or composed commentaries on his works, especially his famed six-volume *Masnavi ye-Ma'navi* (The Spiritual Couplets), which at 26,000 verses has more than the *Iliad* and *Odyssey* combined. The *Masnavi* is "the greatest mystical poem ever written, probably the longest mystical poem by a single author from any religious tradition," according to Professor Jawid Mojaddedi of Rutgers University. His recent English translation of the *Masnavi* is of particular significance — he annotates the dozens of Qur'anic references Rumi sprinkled throughout it. The *Masnavi* draws so heavily from the Qur'an that it's called "the Qur'an in Persian."[2]

Rumi was an Islamic scholar who headed his own madrasah, delivering sermons in the biggest mosque in Konya, Turkey, which is where his family settled after Afghanistan and Hejaz, now part of Saudi Arabia. He issued fatwas and was reverentially referred to as the Maulana, or Mevlana, "the Master." After his death, his son, Valad, and his disciples started the Mevlavi Sufi Order, known as the whirling dervishes for their dancing ritual of spinning around in ecstasy. The whirling came to Rumi in the goldsmith bazar of Konya. When he heard the craftsmen's repeated hammering, he began turning to their rhythm. In my childhood in Hyderabad, I used to hear silversmiths beating pellets into wafer thin shimmering slivers, used to decorate desserts or cooked dishes. In 2019, I went back there and found only one such shop left. Mohammed Imran cut a silver strip into equal little pieces, placed each in between sheets of special hardy paper, bundled the package, and started pounding with a hammer in his right hand while rotating the pouch with his left. Eyes closed, I sat and listened to the rhythm

2 Ram and Rumi

— Tik, tik, tik, TOK. Tik, tik, tik, TOK. I did feel transfixed but did not go into a rapturous dance.

Each of the six volumes of the *Masnavi* focuses on a particular aspect of Sufism. In about a dozen main stories, Rumi tells tales within tales full of anecdotes, fables, homilies, and parables, each conveying some Sufi wisdom. The *Masnavi* was so revered in India that the great Mughal emperor, Akbar (reigned 1556–1605), ordered his administrators to read it. People memorized it, including several of my family members.

Rumi left his lengthy poem unfinished. After nearly 26,000 verses, he gave up, saying, "The sun has set on my heart," adding:

> The flow of words has stopped
> My time on earth is coming to an end.
> The words will come some day
> to someone whose heart is alive.

The beat that moved Rumi into rapturous dance: *tik-tik-tik-TOK*. Silversmith Mohammed Imran in Hyderabad beating pellets into thin decorative wafers.

He died soon after in 1273. Professor Mojaddedi writes: "His death was mourned not only by his disciples but also by the large and diverse community in Konya, including Christians and Jews who converged as his body was carried through the city. Many of the non-Muslims had not only admired him as outsiders but had also attended his teaching sessions."[3] Rumi's mausoleum has since become one of the most popular sites of pilgrimage, visited by people of all faiths. Its serenity is palpable, unlike the crowded chaos one finds at many of the mausoleums of Sufi saints dotted across India and Pakistan, or Senegal.

Five hundred and twenty-eight years after Rumi's passing, the unfinished words of the *Masnavi* came to my great-great-great-grandfather, Muhammad Ilahi Baksh (1748–1829), in Kandhla. He was the older brother of the Baksh who had settled the land dispute over the mandir/masjid.

The senior Baksh was a distinguished scholar of the Sufi Nakshbandi Order, prolific author, poet, physician, and *mufti* (jurist). Like many of the learned in Kandhla, Mufti Baksh was trilingual — fluent in Arabic, the language of the Qur'an and Islamic traditions, both of which suffused the *Masnavi*; Persian, the literary language of Muslim courts in India; Urdu, the indigenous language that emerged as an amalgam of Arabic and Persian.

In this rich literary milieu, Rumi had a following, his manuscripts passing hand to hand. Such affinity with Rumi was remarkable, considering that Persian wasn't the mother tongue of Indians, and that Baksh and his ilk were orthodox and observant, while Rumi believed that spirituality and the inner self of a believer mattered more than rituals. He didn't think that the Qur'an should be taken literally because it contained possibly seven layers of meaning, and that dancing was an ecstatic path to God.

In syncretic India, Rumi was venerated not just by Muslims but also Hindus. Muslims had a particular cultural affinity with him amid the British colonial onslaught on Muslim traditions and institutions. They admired him for reasons decidedly different than what has made him a bestselling poet in North America today. Here Rumi has been denuded of his Islamic content, his verses reduced to pithy New Age sayings intoned by the likes of Madonna, Goldie Hawn, Demi Moore, and Deepak Chopra, who project Rumi as a mystic without God. In India and the Muslim world, Rumi holds sway because his poetry is rich with Islamic references and explorations of mysticism within the boundaries of the faith, even though he pushes those boundaries.

Baksh started translating the *Masnavi* into Urdu but felt a greater calling to compose an ending to Book 6 in Persian verse. His introduction is audacious:

> Maulana Jalal al-Din Rumi
> the sea of knowledge, the tower of gnosis
> Has cast his being on to my heart
> lighting up my body,
> Say that which has been left unsaid
> String the pearls that remain unstrung.

He picked up where Rumi left off — the story of a king's three sons smitten by a Chinese princess. The first two die in pursuit of her, and there's a substory about a man who willed his gold and silver to the laziest of his three sons. Mufti Baksh began his addition by parading the lazy brothers before a *qadi* (judge) to catalogue their indolence, so he could render a fair ruling.

Baksh continued for about 1,000 verses in Rumi's voice and style — colloquial, non-linear, broken up by subheads. Weaving tales within tales of prophets, kings, and beggars. Sprinkling anecdotes, animal fables, homilies, and parables. Going off on tangents such as the story of Moses wandering the desert for 40 years, the tale of a dervish distracted by a gorgeous woman, the account of a man caught between looking for his lost camel and attending Friday prayers, the story of a Sufi spurning the entreaties of the sultan, and ...

He closed with a tribute to Rumi:

> God's sun, the respected Jalaluddin
> himself said at the time of closing [his sixth book]
> The rest of it would come
> in the heart of one whose spirit was alive ...
> This conversation is not the result of my efforts
> It's you who brought me the pearls from the river.

That was 1801. Baksh's addendum remained in manuscripts until 1864 when it was published as *Ikhtetam-e-Masnavi* (Masnavi Completed). Within a year, it was appended to a historic lithograph edition of the *Masnavi* published in Lucknow in 1865. That was acknowledged in 1887 by E.H. Whinfield, the English translator of Rumi: "In the Lucknow edition there follows an epilogue written by Muhammad Ilahi Baksh, giving a continuation of the story of the third brother."[4] Some publishing houses started attaching Baksh's ending to the *Masnavi*, and his work was soon translated into Urdu, Sindhi, and other languages.

Rumi aficionados in India and Pakistan are well versed in Baksh's contribution, which continues to sell, especially in its Urdu translation. During a 2019 trip to India, I visited an Urdu bookstore, my second, which had a six-volume *Masnavi* with Baksh's work appended to it, both in the original Farsi and their Urdu translations. But in the West, Baksh remains unknown, even as our fascination with Rumi grows by leaps and bounds.

* * *

How Baksh came to his *Masnavi* mission is itself quite the tale. He was said to have dreamt of Rumi and asked him about the unfinished poem. "You complete it," Rumi responded.

Rumi reappeared in Baksh's dream and told him to "sit down with ink and paper between *Asr* and *Maghrib* [the evening and dusk prayers] and the rest of the story will come to you."

And so it did. An inspired Baksh wrote page after page.

Such *ilham*, "celestial guidance," evinces skepticism. Yet they are real to believers and also several contemporary scholars of Sufism. Baksh did what Allah willed for him in fulfillment of what Rumi envisaged. Coleman Barks, the American translator who has done more than anyone else to make Rumi a bestseller in the West, credits just such a *wahi*, "revelation/inspiration," for his own Rumi mission.

Barks, a professor of English literature at the University of Georgia and a poet, often tells the story of how he'd never heard of Rumi until the 1970s when the American poet, Robert Bly, handed him a copy of Rumi translations by British Orientalist A.J. Arberry and said: "Release these poems from their cages."

The professor didn't know Farsi or Islam but soon had a dream in which a stranger bathed in a circle of light told him, "I love you." A year later, Barks saw that man — the leader of a Sufi order near Philadelphia, Muhammad Bawa Muhaiyaddeen, a Sri Lankan mystic who had come to the United States in 1971. "It has to be done," Bawa said, of the need to undertake the Rumi translation.[5] So began Barks's long Rumi journey.

* * *

Baksh's original manuscript in his handwriting is preserved at the Mufti Ilahi Baksh Academy, located in my father's ancestral home, now acquired by a distant relative, Nurul Hasan. The house incorporates a smaller one where Baksh lived and wrote. The academy shares a wall with the house of Dada, my grandfather. The Baksh academy isn't as grand as the title suggests — Nurul Hasan lives there and runs it with the help of volunteers. But its collection is grand. It includes several original Rumi editions published in India, as well as the originals or first editions of Baksh's literary output in Farsi, Urdu, and Arabic — 34 books, 17 commentaries on others, and several pamphlets.

When I held Baksh's 1801 manuscript and gawked at his faded handwriting, shivers ran down my spine.

* * *

Baksh was a *hakeem* (physician) practising *hikmat*, the Unani-Tibbi natural medicine (Greco-Arabic medical system), one of three non-allopathic disciplines with a rich tradition in India, along with Ayurveda and homeopathy. He used to take a *hakimi* potion before going to bed. One evening, his attendant was away, and the substitute staffer prepared the dose. That night, Baksh had convulsions and died the next evening, age 82.

How or why did the attendant get it so horribly wrong? There's nary a recrimination in family history or folklore. An honest mistake, what else? Besides, one's time in this world is fixed — Baksh went when Allah called him. The end.

3

The Milieu That Made Me

THE WANING YEARS OF MUFTI BAKSH COINCIDED WITH THE COLLAPSE OF the Mughal Empire. In 1803, the East India Company captured Delhi and from 1837–57 reduced the reigning Mughal emperor, Bahadur Shah Zafar, to a figurehead. The Muslim literary and religious class that had long benefited from the empire, including our family, became active across the range of the anti-colonial struggle.

It was Mufti Baksh's Sufi masters in Delhi who formulated the first intellectual and political manifesto for independence. They were two noted theologians, philosophers, and prolific authors of the age: Shah Waliuallah (1703–62) and his son, Shah Abdul Aziz (1746–1824), at whose school, Madrasa-e-Rahimiyahh, Baksh studied. Unlike the Wahhabi movement then spawning in Saudi Arabia, the Waliullah school of thought admired Sufi spirituality and provided a bridge between Sufis and the traditional *ulama*, "channelling the streams of the Sufi spiritual heritage into traditional Islam." They opposed not only British rule but also the more than 550 Hindu, Muslim, and Sikh princely states that perpetuated another kind of slavery, feudalism.[1]

A fatwa designating British India as *Dar al-Harb*, "Abode of War," was issued by Abdul Aziz: "Our country has been enslaved. It is our duty to struggle for independence and put an end to the slavery." But what, exactly, did he mean? What were his followers, including Mufti Baksh, supposed to do?

Abdul Aziz wasn't calling for war, nor for *hijrat* (emigration). Muslims didn't have to migrate because they could still practise their faith. They could work for the British, even wear European clothes, as long as that wasn't to curry favour with the colonial bosses. Muslims could learn English, even enroll their children in British schools, but had to be vigilant against absorption into "English culture," and more importantly, slipping into self-loathing because of their faith. Indian Muslims had to remain proud Indians and proud Muslims.

The jihad that Abdul Aziz spoke about was of several kinds — of the *nafs*, "soul," to make oneself a better human being; of the tongue, to spread knowledge or engage in debates; of self-defence, the doctrine of deterrence; and, finally, to wage war, which was to be avoided as much as possible, since initiating one that might be lost was tantamount to suicide, explicitly banned by the Qur'an.

Jihad if necessary but not necessarily jihad — some reasonable accommodation with the British — was to be sorted out by a committee to which Abdul Aziz named Abul Hasan, Mufti Baksh's son.

Not everyone was listening, either on the Indian or British side.

By 1857, anti-British fervour had built up to a series of uprisings culminating in what the Indians proclaimed as the First War of Independence. The British called it the Mutiny. Muslims took part in large numbers. One of my family members led a short-lived rebellion near Kandhla: Imadullah Makki, educated in the Baksh household and who had married a Baksh granddaughter, made a most unlikely revolutionary. He was a frail, soft-spoken Sufi scholar of the liberal Chishti Order and the author of a multi-volume annotation of Rumi's *Masnavi*: "He was a Magus-like figure, a Sufi master, par excellence, one who altered the destinies of his disciples."[2]

The uprising was to commence in Shamli, 17 kilometres north of Kandhla, and to end with nothing less than the liberation of Delhi. Three dozen revolutionaries waylaid a column of British soldiers in a park and captured a few weapons, including a cannon. That inspired a few hundred locals to join them in a march to the Shamli fort where they overwhelmed the British troops. Their victory was short-lived.

Recapturing the fort, the British sent 34 revolutionaries to the gallows, burnt down three neighbouring villages, and launched a manhunt for Makki

3 The Milieu That Made Me

and his closest disciples. He found refuge in Kandhla in a house across from my father's ancestral home that now houses the Baksh Academy. Makki later escaped to Mecca, which is where he died in 1899. In his waning years in exile, he helped guide the publication in India of a new edition of Rumi's *Masnavi*, including Baksh's conclusion.

* * *

After the Mutiny, "the British exacted terrible reprisals as they dispersed the mutineers. Vengeful soldiers lashed tens of thousands of mutineers to the muzzles of cannons and blew them to pieces; they left a trail of destruction across north India, bayoneting and burning their way through villages and towns."[3] Much of Delhi was levelled, its Muslim inhabitants killed or expelled en masse or exiled to the Andaman Islands in the Bay of Bengal. Of the 200,000 slaughtered in Delhi alone, 51,000 were said to be the *ulama*, the learned class, my people. The venerable Madrasah Rahimiyyah of Shah Waliuallah and Shah Abdul Aziz, where Mufti Baksh had studied, was auctioned off.[4] British soldiers took over mosques and stomped into the sacred spaces with their shoes on, a sin since repeated by American and Allied soldiers in Afghanistan and Iraq.

Emperor Bahadur Shah was held captive at the Tomb of Humayun (1530–40 and 1555–56), the mausoleum of the second Mughal emperor. At this jewel of Mughal architecture, British soldiers routinely humiliated him, ordering him to stand and bow to them. It was there that the emperor was informed that two of his sons and a grandson had been shot dead, and on October 7, 1857, he was awakened at 3:00 a.m., put in a bullock cart, and shipped to exile in Rangoon, Burma. There he penned the poem that has since been immortalized by generations of Muslims, including my own:

Kitna Hai Bud Naseeb Zafar Dafn Ke Liye,
Do Gaz Zameen Na Mil Saki Kooye Yaar Mei.

Unlucky is Zafar even in burial
Denied two yards in his own land.

Whenever I'm in Delhi, I try to visit the imposing mausoleum, a UNESCO World Heritage Site, its 12 hectares of gardens restored by the Aga Khan Trust for Culture. For me, this oasis of tranquility evokes melancholy — and anger.

Preserving Islamic Knowledge

Out of defeat and despondency came creativity. Post-1857, Muslim nationalism found a range of expressions, including in my family and its circle. It was best manifested in new, divergent centres of learning. While madrasahs are as old as Islam, spreading Islamic knowledge to new generations, the seminaries started in India at that time were in response to the evisceration of an old Muslim order. Three major madrasahs of differing doctrinal inclinations were set up to preserve Islamic knowledge and protect Muslim culture and identity. Their medium of instruction was the indigenous Urdu language in order to reach the masses rather than just the traditional Arabic- and Farsi-speaking elite. Most prominent of these seminaries was Darul Uloom, "House of Knowledge," established by close associates of Makki. That's the madrasah my father and two uncles studied in and which played a prominent role in India's independence.

Started in 1866 on an auspicious Friday under a pomegranate tree in a mosque compound in Deoband, 145 kilometres northeast of Delhi, Darul Uloom took no funds or favour from the British. Indeed, it safeguarded Muslims from British culture.

Darul Uloom distinguished itself as a seminary on par with Egypt's famed Al-Azhar University. Its orientation from the beginning was reformist. Darul Uloom wasn't literal in its interpretation of the Qur'an and Hadith (the sayings and deeds of the Prophet Muhammad). It opposed ritual excess, especially financially ruinous marriages with their demands for dowries by the families of grooms. It advocated for the remarriage of widows and their legal rights of inheritance in a land where Hindu widows were expected to throw themselves on the fiery pyres of their dead husbands or spend the rest of their lives as widows.

A Deoband stalwart, Sayyid Mumtaz Ali (1860–1935), advocated equal rights for women, including equivalent division of assets, a revolutionary idea for the times. He also opposed polygamy on the Qur'anic ground that up to four wives are permitted only if one is capable of treating each justly, but "you have it not in your power to do justice between the wives, even though you may wish it" (Qur'an 4:129), a qualifier that men have conveniently forgotten over the ages. He opposed the veil and championed women's empowerment: "An educated woman can take care of herself better than an inexperienced, undereducated, mentally confused bundle of veils which has not been allowed to develop self-confidence and cannot take care of herself."

His six-volume *Huquq-e-Niswan* (Rights of Women) in Urdu, published in 1898, was "undoubtedly too far in advance of its times," writes Gail Minault of the University of Pennsylvania, who specializes in 19th- and 20th-century history of India, including religion and women's movements.[5] One Deoband elder, indeed "indisputably the most influential scholar affiliated with the Deoband school,"[6] was Maulana Ashraf Ali Thanvi (1863–1943), a close associate of our family, spiritually and by marriage. His most famous publication was *Behishti Zewar* (Heavenly Ornaments), "one of the 20th century's most influential books, explicating reformist teachings for women," according to Barbara Metcalf of the University of California.[7] In her book *Perfecting Women*, she writes:

> The "heavenly ornaments" of the title are not women themselves as adornments or ornaments. There is no notion that women are the Victorian "angel of the house." The "ornaments" are rather a metaphor for the virtues both women and men must cultivate in themselves. The work treats women and men as essentially the same, in contrast to European works directed towards women at the time. Women are essentially the same as men, neither endowed with a special nature for spiritual or moral virtue nor handicapped in any way by limitations of intellect or character.[8]

Behishti Zewar, aka *BZ*, became a classic gift for millions of Muslim brides who, as the saying has it, "entered their husband's home with the Holy

Qur'an in one hand and the *Behishti Zewar* in the other." My mother came with it. My sisters went with it. Most Sunni households keep a copy of it.

Written in Urdu and translated into many languages, *BZ* isn't a feminist tract. As Metcalf notes, "This is patriarchy. But women were to enjoy the respect accorded those who mastered true knowledge."[9] When Maulana Thanvi was asked to write a companion guide for men, he said that *BZ* would do just fine for men, as well. As Metcalf points out, "It is hard to imagine a guidebook for women written in 1900 in Europe or America that would also be recommended as a proper guide to men."[10]

Thanvi had no children. His scholarly tradition was carried on by his nephew, Maulana Ehtisham Haq Thanvi, who, too, studied in Deoband but migrated to Pakistan. He developed a distinct sing-song recitation of the Qur'an, so much so that my ears perked up in 2019 when New Zealand's Parliament in Wellington commemorated the massacre of Muslims in that country and the televised session began with the reading of the Qur'an. Sure enough, the reciter was a Thanvi, Nizam ul-Haq. I didn't know of him, let alone that he'd settled in New Zealand. But that familiar enunciation, that sound, that melody, at once bridged decades and continents.[11]

* * *

Pursuing a radically different approach from Darul Uloom was a college modelled after Cambridge University. It was unapologetically pro-British, a "Western-style school aimed at cultivating a class of Indian elites who would collaborate with the colonial regime."[12]

It was initiated by Sir Syed Ahmed (1817–98), who had obtained his religious education in the Baksh household and wrote that "their family and mine have known each other for generations." Sir Syed was a civil servant for the East India Company and had condemned the 1857 war, especially "the wholesale butchery of Christians" at some centres of the rebellion. He swore allegiance to "Her Excellency the Exalted Ruler, Queen Victoria, long may she reign."

Sir Syed published *The Loyal Mohammedans of India*, arguing that Muslims were the most loyal subjects because "of the principles of their faith." The British were Christian, a "people of the book and our brothers in religion." Therefore, jihad against the British Raj was un-Islamic.

In 1869–70, Sir Syed went on a subsidized trip to Britain, stayed in London's Bloomsbury, met Thomas Carlyle, attended the last reading given by Charles Dickens, and visited Cambridge, studying its syllabus and governance. Upon return, he established the Muhammadan Anglo-Oriental College in 1874, which evolved into Aligarh Muslim University. Its alumni all over the world are a well-knit group, including in Canada. I've spoken at their annual dinners in Toronto.

In his time, Sir Syed was widely seen as a flunky of the British — an *ibn-e-waqt*, a timeserver, an opportunist. That was the judgment of a people locked in a life-and-death struggle against a brutal colonial power. But Sir Syed has since come to be revered, rightly, for having exhorted Muslims to learn English and acquire a Western education.

Two Mini-Mughal Kingdoms

In E.M. Forster's *A Passage to India* (1924), the protagonist, Dr. Aziz, is acquitted after being wrongly charged with molesting an Englishwoman and says: "I have decided to have nothing more to do with British India, as a matter of fact. I shall seek service in some Moslem State, such as Hyderabad, Bhopal, where Englishmen cannot insult me any more."[13]

Hyderabad in the southern Deccan plateau and Bhopal in central India were the largest and most prosperous Muslim princely states. Both were pro-British and surrendered sovereignty to the Crown in the 19th century but enjoyed considerable domestic autonomy. That meant their citizens were free of British racism.

Both states, especially Hyderabad, were multicultural and major centres of learning and the arts. During and especially after the collapse of the Mughal Empire, both offered patronage and jobs to Muslim intellectuals, scholars, educators, poets, and artists.

Benefiting from the peace, order, and good government in both Hyderabad and Bhopal were my own ancestors. Mufti Baksh worked in Bhopal as a jurist in the late 18th century. A hundred years later, his great-grandson — my grandfather, Dada Ismail — served there as a civil servant. Dada had the standard religious education in Kandhla, including memorization of the Qur'an, but ended up as the state's superintendent of forests, a job that afforded him time for his calligraphy, copying rare Arabic and Persian books.

Bhopal and Its Begums

Bhopal had the unique distinction of being ruled by four women for more than a century (1819–1926), the last of whom caused Dada Ismail to flee the state overnight.

The main objection to female rule came not from the locals but from the British. They exercised suzerainty over the state, plotting more than once to sideline the women rulers, titled begums, who outsmarted the British. They proved effective rulers, initiating several reforms, especially in women's education. They were pious without being puritanical in their faith or sectarian in their statecraft. They usually wore the veil when presiding over the court, meeting foreign visitors, or venturing out into their domains to take the pulse of the populace.

The first begum ascended the throne in 1819. That was 19 years before Queen Victoria's coronation. The second begum slapped the British political agent in public for having the gall to touch her earring while complimenting it. She rode, played polo, and went tiger hunting. Praying in the famous Jama Masjid of Delhi at a time when women weren't allowed in mosques, she became the first Indian ruler to perform the *hajj*, taking along a retinue of 1,500 courtiers. And she published a travelogue in which she portrayed the Sharif of Mecca as an uncouth extortionist and the local Arabs as a people who could "neither sing nor dance."

The third begum was widowed at age 29 and married her chief secretary after court rumours of romance. The fourth begum wore her burka to the 1911 Delhi Durbar marking the coronation of King George V. Sultan Jahan Begum was also the one who caused Dada Ismail to flee Bhopal when she ascended the throne in 1901.[14]

Dada had a difference of opinion with her "on an issue of Sharia" while she was heir apparent, according to a 1977 book by one of his grandsons, my cousin, Mohammed Mian. Fearing her wrath when she became the queen, Dada fled overnight for Kandhla.

3 The Milieu That Made Me

He need not have. Court officials impressed with his integrity convinced the begum that he should be brought back. She dispatched an emissary to Kandhla to convey her wish that he come back. But he declined, offering a note of explanation:

> I've had a difference of opinion with you on a sharia principle. If a similar situation were to arise again and I bite my tongue because of your status as the Queen, I'd be compromising my *deen* ["faith"]. If I speak my mind, I'd end up upsetting you. I neither want to risk angering you nor compromising my *deen*. I'd like to be excused.[15]

Back in Kandhla, Dada switched to the family business — religious writings, besides opening that madrasah at the Jami Masjid. He authored two books but mostly hand-copied rare manuscripts, the most monumental of which took him 19 years (1919 to 1938). It ran to 7,802 pages in 13

Sultan Jahan Begum of Bhopal, London, 1926.

volumes and was an exhaustive commentary on a ninth-century classic, *Sahih Bukhari*. That collection of Prophetic traditions is found in most Sunni Muslim homes even today. Dada knew the book by heart — all 1,139 pages in the original — and used to routinely recite it. The commentary on it that Dada copied is error-free; he didn't rewrite or cross out a single word. It can be seen in the family archives in Lahore, Pakistan, along with five more of Dada's manuscripts, totalling another 2,602 pages.[16] This treasure, which I saw during a 2017 trip, has been preserved in the library of my first cousin, Sadiqa, and her late husband, Maulvi Musharraf Thanvi, a descendant of Shaykh Ashraf Ali Thanvi, the author of *BZ*, the treatise on women.

The elder Thanvi resided at Thana Bhavan, named after Devi Bhavan Temple, 35 kilometres northeast of Kandhla. He was the pre-eminent Sufi shaykh of his age, known as *Hakim al-Ummat*, "Sage of Muslims." Dada periodically visited him at his Sufi lodge, sometimes to invite him to Kandhla to deliver a sermon. My grandfather would hand over an envelope with two rupees for a first-class return train fare, but Thanvi invariably travelled economy and returned the difference. On one of his visits to Thana Bhavan, Dada took along his elder son, Mohammed Idris (born in 1899), and said, *"Ye aap ke sapurd hai"* — "He's yours [to educate]."

Idris eventually went to the Deoband seminary where he graduated with honours in 1921. Within a year, he was hired as *shaykh-as-tafseer*, teacher of the exegesis of the Qur'an. Darul Uloom is where my father, Mohammed Moosa (born in 1909 in Kandhla), also studied; his older brother was one of his teachers. At the madrasah, my father befriended a fellow student, Syed Sarwar Hussain, and the two forged a deep bond for the rest of their lives, making me who I am. My siblings and I called Syed Sarwar Chote Tayabba, meaning "Younger Uncle," while referring to Uncle Idris as Bade Tayabba, "Older Uncle." During their time there, Deoband was a hotbed of anti-British activities.

In 1920, when Mahatma Gandhi launched his boycott of British goods, courts, schools, and colonial jobs, Darul Uloom threw its full weight behind it. And also issued a fatwa of non-co-operation with the British while adhering to Gandhi's non-violence.

Gandhi backed Muslims protesting the end of the Turkish caliphate in 1924 and the British role in the vivification of the Ottoman Caliphate. Indian Muslims had long held the caliph in high regard, since he'd been the Protector of the Holy Cities and Defender of the Islamic Faith by virtue of Ottoman control of the holy cities of Mecca and Medina until 1915.

With the end of the Ottoman Caliphate, Sharif Husayn, the pro-British governor of Mecca, proclaimed himself caliph. His claim was recognized in the Arab lands under British mandate: Iraq, Jordan, and Palestine. But he was seen by Indian Muslims "as an imperial stooge, a traitor to the Turks and, therefore, to pan-Islamic solidarity."[17]

Gandhi's support for the Muslim agitation advanced Hindu-Muslim unity against the British. He and other Hindu leaders were invited to speak to Muslims at leading madrasahs and mosques, including the great Jami Masjid in Delhi.

The nizam of Hyderabad, circa 1930s.

* * *

Uncle Idris at Deoband, absorbed in his teaching and writings, remained aloof from the political firmament. His scholastic fame soon reached Hyderabad where the ruler, known as the nizam, issued a *firman*, a royal decree, dated October 3, 1926, granting him 40 rupees per month for life. Three years later, Hyderabad enticed him to pursue his writing in Hyderabad City, capital of Hyderabad State. My father and Sarwar Hussain followed him there.

That's how our side of the family became Hyderabadis.

The Pull of Hyderabad

As allies of the British, both Hyderabad and Bhopal didn't support the Khilafat Movement, just as neither had backed the 1857 rebellion. That, however, didn't stop the nizam from announcing a spectacular financial rescue of the fallen caliph, granting him a royal pension of £4,000 per year for life. Not just that. In 1931, the nizam arranged the marriage of his older son, Prince Azam Jah, to the caliph's only daughter, Durru Shehvar, then 17. The nizam's younger son, Prince Moazzam Jah, was betrothed to his first cousin, Sultana Nilofar Hanim, great-granddaughter of Turkish Sultan Murad V, the 33rd Ottoman sultan. The twin marriages were performed by the deposed caliph himself in his exile in Nice, France. Six weeks later, the two couples arrived in Hyderabad by train from Bombay, and the nizam broke protocol and received them himself at the railway station. At dinner the band played "The Roast Beef of Old England."

Hyderabad State was larger than Britain, and its finances were of the same order as Belgium's. In 1938, the nizam was featured on the cover of *Time* as the richest man on the planet; his worth then was pegged at "$150 million in jewels, $250 million in gold bars and a total capital of $1.4 billion," more than that of the Rockefellers at the time. Like Bhopal, Hyderabad's population was majority Hindu, but the rulers maintained exemplary religious and cultural harmony.

An equal-opportunity philanthropist, the nizam supported churches, temples, gurdwaras, and mosques, Sunni and Shia. Before Saudi Arabia

3 The Milieu That Made Me

discovered oil, he subsidized the holy cities of Mecca and Medina and contributed to the London Central Mosque in Regent's Park. He donated to both Aligarh Muslim University and the Deoband madrasah, and even more to Hindu University in the holy city of Benares. Asked why, he said, "Because there are more Hindus in India than Muslims." He backed a string of Hindu temples across India, helped restore Hindu paintings by Italian experts at the world-famous Ajanta and Ellora Caves, and subsidized the publication of the *Mahabharata* and other Hindu holy texts.

"Hindus and Muslims are like my two eyes," the nizam was known to say. He sustained a dizzying range of scholars and educators of different nationalities, sects, and theological orientations, as well as both pro- and anti-British activists. The nizam hosted Sir Syed twice, in 1882 and 1891, but also provided a haven for Sir Syed's critics, such as Tayabba. The nizam also employed Sir Syed's grandson, Sir Ross Masood, as director of public education (1916–28). Masood was the man to whom *A Passage to India* is dedicated and on whom the character of Dr. Aziz was based. Masood had been the love interest of Forster, his teacher in England. Forster came to India twice to pursue him, in 1912 and 1922, because "he was deeply in love. The affection was lopsided: Forster had twice declared his feelings, but Masood was straight and couldn't reciprocate."[18]

* * *

In Hyderabad, Tayabba lived across the street from Marmaduke Pickthall, the British convert to Islam who translated the Qur'an into English under the nizam's patronage and also launched an academic journal, *Islamic Culture*, to which noted scholars contributed, including the Canadian Wilfred Cantwell Smith of McGill University, who spent six years in India (1940–46).

One reason Tayabba had been attracted to Hyderabad was its collection of rare books, especially at Dairat ul-Ma'arif (House of Wisdom), attached to Osmania University. Tayabba had a particular interest in a manuscript, said to be the only one in India, of a commentary on *Mishkat al-Masabih*, a 14th-century classic on the Hadith. He wrote his own commentary in Arabic — *Ta'liq al-sabih* (Early Morning) — and went to Damascus in 1934 to get it published.

Deoband Beckons

Just as Tayabba's fame had brought him to Hyderabad, his greater celebrity took him back to Deoband. In 1939, he was invited to head a newly established department of *tafseer* (Qur'anic commentary) at Darul Uloom. In Hyderabad, he was being paid 250 rupees per month and had free accommodation, whereas the madrasah was offering only 70 rupees. He didn't mind, but his wife did. Tayabba took a train to Kandhla to consult my grandfather, who reacted sharply: *"Dar Kar-e Khair beech, haajat-e istikhara neest."* That's a Farsi saying: "You don't need to think too much to undertake a good deed." Or more precisely: "To do a good deed, you don't need to do the *istikhara*," the special prayer Muslims perform seeking God's guidance. So it was that Tayabba left Hyderabad to return to Deoband. His brother, Moosa, my father, had started a construction company and thus stayed behind.

In 1937 or 1938 — that's my best guess, there being no record that I've found — Abba went to Kandhla to get married, to who else but someone from the tight circle of the Mohalla Maulviyan neighbourhood. Amtul Baseer was from a family of *hakeems*, physicians. Her father, Hakeem Rasheed Ahmed, had his clinic in a space rented from the local mosque, 18 metres from where my father grew up.

Abba's business had expanded to Warangal, 140 kilometres northeast of Hyderabad city. He was building dams, water canals, and roads in the interior. At home during the day, Amtul Baseer used her spare time to start memorizing the Qur'an and recite it to Abba in the evenings. Her memorization was letter-perfect, as we discovered as children.

Their first child, Amina, was born in 1940. We endearingly and respectfully called her Abbi. I was born in 1942, Maryam in 1943, Suleman in 1945, Syeda in 1947, and Yousuf in 1948.

4

The End of Colonialism

MY EARLIEST MEMORY OF KANDHLA AS A CHILD IS OF A FALL VISIT. WE
went by train, two nights and a day to Delhi, 1,500 kilometres north, and
then on the smaller, metre-gauge line to Kandhla, an hour and a half away.
Luggage included tiered aluminum tiffin carriers with meals apportioned
for the journey — mostly rotis and dried curries and snacks. Travelling in
the women's compartment, Amma made a little room on the long wooden
bench seat, spread out a *dastarkhaan* (tablecloth), folded to fit the seat's di-
mensions; spread the meat or curry on a roti; rolled it, bottom folded up so
as to ensure no dripping; and handed everything out to the kids one by one,
starting with the youngest. Hot tea for adults and hot milk for the children
came from the endless stream of chai wallahs or samosa wallahs, either at
stations or on the train that the peddlers boarded at one station and got off
at the next.

Samosas and other snacks from vendors were frowned upon, being presumed unhygienic. But the rule got relaxed toward the end of the journey,
either because we were running out of our own supplies or for a desire for
something fresh and warm or different from the changing regional cuisine. Freshly plucked oranges at Nagpur station. *Pethay ki mithai*, pumpkin
or gourd candy, at Agra, home of the Taj Mahal but equally famous for
this delicacy. The whole journey was one long foodfest, with passengers

exchanging portions — keeping in mind that Hindus were strict vegetarians. Strangers were befriended, tales exchanged, and one another's religious requirements respected: Muslims quietly saying their prayers, Hindus closing their eyes, folding their hands, and reciting their mantras and *shloakas*, especially in early mornings and at mealtimes.

Dada died in Kandhla in 1942, but I remember his room fronting the narrow street. That was where he wrote and received male visitors who never entered the private inner sanctum, as per the custom common to both Hindus and Muslims. His wife, my *dadi* (grandmother) was a descendant of Mufti Baksh. I remember her as frail and soft-spoken, dressed in *shalwar, kurta, dupatta*, just like Amma. As for the sari, its use is more contemporary.

I recall my grandmother supervising the slow clay-pot cooking of *gannay ki kheer*, sugar-cane pudding, the foam repeatedly skimmed off the top and mixed with millet — or was it rice? — and topped with walnuts. A perfect foil for the chilly fall weather. I have another memory: of mango orchards by a canal. Abba's younger brother, Mohammed Ayub, also a *hafiz*, who, like Abba, had gone into business, had learned the art of grafting. That was the first time that I saw little grafts all over the grove, covered in cloth and plastic and tied with cotton thread.

Deoband and the End of British Rule

Upon his return to Deoband in 1939, Tayabba found the madrasah to be even more deeply involved in the anti-colonial struggle than when he'd left it. A new rector at Darul Uloom, Husain Ahmed Madani (1879–1957), was emerging as a formidable figure in the freedom movement.

The anti-British struggle had started out as a united effort of Hindus, Muslims, Sikhs, Zoroastrians, and others. But by the 1930s, the idea of carving out a Muslim Pakistan from the rest of India was beginning to take hold. So was the concept of Hindutva, India for Hindus. Hindu nationalists were arguing that India was Hindu land and that Muslims and Christians were foreigners. Some Hindu nationalists clamoured for the division of India well ahead of Muslims demanding Pakistan. The chief proponents of Pakistan were the philosopher-poet Sir Muhammad Iqbal (1877–1938) and the barrister Muhammad Ali Jinnah (1876–1948). The Muslim community was divided. While the majority favoured Pakistan, a fervent minority opposed it, including the Deoband seminary. The orthodox madrasah believed that the fight against colonialism had to be fought in alliance with the Hindu majority. The position wasn't merely pragmatic; it rested on a Qur'anic principle:

Say, O believers! I do not worship what you worship,
Nor do you worship what I worship; Nor will I ever worship what you worship,
You have your religion,
And I have mine (Qur'an 109:6).

Madani redefined the character of Indian nationalism as a Hindu-Muslim alliance, a "composite culture," just as Gandhi's vision of India rested on Hindu-Muslim harmony. He told fellow Muslims that the idea of Pakistan would prove a "poisonous powder for communal warfare ... and for peace and prosperity in India."[1] Madani added: "We should endeavor jointly for a democratic government in which Hindus, Muslims, Sikhs, Christians and Parsis [Zoroastrians] are included. Such a freedom is in accordance with Islam.... Muslims can live as observant Muslims in a religiously plural society where they would be full citizens of an independent, secular India."[2]

Furthermore, Madani contributed a revolutionary idea still relevant to this day. Given the diversity of Muslims — racial, ethnic, linguistic, cultural, and doctrinal — there wasn't likely to be agreement on the nature of an Islamic polity. Only an authoritarian state could define and enforce Islamic conformity. Today's Muslim world shows how prescient he was. But Madani was penalized by both the British and by Muslims. He was jailed several times and was taunted by many Muslims for selling out to the "Hindu" Congress.

Just as Madani's "opposition to the British was grounded not in 'religious' opposition to the British rulers as Christian, his opposition to Islamist politics did not derive from India's not being a majority Muslim country," writes Barbara Metcalf in her landmark book *Husain Ahmad Madani: The Jihad for Islam and India's Freedom*.[3] His was a groundbreaking belief that democratic norms best serve the interests of Muslims. It was "an extraordinary change from medieval precedents," says Metcalf, all the more remarkable because he was making the argument "*from within the Islamic tradition*" [emphasis hers]. In a telephone interview, Metcalf told me that Madani also showed "how the spiritual and moral dimension of Islam was closely related to, and could not be seen as separate from, the political dimension — the opposite of the British notion that religion was a separate domain that dealt only with family law, personal ethics and moral teachings."

The irony of the situation couldn't have been more extreme. The push for Pakistan was coming from Westernized, suited/booted liberals like the British-educated, whiskey-drinking Jinnah and the Berlin-educated Iqbal, while the pious *ulama* of Deoband, visibly Muslim with their beards and traditional clothing, were steadfast against a confessional Muslim state, even though majority Muslim opinion by then had swung in favour of it.

Madani was challenging three forces simultaneously — Hindu nationalists, Muslim separatists, and the British.

Being dragged into the Second World War was something Madani also opposed. He argued that it wasn't India's fight — not unlike Quebeckers who resisted the Boer War in South Africa and both the First and Second World Wars. His position was particularly difficult, given that Muslim soldiers were among the 2.5 million Indians recruited for the war, and the nizam, India's most powerful Muslim ruler, backed the British, contributing a staggering sum of £25 million, making him the largest individual contributor to the Allied war effort.

The many paradoxes and divisions were played out in our family, as well.

Tayabba Idris, immersed in his teaching and writings and being apolitical, began favouring the *deux nations* concept and found himself at odds with his boss and most of his colleagues. He was a minority within a minority within a minority.

Abba, being a product of the Deoband madrasah, also identified with the anti-British struggle, even while living in pro-British Hyderabad. Happily employing and working with mostly Hindus, he wasn't interested in going to Pakistan. Amma was apolitical, though she was a fan of Iqbal's poetry that had stirred Muslims. She had memorized several of his poems and often recited his couplets to us. However, I don't know what she thought of his political ideology as the first theoretician of a separate Muslim state in post-colonial India.

But up north, in and around Delhi, there was no escaping the drama of divided loyalties. Two prominent cousins of Abba found themselves in the centre of it. Shaykh Yousuf Siddiqui and Shaykh Muhammad Zakariyya were the leader and *eminent grise*, respectively, of the Tablighi Jamaat, the pacifist missionary movement started in 1926, an offshoot of the seminary. Both were at the group's headquarters in the Delhi suburb of Nizamuddin on the day of Partition, August 15, 1947, a date that fell that year in the fasting lunar month of Ramadan when the faithful spend time in prayers and spiritual serenity. But both were kept busy rejecting the entreaties of their followers to join them on the aliyah to Pakistan. Tens of thousands of Muslims boarded trains at a nearby railway station, departing for Pakistan. As Barbara Metcalf writes in *Husain Ahmad Madani,* "People would gather at the mosque before the trains departed, only to hear Maulana Yousuf tell them in the strongest possible terms that they had to have confidence and not flee Delhi. Maulana Zakariyya told inquirers that no place allocated to Pakistan could have the holiness and blessedness for knowledge and spirituality of Hindustan."[4]

Both stayed put, and their movement has since spread worldwide, including to Pakistan and Canada. In the post-9/11 period of pointing fingers at anything Islamic, the group was maligned, with no evidence, as "fundamentalist" and "militant," the same charges Hindu zealots in India hurl at it periodically. The group's defining features have been ascetic pacifism and political quietism, attributes criticized by some members of my family, including Abba, who held that religiosity wasn't a licence to isolate oneself from the realities of family, friends, community, and country. The Tablighi rejoinder is that one needs to first purify oneself and turn to God before trying to change anything and anyone else.

* * *

The division of India led to the massacre of an estimated one million Muslims, Hindus, and Sikhs, and the displacement of millions of Muslims fleeing India for Pakistan and millions of Hindus and Sikhs fleeing in the other direction. It was one of history's greatest migrations. But that didn't make Pakistan purely Muslim or India purely Hindu. There remained 45 million Muslims in India and 18 million Hindus in Pakistan. Notwithstanding the horrors, Maulana Madani's response "was to rejoice at the end of colonialism and to summon Muslims in a free India to faithful citizenship and Islamic practice."[5]

In addition to his stellar role in the independence of India, Shaykh Madani gifted our family a personal intervention — exhorting our family members not to abandon Kandhla.

During Partition, Kandhla had escaped the worst of the upheavals — until an uncle was shot dead at close range. Mohammed Zaheeruddin — referred to with the honorific *maulvi*, "the learned" — was among the first in the family to get a Westernized education, a master's degree from Aligarh Muslim University, despite the family's differences with that institution.

A descendant of Mufti Ilahi Baksh, Zaheeruddin is described in different accounts as a model citizen. He was murdered, at age 49, for the same reason that Mahatma Gandhi was a year later — for being a symbol of Hindu-Muslim unity. "When the Sanghis [Hindu extremists] started demonizing Maulvi Zaheeruddin, non-Muslims in the neighbourhood refused to turn against him. They stood by him. But the Sanghis felt the need to remove him."[6] The murder left the family shaken, and many started fleeing for Pakistan.

Cousin Faizul Islam recalls how his own family also prepared to leave. "My father, Ziaul Islam, sent me, my mother, and sister to Lahore to go find a house. My uncle, Riazul Islam, was planning to move to Medina and wrote to Maulana Madani, asking for permission." This was according to the custom in those days to seek guidance from family elders or spiritual mentors at key junctures in life.

Faizul Islam continues: "Maulana Madani rushed to Kandhla. It was Thursday night and he spoke to a gathering at the Jami Masjid. He strongly urged the congregation to stay in India. He said that if the *ulama* and the landed gentry abandoned Kandhla, what sort of an example would that set for the other Muslims in the region? The Do Aab area would be emptied of Muslims.

"At the end of his speech, he walked up to my uncle, held his collar, and said, 'If you abandon Kandhla, I'll catch your *daman* [the flowing bottom of a tunic] and point you out on the day of judgment.' [Meaning he would identify him as a traitor to his home soil].

"So, my people stayed. As did the remaining five or six of our families that had not yet left."

In Hyderabad, far removed from the horrors of northern India, we were safe. But not for long, as we shall see.

Sufism, Which Sufism?

Darul Uloom in Deoband continues to thrive despite periodic collateral damage from the bad reputation madrasahs have acquired in recent years. Madrasahs deserve much criticism, but not for the reasons usually assumed in the West. Much of what has been said of madrasahs has been propagandist in the service of the American war on terror.

The problem with many madrasahs in India, Pakistan, and Bangladesh is not that they're breeding militancy — some might be — but that they're a racket in the American free-enterprise tradition, raking in big bucks but providing substandard education by ill-educated teachers and offering little or no financial transparency. Which is why they ward off repeated government attempts to modernize their curricula and open their books.

The Deoband seminary has little or no practical connection to its post-1947 offshoots, especially in Pakistan. It has even less to do with the "Deobandi" madrasahs in the tribal areas along the Pakistan-Afghanistan border that supplied the much-admired, pro-American, anti-Soviet mujahideen in Afghanistan in the 1980s; the much-derided foot soldiers for the Taliban in the 1990s; and the anti-American, anti–North American Treaty Organization (NATO) militants of the post-9/11 period.

In fact, many of the so-called madrasahs from where the Afghan mujahideen and the Taliban were recruited weren't madrasahs at all but rather "militant training camps that sought to be passed off as 'madrasahs' in order to legitimize their operations and to solicit funds," writes Indian author Yoginder Sikand in his well-researched book *Bastions of the Believers: Madrasas and Islamic Education in India.*[7]

And as Professor Metcalf has observed, the politics of the madrasahs in Pakistan and Afghanistan could not differ more dramatically from Deoband's.

Darul Uloom has also been the target of those who bristle at its long opposition to what it considers distortions of Sufism. Many Deobandis have been prominent Sufis themselves but sharia-compliant ones, meaning they don't excuse themselves from such essential tenets of Islam as praying, fasting, and adhering to a *halal* way of earning a living *sans* corruption. As the German scholar Dietrich Reetz writes, "Most Deobandi divines were themselves active Sufi shaykhs, following the path, or *tariqa*, where they saw it in consonance with the law and word of God, or Sharia." On mystical experience, "the Deobandi position was one of veneration of orthodox Sufis and opposition to the Wahhabis."[8]

What the Deobandis have consistently opposed is the highly commercialized and exploitative culture surrounding many mausoleums of venerable Sufi saints. Pilgrims are peddled religious knick-knackery as well as escort services for prostrating at the graves, kissing the precincts, and petitioning the dead to intercede with God for a variety of worldly wishes. Deobandis see such practices as contravening the fundamental tenet of Islam — one bows only to God. The relationship between the believer and God is direct without intercessors. There's no papacy in Islam. Deobandis also oppose hereditary succession; each Sufi master must earn his (or her but overwhelmingly his) station in life through knowledge and devotion, and not inherit shrines that have become cash cows.

These positions also happen to be red flags for the West, which (a) gets spooked by "sharia" and (b) equates Sufis with those who wear their religion lightly or not at all — a framing that fits with the thinking that the best Muslims are those who are the least Muslim. Deobandis stand as irritating counterweights to such clichéd and distorted thought.

People are entitled to their faith practices, obviously, including shrine worship. But so are those with contrary theological positions that are neither "puritanical" nor "Wahhabi." Such lazy characterizations fly in the face of the Deobandi record as a reformist, pluralistic, politically liberal force in a democratic framework.

4 The End of Colonialism

In recent years, the Deoband madrasah has maintained its long-standing history of friendly relations with Hindus. In 2004, it urged Muslims to avoid cow meat in deference to the Hindu belief in the sacredness of the animal. And Deobandis have endorsed yoga as healthy, suggesting its Hindu incantations might be substituted with recitations from the Qur'an or Allah's 99 names. In fact, there has been no communal violence in Deoband as of this writing.

In 2008, Deobandis came out in support of India's Women's Reservation Bill, which proposed a 33 percent quota for women in India's Parliament. The bill was passed by the Rajya Sabha (the upper house of the Indian Parliament) in 2010 but got derailed by the Lok Sabha (the lower house).

5

The Fall of Hyderabad

WE FLED AT DAWN.

A year after the end of British rule, independent India invaded the independent state of Hyderabad. Indian troops pierced the state's 4,000-kilometre border at five points, starting on September 13, 1948. As they advanced with little or no resistance, mobs followed them in some areas, rampaging through Muslim neighbourhoods. The troops and the mobs might come to Warangal any day, any hour, so it seemed wise to get out while we could to Hyderabad City, the capital.

We were nine in all: Abba, Amma, the six children, plus Sarwar, my *tayabba*. I was living in Hyderabad at that time and staying with Tayabba doing my *hifz*. Both of us happened to be visiting Warangal.

Abba said he'd follow a day or two later, and Tayabba would escort us out immediately. A road trip would be suicidal. Trains were sporadic and probably not safe for Muslims, but we had little choice.

The morning chores were done almost as if life were normal — *fajr* prayer at the local masjid, morning tea, and then quiet preparations to leave. My assignment was to get Suleman, my younger brother, ready. Barely four, he was standing in front of me and was fidgety. I tried to get him to stand still long enough to stretch his arms one by one, so I could slip on his *sherwani* sleeves. The custom was to wear a *sherwani* when travelling, emergency or not. Or perhaps the plan was to make the departure appear as routine as possible.

My Name Is Not Harry

The staff prepared and packed the tiffin. *Tongas* — horse-drawn carriages — took us to the Kazipet Railway Station five kilometres away. There was no train. Abba spoke to the station master, a Hindu gentleman he knew, who agreed the family had to get out. The sooner the better. He could put us on a freight train leaving for Hyderabad. While Abba and Amma debated, the station master said the freight train was the safest way to travel. It was the passenger trains that were in danger of being attacked, as had happened in northern India in 1947 when passengers were dragged out and massacred — Muslims in Hindu areas, Hindus and Sikhs in Muslim regions.

We were hustled into a coal boxcar, its floor covered with black soot. Amma asked for a broom that, of course, couldn't be found. She took out a towel — or was it someone's clothes? — and cleaned the surface as best as

Suleman and me, 1950s.

5 The Fall of Hyderabad

she could, telling us to settle down and Abba not to delay his own departure and to join us in Hyderabad as soon as possible. In his usual confident way, Abba said not to worry about him.

As the train crawled out, we kids were excited about this unusual mode of transport, mucking our hands on the interior walls of the metal car, sticking our noses and eyes in and out of the slats, feeling the air whiz by. The train stopped frequently. When it was stuck at a station for long, Tayabba climbed out to inquire what the problem was and to take the kids to the washroom and refill our depleting water supply. The news wasn't good — the station staff were unsure when, or if, the train would depart. Eventually, it did. Five or six hours later, it pulled into Hyderabad.

When we emerged, we were covered head to toe in soot. Piling into human-pedalled bicycle rickshaws, we were transported to the residential orphanage where Tayabba was principal and where he and I lived. But where was our luggage? It had been left behind on the freight train or at the railway station or in the rickshaws — who knew where? Calm as ever, Amma asked Tayabba for his and my clothes, and for scissors, needle, and thread. In what seemed like no time, she fashioned ill-fitting outfits for the siblings. Bathed and cleaned, we were soon out and about, running and playing in the vast courtyard.

In the neighbourhood lived a friend, Basit Jung, part of the nizam's nobility. He said the orphanage, however roomy, was no place for a family — everyone should stay in his mansion, Baquer Bagh, "Garden of Baquer," named after his eldest son, Baquer Khan. There was no shortage of space there. Basit Jung was part of the landed gentry and had held senior administrative posts. He had been collector — chief civil servant — of Warangal District, where he lived in an elaborate government house not far from our own home. Still, Baquer Bagh was in a league all its own. Spread over hectares and hectares, it had well-maintained gardens on all four sides, with mango and guava orchards at the back stretching nearly a kilometre. The swimming pool was used by men and boys.

A wing was cleared on the main floor and cordoned off for us. We moved in. But soon that neighbourhood, too, was deemed unsafe, being not far off the highway on which the invading Indian forces could be coming. We were on the move again, this time with the Jung family, to the historic "old city," which was mostly Muslim. There we might find safety in numbers.

The far greater worry was that there was no sign of Abba, nor word as to when he'd come. There was no phone in our Warangal house; Tayabba tried calling the two people in the neighbourhood who had them. But the phone lines weren't working. Tayabba then went to the railway and bus stations asking incoming passengers on the infrequent trains and buses from Warangal if they had news of Abba. Nothing. A pall settled on the household. Special prayers were offered asking Allah's mercy on Abba.

Then out of the blue he appeared, smiling as usual and reporting that there had been no way for him to leave or to communicate with us. But here he was just as he said he'd be.

Shukranay ki namaz, a prayer of gratitude, was offered. And Abba told us stories of Warangal.

Police were conducting house-to-house searches to confiscate guns. Abba welcomed them, saying we had none. He confidently led them from room to room, *almirah* (cupboard) by *almirah*, and from one big tin trunk to another. Then he glimpsed the wooden butt of a gun half hidden under a neat pile of women's clothes. Distracting the officer, he moved some clothes on top of it, at which point the enforcers announced that they'd seen enough and departed. Since we didn't hunt, the gun must have belonged to Amma's brother, who had visited us from Kandhla and used to go bird hunting.

But Abba's most uplifting story was this: one day a mob went around our neighbourhood harassing and threatening Muslim households. When they came to ours, they confronted an unusual sight. The cook, Gatti — a diminutive, gaunt, and stooping woman —stood at the gate, announcing to the crowd they'd have to kill her to enter the compound. She spoke Telugu, the language of the majority Hindus, and had a red *bindi*, the coloured dot worn by Hindu women on their foreheads. Gatti stood her ground, even as the crowd demanded to know why she was protecting Muslims. "Because they're my family," she told them.

* * *

In Hyderabad, there was a family crisis. Amma developed hemorrhoids, though nobody used that term in front of the kids, only saying that she was ill. Medicines didn't work, and she got weaker by the day. Soon she was skin and bones. Abba and Tayabba went from doctor to *hakeem* to Ayurvedic *vaids*, but to no avail. Then, one afternoon, Tayabba arrived clutching some leaves — a *hakeem* acquaintance of his had suggested they be boiled and turned into a paste and applied. Amma did recover slowly but remained gaunt all her life.

There was yet another scare. Abba had a younger brother, Zubair ul-Islam. Thin and tall, he was a good field hockey player. Adept at badminton, too. We kids were fascinated by his habit of starting the day by downing raw eggs. Abba had enticed him out of Kandhla after the horrors of the 1947 Partition, hoping to get him involved in the business. But he wasn't interested, being keen on going to Pakistan. One day he joined a caravan of Muslims travelling from Hyderabad to Bombay to sail to Karachi. But the group got hauled out of the train at Sholapur, just across the border in neighbouring Bombay State, and detained in a camp.

Abba started visiting him in Sholapur, taking along two separate packages of Danish cheese, British biscuits, and other non-perishable goods — one set for his brother and the other for the commander of the camp. Uncle Zubair was eventually released and did go to Pakistan.

Mountbatten's Games

The absorption of Hyderabad State into India was months in the making, a by-product of the messy division of India by the departing British. While Pakistan had been carved out in Muslim-majority areas of the subcontinent, there remained one Muslim-majority state in India, Kashmir, ruled by a Hindu rajah, and three Hindu-majority but Muslim-ruled states. Kashmir's maharajah opted for India. But when the Muslim rulers of Hyderabad, Bhopal, and the small state of Junagarh by the Arabian Sea dillydallied over either joining Pakistan or remaining independent, India coerced or crushed them. It was foolhardy of them to think they could keep their old order.

There was hardly any public support in the new democratic India for retaining feudal kingdoms. Hyderabad, for all its glory, had perhaps the most oppressive landholding system and had a literacy rate of barely 2 percent. That was why many Muslims, too, were opposed to the princely states, such as Shah Waliuallah and Abdul Aziz, 19th-century intellectuals and the teachers and mentors of Mufti Baksh.

Months before the Indian invasion, Hyderabad had been put under an economic blockade by India, and there had been cross-border raids from neighbouring states by militias. The nizam appealed to Lord Mountbatten, the last viceroy, who had stayed on as India's first governor general: "Hyderabad is half the size of France and has a population of 17,000,000 ... considerably more than Canada or any other British Dominion outside India."[1] Mountbatten wrote back on April 8, 1948, assuring he'd "never be a party to improper pressure on your State.... Never will I, the constitutional Governor-General of India, be a party to any such procedure."[2]

But plans to invade Hyderabad were well advanced. According to D.F. Karaka, editor of a Bombay weekly, *The Current*, "It is difficult to believe that Lord Mountbatten, as the constitutional head of the Indian government, could have been unaware of them." Karaka made that observation in his book *Fabulous Mogul: Nizam VII of Hyderabad*, a highly informative, even if hagiographical account of the ruler.[3]

The nizam wrote Mountbatten again but got no reply until weeks later, with Mountbatten blaming the delay on the bureaucracy. Sir Arthur Lothian, a former British resident in Hyderabad (1942–46), noted that: Britons should feel "shame at our tacit abandonment of Hyderabad to pressure of every sort from India."[4]

On September 4, Hyderabad appealed to the United Nations Security Council in Paris. By the time the council got that onto its agenda on September 16, Indian forces had already marched in. Any hope that the council would call for an immediate ceasefire evaporated when it adjourned for four days until September 20. Canada abstained, with ambassador General Andrew McNaughton saying he'd "await further information."

The invasion was over in five days. India called it a "police action." Karaka wondered "why the Government of India had to use a Lieutenant-General, three Majors-General and a whole Armoured Division to effect a 'Police Action ...'"[5]

5 The Fall of Hyderabad

Canadian academic Wilfred Cantwell Smith of McGill University wrote after his visit to Hyderabad a year later:

> The Muslim community fell before a massive and brutal blow, the devastation of which left those who did survive reeling in bewildered fear. Thousands upon thousands were slaughtered; many hundreds of thousands uprooted.... In some areas, all the men were stood in a line, and done to death. Of the total Muslim community in Hyderabad, it would seem, that somewhere between one in 10 and one in five of the adult males may have lost their lives in those few days. In addition to the killing, there was widespread rape, arson, looting and expropriation. A very large percentage of the entire Muslim population of the districts fled in destitution to the capital or other cities.[6]

It turned out that Smith, like others in Hyderabad, had exaggerated. Prime Minister Jawaharlal Nehru set up a committee to investigate. It was co-chaired by a Hindu and a Muslim, Pandit Sunderlal, a prominent member of the ruling Congress Party, and Qazi Abdul Ghaffar, the editor of *Payam* (Message), a pro-India Urdu newspaper in Hyderabad. After touring nine of the 16 districts of the state, they concluded that "a very conservative estimate, at least 27,000 to 40,000 people, lost their lives during and after the Police Action." The committee also criticized the military government for dismissing or otherwise penalizing thousands of people in the nizam's civil service.

Just about every family has stories of the horrors of the police action. The family of my brother-in-law, Siddiq Ahmed Khan, husband of Maryam, fled on foot and in bullock carts ahead of a rampaging mob. A niece of his, who happened to be out of the house when the family fled, was shot dead. Another family member jumped onto a truck to escape but it got stopped and all the passengers were lined up and shot. An uncle of Siddiq posted outside the city hid with his colleague in cane fields, and the two walked three days to safety, their feet blistered.

Such oral accounts, including those by Hyderabadis living overseas, need to be collected.

The idea of landlocked Hyderabad joining Pakistan or even being independent was a pipe dream. Still, by crushing the state and its people so brutally, India created a bitter legacy and also violated Gandhi's pioneering achievement of winning independence from the British with *satyagraha*, "non-violence."

The New India

The takeover of Hyderabad so unsettled Uncle Idris in Deoband that he decided to leave for Pakistan. He resigned from the madrasah, went to Kandhla, packed his and Dada's writings and manuscripts in wooden trunks, left everything else in the house, and travelled with his family to Bombay, where he caught a ship to Karachi. His younger brother, Mohammed Ayub, the one with the mango orchards near the canal that I loved so much as a child, also left.

The abandoned homes and mango groves were taken over by the government and allocated to the refugees pouring in from Pakistan. The official assumption was that everyone in our family had bolted for Pakistan. That some of us were still very much in India, in Hyderabad, didn't matter. A court case lingered for decades before Abba abandoned it and counselled me not to be tempted to pursue it after he was gone: "Use your time and energy on something more productive."

* * *

The ideas and ideals of Shaykh Madani, the rector at Deoband, came to be reflected in independent India's 1950 Constitution. India's first president, Rajendra Prasad, visited Deoband and thanked Madani and the institution for their roles in the independence movement. Yet, with a characteristic Deobandi mixture of modesty and independence of mind, Madani politely declined a high civilian award, Padma Vibhushan, due to his "concern that it might create the impression that he was in some sense subservient to the government."[7]

5 The Fall of Hyderabad

* * *

For all the political turmoil and personal trauma, our family emerged relatively unscathed. Back in Warangal, Abba resumed his business and salvaged some of the lifestyle that had been built up through the 1940s.

I stayed behind in Hyderabad with Tayabba, who had no family of his own. The orphanage was a spacious rectangular place with a long line of classrooms along one length and a mosque wall on the other, with a courtyard in between to run around in and play. Some of the classrooms were outfitted for teaching trades — tailoring, carpentry, and cobblery. Tayabba's corner room, which I shared with him, was only slightly more spacious than the others. He and I lived a compact life. We took out the day's clothes from two neatly stacked tin trunks in the corner and kept our other belongings tidily arranged. A limited quantity of groceries was kept in another corner where there was an *angheeti*, a brazier. I took it out into the yard to get the coal briquettes burning while Tayabba cooked. It was simple and minimal fare — roti, rice, and *daal* (lentils); vegetables once in a while; eggs often and occasionally meat for me. Tayabba eschewed a cook or a cleaning person because neither the students nor the live-in teaching staff had any help and did all the cooking and cleaning themselves, so he'd do the same. Several colleagues and students always offered to help. But Tayabba declined. It wasn't their job to do our chores.

Prayer times set the rhythm of the day, starting with the pre-dawn *fajr* prayers. In India, Muslims aren't the only ones to begin early. Hindus do their *puja* first thing in the morning — we could hear their *bhajans* in the neighbourhood while yogis performed Surya Namaskar, "Namaste to the rising sun."

Post-*fajr*, I had my first Qur'anic lesson of the day for about two hours before breakfast. Noon prayers were followed by lunch and a siesta. Most late afternoons Tayabba and I visited his friends, usually in a two-seater rickshaw, the commonest transport. On steep inclines when the *rickshawallah* found it hard to pedal, he'd get down and pull the rickshaw, his left hand on the handlebar, right on the seat. Tayabba, too, got out to push the rickshaw from the back. More fun were the double-decker buses imported from England. I loved the front seat on the upper deck.

Tayabba and I went to Warangal often, frequently by train, the most pleasant of which was a gorgeous yellow one-car diesel locomotive with a driver's cabin on either end. It had plush leather seats, three on each side of a passageway, about two dozen rows in all. The train was part of "His Exalted Highness, the Nizam's Guaranteed State Railway," the first in India to buy the British-made diesel car. Two of them, in fact; the other one travelled from Hyderabad to the historic city of Bidar.

The two-hour journey to Warangal was a good time for my Qur'anic lessons. He gave me a line from anywhere in the Qur'an and I had to pick it up and continue reciting. In fact, most trips, long and short, usually served as a classroom.

Smile, You Are a Muslim

What I recall most from my time with Tayabba was his emphasis on honesty: "Be scrupulous down to a *paisa* [penny]. Make do with what you have; if you ever borrow anything, make sure to return it before you forget." He was against religious rigidity — "the more ignorant, the more intolerant" — and was fond of citing a Persian couplet:

> *Neem Hakeem Khatra-e Jaan*
> *Neem mullah khatra-e Eman.*

> Half doctors a danger to health
> Half mullahs a danger to faith.

Tayabba admonished against showing off religiosity — "Your actions are for Allah, not for impressing others." He counselled against confusing a dour demeanour for piety — "Smile, you are a Muslim."

Friday prayers were a big deal. Tayabba and I often went to Makka Masjid, so called because its bricks were said to have been baked from the soil of the holy city of Mecca. The largest mosque in the city, it was packed every Friday with perhaps 10,000 worshippers in the large hall and vast open courtyard.

I remember mosques as very social places. After prayers, knots of people squatted at various spots, some engaged in *dars*, "discussion groups," others just chatting like Tayabba and his friends. I often stretched out on the *janamaz*, "prayer rugs." Nobody objected, unlike the busybodies in North American mosques these days who have taken on the corporate ethos of not letting anyone linger anywhere in public spaces.

Most of Tayabba's friends had libraries in their homes, which is where they welcomed guests. The floors had lush carpets, with cushions along the walls to lean on, and small, portable, low-lying writing desks angled toward the person squatting in front. While the adults talked or pored over books, I frequently dozed off in a corner and was awakened only at the arrival of tea and refreshments. That was the most enjoyable part, besides being fussed over as the only child among older men.

Often, Tayabba and I ate out, he deferring to my meat choices though he preferred vegetarian. My favourites were mutton kebab, chicken biryani, and chai. For ice cream, he took me to high-end places such as John's Bakery, which also made the best curry puffs, that Indo-British concoction of flaky pastry stuffed with curried veggies or meat; or to Vicaji's, the old hotel on a hill run by a Zoroastrian family, with its musty leather sofas and the biggest billiard table in town.

Tayabba lived an eclectic combination of modern luxuries and the modest style of the *maulvis*, the religious class — the austerities for himself, the indulgences for me.

Living Off Their Silver

The end of Hyderabad State meant the demise of a well-established cosmopolitan culture, the biggest victims being those who had been its greatest beneficiaries, namely, Muslims. The old nobility, having lost their generous government salaries as well as much of their land, were destitute. Some tried businesses, but they didn't know commerce.

Many families survived by selling off their silver. Auction houses took a disproportionate percentage of the sales of beautiful furniture and household goods. The biggest tragedy was that extensive personal libraries were lost — the books sold for their leather bindings, or worse, as wrapping paper. Those who had land sold off chunks or were coerced into doing so — or murdered. Moinuddin Pasha, the son-in-law of Basit Jung, was axed to death close to his lands during an overnight stay in a bungalow in the town of Aler, 70 kilometres out of Hyderabad on the road to Warangal. So haunted were we by that brutality that for years afterward — decades, really — rarely did I or any members of our family drive by without slowing down near the bungalow and speaking of the tragedy.

* * *

I finished memorization of the Qur'an when I was "nine years, one month, and 27 days," according to the handwritten marginalia by Tayabba on a poem he wrote to mark the occasion. The 27-verse ode begins with *Azeezi mukarram, azeezi girami,* "Dear Honoured, Dear Beloved."

Tayabba used to compose a poem for each one of us on important occasions, such as marriages, but also for mini-milestones, as in "Yousuf Recognizes Words." According to his note, I completed my *hifz* on the 11th day of the lunar month of Safar, 1370. That translates to November 22, 1950, which poses a question. If June 1, 1942, was my date of birth, according to my papers, I'd have only been eight years, five months, and 10 days old. Conversely, if I was more than nine years, one month, and 27 days old in 1950, my date of birth would be September 1941. The discrepancy isn't explained by the lunar year being 11 days shorter. Either Tayabba's notation is wrong, which is doubtful, given how fastidious he was, or more likely, my birth year is 1941, and I'm a year older than what the records say — and no doubt the wiser for it.

The casualness of dates is a very Indian, or Eastern, thing. Much of the South floats on a sea of imprecision, whereas the North demands exactitude. And the twain do not meet. An immigrant, or especially a refugee to the West, is expected to square all the dates, which she or he cannot, and is deemed evasive. Similarly, the spelling of a family's last name can differ from person to person — I am Siddiqui, but brother Suleman is Siddiqi. Why's the *u* missing in his? Who knows! When his name was written out for the first time in English, either by a teacher or the office in his first school, it got spelled the way it did and stuck to him for life. English, or French, isn't our mother tongue, nor of 99.99 percent of South Asians; our names are written out more precisely in our respective native languages — Urdu, Hindi, Telegu, Tamil,

5 The Fall of Hyderabad

Malayalam, Kannada, Bengali, Marathi, Punjabi, Gujarati, Kutchi, Sindhi, et cetera. But transliteration of names into English or French is another matter. Fortunately, Suleman and I have never had to prove to a Western bureaucrat, judge, lawyer, or journalist that we're children of the same father.

This clash of civilizations between the North and the South is for real, unlike the conjectures on which Samuel Huntington built his thesis.[8] The imprecision of names, dates, and times manifests itself in a million ways — for example, in this familiar conversation:

> Shall we meet again?
> Inshallah.
> Inshallah, yes? Or inshallah, no?
> Yes, inshallah.
> Great. When shall we meet?
> Someday, inshallah.

In 1951, or thereabouts, Tayabba and I were back in Warangal — I don't remember whether his contract had come to an end or if the orphanage had closed. Back with Amma, Abba, and the siblings, I don't recall adjustment problems, though they might have had a different view.

My secular education would begin at last — not in school but rather at home. Either because the public schools were deemed to be no good, or more likely, because I had a lot of catching up to do. In any case, I entered an even more joyful phase of life, one of unquestioned family love and happiness that marked me for life.

6

Happy Childhood

THERE WAS NO ELECTRICITY IN WARANGAL EXCEPT FOR STREETLAMPS. AS evening approached, my siblings and I helped prepare the chrome Petromax lanterns, pouring kerosene and pumping air to build up the pressure for the mantles to burn bright white. Outside the house, some youngsters studied under street lamps late into the night. In the morning, the poor came to sweep up the moths for food.

There was nothing distinctive about our mostly Muslim neighbourhood except its interreligious harmony. Horrible memories of the 1947 Partition and 1948 Indian invasion of Hyderabad State had been set aside in the spirit of the new, independent, secular India.

On one side of our house, beyond an open shallow space that formed a little lake during the monsoons, lived a Hindu family. They occupied the white lime-washed bungalow that once belonged to a Muslim who had migrated to Pakistan. Three brothers there, Kanhayya Lal, Jawahar Lal, and Kishan Lal became my best friends. Their mother maintained a strictly vegetarian kitchen; outsiders couldn't enter but could benefit from its fresh fried *puris* and veggie dishes.

Across the main road from our house lived nuns. We rarely saw them, ensconced as they were behind walls. But they came out to distribute food and hold free classes as part of their missionary work in a nearby poor locality.

Their neighbour was Fazal Husain, a prosperous Muslim advocate (father of Ali Husain who welcomed me in Montreal in 1967). On his multi-hectare property, he had set up the Sir Ross Masood Memorial Boarding School, named after the grandson of Sir Syed Ahmad Khan of Aligarh Muslim University. My ancestors had opposed Sir Syed as too obeisant to the British, and here 1,400 kilometres away and a few generations later, was his vision of "English education" arrayed in front of us. But old differences had been forgotten with the departure of the British, and Muslims were readily teaching their kids English and sending them to secular schools, as my siblings and I would be.

The only grocery store was run by three Hindu brothers, Pedayya, Yenkatum, and Jaganathan. There was a chai canteen and a few shops providing primitive services: chopped wood for fuel; bikes for rent; a horse-drawn *tonga* service; and a *girni*, "grain-grinder," making wheat and millet flour. A public water tap nearby only functioned mornings and evenings. Beyond those was the local mosque, the heartbeat of the community. Choti Masjid, "Little Mosque," it was called, to differentiate it from the Badi Masjid, "Big Mosque," not far away.

The mosque had only one employee, the *muezzin*, who gave the *azan*, "call to prayers," five times per day from a high platform. He doubled as the caretaker. The bulk of mosque work was done by volunteers. The priestly duties fell mostly to Tayabba and Abba, both being *hafiz*, the only ones in the area who knew the Qur'an by heart. Memorization wasn't a tradition in southern India at that time. Tayabba led Friday prayers and also gave sermons on special religious days. During Ramadan, he and Abba alternated leading the month-long evening prayers, reciting one of the 30 chapters of the Qur'an each night and ending on the 27th evening, it being the auspicious Night of Power when Allah revealed the first verses of the Qur'an to the Prophet Muhammad. When either Abba or Tayabba recited at our mosque, the other recited at another. Being a faster reciter, Abba was finished in two weeks and launched another nightly recitation at a second mosque. As if that wasn't enough, he'd do a third recitation in the special early-morning prayers, *tahajjud*, around 3:00 a.m., in the last seven days of the month. All gratis, the family never monetizing their gift of memorization or their knowledge.

The remarkable thing about Abba was that the heightened night routine didn't seem to affect his hectic workdays, except that he extended his afternoon siesta by about an hour. He had boundless energy and a strong work ethic. When he undertook multiple projects for the Public Works Department (PWD), he'd visit one or two in the morning, go to one PWD office or another to deal with officials, come home for rest, and be off again to other sites.

His afternoon nap is a habit I inherited; all my life I've tried to steal a few winks on my office sofa. It's a luxury my kids don't relate to at all. They think it's a strange Third World habit. I tell them their productivity would increase if they adopted it.

Tayabba and I kept up our routine. After *fajr* prayers at the mosque, he and I often went for a walk to a nearby mountain where he stood at the bottom for the 30 minutes or so that it took me to climb to the top and come back down, boasting that I'd done it in less time than on the previous trip.

My uncle was indulgent in many ways but also tough when it came to my studies. There were times when he spanked or pinched me, occasionally leaving bruises. I cried but rarely complained, and when I did protest to Abba and Amma, they'd say I wouldn't have been punished had I done my homework. Corporal punishment, aka tough love, was common. It angered me and left me frustrated. Yet, and this is the surprising part, once I grew up, I didn't have any lingering anger toward Tayabba. All the good he'd done, his million kindnesses and selfless dedication, obviated my mini-traumas.

I got to lead the evening *taraweeh* prayers in the mosque, the youngest ever there. For a boy, it's a great confidence booster to lead older people in prayer night after night. The recitation being from memory, Tayabba was my prompter. But when he got called to another mosque, it was Amma who took over. She did it from a small open-air alcove behind the back wall — the social mores of the mosques in India allowing men only. The presence of Amma and my sisters in the mosque was unusual. More revolutionary was Amma's prompting from about eight metres away, her soft voice wafting over the lines of men silently lined up behind me, well ahead of her. Her presence challenged the social norm, but so impeccable were my family's Islamic credentials that no one dared object. As years went by, other women of the locality started coming, as well. On a 2019 trip there, I saw that the newly expanded masjid now includes a large section for women.

With such fond memories of the place, I thought I better cross-check with my cohorts of the time who have since dispersed all over the world. I started with Syed Husain of Maryland, brother of Ali Husain, who had welcomed me to Canada at Dorval International Airport in Montreal back in 1967. Syed Husain said his memories ran "deep and dear," especially "the sense of togetherness, care, serenity, and peace around the masjid." The breaking of the daylong fast in Ramadan "used to be a feast, as several families used to send sumptuous *iftar*," drinks and appetizers to recharge the thirsty and hungry.

Mansoor Baig of Chicago said: "Memories of my lovely childhood there are still fresh" — and revelatory. For years he attended post-dawn religious classes where "unfortunately not a single word of English was spoken or displayed. English was still considered un-Islamic in the mosque precincts," a legacy of the anti-British struggle. "This was not rectified until 1955 or 1956." Mansoor had another telling tale, a theological conundrum, when a baby goat fell into the mosque's well. "Questions were raised whether the water was still *halal*, 'permissible,' and, if not, how to make it so again. Dead goat removed, water proportionate to its weight was bucketed out." Talmudic wisdom.

Mumtaz Ali Baig of London, England, wrote me a three-page note in his neatly calligraphed Urdu. He recalled how Fridays were particularly special. "The masjid was a beehive of activity right from the morning, preparing for a full house for the weekly sabbath at noon. We would be putting up the canopy to keep the sun off the courtyard, tying the ropes on top of the roof, a job given to little kids in deference to the privacy of the women of the households nearby who would not want men gawking at them."

All three — Syed, Mansoor, and Mumtaz — also recalled, unprompted, the Qur'anic renditions of both Abba and Tayabba, especially the latter's erudition in sermons. "Your Tayabba was also Tayabba for all of us," wrote Mumtaz.

Snakes, Snakes

As strict an upbringing as we had at home, the boys were given freedom to roam and play outside, as and where we liked. There was no helicopter parenting. Venturing out meant a million things besides playing cricket: wading into wet rice paddy fields, stealing ripe tomatoes and consuming them on the spot, jumping into nearby wells, there being no streams or canals nearby. Step wells with stairs embedded into the circular wall descending were a marvel of engineering unique to India. During summers, we walked down that many more steps to the water. The hotter the summer, the lower the water level — sometimes nine metres or more down in our favourite well.[1]

We tied empty tin cans to our bodies as floaters and waded out while older boys kept an eye out for us. There were jumping and diving competitions from varying heights, using the steps as the takeoff platform. Honoured were those who could leap from the top, or more daringly, dive the whole way down. I never did; I was chicken.

Wells provided the ideal respite from the searing summer heat, and we brought our lunches along and spent hours on end in them. Our summer camp.

The wells served nearby farms, as a communal bathing spot for the poor, and for washing clothes on platforms of rocks. An unwritten code — no soap, no snorting, no food — was generally observed, with the passing parade of people keeping a keen eye. They also served as rotating lifeguards, making sure the kids stayed in line. We obeyed because we knew where the lines were drawn, and also because if we crossed them, word was bound to trickle back to parents. When it takes a village to raise a child, every villager is a potential informant on miscreants.

A childhood memory that haunts me still is the fear of snakes. Once in a while, there was a kerfuffle in the neighbourhood because a cobra, the deadliest of snakes, was spotted in someone's house and people would swarm all over with sticks in hand. The cobra would sit there in a corner, lifting its top third erect, baring its fangs and hissing off and on, sending shivers down people's spines. It wasn't called king cobra for nothing. The drama only ended when someone struck the serpent dead.

In case there was no such happy ending, inevitably, one or two people in the crowd would claim to have just the right antidote: a prayer or some *abracadabra* incantation, or a home-made potion from a secret recipe. Curing snake bites has a long and storied history in India. The last Mughal king, Bahadur Shah, believed that being the emperor and a Sufi saint, he possessed special spiritual powers to defang snake bites. He would send "a Seal of Bezoar, a stone antidote to poison, and some water on which he had breathed" for the victim to drink. The king's success rate wasn't recorded.

For years I had bad nightmares about snakes, especially those skulking in water. To this day, the rush of water from a pipe in a swimming pool can send a jolt of fear through my body. Whenever I return to India, the fear of snakes returns, especially at brother Suleman's house in Hyderabad, which is next to a ravine. Maryam also developed ophidiophobia and wrote about it in an essay for a magazine in Montreal.

Not far behind was the fear of scorpions and spiders. On a trip to Oman in 1999, I spoiled a family outing to the desert on a glorious moonlit night by kiboshing the overnight camping after being told that the sands were crawling with scorpions.

Culture of Food

Meals were family rituals, with everyone present for all three, unless we weren't home for a good reason. Our tradition was to eat sitting on a carpeted floor, with a *dastar-khan*, a tablecloth minus the table. We sat cross-legged, the yoga easy pose. But Tayabba preferred to kneel and tuck his feet under his buttocks, as in the daily prayers. An anti-slouching posture, it also followed the Prophet's dictum and practice of avoiding overeating: "Stop eating when you can still eat some more."

Most meals had two courses — fresh homemade roti followed by rice, both eaten with a vegetable or meat dish, mutton or chicken but not beef; a lentil dish, there being dozens of varieties of pulses, each cooked either *sookha* or *patla*, "dry" or "wet," the first where the pulses keep their shape, the second cooked in water or tomatoes and turned into gravy. Rice was mostly for the kids. The elders, being northerners, preferred rotis. A roti had to be rushed from the kitchen hot and puffed up off the *tawa*, the inverted griddle. That was especially so for Abba and Amma, while Tayabba wasn't fussy. For the rest of us, the rotis were precooked, but only by about 10 minutes, so that they were still warm.

There was no prepackaged flour. We had to buy wheat and take it to the local *girni*, "grain grinder," in our case, run by a friend, Mustafa Bhai, older brother of Mumtaz in London. The family was impeccably honest — a guarantee that "A grade" wheat or millet wouldn't be mixed with cheaper varieties.

Seasons dictated our menu. In the winter, we ate heftier, denser dishes — meat pilafs and *khichdi* (a rice and lentil dish) — usually with a heap of *ghee* (clarified butter) to fortify the body for the cold weather, which, in fact, wasn't all that cold in Warangal. In the summer, the meals were lighter, and there were frequent thirst quenchers: *aab-shola* (raw mangoes baked and squeezed, mixed with sugar and a touch of lime), melon juice, or *limboo-pani* (squeezed lemon, water, fresh mint, and sugar).

Abba was a big meat eater, and so were the boys. Particular about the quality of meat, he trained staffers Lal and Wazir Mohammed to buy only the choicest cuts. The brothers had been with us for as long as I remember. When either was away, Abba went himself, rather than trust anyone else. He was disappointed that his sons, especially the eldest, showed little or no inclination to learn meat shopping, even while being carnivores.

I was even more leery of the annual ritual of sacrificing animals on Eid al-Adha. It's the festival that coincides with the conclusion of the annual *hajj* pilgrimage in Mecca and marks Abraham's readiness to sacrifice his son, Ishaaq (Isaac), on God's instructions, only to discover he was sacrificing a ram. Up to a dozen goats were sacrificed over three days. Then the meat was sent to friends and neighbours, with a designated portion distributed among the poor.

As gruesome as I found the scene, I liked the fresh kidney and liver that got cooked within minutes. That was an Eid delicacy, which everyone enjoyed, including the drop-in guests. But Lal Mohammed ate the liver and kidney raw, saying that was the custom in his village to stay in good health. Only after coming to Canada did I learn that the Inuit eat raw meat, especially in winter.

* * *

For bigger parties, we kids were the waiters, manning the plates and dishes and cutlery, the latter limited to serving spoons of varying sizes because everyone still ate the Indian way with hands, the right hand. Woe be to us if we didn't ensure enough of everything, including wash basins near a drain, and soap and towels. The boys didn't get to eat with the adults — we were bearers, fetching rotis, re-topping the dishes, filling water glasses, anticipating every guest's needs. Sequencing and timing were the keys. Abba had a habit of inviting people over for lunch or dinner from the mosque or workplace, causing Gatti and her assistant cook, Husaini Bi, to grumble, "Why doesn't your father give us some notice?"

Anyone dropping in at the house had to be fed, at least given tea and snacks. A habit I inherited — and came to regret, especially during the building of an extension to my Toronto house that turned into a three-year nightmare. As contractors and tradespeople absconded with money without finishing their jobs, I got more and more resentful at having kept up an endless supply of tea, coffee, and cookies for them. "I'm foolish. I shouldn't be doing this," I kept telling myself. Yet I couldn't help it.

Abba's generosity was most evident during Ramadan. For the breaking of the fast at dusk, several dishes were sent over to the mosque. If Ramadan fell in the summer months, big blocks of ice procured from an ice factory were dispatched for the thirsty congregants. The Islamic concept is that the more people fed, especially those who have fasted, the greater Allah's reward will be. Ditto for generosity with the less fortunate, as long as a show isn't made of it. The best way to give is anonymously. To this day, I cringe when I see buildings, schools, halls, chairs, and benches named after donors, or big philanthropists feted in newspaper ads.

Mangoes Galore

Abba was a mango aficionado. He was familiar with dozens of its ostensibly 99 varieties and knew where to procure which kind. The sweetest mango came from the hottest regions. As people fried, mangoes thrived. Abba dispatched either Wazir or Lal Mohammed to districts that were hotter, such as Khammam, a two-hour train ride. They returned laden with the fruit in different states of ripeness. The ones ready to be consumed were cooled in a bucket of ice water, and we all took positions on veranda steps in the inner courtyard. Abba handed out the mangoes, whole or in slices, and they were passed on in the human chain.

Mangoes fall into two broad categories — ones to slice and eat like any other fruit, the other a juicy variety that was sucked. To soften the pulp, we held the mango in one hand, thumb at the bottom, index finger at the top, and used the other hand to press the pulp gently while rotating the mango on its axis. Soon the fruit turned into a sack of juice, at which point we plucked out the top with our teeth to make a tiny opening to suck the juice into our mouths, ideally in stages. If the opening was made too large, the juice spurted out and we were deemed persons insufficiently trained for polite company. All the sucking done, the skin with the seed still inside was tossed into a bin.

Mango ice cream had pride of place over that made from papaya, coconut, and other fruit. Mango juice, preferably squished pulp, mixed with whole milk made for a creamy and smooth end product. Suleman, Yousuf, and I had the job of turning the crank of the manual machine in which the drum rotated in a tub of ice cubes and coarse salt. As for sherbet, I'd never heard of it until I came to Canada.

Abba was particular about his tea — it had to be Lipton's Darjeeling, brewed just right and piping hot. I've remained a diehard fan of the brand, along with Akbar's Tea from Sri Lanka. Neither brand is readily available in Canada, let alone the United States, which must have the world's most insipid teas. Worse, American corporate culture has caused great grief for tea drinkers in Canada: most restaurants no longer boil the water to the temperature required, presumably to avoid being sued for possible scalding. Many hotels and motels no longer stock teakettles, expecting their pipsqueak little coffee machines to double as tea-makers. I've taken to carrying not only my own tea but a kettle. Idiosyncratic, for sure, but I do get a good cup of tea.

* * *

When the grocers Pedayya, Yenkatum, and Jaganathan split the business into three stores, Abba divided his order into three. Instead of one running account paid at the end of the month, there were now three. Abba rarely looked at the bills, believing that one either trusted a person or didn't. Someone was telling the truth unless proven otherwise. That dictum popped up in my head decades later in Toronto when I told the middle school teacher of my son, Fahad, that I assumed he told her the truth. She said, "Most kids lie," to which I replied that the burden of proof was on her, not him. The teacher looked at me as though I were from an alien world.

Family Life

The house kept expanding with the family. Abba bought up a neighbour's house and extended ours into it, doubling the inner courtyard and duplicating whatever there was on our side. We ended up with four toilets, four shower stalls, two kitchens, and two pantries. Very utilitarian but no style, architectural or otherwise. About three-quarters of a higgledy-piggledy hectare.

The inner courtyard had trees: a papaya, a guava, and a *sithaphal* (custard apple or sugar apple). The crop from the papaya was more profuse, but the one from the guava more fragrant, scenting the area. Outdoors, a few coconut trees lined the long driveway. Inadvertently, I killed a row of small palms by pouring leftover ice and salt water from the ice-cream machine into the concave base of the trees. Within days, they wilted and turned brown, with everyone wondering why. Then it dawned on me that I may have been the culprit. I fessed up and was admonished with gales of laughter at the depth of my ignorance.

For a time, we had a buffalo for fresh milk every day. That meant losing the makeshift badminton court in the front yard. It wasn't a proper court, only a marked space with two poles and a fraying net. We whined about the loss, but the benefits and popularity of the fresh milk, cream, and curd was deemed far more important — until my sisters joined the protest. They complained that while boys got to go out to play cricket or whatever, there was no similar organized activity for girls, the concept being alien to societal mores. That was the end of the buffalo project. Sisters had clout.

A garden patch produced different crops throughout the year — white radishes, cauliflower, carrots, potatoes, tomatoes, tiny green hot peppers, coriander, and mint.

6 Happy Childhood

Summers could register up to 48 degrees Celsius. Mitigating the heat was an elaborate yet engaging exercise, indoors and outdoors. During the day, curtains of vetiver *khas* (grass), of which perfumes are made, were unrolled and hung over the doors and windows. Frequently, they were watered so that when the *loo*, "hot wind," blew, it came through the grass screen and arrived cooled — a natural air conditioner. When the wind subsided, the backup was a *punkah* — literally, "the wing of a bird" — a rectangular piece of heavy cloth tied to a bamboo stick hung from the ceiling and moved back and forth by pulling on a string to create a draft. The one who did the pulling was the *punkah-wallah*, a colonial British coinage. We didn't have a designated person — whoever happened to be around did the chore. In the living room, heat escaped from vents high on the five-metre walls. In a chamber that served as the family room in summer, sawdust was spread on the floor and sprinkled with water.

During evenings, the inner and outer courtyards were sprinkled, the first sprays evincing hot vapours off the soil before eventually cooling. Sleeping cots were laid out. On the hottest nights, the younger ones slept on the flat roofs of the verandas for better breezes. That felt special on moonlit nights.

Most of these arrangements were labour-intensive, but in retrospect, environmentally sound. One of the worst things that's happened to India in the modern era is the proliferation of reinforced concrete box houses that turn into ovens, needing constant air conditioning that's unreliable due to electricity shortages. My brother Suleman's house is like that; during summer visits, he and I talk about the irony of a contractor's son having built himself such a trap.

In the mosquito season, all beds were fitted with nets. The first chore after tucking under the net was to make sure not a single mosquito was left inside, otherwise you'd be a sitting duck all night. To this day, I can't stand the buzz of mosquitos that inevitably find me. It's one reason I dislike cottaging, not to speak of all the driving and traffic hassles. This sounds very un-Canadian, but for me, the great outdoors don't quite compensate for such irritations.

There were no fridges, necessitating vegetable and meat shopping every morning, and fresh cooking thrice per day. Milk and leftovers were stored overnight in the inner courtyard in an *almirah* (cupboard) that had screen netting for air circulation and legs that sat in small tin cans of water,

The House in Warangal

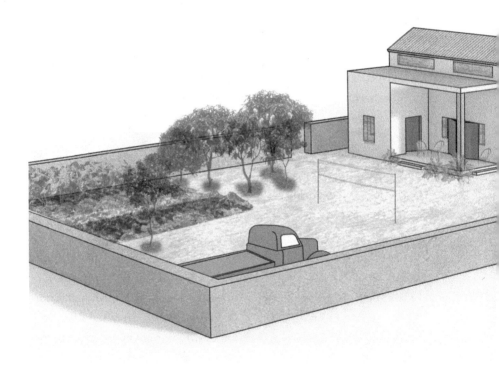

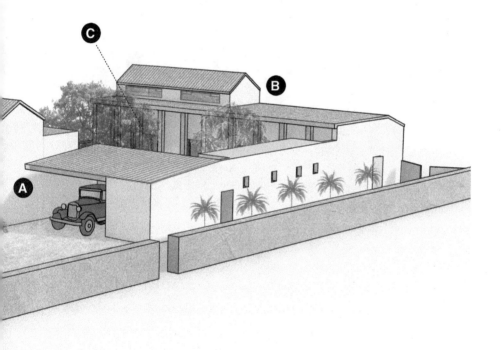

- **A** Reception room/guest parlour
- **B** Bedroom block
- **C** Inner courtyard

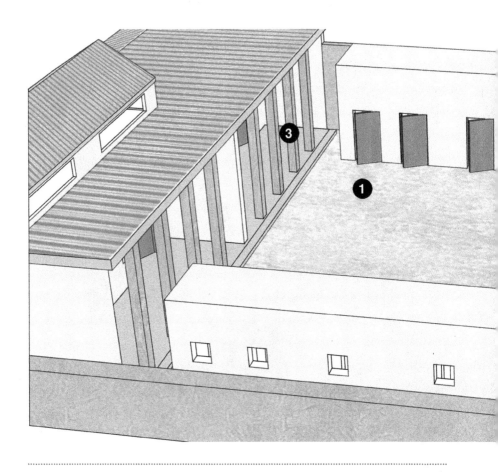

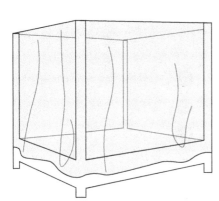

❶ In mosquito season, beds with netting — indoors and in courtyard

❷ *Almirah*, which kept food cool and ants out

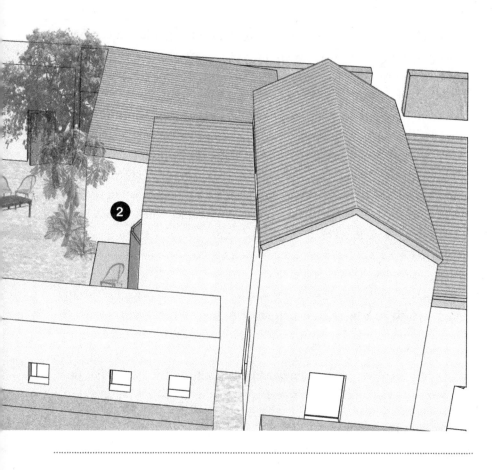

③ Eating mangoes on veranda steps of the bedroom block

periodically topped up to keep ants away. Midmorning, the contents were brought indoors and sheltered from the sun.

Our well-ordered world at home was turned topsy-turvy at times by the dictates of the construction business: a group of labourers, 20 or 30 of them, en route to a new worksite in the interior camped overnight on the house grounds. They had to be fed, of course. Usually, there were enough staples in the pantry. Fresh vegetables were picked from the garden or sent for, fires were lit outside, and a mega-cooking session began. The workers all slept outdoors and had access to a washroom attached to the godown next door.

Sometimes, even construction materials were deposited by our 1950 Bedford lorry in various corners. A load of sand or gravel here and there, and once, a few barrels of bitumen, some of which leaked on a hot day, trapping a mongoose, a few lizards, and much to our delight, snakes.

As patriarchal as the household was, with Abba as its head, he was unambiguous about how women were to be treated. When Amma informed Abba that Wazir was physically abusing his wife, Abba started handing Wazir's pay directly to his wife. Abba also put him on notice that he'd be fired and booted out of the house compound if he didn't change, but that his wife and kids would be free to continue to stay with us. Wazir changed.

Picnic, Picnic

Abba often took us to construction sites or good picnic spots — a river, a lake, a dam, or some open space between lush paddy fields. Mats were rolled out, tiffin opened, a fire lit, and tea brewed. On overnight journeys, we stayed at dak bungalows, lodges from the British era that had served as staging posts for the *dak*, the imperial postal service, and also accommodation for *sahibs* on tour. Post-independence, the bungalows served the same lodging purpose for the Indian officer class. The rent was negligible, the service by the resident staff commensurate with the tip, usually sent in advance with the groceries to ensure not only a hot meal but clean cutlery and dishes, mopped floors, disinfected washrooms, and a controlled burn of dry *neem* leaves to smoke out the mosquitos in time for our arrival.

Some of the more memorable picnics were deep in the interior, such as picturesque Pakhal Lake, now a wildlife sanctuary, and the nearby

Lakhnavaram Forest, about 60 kilometres east of Warangal. A tiger by the edge of the lake water was an awesome sight, etched in my mind ever since. Fodder in Canada for my bedtime stories for sons Fahad and Faisal, spiced up with invented details they lapped up until they realized I was winging it.

One familiar fixture on rural roads was toddy tents, gathering places for the poor. What gin was to London's poor in Charles Dickens's time, so is the fermented sap of palm trees in India. The palm sap consumed immediately after the tapping makes for a nutritious drink, but it begins to ferment instantly. Abba once asked our driver, Farooq Ali, to slow down the car so we could hear the loud, drunk voices and be warned.

Farooq Ali was the one who taught me to drive at age 12. Rules for the road being loosey goosey, no policeman ever asked to see a licence. But just in case, Farooq Ali obtained one for me from the local transport office by overstating my age. That was fraud, all right, but was deemed the acceptable *ha-ha-ha* kind.

Trips to Hyderabad by car were the most fun. We travelled that route countless times, knew every curve on the road, every village along the way, and the seven railway crossings that stopped the road traffic when the trains came. As cars, buses, *tongas*, bullock carts, cattle all came to a halt, we kids walked up to the railway tracks and placed various coins — silver annas, nickel *paisas* (pennies) — on the tracks to be rolled over by the passing trains and collected the pressed metal. The freight trains squished the best — the heavier the load, the thinner and wider the souvenir.

Secular Education

Following *hifz*, I was started on secular education. Not in a school, perhaps because they weren't very good, or more likely, because I had a lot of catching up to do. Private tutors were arranged at home. Ramchandar Rao taught me English and math. He was a veteran Public Works Department officer who moonlighted as Abba's clerk. Teaching Maryam and I was added to his other responsibilities. He was big on the Wren and Martin grammar book; we weren't.

Once a month, I went to Rao Sir's house for lessons. He said those were the days when he had to stay at home. Only later did I learn that during his wife's monthly period, she didn't enter the kitchen and he did the cooking, per the custom in many Hindu households. At that time, I didn't know what periods were.

Pundit Chakrapani came to teach Telugu, the regional language. He, too, was a Brahmin but more religious than Rao Sir — visibly so, his forehead smeared with a *tilak*, the vertical whitish mark made with ash or a paste. Not only did Messrs. Rao and Chakrapani not eat meat, they wouldn't drink or eat out of utensils that might have been used for meat. A separate set of teacups and plates were duly set aside for their tea and refreshments or the occasional meal. They felt further reassured that the kitchen was run by Gatti.

We were taught math by Aziz Ahmed Bhai, an ace accountant who worked for the railways. A non-nonsense type, he wasn't interested in chitter-chatter, even about the tea and snacks served to him. But he did make sure we knew our tables by heart and did our additions and subtractions in a jiffy. That came in handy later, keeping Abba's books, and in Canada, doing expense accounts down to the penny without a calculator.

Middle School

When I was deemed ready at about age 10, Abba took me to the local middle school to be tested for admission to grade 6. The principal pronounced me fit for grade 7. I had caught up with Abbi, who was at a nearby girls' school with Maryam. The two might have been the first girls from the Kandhla clan to go to public school. Amma sent hot lunches every day. The girls were the first port of call. The leftovers were brought to me. My lunch was set out on a mat under a tree, a sight that didn't go unnoticed by my homeroom teacher, Mr. Jabbar. One afternoon right after lunch, he started the class by asking if I had had my lunch and whether it was *khichdi*, rice cooked with lentils and *qeema*, a ground meat dish. It was a classic combo that was said to induce sleep.

"What about my lunch, Mr. Jabbar?" I said, standing to attention.

"What, you called me by my name? I am Sir, you call me *Sir*!"

"Sorry, I didn't know. I was taught to address adults by calling them Mr. So-and-So."

That flared him up even more. "You are questioning me? Stand up on the chair!"

I didn't.

"Stand up on the chair."

I still didn't, thinking there was something wrong with the guy.

"Out!" he barked. "Get out of my class. Now!"

I happily left, only to see him following me and ordering me to the principal's office, where he left me outside, talked to the principal inside, then stormed out. The principal emerged, motioned me in, and said gently that I was new to the school and should learn its ways, especially Mr. Jabbar's. He had to be addressed as Sir.

I said, "Okay, Mr. Jabbar, Sir."

"No, no. Just Sir. Yes, Sir, no, Sir."

"Yes, Sir."

The principal cracked a smile. I took that to mean he knew Mr. Jabbar was a meanie who had to be managed.

That evening at home the story caused much amusement. But Abba added, "Address him as Sir but also keep your lunch out of his eyesight!"

Meaning?

Abba was upholding the need to respect the teacher yet implying that Mr. Jabbar's ire might have been triggered by his irritation at the assumed elitism of my lunch arrangement.

Grade 7 done, I went to Hanamkonda Public High School, not far away. It was Urdu medium, and like the middle school, just as ineffective. Teachers didn't care or perhaps didn't know much about their subjects. In history exams, for example, regardless of which bygone kingdom or ruler we were asked about, we wrote that it/he/she built roads, planted trees on both sides, and dug up wells along the way for the comfort of travellers. No teacher ever questioned us for such generic answers.

Most of my time was spent on the cricket field.

When it was time to write the grade 10 matriculation exam, I was 13 years and 10 months, way below the minimum age of 15. The required "doctor's certificate" was obtained, attesting to a maturity I lacked, and which showed up in spades in the aimless years that followed in college.

Abbi's Wedding

That summer, Abbi also finished high school and got married. She had had two proposals, both from first cousins in Pakistan, ironic in retrospect given the family divide over India and Pakistan. One proposal for Abbi was from Mohammed Mian, a son of Uncle Idris, the famous scholar in Lahore, the other from Mohammed Hamid, son of Abba's sister in Sindh. Arranged marriage it was to be, and both prospects were persons of known pedigree. But still each had to be checked out, given that we hadn't observed them at close range since the Partition. Tayabba was dispatched to check the young men out. He returned nearly three months later with his assessment that while Hamid was better educated and had a job in a reputable madrasah, Mian seemed a more suitable candidate. Quiet consultations ensued between Amma and Abbi, and Mian it was to be.

Shaykh Idris came, with Mian in tow. That was the first time I met him, after hearing so much about him. He was a saintly figure in a simple

Elder sister Amina, affectionately called Abbi.

white *kurta* and pyjama, vest, and cloth cap. Modest, soft-spoken, smiling. It was a family tradition that the *nikah* (marriage ceremony) be performed by a member of the family, so who better than Shaykh Idris? He did in our masjid, with a few people present, and we came home for a big dinner for family and a seemingly endless stream of guests.

My First Photograph

Mian had come armed with a Kodak. And so I was photographed for the first time at age 14. The legacy of religious prohibition against graven images — shared by Jews, Christians, and Muslims — had lingered longer in India than Europe or elsewhere. Abba and Amma had never had their photos taken. Tayabba had one mug shot, snapped after much grumbling, for his Indian passport in order to visit Pakistan. Amma, first, and then Abba had their mug shots taken only when applying for passports to visit Abbi in Pakistan. Posing for cameras was seen in our household as the sin of self-absorption, best avoided. The attitude was summed up in Abba's morning mutterings upon seeing newspapers with pictures of Prime Minister Jawaharlal Nehru impeccably dressed in his white *sherwani*, long Nehru jacket, bedecked with a rose, and smiling: "He sure knows how to pose!" Abba would say.

But here was Mian, son of an eminent scholar, shooting pictures! We were ushered into the age of photography. I, however, never did learn to be comfortable in front of a camera, even after a lifetime in Canada, as attested by my forced, awkward smiles in family and professional photographs. And I still don't relate to all the self-preening before iPhones by the younger generation in the family.

Abbi couldn't travel to Pakistan with her husband. Given the on-again, off-again relations between India and Pakistan, much paperwork had to be undertaken in both countries. That done, a few weeks later, I was assigned to escort her and Amma to Pakistan, nearly 2,000 kilometres north.

Trains weren't interconnected in those days. I had to get down at various stations, hurry to the women's compartment, inquire after Amma and Abbi, fetch them what they needed, and rush back to my car. Doors were invariably left open as the train crawled out of a station, so you could always time a run-up before jumping aboard.

It took more than 30 hours to get to Delhi. After a daylong wait there, we boarded an overnight train to Amritsar, the city of the Golden Temple. From there, we took another train for the 30-kilometre journey to Attari, the northernmost point in India. All passengers had to get down with their luggage, which was carried by porters past the first immigration checkpoint through a no man's land, a 200-metre walk, to the Pakistani checkpoint of Wagah. Papers processed, we boarded yet another train for the 30-kilometre ride, past Bata Nagar, the shoe factory town, to Lahore, our destination. Not that I knew that Bata was a Canadian company, for which Chacha Ayub, Abba's younger brother, would be a franchisee in Pakistan.

No sooner had we been welcomed at the Lahore station than a cousin asked, "Did you bring bananas?" I didn't know that Pakistan grew none. Nor mangoes. Both deficiencies have long since been rectified.

* * *

In Warangal, Maryam shifted to a newly opened private Christian school. It had a proper curriculum and high academic standards. She was the first woman in the family to go to a school run by nuns. She was more diligent than the rest of us, and she emerged with a solid foundation that stood her in good stead right through to her master's degree in botany from Osmania University in Hyderabad, where she topped the class, and another master's degree from McGill University in Montreal, again the first woman from among the Kandhlavis to do graduate work.

Meanwhile, my meanderings continued.

7

The Making of a Journalist

IN THE FALL OF 1956, AGE 14, I ENTERED WARANGAL COLLEGE OF ARTS AND Science. But top of mind was the Australian cricket team tour of India. Hyderabad wasn't one of the venues. The nearest was Madras, nearly 700 kilometres south. Abba said I could go and had Farooq Ali, our driver, take me to the station, buy my ticket, and get me boarded. By now a veteran of long-distance train travel, I slept through the night. The next afternoon, the air started smelling coastal. Swaying palms and wetlands whizzed by. This was a sight I hadn't seen before. At the station, I felt lost in the sounds of Tamil, which bore no resemblance to Telugu. Hindi wasn't spoken there, indeed resented as the language of the ruling northerners, who had tried to impose it in the south, triggering riots. But English was understood by enough people to get by.

The hotel was near a mosque, handy for *halal* food. At the Chepauk cricket ground, Ray Lindwall opened the bowling for Australia. His smooth, loping run-up was a sight to behold. "If one were granted one last wish in cricket, it would be the sight of Ray Lindwall opening the bowling in a Test match," according to English cricketer John Warr. There was the stylish Ritchie Benaud, who beguiled Indian batsmen with his spin bowling. He went on to an illustrious career as captain, and post-retirement, as a radio and TV commentator.

Most Indian players were plodding by comparison, except for captain Polly Umrigar of Bombay. Tall, stocky, and fair with curly hair, he had presence. So did Gulabrao Ramchand with his swagger. The spin duo of Subash Gupte and Hyderabad's own Ghulam Ahmed were ineffective.

The visitors rolled over the home team within four days. I felt robbed of a fifth day's cricket. North Americans might snicker at how long a test lasts but that's precisely the beauty of it — the stately pace, the breaks for lunches and teas, yet each of the 15 two-hour sessions a test of resilience and character through unpredictable and sudden twists and turns.

Play, Not Study

In college, standards seemed high and some of the professors good. But I was skipping classes, learning tennis, playing too much cricket, captaining the team. Unlike in baseball, soccer, or basketball, where coaches make most of the decisions, in cricket the captain is king. It's he — and lately she with the advent of women's cricket — who makes all the calls during the game: which bowler to bring on when, where to place fielders, what order batters should bat in, when to calm excitable colleagues or ignite disheartened ones, and whom to turn to in a clutch and convey such confidence in him that he's inspired to create the magical moment that turned a game around. In my days, the captain even got to pick the team — who was in, who was out. You had to be fair, seen to be fair, or you lost respect and couldn't be an effective leader.

The college, an English medium institution, had an annual magazine, the editorship of which was given to the winner of a speaking-and-writing competition. I got it in my final year and "brought out a very good magazine," according to a letter by the principal. "He was successful in getting messages from eminent personalities like Mr. Bertrand Russell, and Dr. S. Radhakrishnan, and an article from a Reader in English from London University," the principal wrote. "These were quite unique and new for the college magazine." There being no easy access to a phone, let alone long-distance calls, I must have posted letters to the vice-president of India in Delhi, as well as to Mr. Russell and the gentleman at London University. But I have no recollection of how or where I got their addresses. It must have been with the help of English lecturer Isaac Sequeira, who went on to be a Fulbright Scholar in the United States, a distinguished academic, and later director of the Indo-American Centre for International Studies, Hyderabad.

The cricket captaincy and the magazine editorship gave me a licence to take a near-holiday from studies. I tried pre-medicine one year and pre-engineering the next and failed at both. Exam results weren't conveyed individually but rather published in newspapers by the ID numbers students were assigned. You nervously waited for the morning paper and then frantically scanned the long agate to locate your number, starting at "First class," those with marks higher than 60 percent, then "Second class," between 40 to 60 percent, and then just plain "Pass." If your number wasn't on any list, you looked for it again … and again. Finally, your heart sank. How to inform the parents? I consulted sister Maryam. Although younger, she first issued her own admonition and then accompanied me to Amma who, in turn, offered to tell Abba and Tayabba. The buffer worked. "I hear you failed," Abba said. Tayabba was sarcastic: "Perhaps you want to play more cricket?"

Awaiting exam results could be traumatic. Many students turned up at mosques to make supplications: "Please, God, let me pass my exam," or more ambitious, "Let me pass in the second division." To make doubly sure, some trekked to Sufi shrines, besieging dead saints to intervene with God on their behalf. Hindu kids made beelines to temples, with extra flowers, and came out with ashes smeared on their foreheads, blessed by the priest. The sad part was that you read in newspapers that some kid somewhere had committed suicide, such was the pressure applied in some families. I never prayed for marks. As Tayabba, Amma, and Abba would say, "If you want good marks, study for it — Allah doesn't reward the lazy."

* * *

The only off-field attraction lay in the English department, more its eclectic faculty — a Christian, Muslim, and Hindu, the last a Brahmin with a long and unpronounceable name, T.G. *Vaid-ya-na-than*, shortened to TGV, which, he said, we could use without being thought of as disrespectful. Going by initials was the South Indian way.

TGV was tops. He was different. In an age when people rarely moved out of their regions, he'd migrated from the south, from Madras to Warangal. TGV laughed out loud even among strangers. A contrarian, he had definite ideas and opinions. He dismissed those who, reflecting the simmering nationalism of post-British India, advocated teaching less William Wordsworth and more Rabindranath Tagore. The debate was framed in the plaintive cry of an Indian child: "What are daffodils, please?" TGV thought students didn't need to see the damn daffodils any more than they had to glimpse a visage of Wordsworth or had to witness God or other intangibles of life to ponder them.

He agreed to mentor me. I biked down to his house because Abba had banned using the car to visit those who didn't have one. I went after predawn prayers. TGV waited, smiling, in his white cotton *lungi*, the South Indian sarong, but no shirt, one hand playing with the sacred Brahmin thread strung from the neck across his hairy chest, the other holding a book he'd chosen for discussion.

English professor and dear mentor, T.G. Vaidyanathan.

7 The Making of a Journalist

TGV's wife, Indira, was more religious than he, praying to her gods longer and keeping a vegetarian kitchen. That ruled out offering her food that had been cooked elsewhere. But giving her produce from our garden was kosher. The arrangement that ensued suited all parties: my vegetables, her cooking, his teaching. His enthusiasm for his subjects was infectious, especially when he got rhapsodic about good writing on cricket: "Read Neville Cardus. Must read Cardus." Yes, sir. This was the teacher who ended up changing the course of my life.

In 1959, the Dalai Lama came to India, escaping China through the Himalayas. A grainy picture of him on a horse on newspaper front pages is imprinted on my mind. That he was a member of a minority who fled religious persecution had resonance in our household. That he chose India and that India welcomed him made us proud.

* * *

We moved back to Hyderabad from Warangal, principally for our higher education, while Abba stayed in Warangal for his business and commuted often. I joined Nizam College, which had a pedigree. Established in 1895, its first principal, Aghorenath Chattopadhya, was the father of the famed Sarojini Naidu, novelist, poet, and freedom fighter. She had shown such promise as a writer at a young age that the nizam of Hyderabad sent her on a scholarship to Cambridge. Upon her return, she worked with Gandhi in the independence movement. By my time, Nizam College was known for less lofty endeavours — cricket and cheating in exams.

Getting onto the college cricket team wasn't easy. In Warangal, I was a big fish in a small pond. This college crawled with talent. It had stars of the stature of M.L. Jaisimha, who played for India, and Asif Iqbal, who migrated to Pakistan and ended up captaining the Pakistan team. I got relegated to the B team, getting over my bruised ego by basking in the reflected glory of training with them. One cracking shot by Asif hit my shin before I could get out of the way, though I was a good four and half metres away. Such was his wrist work and timing! Unlike Asif and some others, I wasn't a natural talent and had to work hard on my game, but the joy of it kept me going.

The college was across the street from a cricket stadium where I saw a touring West Indian team play Hyderabad. The visitors had big names — Wesley Hall, Lance Gibbs, and Rohan Kanhai. The home team was captained by Ghulam Ahmed, well past his prime by then, but it had rising stars Jaisimha and Habeeb Ahmed. I have two memories of the game: opening bowler Hall, a hulking 1.8 metres, hurling down thunderbolts, yet Habeeb hitting three deliveries in quick succession out of the park, electrifying the audience; and of boys and girls fawning over the stylish and handsome Jaisimha, tall and lithe with not an ounce of fat on him, pants and shirt perfectly pressed, collar turned up. Satya Nadella, CEO of Microsoft, a fellow Hyderabadi, recalls how his father put up a poster of Karl Marx, which his mother countered with a poster of the goddess Laxmi, while "the only poster I wanted was of Jaisimha." The trinity a perfect distillation of the zeitgeist of the age — the lingering leftist romance of communism, the God-fearing ethos of India, and the growing obsession of the young with cricket.

I saw my first movie, *Mughl-e-Azam* (The Magnificent Mughal), when I was 18. It was the overwrought tale of Crown Prince Salim, who became the third Mughal emperor, Jahangir. He was in love with a court dancer named Anarkali (Pomegranate Bud). The movie was more than three hours long, but it stirred the public's imagination. I remember that when a dance of Anarkali was shown reflected in hundreds of little mirrors, the audience gasped in the darkness and clapped. The love story became the highest-grossing Indian film of the time.

Movie-watching remained my little secret for years until it was deemed tolerable in our household.

Journalism Beckons

I received my bachelor of science, barely, in 1961. By now, I was convinced I wasn't cut out for the sciences. By then, TGV had moved to Hyderabad and was teaching graduate school at Osmania University. He suggested I see the head of his English department, S.K. Kumar, who had an aura around him, having studied at Cambridge University and interviewed E.M. Forster there. Dr. Kumar was blunt: "We don't admit science students here." But given TGV's word, he said he'd give me a writing test. I was in. All those years of

7 The Making of a Journalist

taking dictation from Abba in Urdu and turning it into correspondence in English had done some good.

Soon, I did another about-turn and got drawn to journalism when it was announced that the diploma course at Osmania was upgraded to a graduate degree. Without showing any impatience, TGV suggested I see the newly installed head of the department, S.A. Govindarajan. He, like many South Indians, went by his initials. SAG had been a senior editor at the *Hindu*, the English daily in Madras. Notwithstanding its name, it was a staunchly secular paper and a model of accurate and fair reporting.

SAG couldn't have been more different than TGV — short, bespectacled, serious, and with a no-nonsense demeanour. Peering from behind his owlish glasses, he got straight to the point: "Why do you want to do journalism?" I gave some meandering reply to which he didn't respond. It was only after two or three days of agonized waiting that he informed me I was in.

I apprised Abba about my latest inclination.

Journalism professor S.A. Govindarajan.

"Have you asked TGV?"

"I already have and he thinks journalism will suit me."

"If it's fine by him, it's fine by me."

An observant Muslim, Abba had full confidence in this Brahmin suggesting admission into a faculty headed by another Brahmin for a career that was alien to anything the family had ever done. Parent and teacher, high up in the pantheon of the Indian multicultural cosmos, respecting each other across lines of faith, language, and culture, these disparate beings were far more secular than many secularists today, far more liberal than many of our liberals who turn out to be closet bigots, as we saw after 9/11.

Later, Abba said, "I hope you know you won't be rich being a journalist" and "Nobody will want to give you their daughter in marriage," given the prevalent and not too inaccurate view that one became a journalist having failed at everything else. But he added that it could be an honourable profession, provided one resisted the temptation to be popular. "It's easy to be popular but difficult to be respected." As for Tayabba, his reaction was to cite a Qur'anic line:

يَا أَيُّهَا الَّذِينَ آمَنُوا اتَّقُوا اللَّهَ وَقُولُوا قَوْلًا سَدِيدًا

I didn't know the meaning of it and had Amma translate it for me: "Be mindful of Allah and always speak the truth" (Qur'an 33:70).

The journalism department was housed in Osmania University's signature arts college building, one of the wonders of India. A favourite project of the nizam's, it had been designed by Belgian architect Ernest Jasper and opened in 1939. You felt important just being in it.

To Sir, with Love

TGV's English department was next door, and he'd corner me in corridors to ask if I'd read this book or that one, and if not, why not — by Rudyard Kipling, P.G. Wodehouse, Aldous Huxley, and, again, Cardus on cricket.

The year I left India, 1967, TGV moved to the southern city of Bangalore. He went briefly to the United States as a Fulbright Scholar and began writing newspaper columns on movies, cricket, or whatever moved him, becoming

7 The Making of a Journalist

a cultural critic long before the genre was invented. His book *Hours in the Dark: Essays on Cinema* won acclaim, and he edited a book about Sunil Gavaskar, India's greatest cricketer.

In 1977, I unexpectedly found myself in Bangalore. With three hours before the next flight, I taxied to the university campus with no idea where to find TGV. Several people knew where he would be at that hour. Peeping through his classroom window, I saw that he hadn't aged a day or lost his spellbinding hold on students.

After 10 minutes, I couldn't resist edging closer to the door and waving. In a flash, he was out, beaming, arms stretched to enfold me in a tight embrace. "Finish your class," I told him. He agreed. But no sooner had he gone back in than he announced that he couldn't continue.

In an hour of catching up, he explained why he hadn't stayed on in the United States. "There was great order in society but little inside the home. Here in India, it's all chaos outside but there's peace at home." He had discovered his Indian-ness, something he later explored in his book *Vishnu on Freud's Desk*.

Osmania University, architectural jewel and the alma mater for Suleman, Yousuf, and me.

As we dashed off to visit his wife, Indira, he mused that it was a very Western thing to do: shoehorn so much into such a short time, something he said he admired.

Indira made her famous coffee — by decoction. On the way to the airport, I ventured to say that it couldn't be easy for Indira to be his wife. He said he was working on being considerate and that their daughter, who was at school at that hour, had brought the couple closer.

In 1992, TGV came to Toronto on a side trip from New York City. He had admirers everywhere. Two of them came with him to dinner. He was in his element, catching up. Midway through the evening, he lowered himself from the sofa to the carpet and sat cross-legged. Instinctively, we followed him down. He held court until well past midnight.

In 2002, news came that he had died after a brief illness, age 73. He was cremated with his cricket bat beside him.

"His death marks the beginning of the end of a style of scholarship — a total disregard for contemporary fashions and trends, a Brahminic pride in one's simplicity and cultivated poverty, and the tendency to give priority to a life of mind over demands of career, fame, media exposure and even public acceptance," wrote author Ashis Nandy.[1]

I hadn't thought of TGV that way. But Nandy could have been writing about some of my ancestors who had been dedicated to a life of study and contemplation, content with what little they had, contemptuous of compromises with the rich and the powerful.

I devoted a column to TGV, "To Sir, with Love," in the *Toronto Star* on June 16, 2002. One of the commiserating respondents was Ram Guha, one of India's foremost scholars and the author of definitive biographies of Mahatma Gandhi. Guha lives in Bangalore. He said he was a friend and admirer of TGV and that cricket had brought them together. In death, TGV brought Ram and me together.

* * *

Getting me into the graduate journalism program was the best gift TGV could have bestowed. Covering events for the journalism lab weekly, the

7 The Making of a Journalist

Osmania Courier, meeting and interviewing people, was what I was made for, I thought. Writing seemed a cinch. The most energizing realization was that journalism was a passport to go where others couldn't, talk to VIPs, and travel on someone else's dime.

Classmate Sajjad Hyder and I worked as a team. We covered King Hussain of Jordan, who came to Osmania to receive an honorary doctorate. We got to know the grandson of the nizam of Hyderabad, Prince Mukarram Jah, chancellor of Osmania, and his wife, Princess Esra. We had full access to Dr. D.S. Reddy, vice-chancellor (president) of the university, who held frequent receptions at his official residence, a bungalow atop a small mountain overlooking the 560-hectare campus. (Forty years later, when brother Suleman became vice-chancellor, he refused to live there, preferring his humble house just outside the campus — much to the family's disappointment, depriving us of the joy of staying there on visits.)

One of our journalism lecturers was Allen Bradford, a U.S. Peace Corps volunteer. Hyder and I misled him for a lark when he did a survey about rural Indian awareness of things American. We accompanied him to a nearby village as interpreters. Locals were lined up, and Allen

My brother Suleman.

prompted us, "Ask him if he's heard of Alan Shepard," the first American in space.

"No," said the villager emphatically.

"Ask him if he's heard of Yuri Gagarin," the first person in space.

"Yes, yes, that Russian fellow who went up in the sky."

Allen was flabbergasted. "How does he know about Gagarin but not Shepard?"

The villager replied, "Gagarin came to Hyderabad, no?"

The Soviet cosmonaut indeed visited Hyderabad in November 1961 within months of his epic journey into space, Indo-Soviet friendship being at its peak. But Hyder's translation was: "He doesn't know how he knows but he knows Gagarin, and he doesn't know Shepard."

Allen concluded that America was failing to tell the world about its great achievements. The U.S. Information Services, which had an office in Hyderabad, obviously wasn't doing its job. I felt guilty about it and tried unsuccessfully later to locate Allen and apologize. Only recently did I see a 2002 *Washington Times* obituary that he had died of cancer, age 64. Allen had joined the paper in 1985 after spending a dozen years in Delhi as a radio and TV correspondent for ABC. I wish I'd tried harder to find him.[2]

Being the first batch of the graduate journalism degree program, our class was pampered. We were taken on a tour of Bombay to visit newspapers and advertising agencies and meet the governor of the state, the legendary Vijaya Lakshmi Pandit, Nehru's sister. She had been India's ambassador to the Soviet Union, the United Kingdom, the United States, and also the United Nations. Pandit was the first female president of the U.N. General Assembly (1953). More colourful was the story that before she married Mr. Pandit, she was in love with, or had already secretly married, a dashing Muslim journalist, the Oxford-educated Syed Hussain. But given the nation's growing Hindu-Muslim tensions in the 1930s, the relationship was nipped in the bud. High-level machinations involved even Mahatma Gandhi. He had her over to his ashram in Allahabad to dissuade her. I didn't know anything concerning that until Tayabba told me about it a few days before our trip. "You may want to ask her to about it," he said mischievously.

I conveyed the suggestion to the journalism professor escorting us, Mr. Thakur, a sourpuss, who got all flustered. "It's a joke, sir, a joke," I said.

The governor's residence, a relic of the British Raj, was breathtaking: bigger and better than the stately mansions of old Hyderabad. Perched on a high ridge jutting into the Arabian Sea, water on three sides, it featured a beach, a forest, and a series of lush lawns — the 20 hectares within eyesight of Marine Drive, the world's most expensive real estate, where every square metre cost a fortune.

The best part of the trip was that all three girls in the class — Devi, Asha, and Romi — came along, their parents assured by the presence of not one but two professors, Mr. Thakur and Allen Bradford. Hyder fancied Romi, and Srinivas, fellow student and friend, was enamoured of Asha, and I of Devi. None of us ever said a thing to any of them, that being the social norm. We were besotted from a distance.

One of my favourite journalism professors was Syed Bashiruddin, a hulk of a man, gregarious, energetic. He did the university proud when he was named India's ambassador to Qatar. It turned out that the real reason for his appointment by Prime Minister Indira Gandhi was that he had been recommended to her by his guru, the (in)famous Satya Sai Baba, who was notorious for pulling off hand tricks as holy miracles. Either she was also a disciple or someone in her circle was.

Muslims at the *Hindu*

SAG was a kind man. He invited students to his house for lunch or dinner, made by the cook he brought with him from Madras. Multi-course South Indian vegetarian meals, one of the many distinct regional haute cuisines of India, were a treat. The dishes included *idli*, ground rice steamed; *vadas*, a fritter made with urad lentils; *dosa*, a thin crepe made with fermented ground rice and eaten fresh off the griddle plain or stuffed with spiced potatoes; *puri*, a small fried puffed roti; two or three vegetable dishes; white rice; and three must-haves — home-set yogurt; *sambar*, a southern version of lentil; and *rasam*, a light lentil soup featuring fresh ginger, tamarind, and black pepper. SAG insisted that we consume each course but was especially particular about *rasam* — "Have it, have it — good for digestion, good for health."

Thanks to SAG, Hyder and I were selected for internships at the *Hindu* in Madras. The paper was owned and operated by the Kasturis, the venerable Brahmin family. When I reported for duty, Gopalan Kasturi, then joint editor — or was it his older brother, Gopalan Narasimhan, the editor? — asked, "Have you found accommodation?"

"Yes, I have — a hotel near the mosque I used during my previous visit for the cricket test."

"Good that you're staying in the mosque compound." Meaning he was happy I wasn't at some seedy place. Next he asked, "How much money have you brought?"

"Five hundred rupees, which Abba gave me."

"Too much. Don't waste your father's money. Eat in our subsidized cafeteria. Give me 300 rupees. I'll keep it for you."

At the end of the internship, he handed back the money and said, "Now, go and return it to your father."

What I didn't see then but do now — a parallel between Mr. Kasturi taking comfort at my staying close to a mosque and my father having complete confidence in TGV and SAG guiding me. Despite the legacy of 1947, there was mutual respect and trust across faiths and cultures in the India of my childhood, especially in South India. That part of the country wasn't scarred by the sectarianism of the North where Muslim invaders had come from Central Asia and Persia, whereas Islam came to the South peacefully through Arab traders plying the historic route between the Middle and Far East. South Indian Hindus, Muslims, Christians, and Jews were culturally more assimilated, wearing the same clothes, sharing much of the same cuisine. The thriving Christian community, Syrian Orthodox, dates back to the 52 CE arrival of St. Thomas, apostle of Jesus. And before modern-day migration to Israel, there once was a prosperous Jewish community along the Malabar Coast, the Malabar *Yehuden*, whose ancestors fled persecution in Portugal and Spain. They thrived especially in Cochin, now renamed Kochi, which has the oldest synagogue in India.[3]

South Indians have clearly been less bigoted, less volatile, and more disciplined than northerners. I came to admire them even more because of TGV, SAG, the folks at the *Hindu*, and also vague familiarity with such historic

South Indian figures as Srinivasa Ramanujan, the mathematical genius who dazzled Cambridge University in the early 20th century; Nobel laureate physicist Sir C.V. Raman; and philosopher Dr. Radhakrishnan, India's second president, who wrote that letter to my college magazine when he was vice-president.

The final exam for the journalism program was easy — the first time in my life that I neither dreaded the arrival of the annual ordeal nor was nervous during the tests or wait for results. I missed the gold medal by a whisker to Devi. I had no trouble consoling myself that she won because she was a bookworm, whereas I had been such a productive busybody.

On to Bombay

In 1963, I got a job as a junior copy editor at the headquarters of the Press Trust of India (PTI), the national news agency in Bombay. The salary was a paltry 250 rupees per month, half of which went for rent. The rest lasted roughly 10 days, following which I fired off "send-money" telegrams home. Abba got so used to those requests that he told Amma not to bother opening the telegrams, just send some money.

Journalism classmate Hyder got the same job ahead of me. When looking for accommodation in Bombay, Hyder ran into a fellow Hyderabadi who said he was a paying guest at a Zoroastrian gentleman's place and would ask if Hyder could crash there, as well. Mr. Moose said yes. In turn, Hyder got me in. We shared a room, never argued, never got cross with each other. It helped that he got up late and I was done showering well before he saw the light of day. I used to kid him that had he been used to getting up for the pre-dawn prayer, he, too, could get on with his day in proper time. "I'm a Shia, our rules are more relaxed," he'd respond, pronouncing a fatwa to suit his laziness.

The flat was unusually large and had four bedrooms. It was in central Bombay, in Colaba, not far from the iconic Taj Mahal Hotel. Close by was a Zoroastrian colony where years later Rohinton Mistry located his *Tales from Firozsha Baag*, the 1986 award-winning stories about Bombay Parsis. And it's the same area where we saw the great Indian painter M.F. Hussain enter or exit the Jehangir Art Gallery. He couldn't be missed — tall, gaunt, flowing beard, no shoes, because he said he wanted to feel the earth like the poor.

The city was intoxicating. It had cosmopolitan camaraderie and egalitarianism. The smell from Colaba's fish market got into the nostrils of paupers and billionaires alike. The sacred and the profane coexisted. Red-light districts thrived near churches, temples, and mosques, the streets shared by hookers and priests. People of all faiths lived cheek by jowl. Our apartment's Zoroastrian owner had welcomed Hindus, Muslims, a Christian, and a Jew, Rosalind Samson. She worked at the American consulate and went to the local *shul*, Chabad House, which was stormed in 2008 in a terrorist attack.

Breakfast was at home, but we were on our own for lunch and dinner. The standard of our meals out was high at the start of the month and steadily declined as the money supply eroded and we ate at the cheapest holes in the wall. Iranian cafés were famous for their tea — and a free banana, the poor man's protein for the day. The banana has persisted as a habit throughout my life.

Amid our deprivation in Bombay, we dreamed of having a meal at the luxurious Taj Hotel. We walked by it often and sometimes went into the lobby to gawk. One day, flush with our pay at the beginning of the month, we had tea in the hotel, the cheapest item on the menu. We admired the crockery, cutlery, linen, and liveried bearers serving tasty biscuits that came with the tea. Hyder and I didn't feel intimidated by the surroundings — it just seemed like old Hyderabad — but when we lingered well past every other afternoon guest, we felt we might be thrown out, but weren't.

The Taj abuts the Arabian Sea, not far from the port where British colonials came in the 16th century and departed in 1947, and from where the British traded opium to China. Nearby is the grand Gateway of India, begun in 1911 to mark the visit of King George V.

Bombay is where the maharajahs and maharanis from British India's 556 states came to party in "Little London," the city with the most Gothic buildings outside Victorian England. It's also the location of the preserved birthplace of Rudyard Kipling, the great storyteller and apologist for colonial India.

Post-colonial Bombay married old money with new. It became a bigger financial hub, with many corporate headquarters and the gold and diamond bazaars, along with the dream factory called Bollywood. Bombay had celebrities and celebrity-watching long before the world succumbed to celebrity culture.

7 The Making of a Journalist

One day we had walked out of our PTI office when Hyder spotted Nutan, a famous actress of the time. She got out of her chauffeur-driven car and crossed the sidewalk into a building. *"Nutan hai, baap"* ("That's Nutan, bro"), said Hyder, instinctively following her and telling me to "Come, come."

"Come where?"

"Just follow me."

Nutan crossed the lobby, so did we. She entered the elevator, so did we.

The elevator operator knew what floor she was going to and glanced at us. *"Tum kidhar?"* ("You, where to?"), he asked in that dismissive Bombay slang reserved for the common man.

"Same floor, same floor," Hyder replied.

There was awkward silence as the elevator whirred up, seemingly forever. While I mostly stared at my toes, Hyder couldn't take his eyes off Nutan, transfixed by her pristine skin and calm demeanour. She was obviously accustomed to gawkers. She seemed to be gazing at nothing and into nowhere until the elevator stopped, the operator clanged open the accordion metal door, and she stepped out silently and majestically, leaving the two of us speechless.

The operator inquired, *"Utarna hai?"* ("Getting off?")

"No," said Hyder sheepishly.

The operator, obviously used to seeing VIPs come and go to the high-end lawyers' offices, admonished us, *"Nutan ko kya ghoorta tha!"* ("Why were you gawking at Nutan?")

We had no answer, only embarassed silence.

Hyder dined out on the story — how he managed to see the great actress, away from the crowds, up close, all by himself and his buddy for a full minute or two!

Clearly, Hyder had more gumption and initiative than I did. He once wangled an invite to see the leading actor of the day, the legendary Dev Anand, at his house in Juhu Beach by the sea. He even got lunch. We never heard the end of that story, either.

I had my own little brush with Bollywood by default. My developing love interest, Shehla Burney, a college mate from the literature class in Hyderabad, had family connections with the leading poet of the age, Kaifi Azmi, whose daughter, Shabana, became a leading actress. Kaifi wrote songs for movies, as did the other leading poets of the time: Majrooh Sultanpuri, Ali Sardar Jafri, and Sahir Ludhianvi. They were leftists, poets of the dispossessed, part of the Progressive Writers' Movement. Each of the poets had a mass following outside of Bollywood and attracted thousands to poetry gatherings all over India. Kaifi's signature poem was "Aurat" (Woman), a clarion call for women's empowerment that he wrote during the 1940s in the final stages of the independence movement. It had so seeped into the Indian consciousness, long before contemporary Western feminism, that Kaifi couldn't leave a poetry gathering without reciting it. Audiences called out for *"Uth meri jaan,"* "Rise, my love," the poem's refrain, and he always obliged in his booming voice:

Rise, my love, march with me.

Patience won't help you through life
You will fly only when you are free
Heaven is not merely in the arms of your man
Walk unfettered on the path of freedom with me.
Rise, my love, march with me.

History hasn't known your worth
You are like burning embers, not merely tears
You are a person, not just a young beauty
Change the course of your history.

Rise, my love, march with me.

Break free of ancient bondages, break the idols of tradition
Shatter the vows that have become shackles
Raise your forehead from the altar of fate
I am not going to pause, nor will time.

Rise, my love, march with me.

This was the poem that brought together Kaifi and Shaukat, his theatre actor wife. She heard him recite it at a gathering, and as she recalls in her memoir *Kaifi aur Mai* (Kaifi and I), "I fixed my gaze on Kaifi, convinced that he had written this poem for me, and I alone had the right to march with him."

The poem's popularity was evident whenever Kaifi was invited to Toronto in the 1980s and 1990s, by which time he'd suffered a stroke and was wheelchair-bound. When the audience beseeched him for "Aurat," he smiled and said, "You can see my condition. I cannot run away. But first, let me recite some of the more recent compositions."

When I first knew Kaifi and Shaukat in Bombay, they were renting a shack in a bohemian artists' commune by the beach in Juhi, a suburb of Bombay. Theirs was an open house, with people coming and going, being served tea and biscuits, and when it was time for lunch or dinner, being asked to join. By the late 1970s, when Kaifi was becoming known as the father of Shabana Azmi, the actress and activist, he took great pride in letting it be known that he was walking in her shadow.

* * *

Hyder and I often sought out senior journalists to talk to. I particularly admired K.N. Prabhu, the veteran cricket correspondent for the *Times of India*. I envied his elegant writing — and his travels with the Indian team at home and abroad. When I caught up with him, it didn't take long for him to realize that he lived, literally, within 45 metres of where we did in Colaba, and he invited me to dinner. He and his wife then issued an open invitation to come anytime I wanted a home-cooked meal.

Although Hyder and I were copy editors, we could accompany senior reporters on their rounds or initiate some marginal assignments ourselves. One lucky break came when I got assigned to assist the reporters covering a key cricket test between India and Australia. It was the second of a three-game series, the first having been won by the visitors. This one was in Bombay at Brabourne Stadium, the temple of cricket, which, not being far from the office, I had made multiple pilgrimages to. The stadium had been the site of the most talked-about moment in Indian cricket, the one I mentioned in the opening chapter, the 1960 kiss planted on Abbas Ali Baig by a besotted fan who ran onto the field as he was walking back to the pavilion after a fine batting performance. The team was led by the nawab of Pataudi, the scion of a principality north of Delhi, a prince of a man and a charismatic cricketer. At age 21, he was the youngest man in the world to lead a national team and was the first Indian captain to mould the team into a national unit, not just a conglomeration of players from various regions. His more remarkable achievement was that when he lost his right eye in a car accident while studying, and playing for, Oxford, he trained himself to play with his other eye and still set the cricketing world on fire.

The PTI coverage of the match was standard wire-service fare — filing running commentary every few minutes, putting new leads at breaks, wrap-ups at lunch, at tea break and at the end of each day. News agencies didn't give bylines in those days, only initials at the bottom of every take that went by telex — MHS/URW/AMH or MHS/URW/MKG/GKS, et cetera. The MHS was for Mohammed Haroon Siddiqui. By the time the newspapers picked up the wire copy, even the initials were gone. It didn't matter. I had helped cover a test match, especially one that India won in an exhilarating finish at the tail end of the fifth day.

A side benefit of combining journalism and cricket was to land a gig on All India Radio to do commentary on an interstate match in Hyderabad. In the booth was veteran broadcaster Bharat Chand Khanna, himself a first-class cricketer who had played for Cambridge University and Hyderabad and was a senior government officer. He was kind and helpful and told me to slow down. Obviously, I yakked too much too fast. That stint helped land some periodic commentaries on the air, first in Hyderabad and later in Bombay. I still do a silent play-by-play of imaginary games many a night to switch off my mind and go to sleep. Or, better still, fantasize that I'm in a game, the team is in deep trouble, and I'm singlehandedly rescuing it with a great piece of fielding or bowling or batting — a great escape from the ground reality of my mediocrity.

Another Lucky Break

Our flatmate Rosalind, the one who worked at the American consulate, had her own room, unlike the rest of us. She fell in love with the other Hyder in the apartment, whom we called Hyder Senior. He was a Britain-returned brown Englishman, prim and proper, who used to admonish the younger ones if we hadn't shaved or weren't properly dressed. "You should always be presentable, for you never know when opportunity will knock," he always told us.

Knock it did in my case, in December 1964, when the PTI news editor handed me a last-minute assignment to cover the visiting crown prince and prime minister of Kuwait, Shaykh Sabah al Salem al Sabah. I met him at the governor's mansion. During our conversation, I must have displayed near-total ignorance of Kuwait. He responded by inviting me to go along with him on his return journey home. "Come and see for yourself," he said. I kept quiet.

Back at the office, I talked to a news editor who said, "Go talk to the chief editor." I did.

"It should be all right," said the chief editor, giving the go-ahead to a freebie that I wasn't even sure was a serious offer and not just a throwaway line from a head of a state to a cub reporter.

That evening, I recounted the story to Hyder Senior.

He sat bolt upright and got straight to the point. "You have a passport?"

"Yes, I do, but it's expired."

"Get it renewed first thing in the morning."

"That's impossible with Indian bureaucracy, and the shaykh leaving the day after that."

"Talk to your editor. He'll get it done."

Sure enough, the editor wrote a letter to the passport office. There, I couldn't get past the peon, that ubiquitous gatekeeper to the bureaucratic *babu*-dom. I begged him, but to no avail. Then, when no one was looking, I slipped him a 10-rupee note. Soon I was in. Said the officer, "Come back tomorrow morning. It'll be ready."

The following afternoon, I was at the airport being ushered through to the shaykh's plane. I'd never been on a jet. The shaykh's entourage when it finally arrived occupied about four or five rows. Then came the shaykh himself with two assistants, and he took his front-row seat. Airborne, I hopped from one empty row to another, taking the window seats and admiring the Indian Ocean below. As we descended into Kuwait, I was summoned to the front to sit next to the shaykh. "India big, Kuwait small," he said. "Small but beautiful."

As the plane dipped toward the airport, I was awestruck by dozens of lit torches on the ground, well spaced out, glowing. "Nice lights," I said.

The shaykh smiled. "Oil wells, oil wells."

Oil wells? Burning?

We landed, and the shaykh took me by the hand as we went down the stairs to a waiting reception party, all men, in full Arab regalia of flowing robes, all kissing his hand, hugging him. The shaykh introduced me to each one in Arabic, translated from behind my back by one of his aides: "This is my young friend, a journalist from India." Then we went into a tent, lushly carpeted, plush chairs laid out in a rectangle. As we sat down, attendants handed out tiny handleless glass cups and poured small shots of dark black coffee, too bitter to swallow, but I did, anyway, out of courtesy. The attendant refilled it in a flash. The translator advised me that unless I wiggled the cup side to side, indicating I'd had enough, they'd keep refilling it.

As we left, the shaykh motioned me to get into his limousine, the longest car I ever rode in. He and I sat in the back seat, the translator facing us from a foldout seat, conveying the shaykh's running commentary on the passing landmarks. When we reached his home, which was modest compared to the gilded palaces of the maharajahs and sultans back home, he led me to his living room where he announced through the translator, "You will stay in my house."

I protested mildly, saying, "That's very kind of you, but I'll find a hotel."

"You can do so the next day, but for now you are my guest. Now if you will permit me, I will go and see my wife and family."

They had remained in their private quarters.

An attendant showed me to my room and announced, "I will be sitting outside should you need anything during the night."

"That's not necessary," I told him. "You should go and sleep yourself."

"No, it is my job to attend to guests," he insisted.

7 The Making of a Journalist

As I closed the door, it hit me that his suit was far superior to mine.

In the morning, the breakfast featured alien items — a large flatbread that was neither hot and puffed up nor tasty like our Indian rotis (it was a pita, which I didn't know then), an oil that was said to be from olives, some beans, and an egg so vast that I wondered if a camel had laid it. This was decidedly not a princely meal from an Indian point of view.

Over the next seven days, I was easily dazzled. Oil- and gas-rich Kuwait, independent of Britain only since 1961, had the highest per capita budget in the world, no taxes and free medicare, the world's largest water distillation plant, its capital the world's most air-conditioned city. The era of the profligacy and vulgarity of Gulf oil princes was yet to emerge. Kuwait's ruling family lived relatively simple lives. On subsequent trips to Kuwait, especially since the First Gulf War, I've seen a greater Americanization of Kuwait, and with it, a preponderance of fast food and fat people.

8

End of the Good Life

OUR WORLD CHANGED WITHIN MINUTES.

Abba had a heart attack in Warangal. Amma and the kids — Maryam, Suleman, Syeda, and Yousuf — were in Hyderabad, having shifted there for education. I rushed from Bombay. Abba was in hospital, Amma with him. Cardiology was still primitive. He was prescribed some pills, told not to exert himself and just rest. When he got chest pains, he'd simply have to lie down until the episode passed.

His sense of helplessness hit him hard. My father was 1.85 metres, heavy-set, with broad shoulders, a little tummy, and tanned skin from being out and about in the sun. He had his head shaved and beard trimmed to a stubble. Abba wore a red fez, *sherwani*, white pyjama, and shoes that were forever being cleaned and polished. He was a man of dignified bearing and purposeful strides. Hyperactive, always in charge, impatient with slowpokes. But he bore physical limitations with forbearance, resigned to Allah's will.

He was calm in coaching me how to keep the business going with the help of his long-time staff, the brothers Wazir and Lal Mohammed and Pyarelal Sa'ab, the projects supervisor. Soon, Suleman was roped into the task, as well.

He and I shuffled between construction sites and Public Works Department (PWD) offices, attending to a million things. Is the labour crew

My Name Is Not Harry

sufficient? Has the steel shipment come? Cement? Gravel? Enough gas for the cement mixture? Water? Project management wasn't taught in those days but learned on the job without Excel sheets. There wasn't even the culture of making to-do lists; every task was uploaded into the head and regurgitated as a reminder, usually at night in bed. There was also the shepherding of files and payments through PWD officials who seemed bent on teaching us that nothing would get done unless their palms were greased. Abba had refused to bribe them in the past but had begun to relent, much to his personal dismay. For Suleman and myself, the officials made it even more difficult, given our inexperience. Everywhere we turned, Murphy's law seemed to apply: whatever could go wrong did. I prepared myself for the worst at every turn.

Evenings were spent doing accounts, jotting down income and expenses in a big, thick ledger under Abba's instructions. We suspected pilfering by some staff members. When Abba was told, he smiled and suggested such things were part of the equation: "Just let it be, as long as the leakage is at a tolerable level." The most honest and scrupulous employee was a Hindu, Durgayya, the carpenter. He was initially hired to work on construction jobs but was then brought on permanent payroll. Between construction jobs, he was kept busy making house furniture, bed frames, *almirahs*, children's toys, et cetera. A dining table with six chairs, plus a sofa set he made out of *sheesham*, "rosewood," are as intact today as they were when he made them nearly 70 years ago.

In April 1965, Abbi and her husband came down from Pakistan. But Abba advised them to go back because Indo-Pakistani war clouds were gathering. Mian recalled for me later: "Your Abba told us, 'You better go back, or you'll get stuck here for months.' He was always thinking of others."

Abba was eventually brought home from the hospital, but his chest pains would send us in panic to fetch Dr. Waghray. The good doctor unfailingly obliged, but now that I think about it, there wasn't much more he could have done to help Abba.

The siblings in Hyderabad had to be attended to. That meant a maddening shuttle between Warangal and there three to four times per week, made worse by bad train and bus service — and nosy fellow travellers. India being one big village, privacy is at a premium, not only in extended households and closely knit neighbourhoods and villages but everywhere. Within a few minutes of boarding a train, someone is bound to ask: "What do you do? How much do you earn? Not working — why not? Not married — why? Married, yes — how many children? No kids, *ay-yayyo*, wife having trouble conceiving?"

One afternoon, on November 18, 1965, I was getting ready to catch my usual 3:00 p.m. bus to Hyderabad and was saying goodbye to Abba when he said out of the blue, "Don't go today."

My first instinct was to ask why. But one look at his face — drawn, almost haunted — and the near-pleading in his voice telegraphed that something was amiss.

Setting my travel bag aside, I said I'd arrange tea for him. I asked Gatti to make some and was coming out of the kitchen nine metres away when I saw him double up. Amma was holding him by the side of the bed and calling out for me. I yelled at Wazir to go get Dr. Waghray, held Abba as he was losing consciousness, cradled his head on my shoulder, and slowly lowered him down. He was soon motionless, amid our rising cries. Even Tayabba, always composed, began sobbing, *"Aray, meray bhai, aray meray bhai!"* — "O my brother, O my brother!" — and intoning Qur'anic verses. But Abba was going, going, gone. It was 3:15 p.m., about the time I'd have been boarding the bus that had a stop in walking distance from home.

Dr. Waghray came. He lifted Abba's hand, checked his pulse, lowered his hand, embraced me, and said, "Sorry, am very sorry. He was like a father to me, as well." He bowed to Amma and Tayabba and quietly walked out, letting us be.

Tayabba closed Abba's eyes, aligned his jaw, covered his body, and pronounced *Inna lillahi wa inna ilaihi raji-un*, the Qur'anic line signalling the end: "To Allah we belong and to Him we return."

We had no phone. A call was placed from a nearby store to Hyderabad. It took forever to connect. I don't recall the conversation, only the cries on the other end of the line. Maryam, Suleman, Syeda, and Yousuf arrived around 9:00 p.m., crying uncontrollably. Maryam wailed throughout the night.

The Qur'an was recited all night next to the body. In the morning, the corpse was washed at home with hot water soaked in *neem* leaves. Wazir and

Lal held a sheet above Abba's *awrah* (private parts), while Tayabba and I did the rest, then shrouded him in a white unsewn cloth.

The body was borne on the simple rectangular wooden frame of slats sent over from our masjid, which was where the funeral prayers were offered after *zuhr*, the regular noon prayers. The coffin was carried the one kilometre to the neighbourhood cemetery, with men taking turns lending their shoulder, per Muslim custom.

As soon as the grave was closed, it hit me that I, age 23, was now the head of the family, responsible for Amma and my siblings and the household. I told myself I couldn't cry, that I'd have to get on with what all lay ahead.

The ensuing weeks and months were to show the tragic effects of the cult of indispensability that envelops so many Indian families — wholly dependent on one person, almost always the father or husband. When something happens to him, the entire family edifice comes crashing down. It did in our case, made worse by the fact that Abba, for all his qualities, wasn't good at handling finances. He didn't have a budget. No savings, either. It was feast or famine, his generosity trumping fiscal prudence. Generous to a fault, he couldn't turn anyone down.

I was told by several people — an engineer, a businessman, an elected member of the state legislature — that Abba had seen them through tough times, especially during college. "I am what I am because of him." That was the refrain.

People in Pakistan told me how during Abba's visits there in 1961 and 1964 he had helped out a number of people. Cousin Mohammed Mian told me about a cousin who had been forced to do his *hifz*, according to family tradition. "But his mind wasn't in it. He didn't want to do it. Your Abba got him admitted to a polytechnic college and paid his fee. That's where the young man did his marine engineering. Your father also gave me 6,000 Pakistani rupees and told me to pay the young man in installments every month." Mian said Abba made similar arrangements for some other struggling family members. Another cousin, Umair, recalled how Abba used to book daylong taxis when he was in Karachi to take nephews and nieces all over the city.

It was moving to hear all that and meet the beneficiaries. But it didn't mitigate our own plight.

Abba's business had also been affected by the renaming and reorganization of the old Hyderabad State in 1956 by the federal government, ceding parts of it to neighbouring states and incoporating an area from the southern state of Andhra, a move widely seen as designed to erode Hyderabad's Muslim identity. The people who came from Andhra along the Indian Ocean were peaceful, tolerant, and wealthy. They seemed free of anti-Muslim bias, and their investments were welcome. But many had a different way of doing business, particularly in construction. They bought off potential bidders to be the sole bidder at inflated prices that allowed for bigger kickbacks and bribes to colluding officials. Abba wouldn't play that game. He put in his usual low bids and suffered, since officials in government procurement departments resented his getting in the way of the new lucrative arrangements.

So Abba's bank accounts were nearly empty. He had cash-flow problems. His accounting books, despite my growing familiarity with them, couldn't quite be deciphered concerning monies due, how much from which project, even whether the requisite invoices had been submitted, and if they had been, at what stage of processing they were in the government's labyrinthine bureaucracy. This lack of knowledge emboldened many officials to demand extra bribes just to locate the files. The process also revealed not only who was corrupt, almost all of them, but also who were the more bigoted, tagging us as the sons of *Turkodllu*, the one who wore a Turkish cap, a derogatory moniker for Muslims. The more time we spent chasing officials, files, and payments, the less time we had for the projects themselves. It was a vicious cycle.

But there were honourable people in the PWD. Abba was fond of telling a story to which he added an ethical quandary for us to ponder. In a competition to recruit junior engineers, candidates were interviewed by a three-member panel of senior engineers, one of whom recused himself, saying the next candidate was his son. Competition done, the son was among those selected. It turned out that another candidate who didn't make the cut was the son of another panel member who hadn't disclosed his kinship. Abba's query to us: "Which of the two panellists was more ethical?"

Abba's physical limitations didn't affect his usually pithy observations. "Either you know, or you don't," about what's right and what's wrong. "Non-answer is an answer," about the absence of a response from somebody. "Give him the gravel division and have him report directly to you," to a fellow contractor who asked how to stop his younger son from bickering with his older sibling. "Dogs bark, donkeys bray," about the need to ignore detractors and just keep going. *"Aaj nahee"* ("Not today"), the ethic of setting aside all differences on special days such as weddings or religious holidays, regardless of faith.

* * *

My siblings continued their studies in Hyderabad. Only Maryam, always diligent, was doing well. Unlike Abbi, who married after high school, Maryam and Syeda went on to university. Suleman was distracted between business and studies. Both he and Yousuf were enrolled in two poorly run affiliates of Osmania University. After his undergraduate degree, Suleman was unsure what to do, so he joined the Master's in Islamic Studies program at Osmania. He got lucky; one of his academic advisers was a visiting professor, Dr. Hans Kruse, an eminent Islamist scholar from the University of Göttingen in Germany. He directed Suleman toward an unexplored aspect of Sufis in the Deccan. With Professor Kruse at the university and Tayabba — the walking, talking encyclopedia of Islam — at home, Suleman went on to distinguish himself as an authority on the subject and as a professor. Later, he moved into administration where he thrived as principal of the graduate school and finally as vice-chancellor (president) of our alma mater, one of the biggest universities in Asia, with an enrollment of 300,000 students. The day he was named head of the institution, some of the staff came to the house with drums and pipes and distributed sweets.

During Abba's lifetime, a proposal for Maryam's marriage had been floated. One of the houses we owned was rented to a provincial civil servant, Syed Ahmed Husaini, during his posting in Warangal. He'd become friends with both Abba and Tayabba and often came to sit post-dinner in the front courtyard and chat. Syed asked for Maryam's hand for his brother-in-law,

8 End of the Good Life

Siddiq Ahmed Khan, who had migrated to Pakistan and was working for KLM Airlines there. Both Abba and Amma hesitated, given the difficulties of travel to Pakistan in the case of Abbi.

With Abba's death, the proposal got frozen for months. Revived by the Husaini family, the decision came down to Tayabba, Amma, and Maryam. They felt that Abba's involvement must have been a good omen. Thus it was that a date was set, and Ahmed came down from Karachi for the wedding at Hyderabad in the fall of 1966. What I remember most was a great deal of crying, including by myself, because Abba wasn't there to witness what he'd considered. As Maryam and Ahmed were leaving, I held a copy of the Qur'an over my sister's head, sending her on the new journey of her life under God's protection. I don't know if Amma gave her a copy of the *Beheshti Zewar*.

Tayabba wrote a *sehra*, a poem of felicitation. But he was too emotional to recite it. A framed copy went with the bride and groom, who displayed it in

Maryam's wedding, 1966. Syeda in middle, Amma at right (partly hidden), and me at left.

their homes all their lives, including in Montreal. We've since included that poem in *Kalaam-e-Sarwar* (Sarwar's Poems), the collection of Tayabba's poetry that we published in 2018.[1] His poetry ranges from searing political and social commentary, to humour, to the family. A section titled "Poems for the Family" runs to 38 pages, expressing love or extending advice and good wishes. The family included staff, as in this couplet that references Gatti, the cook:

> *Khat ke raqim hain bhai bahn sub*
> *Haal Gatti ka, aur Amina ka*

> Brothers, sisters, all eagerly await letters
> bearing news of Gatti and Amina.

The above was written after Amina moved to Pakistan and the family had relocated to Hyderabad while Gatti watched over the house in Warangal.

A year after Maryam's marriage, she returned home for the delivery of her first-born, Abdul-Basit Khan, in Hyderabad on November 2, 1967. That was the tradition then, that expectant moms went home to their mothers for help, caring, and comfort. But she couldn't take the baby with her because of the Indo-Pakistani bureaucratic rigamarole. He stayed with Amma and Suleman, to their delight, but to the dismay of the young mother. The boy didn't join his parents until 1974, by which time they had immigrated to Canada. It was easier to get him there than across one border to Pakistan.

Life at the Club

I joined the Warangal Club, housed in a stately, high-ceilinged, lime-washed, two-storey building not far from our house. I took to going there after dinner to play 13-card rummy — for small amounts of cash — and came home late. Tayabba and Amma couldn't have approved of those late nights and certainly not of the gambling, if they knew. It gnawed at me that perhaps they were letting it be because they were dependent on me. I didn't ask, but in retrospect should have.

One legacy of club-going in Warangal and later in Hyderabad has been that I developed an affinity for the fuddy-duddy but majestic and leafy

8 End of the Good Life

vestiges of British India dotted all over the country and took to staying in them on trips back home.

* * *

My old buddy Hyder got himself transferred from the Press Trust of India headquarters in Bombay to Hyderabad. He and I did some freelance assignments for the Delhi-based India bureaus of the British Broadcasting Corporation and the Associated Press news agency. The biggest story came in 1967, with the death of the nizam, His Exalted Highness, at age 80, signalling the end of an era that stretched to 1911 when he had assumed the throne. His death had drama. It was said he was dead but then he wasn't. The announcement was delayed for the arrival from London of his heir, grandson Mukarram Jah, whom Hyder and I had known from our days at journalism school. The prince was pro-chancellor. Jah arrived nearly two days later, and the first order of his business was to have truckloads of treasures moved from the nizam's palace to his.

What came next surprised everyone.

The nizam had been a forgotten figure, living in obscurity behind the high walls of his palace. Yet half a million people thronged the streets for the funeral — Hindus and Muslims, men and women, old and young. Some women broke their bangles in the traditional farewell to a dear departed.[2] The seven-kilometre journey to Makka Masjid for his funeral prayer took two hours. The mosque and its open courtyard, which hold 10,000 people, were packed, congregants spilling over into the marble and canopied cemetery where five of the nizam's six predecessors were buried. But this nizam had chosen to be interred next to his mother in a small mosque near his palace. The return journey on the gun carriage took hours. As we finally crammed into the tight spaces of Judi Mosque, the Sandhurst-trained Mukarram Jah, 34, stood ramrod-straight until he went down on his knees to sprinkle water on the grave, his white pyjama soiled by the brown mud.

Three days later, he was recognized by Dr. Radhakrishnan, the president of India, as "the sole successor" to the nizam and was conferred with the inherited title of His Exalted Highness. The honour was as empty of meaning as the elaborate "coronation ceremony" concocted by nostalgic courtiers and staged at one of the palaces. Even at my impressionable age, the ceremony came across as farcical. Still, it was quite the spectacle, the old durbar re-created. It can be seen on YouTube *sans* sound. I looked for my handsome young self in it — in vain.[3]

Guests wore the old court dress of *sherwani*, a belt around the waist, and high-peaked headgear. Those not conforming to the dress code, including journalists, were dismissed to the balconies.

The guards with swords who stood three metres apart were drawn from the nizam's dismantled private army, descendants of an Arab militia that had been recruited from Hadramaut in Yemen. As cannons boomed, they presented a guard of honour as Jah entered with his Turkish wife, Princess Asra — he resplendent in a *sherwani* of green brocade with golden threads, she in a chiffon sari with a silver border and bracelets of jewels and a necklace of pearls. He sat down on a yellow velvet cushion placed on a metre-high marble throne.

As the hall echoed with verses from the Qur'an, all was silent for two minutes. Then the proclamation from the president of India was read. Muslim priests wearing long white robes presented a copy of the Qur'an compiled two centuries ago in 28 closely written pages. The prince kissed the holy book. A sword with black jewels embedded in it was given to him. It had once belonged to Jah's maternal grandfather, Abdul Majid Khan II, the last caliph of Turkey, whose daughter, Jah's mother, Princess Durru Shehvar, sat in front of her son. Jah came down from his throne to bow to her as well as to his father, Prince Azam Jah, whom the nizam had disinherited for his profligate ways.

A Hindu, a Muslim, and a Catholic priest prayed for Jah's health and prosperity. Then came *nazrana*, the offering of a golden coin, a practice instituted by the old nizam. But Jah didn't accept and merely blessed each coin, breaking the extortionist tradition.

As Prince Jah drove away from the ceremonial palace, thousands of Hindus and Muslims greeted him. People put up welcome arches, decorated their shops on the roadside, and strung up banners. Three decades after the end of Hyderabad State, the nostalgia and goodwill for its last ruler and his family were palpable.

8 End of the Good Life

* * *

Periodic news assignments like the nizam's death provided brief deviations from the drudgery of the construction business, which wasn't getting any easier, no matter how hard Suleman and I worked. The margins were low. The economy was in doldrums. There were food shortages and high unemployment. Anti-Muslim bigotry, overt and subtle, manifested itself in communal violence in this city or that, fanned by hard-core Hindu Jan Sangh elements, with the mostly Hindu police looking on or aiding and abetting the rioters. Following the 1965 war between India and Pakistan, Indian Muslims were suspected of being fifth columnists. Young men, especially Muslims, left for the oil-rich Persian Gulf and the West. It was said that it was easy for a Muslim to be named president of India, a token, but difficult to get a job as an office peon.

Prince Mukarram Jah of Hyderabad and his wife, Princess Asra of Turkey, at his "coronation," Hyderabad, 1967.

I wanted to get back to journalism, but there wasn't a decent living wage in it, as Abba had warned. But unlike what he'd jokingly said, someone was willing to marry me — Shehla Burney. But my family didn't quite approve. Tayabba told me that opposites might attract, but this marriage likely wouldn't work out. It wasn't merely that her family were leftists, but in his opinion, they were fashionably progressive. But I was determined. Marry her I would, and leave India, as a solution to my mounting dilemmas. Not to Yemen, where I had a job offer from a newspaper in Aden. Not to the United States to do a master's in journalism at Syracuse University. I needed a steady income. To England or Canada then. The paperwork for Canada was all there, ready.

We set the wedding date for October 7, 1967. Amma remained lukewarm but said she would attend. Tayabba was in Warangal then, so Suleman and I dashed off to see him the day before the wedding. He was noncommittal, meaning he wasn't approving. Dismayed, we were returning to Hyderabad when Suleman's Vespa hit a goat in a herd rushing across the highway. We were both bruised, me more than him. I went to the wedding all bandaged up.

Within days, Shehla and I emigrated — a welcome assertion of one's independence in the West, flying the coop, et cetera. But in the East it was an act of selfishness, an abrogation of responsibility. It was the toughest choice of my life — leaving Tayabba, Amma, and siblings behind. I rationalized that I'd be able to support them better from Canada. On the plane to Montreal, I was guilt-ridden the whole way. Such are the gut-wrenching choices many immigrants must make.

There was, however, a pleasant interlude. I'd arranged a flight that had a stopover in Karachi, which was where Maryam and Ahmed lived, and where Abbi and her husband, Mian, could fly to from Lahore, 1,600 kilometres away. Ahmed, a KLM Airlines accountant, got permission for all four of them to come into the transit lounge. We had a short but lively visit. Little did I know that that would be the last time I'd see our dear Abbi.

9

An "Indian" on the Prairies

AFTER MY ARRIVAL IN CANADA IN 1967 AND SPENDING TIME BRIEFLY IN Montreal and Toronto, I headed to Manitoba to take the job on the *Brandon Sun* that Clark Davey, the *Globe and Mail*'s managing editor, recommended me for. Shehla took admission in the teacher-training course at Brandon University.

The decade I spent there from 1968 to 1978 was the best thing that could have happened to me personally and professionally. It made me a Canadian journalist and let me experience the vast expanse of the Prairies and their rolling hills, and beyond, to the Rockies, the West Coast, and parts of the North that I'd have known only fleetingly had I remained in Southern Ontario.

The people of the Prairies were more multicultural and multilingual than Toronto ever was in the 1960s. Friendlier, too, once they got to know you. They had an ethos of interdependence forged by the extreme weather — if your car was ever stuck anywhere in winter, the next traveller would stop and bail you out. And upbraid you if you were ill-prepared for the killer cold.

I'm not one to see racism under every rock but am not blind to bigotry. I faced no racism, only curiosity and ignorance at being an "Indian" or "East Indian," to differentiate us from West Indians and Canadian "Indians." At a remote northern community, a little girl kept staring at me, for which her mother apologized — "She's never seen an Indian." Being an Indian was, in fact, an advantage: there were so many Indian doctors dotted throughout western Canada that people often addressed me as "Doc."

The "Indians" who faced real racism were Indigenous people. But that wasn't recognized; indeed, it was assiduously ignored. There was a residential school in plain sight five kilometres from Brandon on the north bank of the Assiniboine River where friends fished for perch and pike. The bigotry toward Hutterites and the Amish was couched in the complaints that they gobbled up too much farmland and that working in collectives constituted unfair competition. Anti-French prejudice was palpable, an acceptable part of political discourse, and anti-Semitism was just below the surface.

There was a liberal side to Brandon — a well-entrenched co-operative movement and strong labour unions, a spillover from the government in neighbouring Saskatchewan, the old Co-operative Commonwealth Federation (CCF), predecessor of the New Democratic Party (NDP). Brandon University was a liberal arts college with lefty academics and international students, principally from India and the Caribbean, including my younger brother, Yousuf, who came in 1969. The United Church had a dedicated following, some of whom I got to know well after covering Bruce McLeod, the first lay moderator of the church. He was a new kind of God guy, a medical doctor who had served in China and India, and quoted Gandhi often. The United Church could always be counted on to be on the same side of an issue as the *Brandon Sun*.

Sisters Abbi, Maryam, and Syeda

In July 1969 came the shocking news that Abbi had died in a freak accident — the table fan she was sitting close to in the oppressive heat of the Lahore summer had fallen on her, electrocuting her with its 220-volt current. We were all especially desolate being so far apart: Amma, Suleman, and Syeda in Hyderabad; Maryam and Ahmed in Montreal, having immigrated to Canada a year earlier; and Yousuf and I in Brandon. Amma consoled us from a distance but never recovered from the loss. Abbi wasn't even 30.

9 An "Indian" on the Prairies

While still in Karachi, Maryam and Ahmed had befriended a young man, Ghulam Ali Hasan, a transplanted Hyderabadi. His family was so taken with Maryam that they sent a proposal for him for Syeda. That came to fruition in 1969. The irony of a third sister getting married to a Pakistani was glossed over. I picked up Amma and Syeda from Hyderabad and flew to Karachi. Two years earlier at Maryam's wedding, we had dearly missed Abba; now at Syeda's, we missed Abbi, more so because her loss had been so sudden and so recent.

Canadian Experience

The *Brandon Sun* was called the Cadillac of small newspapers in Canada. The best thing about it was Lewis D. Whitehead, its owner/publisher.

Tall and lithe, Lew was a suave bachelor who dressed impeccably, his clothes perfectly ironed, shoes always polished — "know a man by his shoes," as Abba used to tell us. He knew his cutlery, how to use it and not to — tines down and no waving around of knife, fork, and spoon, their movements limited to the space between the crockery and the mouth. Lew never chewed and talked at the same time. His wood-panelled office with carved, cushioned chairs and a polished desk exuded understated elegance. Lew's cars were the latest luxury models, which he let some of us drive to Winnipeg's airport and back, 200 kilometres each way, when he flew off to New York City where he had an apartment and a friend. He trusted us with his beloved Lincolns and Eldorados. Lew had confidence in our driving or thought it impolite to issue a list of dos and don'ts to anyone doing him a favour. For me, the chauffeuring was quite the deal — in India we had a limited supply of cars, most prominently the Hindustan Ambassador, a clunkier version of the Morris Oxford. Our family had upgraded to it from the workhorse 1928 Ford.

Lew had inherited the *Brandon Sun* but transformed it with his money and idealism. For a paper with a circulation of 15,000 and an average of 22 pages per day, it maintained more editorial staff (22), more local columnists (12), more regional freelancers (nearly 60 sprinkled throughout southwestern Manitoba), and subscribed to more news sources and syndicates than any paper of comparable circulation in North America. It was well designed, too, winning awards, including the prestigious Inland Daily Press Association and Northwestern University Medill School of Journalism Award, the only Canadian newspaper so honoured.

Staff were sent by Lew to journalistic and managerial training across Canada and the United States — to Winnipeg; Regina; Montreal; Toronto (several times); Easton, Pennsylvania; Reston, Virginia; New York City; and Cosa Mesa, California. The editorial and management sessions and seminars were arranged by the Canadian Daily Newspaper Publishers Association, the American Newspaper Publishers Association, the American Press Institute, the Columbia School of Journalism, the University of Chicago, and others. Such collective efforts at upgrading staff and journalistic standards used to be the norm in the industry, then flush with money. If some of us succeeded, it was primarily because of the investments made in our careers, something

Lew Whitehead, owner/publisher of the *Brandon Sun*.

denied today's journalists. All of that helped me develop as a reporter, city editor, and managing editor.

Lew was cosmopolitan long before the advent of official multiculturalism. He had made Lubor Zink, the fire-breathing anti-communist from Czechoslovakia, editor of the editorial page. Zink wrote more passionately and more frequently about his former homeland than about anything local. After he left, Lew hired an exact opposite, Charles Gordon, the very liberal son of J. King Gordon, a former United Church minister who had worked at the United Nations in New York City.

Once himself a reporter and editorial writer, Lew had journalistic vision. While the *Sun* was heavily local, he ensured that it wasn't parochial. He let reporters roam the province and beyond. He had ethics. He believed in fairness and balance, especially in a one-newspaper town. He stood by his staff.

All those attributes came in handy when a socialist revolution swept the province in the summer of 1969 and the NDP won power for the first time. Even though the NDP didn't win a single seat in the *Sun*'s bailiwick of southwestern Manitoba, we provided fair coverage. Reporting on the new government made me a better-informed Canadian, and to be crass about it, gave me dozens of journalistic scoops over the province's main news outlets in the Legislative Assembly's own backyard — Winnipeg's *Free Press* and *Tribune*.

"Ed the Red"

Most Canadians remember Ed Schreyer as a lacklustre governor general (1979–84). But in Manitoba he was a charismatic trailblazer. Blowing in like a whirlwind, he won the NDP leadership and a general election within a span of 18 days and became the province's youngest-ever premier. At 33, he had already been in elected office for 11 years, seven as an MLA and four as an MP. He had four degrees and spoke four languages: English, French, Ukrainian, and German. His was a coalition of minorities long denied office — francophones, Indigenous people, Ukrainians, Poles, people of Austrian-German stock like himself, and others. Schreyer was a pioneer in conceptualizing a multicultural society in which "cultural groups can feel secure in their ability to thrive."

"Ed the Red" unleashed a tidal wave of reforms. He nationalized auto insurance, banned extra billing by doctors, subsidized seniors to repair their homes, and legislated the equal division of shared marital assets in divorce, a first in Canada. He displayed nerves of steel in the face of unprecedented opposition from doctors, insurance agents, and their comrades at the upscale Manitoba Club.

There was the added melodrama of whether his minority government would survive, being one seat short of a majority. The teeter-totter wasn't stopped until the NDP won two by-elections in 1971, including one in nearby St. Rose, north of Brandon. The riding was won almost single-handedly by Howard Pawley, the minister who had ushered in public auto insurance. An unusual politician, he rarely raised his voice, had zero charisma, but possessed an abundance of innate decency that showed through and eventually carried him to the job of premier in 1981. His wife, Adele — née Schreyer, a cousin of the premier — was equally unpretentious and even more at ease on the campaign trail than he was.

In those days, ministers didn't need security, weren't chauffeured around, not even the premier, and had an easy, informal relationship with reporters with whom they hitched a ride or to whom they gave one. On the eve of the by-election, after a long day of campaigning from farm to farm, Pawley politely ushered me out of his battered Chevy, saying he had to go off on "a sensitive mission." It turned out that he'd gone to persuade the local priests, especially the Catholic one, to refrain from endorsing either the Conservative or Liberal candidate. None would have endorsed the NDP, Pawley said, but as "long as they just stay neutral we can win."

Pawley and I had something in common — he, too, had grown up in a conservative family of believers. His paternal grandfather, Thomas Pawley, was a strict Methodist for whom Sunday wasn't a day for sports or games or any other activity. Alcohol, tobacco, dancing, and cards were banned on all days. The young Howard blurted out at one Sunday breakfast that the night before, the family had enjoyed *How Green Was My Valley*. "Grandfather stormed from the kitchen, accusing my parents of setting a bad example for their son."[1] Post-politics, Pawley moved to the University of Windsor as professor of politics, and we kept in touch.

9 An "Indian" on the Prairies

* * *

The *Sun* was also even-handed on the Israeli-Palestinian issue, as noted by Dr. A.C. Forrest, editor of the *United Church Observer*. When I reviewed his book, *The Unholy Land*,[2] he wrote to me to say that the *Sun* was "one of the few papers in Canada which gave balanced coverage and some intelligent editorial comment on the Middle East."

Pressured by a particularly irascible mayor, Bill Wilton, who wanted me fired from the municipal beat and Bill Morgan removed or tamed as editorial page editor, Lew refused to comply. Bill, an eclectic immigrant from Australia, promptly penned a funny column on how the riled-up Wilton forgot to take the fedora off his bald head the entire time he was berating Bill in his office.

Lew stood by Charles Gordon, too, who editorially supported the 1969 Official Languages Act and opposed the 1970 War Measures Act, one of a handful to do so. He also let us advocate for the abolition of capital punishment, which was eventually passed in 1976 by a close vote in the House of Commons, 130 to 124.

There was much local flak over most of those stands. Brandon's long-serving Conservative MP Walter Dinsdale and the three others from the region were among the 17 from the West who bucked leader Robert Stanfield's support for bilingualism, reflecting the grassroots venom against French and Quebec. Similarly, while Stanfield had expressed reservations about the War Measures Act, his Prairie MPs were solidly in favour, the only time they stood with Pierre Trudeau because he was, in local parlance, "keeping the frogs in line." When Stanfield campaigned in a by-election in nearby Portage la Prairie in 1970, he was booed, much to my shock.

* * *

Social conservatism manifested itself on the university campus. In tune with the times, there were student protests — by "long-haired radicals," according to city councillor Marie Kotyk — against the Vietnam War, for student empowerment, and more controversially, for prophylactic dispensers in campus washrooms. A prominent member of the board of governors, Reg Lissaman, a former Conservative in the Legislative Assembly, quit, complaining of promiscuity. And the ever-agitated Dinsdale said the university was "abdicating its responsibility" by only "protecting students from an epidemic of disease and illegitimacy."

The campus controversies so rattled university president John Robbins, a distinguished former head of Statistics Canada, that he resigned. What had disturbed him even more than the student demands was how rowdy the kids had been — crashing into administration offices, shouting, putting up their feet on desks. He also let it be known that the *Brandon Sun*, mostly me, was giving too much ink to the troublemakers. That prompted 32 members of the faculty and administration to come to my defence, writing to Lew to express their "personal appreciation to the *Brandon Sun* for its highly responsible reporting and editorial comment concerning recent events at the university." Dr. Robbins ended up being tapped by Pierre Trudeau as Canada's first ambassador to the Vatican.

The university was liberal; the locals weren't. Tariq Ali, the leftist British firebrand activist, was invited by my friend, P.K. Nambiar. Known as P.K., he was a self-confessed Marxist atheist from Bombay. The hall on the campus was full when the long-haired, moustachioed Ali lit into "American imperialism" and issued his usual demands to "smash capitalism" and "end the Vietnam War." He was greeted with pin-drop silence. Later that evening, I said he'd laid it on too thick and was unmindful of local sensitivities. Ali waived me off, saying, "They need to hear it." We moved on to the more important discussion about the respective merits of my Hyderabadi biryani, saffron chicken rice versus the Pakistani pilaf, rice boiled in meat and fat. That prompted P.K. to pronounce that Ali was just another closet bourgeois.

P.K. was like that: blunt, honest, funny. When he heard the newly arrived Muslims in Brandon saying goodbye to one another with *"Khuda Haafiz"* ("God be with you"), he cracked, "What's this *khuda's* office? When does it open and when does it close?"

9 An "Indian" on the Prairies

My Brother Yousuf

My younger brother, Yousuf, enjoyed Brandon University and also campus living but not the food, of course. Food had long been an issue for students and immigrants from the Indian subcontinent to the West, having grown up on a spicier haute cuisine, vegetarian and non-vegetarian, with regional variations galore. Most Indians are familiar with the oft-told tales of the vegetarian Gandhi's plight throughout his student years in England (1888–91), and that of Srinivasa Ramanujan, the mathematical genius at Cambridge University (1914–16), who barely ate anything outside of what little he cooked spasmodically. Yousuf ate with me and the other Indian families frequently until he got hired part-time as a waiter in a high-end steak house. Besides being attentive to guests — childhood training — he Indianized the restaurant's menu, first for his own consumption, then for colleagues, and finally, for the customers who raved about his pepper steak that tasted the way it sounded. They tipped him generously, sometimes $100 or more per shift — big money then.

When Yousuf graduated with a teaching degree, his first jobs were up north — at the Indigenous reserve at Pukatawagan, 700 kilometres north of

My brother Yousuf.

Winnipeg, and then at Lynn Lake, yet another 400 kilometres north. Such isolation and the severe cold were usually countered by visiting workers with alcohol. But by Yousuf with his daily prayers and regular recitation of the Qur'an, since he, too, is a *hafiz*.

His sojourn at Pukatawagan had come by default. He'd been hired as an adult education teacher at the community college in The Pas, but the course hadn't attracted a single student despite the stipend of $500 on offer. However, 10 students had registered 215 kilometres north at the reserve. Would Yousuf like to go there? Sure. "My supervisor got excited and said, 'It's a nice reserve on a lake where you'll enjoy fishing. You can start the following week.'" The train only travelled on Thursdays. On the appointed day, Yousuf was at the station with his teaching manuals and sparse belongings for the 10:00 a.m. departure. But he told me:

> We were still there at 3:00 p.m. Could we drive instead? No. There were only two ways to get there — fly or take the train.
>
> We didn't get to Pukatawagan until 3:00 a.m. The temperature was minus 35 and the wind chill minus 52. Yet there were many people waiting for their supplies at the station that had no platform. It was the first train in after three weeks because parts of the track had been frozen.
>
> I was put up in a bunkhouse with no heating and no running water. The students were kind enough to fetch me ice from the lake and boil it for me. It was their first encounter with a Muslim. It was my first experience seeing the living conditions of an Aboriginal community. I could find relief most weekends flying to The Pas or Winnipeg, not they.

Amma's Death

In 1971, Suleman called to say he had bad news. Amma had been diagnosed with esophageal cancer. He was taking her to Bombay for treatment. I drove two hours to Winnipeg and took a flight to Toronto, another to Europe, and

9 An "Indian" on the Prairies

a third to Bombay to land there 36 hours later. Dawn was breaking. "To the Tata Institute," I said to the *taxiwallah*.

"Who's ill?" he asked.

We drove the next half-hour mostly in silence as he coaxed his beat-up, rattling old Fiat. I dashed out when we arrived and made my way to Amma's ward. She looked pale, weak, and sad. After much hugging and crying, I told Suleman I needed to go downstairs to fetch my suitcase. An attendant there said the taxi fellow would be long gone, absconding with my belongings. I didn't think so.

In the lobby, no sooner had the driver laid eyes on me than he said, *"Mata ji theek hain?"* ("Your dear mother all right?")

"How much do I owe?" I asked him.

"Nothing," he replied, handing me my suitcase.

"I insist, though."

Amma at Syeda's wedding, Karachi, 1969.

"Let me start the day with this one good deed," he replied. Then he folded his bony hands into a *namaste*, saying, "May *Bhagwan* [God] cure your mother," bowed his head, and slipped out.

I've never forgotten his weathered face, hollow eyes, frail frame, fraying shirt, bare feet, quiet dignity, and humanity. A dirt-poor Indian of the highest moral compass.

Such is India. It can be one of the most inhumane and cruel places on earth, yet also the nurturer of the most extraordinary acts of kindness and generosity among strangers across barriers of race, religion, and class.

Yousuf, too, rushed to Bombay from Brandon, and Maryam from Montreal. But Syeda, barely 800 kilometres away in Karachi, couldn't. She and Amma couldn't even talk on the telephone. India and Pakistan had cut off diplomatic relations after the 1971 Bangladesh War, severed postal and telecommunications links, and banned travel. Appeals on humanitarian grounds to both Pakistani and Indian governments proved fruitless.

Amma's diagnosis wasn't good. We took her home to Hyderabad. When it was time to leave for Canada, I felt I was hugging her for the last time. I cried frequently on the return flight. Not long after, in November 1971, Suleman called to convey the bad news.

A saintly figure, Amma was selfless, never demanding anything for herself. I don't remember her ever raising her voice. Her admonitions were gentle, unlike Abba's or Tayabba's. She didn't fuss over food and ate sparingly. Her only regular wants were the glass of warm water with which she started her day, tea twice or thrice per day, and her frequent *paan*, the Indian specialty of green betel leaf with *chunna*, slaked lime, betel nut shavings, and *kattha*, boiled bark from an acacia tree, which is what produces the red colour in the mouth. Many people add tobacco to the mix, but Amma never did. Betel nut wasn't then well known as a carcinogen, but that's what likely caused her cancer.

Dief, Douglas, and David

In Brandon, a steady parade of politicians provided a close-up of some legendary figures. John Diefenbaker, Tommy Douglas, and David Lewis were all fine specimens of extempore speaking, with nary a note in front of them. Lewis was especially spellbinding during his 1972 election campaign against "corporate welfare bums." He spoke in proper sentences and all one had to do as a reporter was to add punctuation. Diefenbaker, or Dief, embittered at being toppled by Robert Stanfield, railed against Dalton Camp, the party president, whom he blamed for engineering the 1967 party coup. Invariably, Dief spoke too long — just as he'd be winding down, he'd start on something new and gather steam afresh. Unlike him, Douglas was at ease with himself and his audiences and was self-deprecating. "The secret sauce of my little success was that I always surrounded myself with people smarter than myself" — a sound management principle best illustrated in the breach by insecure CEOs hiring people more mediocre than themselves.

Anti-Semitism

In a glorious moment of multicultural triumph, the Manitoba Liberal and Conservative Parties elected their first-ever Jewish leaders in Izzy Asper and Sidney Spivak in 1970 and 1971, respectively. But that also let anti-Semitism emerge from the shadows. When either of them went to smaller towns, scuttlebutt had it that the leader demanded kosher food (similar rumour-mongering befell Larry Grossman in Ontario when he ran for the Progressive Conservative Party leadership in 1985). Even Schreyer took to calling Spivak and Asper "gold-dust twins from River Heights," the ritzy Winnipeg neighbourhood. And he smeared Asper as "a disgusting little shyster."

Losing the 1973 election, Asper quit two years later. Spivak persevered in the face of growing internal dissent that he wasn't conservative enough — or was too Jewish, a sentiment all too palpable at the 1975 party convention in Winnipeg. He and his associates decided the topic could no longer be ignored. Ernie Petrich of Winnipeg introduced Spivak thus: "Some say the party needs a messiah to win. What this party needs is Moses. Ladies and gentlemen, what I give you now is Moses."

Spivak responded: "I appreciate the reference to Moses. I promise to lead you through the Red Sea and out of the wilderness." Fifteen minutes into his address, though, he spoke bluntly about anti-Jewish sentiments in the province and within the Conservative ranks. As a hush fell over the hall and several delegates shifted awkwardly, he continued. "The issue that some are trying to raise, the prejudice to which some are trying to pander, is basically no different than that which Kennedy was confronted with prior to his becoming the first Catholic president of the United States."

Still, Spivak lost the leadership at the end of the year to Sterling Lyon, who was as parochial and pompous as Spivak was cultured and cosmopolitan. Spivak was one of the nicest politicians I've covered. Once he was out of politics, I visited him and his wife, Mira, at their house. When I moved to Toronto, we had lunch during his frequent business visits. Asper, too, developed business interests in Toronto — Global TV — and we got together, sometimes at his apartment, "So I may smoke in peace," he'd tell me.

Spivak was very much a Progressive Conservative, Asper a conservative Liberal. Spivak was born rich, Asper worked his way up. The son of a movie theatre owner in Minnedosa, 50 kilometres north of Brandon, Asper liked to recount how he grew up scraping gum from the seats and being an usher and cashier for the family business. It later included the theatre in nearby Neepawa, where a young Margaret Laurence "cut quite a figure in those days," he recalled to me later. But he was already dating Lorraine Rykiss, the daughter of Minnedosa's only other Jewish family. The Aspers and the Rykisses were "ostracized." Lorraine moved to California and became a concert pianist and more famous as the mother of pop singer Paula Abdul.

"In my youth, Eaton's didn't hire Jews," Asper told me. "The banks didn't, either. They didn't hire Indians. Or blacks. We've come a long way … the mongrels are all okay now," thanks, by then, in part, to official multiculturalism. But in western Canada, "we were always multicultural. That's why this two-founding-nations bullshit was hard to take for western Canadians."

Asper didn't bear grudges against Schreyer for calling him a shyster. "It was a racial slur, but I hope he didn't intend it racially. Eddie was a political scrapper, but I hope he regrets it now."

That was the cordial nature of politics then. Adversarial politics weren't allowed to intrude into personal relations. Walter Weir, the Conservative premier, defeated by Schreyer in 1969, told me a year later: "Ed Schreyer is certainly a capable individual…. My personal relationship with him is very good."

And Spivak told me this about Schreyer: "On national issues, he was not partisan." Spivak recalled that when Asper was flirting with western alienation, Schreyer "was ruthless in his attack because he thought it was irresponsible to speak of western independence. Every time debates in the legislature took an unnecessary partisan tone with respect to national unity, he gave us forthright lectures."

Ahead of His Time

While some premiers were ready to do business with René Lévesque, Schreyer refused. When the Quebec premier suggested a series of bilateral deals with other provinces on reciprocal minority language rights, Schreyer would have none of it. "We'll avoid bilateral agreements with Quebec like the plague," he told me in a widely quoted exclusive.

Equally unflinching taking on the NDP and labour union hierarchies, he supported Trudeau on the War Measures Act, and later, on wage-and-price controls. He was an ardent environmentalist long before Canadians heard of the impending doom, and by 1976, was calling for public investments of $100 billion over 10 years — a substantial sum at the time — to generate renewable sources of energy. In fact, he was the first person I saw driving a hybrid Japanese car.

Schreyer was his own man, an original, perhaps too much so. Defeated in 1977 after a lacklustre campaign in which he seemed to float above the fray, he took his defeat in stride and started a fire log company: "No, no, there's no wax in our logs — pure woodchips and sawdust, pressurized. No petroleum by-products there."

He wasn't full of himself, either. On a campaign swing through southern Manitoba in a light aircraft, I got dizzy when the plane swayed in gusty winds and asked to be let off. We were near the abandoned air force base at Rivers, north of Brandon. Schreyer asked the pilot if we could land on that ill-maintained strip, and we did. Taking in fresh air and walking about would help, he told me. Even though on a tight schedule, he stayed there until I felt better and suggested I should be good to get back on the plane. But I wanted no part of it.

"How will you get back home from here?" he asked me.

My Name Is Not Harry

"Somebody's sure to come along, and in any case, the highway's just on the other side."

"You sure?"

"Yes."

Covering elections in Manitoba was a culinary delight. Small-town rallies in legion halls or churches were catered to by volunteers. The New Democrats usually provided the best homemade perogies and doughnuts. During election campaigns, candidates lose weight pounding the pavement, but reporters generally put on pounds. After one of those campaigns, I happened to visit my family doctor, Mike Samuels. He took one look at me and said, "Get on the scales."

"Why? I know my weight. It's around 180."

"Get on the damn machine."

The needle settled at 204 pounds!

"Go and lose 25 pounds, or don't bother coming back here."

An immigrant from South Africa, Mike was a good friend, and his admonition worked: heavy lunches abandoned, cheese and desserts banished, and the first course at every meal became a glass of water. The recipe succeeded. I've stayed around 175 pounds, 79 kilograms, since. A few years later, Mike came to Toronto East General Hospital for a complicated surgery to straighten out his worsening stoop. He stayed cheerful, talked cricket, and nibbled at the Indian dishes I smuggled in. That was the last I saw of him. He didn't live long after returning to Brandon. I miss him whenever I think about my health.

* * *

In 1974, Charles Gordon, the *Brandon Sun*'s managing editor, left for the *Ottawa Citizen*. Lew intimated that I'd succeed Charlie, but in an unusual twist, asked what I'd done in India before coming to Canada. I recited my juvenile journalistic exploits, but he pressed. What else? He kept at it until I got to the part when I acted as Abba's assistant for years and ran his business during his illness. "That's it!" Lew said. "Those are portable skills." He then extended his hand to wish me well in my new job.

Here was a Canadian who valued something more than "Canadian experience." The attributes that appealed to him aren't all that different for journalism than for a business or farming: prodigious energy for multi-tasking for long hours; a determination to overcome seemingly endless adversities; and doing what needs to be done when it needs to be done rather than procrastinating. There's no postponing a brewing management crisis, no not doing the chores that need doing ahead of the impending rain or snow, no wishing away the deadline. Those invaluable skills, however, don't get points on Canada's immigration selection system.

Family Matters

In 1974, Uncle Idris, the eminent scholar, died in Lahore, Pakistan, age 75. Of the thousands who turned up at the funeral, so many wanted the honour of carrying his bier on their shoulders that long wooden poles were added. He was buried close to his daughter-in-law, my sister, Abbi, the one who was accidentally electrocuted five years earlier.

Uncle Idris had authored nearly 100 books and essays in Arabic and Urdu. His Friday sermons drew thousands, including from outside Lahore. He'd start preparing his *khutba* (sermon) after the pre-dawn prayer. "Maulana, why do you, of all people, need to prepare?" someone asked.

"Everyone must prepare for every *khutba* every time," he replied. "Speaking without preparation is nothing to be proud of." A point repeatedly proven by too many imams winging it in their sermons, a fusillade of unfocused, repetitive, empty rhetoric.

Tayabba lived a spartan life. He wore simple clothes, had vests mended, and never bought any furniture for his office, where he sat on the carpeted floor. Family and friends repeatedly suggested he get some chairs and a table for visitors, but he wouldn't budge. "They can meet me where I am — mine is a *darveshi dhanda*" — Sufi lifestyle. But he never took disciples. His was a solitary spiritual quest.

Whenever I visited him, I found him moving between three — or was it four? — mini-desks with ink pots and pens, where he'd been writing on different subjects.

He never asked for personal favours from the rich and the influential, saying, "Had I done so, perhaps neither I nor my children would ever have to work. But not compromising oneself is far better."[3] A constant theme throughout the ages for much of my family.

* * *

Nineteen seventy-five was the year of weddings in my family. In August, Yousuf and I travelled to Hyderabad for his. I went back to Hyderabad for the Christmas Day wedding of Suleman. Those were the first family weddings without Amma. Her absence was very much present in our minds and souls.

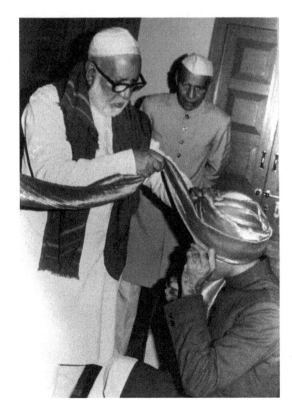

Tayabba Sarwar tying the wedding turban on my brother Suleman, Hyderabad, 1975.

9 An "Indian" on the Prairies

I had a sense of duty done, both brothers and both sisters married, over what had been a roller-coaster decade. To Westerners, that would come across as too much interference in the lives of siblings. But to an Indian — or Pakistani, or Bangladeshi, or Sri Lankan, indeed most Easterners, regardless of faith — it's part of the responsibility of being the first-born in a family. It would be self-centred to think otherwise. And be deemed so.

Suleman's marriage was a love one like mine. Neither lasted. The arranged ones of the three sisters did, as has Yousuf's. No thundering conclusions can be drawn about arranged marriages or India.

One uplifting part of Suleman's wedding was this: people came out of the woodwork to help us. They kept filing in and out of the house, exchanging greetings, taking care of little chores. The neighbourhood barber refused to be paid for the groom's haircut. He, along with the butcher, grocer, florist, vegetable vendor, all came to dinner, bringing modest gifts and embracing the newly married couple in a genuine outpouring of goodwill. A reminder of the protocol of a million little considerations that ordinary Indians live by.

Foreign Reporting

Lew Whitehead also encouraged foreign reporting, which allowed me to use my frequent trips to India to drop in on countries en route that interested me and file reports and columns. Rereading those dispatches, I see a sort of indulgence that perhaps no other paper would have provided for, let alone encouraged.

On my way to and back from Syeda's 1969 wedding, I visited 18 cities in 13 countries in a six-week marathon of 34,000 kilometres. The first dispatch was a rhapsody on the open-faced sandwiches of Copenhagen. My sole reason for being there was that Scandinavian Airlines offered the cheapest ticket through Europe and the Middle East. Then it was on to Zurich to visit the International Press Institute, next Geneva and Rome, and finally overnight travels east to avoid hotel expenses. To Lebanon, Iran, Kuwait, and the shaykhdoms of Dubai, Abu Dhabi, and Qatar, which were still under British control, sleepy places that shut down at dusk.

In Qatar, I asked a taxi driver, a fellow Indian, what he and his friends did for entertainment. He said they mostly watched Bollywood movies and could pick me up later for a show. As we drove into the night, the city lights disappeared, and we were soon into the desert. I wondered whether I'd been had. "Not to worry," he said, "just another few minutes." Indians were getting around an official ban on movies by gathering in the desert, stringing up a white sheet on sticks, and connecting a movie projector to a car battery. There we were, squatting or sprawling in sand, enjoying the cool breeze, hot samosas, and an action-packed *dhishum-dhishum*, a Bollywood coinage to denote the sound of the hero boxing his adversaries into pulp.

* * *

In 1975, I took a stab at a mailed-in interview with Shaykh Zaki Ahmed Yamani, the powerful Saudi oil minister, then the most high-profile figure in the Organization of Petroleum Exporting Countries (OPEC). Sure enough, he answered, combatively at times: "Oil is not the first strategic commodity to be utilized in achieving a political goal. Wheat and soybeans are being used for political purposes. These two commodities are needed for human subsistence and survival much more than oil."

Preparing for Suleman's Christmas Day wedding that year, I was a beehive of activity phoning and writing to embassies in Ottawa and Washington. An urgent telex to the Imperial Embassy of Iran in Ottawa, requesting an interview with the shah. To the Saudi embassy in Washington, D.C., asking for interviews with no less than King Khaled and Crown Prince Fahd. To the ruler of Qatar, Khalifa bin Hamad al-Thani, asking to see him on "Dec. 9, 10, or 11," since I'd "be operating on a very tight schedule." To the embassy of Oman in Washington, applying for an audience with Sultan Qaboos on the two days I'd allocated for Muscat. To the embassy of Kuwait in Washington, requesting an interview with the ruler, Shaykh Sabah, recalling my trip to Kuwait in 1963 when I interviewed both the then ruler and the crown prince. To the embassy of the United Arab Emirates in Washington, asking for interviews "between Dec. 8–12 or Dec. 25–Jan. 2" with Shaykh Zaid, ruler of Abu Dhabi; Shaykh Rashid, ruler of Dubai; and Shaykh Khalid, ruler of Sharjah.

9 An "Indian" on the Prairies

My moxie didn't impress anyone. Nobody replied.

But I did get to Tehran, my second trip there, and wrote articles exposing the underside of the so-called reforms known as the "White Revolution." If that was what it was, it was one with an iron hand. Contrary to the prevailing view in the West, "the king of kings" was a dictator, a megalomaniac who wielded enormous power through SAVAK, his dreaded secret police. The shah had created a cult around himself and the royal family, controlling the media to ensure endless praise for him.

I saw the same things other journalists must have. But I'd seen them with different eyes — and was viewed differently by ordinary Iranians. In the bazaars and mosques, they perceived me not so much as a Muslim — religion having been driven underground by the shah — but rather as a man from India, a historically friendly nation. Whatever the chemistry, it produced copy, which though neither authoritative nor poetic, did manage to portray Iranians as human beings worthy of the same dignity and human rights as us, not as a species to be herded into line by an autocratic stooge of the West.

Democracy Endangered

From 1975 to 1977, India was under Emergency Rule, imposed by Prime Minister Indira Gandhi, who had suspended elections, civil liberties, and press freedom. Hundreds of opposition politicians were jailed — among them, my cousin, Faizul Islam in Kandhla, though I didn't know it then. He was jailed for three months on a trumped-up charge that he'd been ripping up railway tracks! His real crime was that he was often visited at home by an opposition leader, Charan Singh, who later became prime minister.

The Emergency was the most traumatic moment in independent India's history, and I was lucky to be there to observe and capture it in "An Undeclared Dictatorship," a series of reports. Like the shah of Iran, Gandhi had built a personality cult around herself. Like him, she had muzzled and intimidated the press into subservience, except for one newspaperman, Ramnath Goenka, the proprietor of the mass-circulation English daily, the *Indian Express*. When other media moguls fell silent, he roared. With a famous blank page on June 28, 1975. With news reports, columns, cartoons, and editorials highlighting the many draconian measures imposed by Gandhi and her thuggish son, Sanjay.

Two years later, when Mrs. Gandhi finally called an election, I went back to cover it for the *Brandon Sun* and also the *Globe and Mail*, courtesy of Clark Davey, its managing editor. That was my first real foreign reporting trip, one not on my own dime. It was doubly exhilarating: on assignment for the *Globe* to my homeland, which had taken an undemocratic turn. I'd be able to convey it with the confidence and authority that comes with knowledge — and caring.

It took only a few forays into the streets and bazaars and chatting with people in Hindi and Urdu to see that the public anger of the previous years was gelling nicely into support for the opposition. The headlines of my articles tell the story: "Religious Leaders Join the Fight" (after a visit to Delhi's largest mosque) and "Atmosphere of Defeat for Indira Gandhi." Or anticipating a new government, an assessment: "No Lack of Talent in the Opposition," signifying a coalition of parties that had come together as the Janata Party (People's Party) but had yet to identify its prime ministerial candidate:

> The man most likely to emerge as leader, and prime minister, is Morarji Desai, an 80-year-old former deputy prime minister who lost the Congress leadership in 1966 to Mrs. Gandhi.... Desai will likely face stiff opposition from Jagjivan Ram, the 68-year-old leader of India's 80 million Hindu untouchables.

The election results were more decisive than anticipated — the prime minister lost her own seat in the family bastion of Rae Bareli, as did Sanjay Gandhi in a neighbouring riding. I'd been to both ridings, and at an Indira Gandhi rally from where I reported that she was a more disciplined and linear speaker than her father, Jawaharlal Nehru, independent India's first prime minister who, as I recalled from my childhood, tended to be loquacious, meandering, and lovable.

Within hours of the election results, there ensued a quiet power struggle. The éminence grise of the opposition met in a secret enclave to pick a leader. As predicted, Desai emerged the winner over Ram — at the expense of the country failing to "fulfill a much-touted dream of Mahatma Gandhi to see a Harijan, a low-caste untouchable Hindu, in the country's top job." India is yet to have a prime minister who's a Dalit, as the untouchables are now called — from the Hindi word *dalan*, "oppressed."

The toppling of Indira Gandhi represented the greatest triumph of democracy, brought about by the most ordinary and mostly powerless people. It was fitting that the universal franchise was the legacy of her father, who had brushed off strong objections to bestowing the right to vote on illiterate people with no experience of choosing their representatives. "The only way to learn to swim is to get into the water."

Back in Manitoba

Pierre Trudeau visited Brandon with his three sons after his 1977 separation from Margaret. His travel by Canadian National Railway's cross-country Super Continental was supposed to be secret. But *Sun* photo editor Dirk Aberson and I were at the Brandon North railway station when he alighted, wearing his dark aviator glasses, cradling Michel, the youngest, on his left arm, his biceps bulging out of his T-shirt, as Justin and Sasha walked along. His lovely, mischievous expression quickly turned to an icy frown at the journalistic intrusion into his private time, and he snapped, "What, you guys never seen a dad holidaying with his sons?" Intimidated into silence, we watched the Mounties escort him out to drive the family to nearby Riding Mountain National Park. There the family stayed for two days, and Dirk captured the Trudeau kids' thrill at seeing the mighty bison in their 500-hectare enclosure.

* * *

Maurice Strong, the iconoclastic businessman and first executive director of the United Nations Environment Programme, visited Brandon in 1978 with the idea of running in the next federal election as a Liberal against incumbent Walter Dinsdale. He'd been enticed back to Canada two years earlier by Trudeau to be the first chair of Petro-Canada, based in Calgary. Strong's only connection to southwestern Manitoba was that he was born at Oak

Lake, just west of Brandon. While scouting the Brandon riding, he asked me what I thought of the idea. "I'm not in the business of giving political advice," I said, but if his question was whether Dinsdale was vulnerable after being an MP for more than a quarter-century, the answer was an emphatic no. Strong abandoned Brandon but not his political ambition. He shopped the idea around in a Toronto riding, Scarborough Centre, and didn't make much headway there, either, and gave up. Canada lost a potentially great Cabinet minister, a seasoned executive in both the private and public sectors, and an environmentalist before the term came into vogue.

* * *

In Brandon, Shehla proved to be a popular English teacher, but ever acquisitive of knowledge, she enrolled in literature at the University of Manitoba in Winnipeg and then the University of Toronto. We commuted often but drifted apart. For an Indian, the instinct is to make it work somehow. That cultural stranglehold was only erased for me on a trip to India where Tayabba asked out of the blue, "How is your marriage going?"

"Not well," I said.

"Why are you torturing each other? Divorce is an option for a reason."

Only on the long return flight back did I realize he had released me from my cultural and religious bondage. With no children, divorce was easier but no less painful. Shehla went on to become a professor of cultural studies at Queen's University. An expert on Edward Said and post-colonial theory, Dr. Burney held several doctoral and postdoctoral fellowships. It was on a trip to her beloved India that she died in 2022.

Goodbye to Brandon

In 1978, I told Lew I was thinking of moving to Toronto. He was most understanding: "You're 36, and if you don't move now, you probably never will." He wrote his friend, Bill Callaghan, publisher of the *Edmonton Journal*, to see if the Southam chain of newspapers had a suitable job for me. Before anything came of it, I had job offers from the *Globe and Mail* and the *Toronto Star*.

9 An "Indian" on the Prairies

We kept in touch. He sold his sprawling bungalow on the outskirts and moved downtown into an office-cum-condo building with his mother. In April 1985, when he went out with his dog for the evening walk, he was attacked by two drunks who stabbed him repeatedly. Extensive surgery that night by my friend, Dr. Ram Davloor, also from Hyderabad, saved Lew's life. A year later, he was awarded the Order of Canada. A year after that, facing more surgery — and "knowing what I know of my health" — he reluctantly sold the newspaper to Thomson Newspapers, retired to Arizona, and died in 1996, age 69.

Charlie Gordon, the *Brandon Sun*'s former managing editor, wrote a moving tribute in *Maclean's*:

> If Whitehead had died 20 years earlier, the funeral would have been at the Anglican cathedral and the Anglican cathedral would have been packed. The mayor of Brandon would have been there, the member of Parliament, the premier of Manitoba and the entire staff of the Whitehead family newspaper, the *Brandon Sun*.... Speakers, including prominent representatives of the newspaper industry, would have lauded his courage, his generosity. But the *Brandon Sun* hadn't been Whitehead's paper for the past 10 years, and he had largely dropped out of sight. The service, on Aug. 20, was at the funeral home. About 100 people were there, none of them famous, and the paper was largely represented by retirees, bolstered by a good contingent of long-time workers from the composing room. There were no eulogies, aside from a brief attempt by the minister, who said that Lew had known triumph and tragedy, joy and sorrow, etc., etc.
>
> It was a sad and unfair ending.[4]

10

Good to Go at a Moment's Notice

IT WASN'T ALL THAT LONG AGO THAT MAINSTREAM MEDIA WERE FLUSH WITH money. They maintained large newsrooms, provided stable and well-paying jobs, spent lavishly to hire and keep talent, and spared no expense in covering the big stories. Lucky were those of us who benefited from that era.

In fall 1978, I was headed from the *Brandon Sun* to the *Globe and Mail* when *Toronto Star* managing editor Ray Timson called. He'd offer $5,000 more and an extra week of annual holidays. The paper would, of course, pay for moving expenses, including shipping my eight-cylinder Ford Gran Torino, the first new car I owned. The newspaper booked me at the newly built Harbour Castle hotel on the waterfront, across from the *Star*, and told me to take my time finding accommodation. I stayed there for weeks and liked its swimming pool so much that I used it for the next 42 years until Covid hit. When I finally found an apartment, the *Star* gave me "curtain money" for furnishings — that's what tea estate managers in India got with every new posting, a luxury dating back to British colonial rule.

I was rotated through various departments, including copy-editing. Bereft of an office of my own and with no staff to direct, I felt devalued. But I didn't have the luxury of feeling sorry for myself, since the editing process was exacting, headline writing even more so, especially for page 1. You wrote headline after headline until you got it just right, declarative and enticing but not outright misleading, though it could often be sensational. Still, that wasn't what I'd signed up for. Running into Ray in the elevator, I asked what he'd hired me for. Jabbing his fat finger into my chest, he announced, "You should know something about the *Star* — we pay you for what you know, not what you do."

Imagine a manager anywhere in any line of work saying that these days.

An opportunity soon appeared out of the blue. Pierre Trudeau named Ed Schreyer governor general. He and Lily transited through Toronto. She said he had very few clothes. I took them to Bloor and Yonge. He got fitted in tux and tails.

For the swearing-in on January 22, 1980, the family was housed in Rideau Gate, the guest house on the 36-hectare grounds of Rideau Hall, the governor general's residence. On the eve of their big day, the Schreyers let me in. Ed gave an interview that stretched to four hours between the bedlam of family, friends, and four kids, especially the youngest, four-year-old Toban. The headline for the story the next day was "Schreyer's Son: 'Holy Terror' of Rideau Hall." As the family worried about how the little tyke would behave, the chef at Rideau Hall was gracious: "The sounds of your children will cheer us up; this has been a sleepy place for too long," no children having lived at the vice-regal house since the grandchildren of Vincent Massey, whose son, Lionel, was his secretary.

Schreyer's guest list of 240 for the ceremony was a parade of the people of the soil: his 71-year-old widowed mother, Elizabeth, who had flown in a plane for only the second time in her life; three brothers — a farmer, a farm implement dealer, and a salesman; Lily's brother, an insurance salesman; and in a lovely touch well ahead of its time, two Indigenous chiefs from northern Manitoba and two Hutterite elders. And in a western twist, Schreyer included in his bilingual speech a message of multiculturalism in German, Ukrainian, and Polish. All this was too much for some of the old denizens of Ottawa. One was quoted as saying, "Well, Rideau Hall can now serve perogies and *holopchi*."

But there was no questioning the spark that Lily could provide, given her upbeat personality and sharp wit. An oft-told story in Manitoba was that when she and Ed stopped at a gas station, the attendant turned out to be her old boyfriend. Ed cracked, "Where would you be today if you'd married him?"

She responded, "I'd be the wife of the premier of Manitoba."

Foreign Ports of Call

If nine years of knowing Ed Schreyer distilled into two days of informed reporting from Ottawa, a lifelong knowledge of Islam, Muslims, and Iran was good preparation for the February 1979 Islamic Revolution. And for the Soviet invasion and occupation of Afghanistan later that year.

When the Iranians seized 52 American diplomats and held them hostage at their embassy in Tehran, Timson and foreign editor Mike Pieri tapped me and said it was time to go. Timson, who believed in hiring people for what they knew rather than what they did, was also fond of saying that whenever he looked out of his glass office into the newsroom, he saw "a dozen foreign correspondents, good to go at a moment's notice." A moment's notice is what he and Pieri gave me. The administrative machinery of the newsroom arranged for the most flexible air ticket, a wad of American Express travellers' cheques, and a portable typewriter with a spare ribbon. All I had to do was get myself to the airport on time, which not all *Star* reporters could be counted on to do, too many being pampered drunks.

Outside the iron gates of the American embassy in Tehran, there were crowds 24/7. But they didn't seem as angry and agitated as portrayed on Western, especially American media. No sooner did a camera appear than a clutch of the crowd performed, shouting blood-curdling slogans — *Marg baar Amrika*, "Death to America," *Marg baar Shah* — and burned Uncle Sam effigies. But the moment the TV lights were turned off, they smiled, extended a friendly handshake to American reporters, and offered pistachios and cigarettes. This unnerved the visitors. Some were hostile in refusing the hospitality. Others accepted it reluctantly. None reported such vignettes, sticking instead to the narrative of crazed "Eye-ray-nians."

I was more or less in the same trap, filing stories with headlines such as "The Giant of Islam Awakens," "Foreigners Hide in Tense Iran," and "Iran's Soldiers of Allah." But I was beginning to feel that we were peddling fake news, though the term was yet to be coined. My apprehension was confirmed by Dilip Hiro, a veteran British journalist of Indian origin. Over dinner, he said, "Western journalism on Iran is mostly bullshit." He was especially disdainful of the ignorance of Americans covering a country and a nation they knew nothing about and didn't seem to want to learn. And then he offered this wisdom: "The real story is not at the embassy." As scandalous as the hostage-taking was, it was only a symbol of something much bigger.

It was time to break out of the bubble of the 370-odd foreign journalists. And out of the Intercontinental Hotel into the streets, bazaars, and especially mosques, to pray and talk to the faithful. I found no fanatical Iranians out harassing foreigners. Indeed, they were polite to a fault as befitting their refined culture. They were overjoyed about the overthrow of the shah. He, like his father, had been kept on the throne by the British and Americans dating back to a Central Intelligence Agency–engineered coup in 1953 against an elected government. They were relieved at no longer being shaken down for bribes by civil servants, and crucially, not being harassed by the dreaded SAVAK. Amnesty International had said as early as 1976 that Iran had "the worst record of human rights violations in the world." Such reports had gone mostly unreported in the West.

I found Iranians much friendlier than on my previous trips. My very Sunni name — from the first caliph, Abu-Bakr Siddiq — no longer evinced negative vibes in this Shia nation. The revolution led by the Shia clergy using Shia symbolism of martyrdom to end tyranny had, paradoxically, forged an ecumenical sense of solidarity among the Muslim proletariat. This was one of Khomeini's earlier triumphs. The new reality was dramatically brought home to me in a mosque in the old part of Tehran where I struck up a conversation with its Shia cleric. At prayer time, as people dribbled in and began lining up for the service, the black-turbaned *hojatollah*, a junior ayatollah, stepped forward and said to his congregants that they had a Sunni visitor from Canada whom he was going to ask to lead the prayers. I demurred, but he insisted. This couldn't have happened in pre-revolutionary Iran, nor anywhere else. The reverse proposition — a Shia man being asked to lead a Sunni congregation — would be remote, even today.

People saw Khomeini as a miracle man. He wasn't just an *ayat-o-Allah*, "the spirit of Allah." He was one of the five *ayatollah-ul uzama*, "grand aya-tollahs," at the apex of the Shia clerical hierarchy. Post-revolution, he was elevated further by popular will to *naeb-e-imam*, "deputy to the imam," referring to the revered 12th and last of the original Shia imams, dating back to the Prophet Muhammad's time. That imam went into occultation, meaning he disappeared, in 873 CE, according to Shia belief, and would re-emerge at the appropriate hour as the *mehdi*, "redeemer," to liberate the oppressed and institute a reign of justice. Until that day, the ayatollahs must guide the faithful. That collective role, however, got fused into Khomeini's single personality, and the *naeb* in his title got dropped and he came to be called Imam Khomeini or simply the Imam.

Having brought about the revolution, he retreated to his modest home in the holy city of Qom, the historic centre of Shia Islamic learning, 150 kilometres south. In a ragtag neighbourhood of open sewers and barefoot kids, his house was in a tiny alley. He had no office. Two assistants manned rotary telephones in a small room in the house directly across from his. The setup seemed Gandhian, as simple and ascetic as the colonial British masters were grand, as was the shah.

Khomeini rarely ventured out and relayed most of his orders through his son, Syed Ahmed, 46, who lived next door. There was more political, religious, and moral power in that narrow piece of real estate than in the rest of Iran.

A referendum was to take place to make Khomeini the constitutional head of state, *vilayat-e-faqih*, "supreme leader," conferring on him unlimited powers. But he already was all-powerful. The prime minister and other high officials regularly trekked to his abode. They reported that he spoke in whis-pers, that his was a mesmerizing presence, that he had little patience for detailed briefings on the affairs of the world, that he could be philosophical and brutal, by turns, as the world would discover. When President Jimmy Carter's hostage-rescue mission failed after a series of mishaps — a heli-copter swirled in a sandstorm, another crashed into a transport plane, yet another developed hydraulic problems — the Imam opined: "The problem with Carter is that he does not understand metaphysics."

In the alley, two young soldiers managed the crowds gathering periodically, chanting the Imam's name and wanting a glimpse. Sometimes, Khomeini climbed the stairs to the flat roof of his house and waved. Not a vigorous triumphant wave but a slow raising of one hand while he clutched his robe with the other.[1]

Khomeini derived his named from his village, Khomein, 160 kilometres farther south. It wasn't much of a place, and his empty ancestral house was watched by a caretaker. A black-and-white photo of me standing in front of the wooden door to the house served as my passport to events and places — the pilgrimage having elevated my credibility into the stratosphere.

At the besieged embassy in Tehran, there was one haunting sight — hundreds of photos on fences, walls, lampposts, and in the hands of protesters. "Martyrs" of the revolution, mostly young men, killed by the shah's troops quelching protests. The toll was said to have been 60,000, more than the number of American casualties in the Vietnam War. The resting place of many of the victims was 20 kilometres south at the Behest-e-Zahra Cemetery. There rows upon rows of graves had framed pictures of the dead as headstones. The day I was there, there were several widows and mothers in black, and a few fathers and brothers, weeping quietly or crying loudly, some thumping their hands on their chests in the traditional Shia method of mourning. The hostage takers were at the American embassy because the dead were here.

"This, you see, was my son," a woman who looked to be in her forties told me, pointing to his picture. "He was shot by [the troops] of the Shah in Jaleh Square," referring to Black Friday, a particularly gruesome event the year before when at least 100 demonstrators were shot dead. "A bullet had gone through his eye into the head," she said, wiping a tear with her chador. "I didn't find out about it until the next day when friends and a *hojatollah* brought his body home. Here he lies, my son. And where's the Shah? He left in his big plane with our money, jewels, gold."

A visit to the shah's abandoned gilded palace in Tehran, and those of his twin sister, the tactless and tasteless Princess Ashraf, and their younger sister, Princess Shams, provided ample proof of the people's pent-up anger: gold phones, gold ashtrays, gold candelabras, silver urns, baroque chairs, and gaudy trinkets, especially in the six-room apartment of Princess Leila, the

10 Good to Go at a Moment's Notice

six-year-old daughter of the shah and his third wife, Princess Farah Diba. There was nothing Iranian, let alone Islamic, about their lifestyle, which was out of tune with the history and culture of the land and its people. It wasn't known what treasures the shah had absconded with on his private jet when he went into exile, but the new revolutionary government did release a dossier of his largesse abroad, including hefty contributions to Richard Nixon for his 1972 election campaign and to members of Congress, especially Republicans; trips for journalists; and gifts to such celebrities as Elizabeth Taylor.

Not far from the palaces was a mountain village. Sohanak had one dirt road, three wells, nine shops, and about 100 mud houses. Once isolated, it was getting hemmed in by mansions of the nouveau riche, mostly beneficiaries of the shah's crony capitalism. Lambs and goats from the village were being shooed off their traditional grazing grounds. The villagers petitioned, but no one listened until the revolution. A people's committee allowed the cattle to roam; let the villagers take tours of the abandoned royal palaces; and helped them lay a much-needed water pipe. "Revolution Brings Smiles and Water to Village" — that simple tale turned out to be the most read of my dispatches. Readers related to its symbolic importance, which had escaped me when I wrote it.

Stories like that and the insights they provided weren't a function of great talent but rather of luck and who I was — not American, not British, but a Canadian Muslim from India with whom people felt at ease and whose dignity I wasn't violating.

Foreign reporting in the West had mostly been war propaganda, from the two world wars to the Korean War, to colonial warfare in Algeria, India, and elsewhere. The only honourable exception was the Vietnam War in which forthright media coverage had sparked the anti-war movement. The enemy, usually non-white, made a juicy target — the more crudely portrayed the better. Non-war reporting wasn't much better. It consisted of Orientalist exotica — the sultan's harem, the belly dancer's pelvis. Or it was outright racist. The *Toronto Star*'s Gordon Sinclair, to cite just one example, won fame in the 1930s with his dispatches from India — "the pagan peninsula" with its "wild and woolly Hindus," "Brahmins, the supreme high hooper-doopers of this impossible land," "scrawny, underfed untouchables," "impossible-looking beggars," and "yowling idiots." Not only did the *Star* publish and promote such writing, in tune with those times, but it was still going ga-ga over Sinclair well into my own time. While Canada was slowly opening up to immigrants — the *They* of far-off lands were becoming part of *Us* — the media remained mired in caricaturing foreigners. Reporters knew the formula — the farther away from home base, the greater the licence to demean and dehumanize the natives. On Iran, the only Muslim "experts" and commentators featured on both TV and in print media were those who were anti-revolution or anti-Khomeini, authenticating the worst of Western prejudices.

Some of this legacy was at play in the reporting of the Iranian Revolution. Anything different, such as mine, must have been a welcome novelty, especially to Canadians, brought to them by Canada's largest newspaper. It had no equivalent in North America or Europe — there being few or no Muslim reporters from the Western media in Iran at the time.

Autocratic Khomeini

As much as the revolution was popular, opposition was building up to the increasingly autocratic Khomeini. The most significant was by a rival ayatollah, Kazem Shariat Madari, who lived 182 metres from Khomeini in Qom. Madari had been a grand ayatollah long before Khomeini. Unlike Khomeini, he was a "quietist," apolitical. He objected to Khomeini being made "supreme leader." Madari also denounced the taking of American hostages. A pro-government mob attacked his home and killed two of his guards, the first sign of the thuggery that came to mark Khomeini's rule. Madari's followers rose up in anger in his home province of Azerbaijan. In the provincial capital of Tabriz, 600 kilometres northwest of Tehran, they took over all federal institutions — a revolution within a revolution — but were as quickly crushed.

I rushed back from Tabriz to Qom on the off chance that I might interview Ayatollah Madari before he, too, was arrested. His assistant said the cleric wasn't giving interviews.

"Not even to a Canadian?" I asked.

"No. This is a dangerous time."

But the assistant was interested in hearing first-hand reports from Tabriz. He soon excused himself and returned a few minutes later to say the ayatollah would see me. There entered the saintly-looking figure in a black turban, round black glasses, white beard, and a long robe over a long white *kurta* and pyjama. He whispered *"Salams,"* smiled, lowered himself gracefully onto the carpeted floor, and tucked his hands into the pockets of his robe, elbows close to the body, as though mindful of occupying as little space as possible. Madari spoke softly, didn't use a harsh word, never berated Khomeini by name. But his rejoinders to the leader were loud and clear. The constitution should assert "the sovereignty of the people," not a person. Those who revolted in Tabriz weren't, as Khomeini said, "non-Muslims, imperialists, and pro-Zionist forces." No, he wouldn't order his followers to disband their People's Republican Party. "It is an independent party. I know the people who established it. They are real Muslims. Its members, I am told, are between two to three million, especially in Azerbaijan. I hope the country does not have that many imperialists and Zionists."

He answered every question patiently for nearly two hours. That was his only interview in the wake of the revolt. It was to be his last. He was placed under house arrest and cut off from the world soon after until his death six years later. I hope to hand over that historic tape to one of Madari's foundations, ideally in Canada.

In Qom, I saw two other senior clerics, Mohammed Reza Golpayegani, 80, and Morteza Pasandideh, 82, Khomeini's older brother, who, unlike his killjoy sibling, wasn't a forbidding figure but rather jovial. Both Golpayegani and Pasandideh looked as serene and healthy as Khomeini and Madari. What was their secret? They lived sedentary lives, none ever did anything resembling exercise beyond their daily prayers at home or walking to a mosque close by. Except for Golpayegani, they were trim. Their diet was sparse — very little meat, cooked veggies with thin Iranian bread and fine refined rice, goat's milk, yogurt with honey, and fruit. They lived stress-free lives, had an inner peace. Khomeini lived to be 87, his brother 88, Madari 80, and Golpayegani 94.

I didn't know that holy Qom was also famous for a heavenly dessert, *sohan halwa* — *sohan* meaning "sweet," as in a sweet dish or a sweet person.

Unlike the Indian *sohan halwa* that's brittle and has to be chewed, this one melts in the mouth, a function of not just blobs of butter but rather how it's folded slowly and at the right temperature into the ingredients — wheat flour, oodles of saffron, sugar, pistachios or almonds, and crushed cardamom. When *sohan halwa* began to be readily available in Toronto in the 1990s, I took to giving the imported tins as Christmas gifts and serving it to family and friends. To the ardently anti-Iranian, I'd say, "*Psst!* This is from enemy country," and still gladly they took it. When I offered it to author John Ralston Saul without telling him what it was, he took one bite, paused, savoured the taste, and said, "Whatever it is, it could only have been made by a great civilization."

The Canadian Caper

As the hostage crisis wore on, I got to know some of the captors. The toughest was "Mary," their English-speaking spokesperson, who never flinched in the face of hostile questions and remained cool and composed in TV interviews. I got a partial tour of the 11-hectare compound with its main three-storey chancery, long barracks, and residence at the back nestled under fir and birch trees. After several interviews, I put together what was by then perhaps the most detailed description of how the students had planned and pulled off the siege, overpowering the bulky Marines. They said their resolve got strengthened after seeing a large-size picture of Khomeini on a dartboard and also discovering several crude cartoons of Khomeini from American and British newspapers in the embassy.

The captors claimed they were feeding the hostages better than what they ate themselves. At Christmas, they made cookies for their captives. This was corroborated by two well-known American priests, Bishop Thomas Gumbleton and Reverend William Coffin, who had come to perform the Christmas Mass. Coffin also noted: "We should be grateful that we are in a Muslim country and that there are not drunk guards." An American reporter wanted to know whether the hostages were getting bacon and eggs for breakfast. Foreign Minister Sadegh Ghotbzadeh, who was educated in Canada, snapped, "Jesus Christ! They are not jumping for joy, my dear, but they are fine."

Amid all the Iranian anti-Americanism, there was little or no anti-Canadian sentiment, a fact confirmed at the Canadian embassy, a modest building with a single door opening onto a relatively busy street. Ambassador Ken Taylor told me: "There are no anti-Canadian feelings here and there's no evidence any Canadians are being harassed." As for his 16-member diplomatic staff, "No one has indicated any inclination to leave Tehran. They are a bit concerned and hence generally careful but there's no panic."

Roger Lucy, first secretary, added, "Actually, people are incredibly friendly."

Taylor — confident, charismatic, always well dressed — never gave a hint that he and a staff member were hiding six other Americans in their residences. At the time, Taylor was sheltering four of them in his personal residence.

It was a very risky business, but Taylor never let on, never gave a clue. The guests were spirited out on false Canadian passports — a story told in the movie *Argo*, which falsely made it seem an American rescue mission whereas it was a Canadian operation through and through. A more accurate version appeared in the Canadian documentary *Our Man in Tehran*. Taylor was showered with honours and accolades, especially when he was posted as Canada's consul-general in New York City. When I met him later, I said, "Mr. Taylor, you're a great liar."

"That's what I got paid for," he replied.

He was writing his own version and "had all his papers neatly boxed," book agent Michael Levine of Toronto told me. "We met a few times in Toronto and even once at his apartment in the Carnegie Towers in New York on 57th Street next to Carnegie Hall. Sadly, his housekeeper collected all the boxes and recycled them. The book never was written."

* * *

Transmitting news copy from Tehran back to the office wasn't easy before laptops and iPhones. Too few telex machines, too many foreign journalists. But the clock worked in our favour, North America being more than eight hours behind. We could file late into the night. But, given the next day's work, it meant very little sleep. After five weeks of the grind, I was done. I wanted out. Foreign editor Pieri tried to keep me going. But I said, "Mike, you don't want to hear this, and I don't want to say it, but if someone came and said the hostages have been shot, I wouldn't be able to muster the energy to do anything."

After a long silence, the telex machine clattered: "In that case, take tomorrow off."

That was it. But such was Mike's drive and enthusiasm — combined with a rare openness to ideas from the field — you'd do anything for him.

Kabul Calling

On Christmas Day 1979, the Soviets invaded neighbouring Afghanistan. Radio Moscow and Radio Kabul announced that all Afghan borders had been sealed. Really? Historically, Afghanistan's borders have always been porous, Pashtuns crossing the mountains into Pakistan, Tajiks and Uzbeks trekking in and out of Tajikistan and Uzbekistan, Baluchis routinely travelling to Iran and Pakistan.

I flew from Tehran to Zahedan, 1,500 kilometres southeast, the capital of the Iranian province of Baluchistan, picked up a Baluchi tribal leader, Mohammed Sharif, and drove across the border nearly 50 kilometres into Afghanistan. No Soviets, no Afghan soldiers, only goats and their herders. The Baluchi controlled the 700-kilometre Iranian-Afghan border, plus hundreds of kilometres deep inside Afghanistan. "We know the territory like a mother knows the body of a child," said Sharif. "Strangers are lost here. They can't fight. Let the Russians come. We're ready for them. We've been fighting the Russian puppets. Now we'll fight the Russians themselves." Sharif's people had been fighting the communist regime in Kabul that had come to power in a coup 22 months earlier. He was among the estimated 30,000 to 60,000 Afghan refugees who had already fled to Iran, and a greater number to Pakistan.

At sunset, Sharif, his two assistants, and the driver lined up to say their evening prayers. It was a sight to see: Four Baluchis in their baggy pantaloons, long shirts, Western-style jackets, and big turbans standing erect, shoulder to shoulder with a visitor, united in Islam and with nature. At the

10 Good to Go at a Moment's Notice

end, they prayed for divine intervention in the battle against the atheist Russians and their puppets in Kabul.

* * *

"Can you get to Kabul?" asked Pieri. Translation: Get to Kabul — now.

One way there was via Moscow — not a good idea. Or from Pakistan or India, preferably the latter, given the good relations between Kabul and Delhi. At the Afghan embassy in India, the officer in charge did ask, out of curiosity or duty, "You Indian?"

"Yes, absolutely," I replied.

While waiting for his decision, I dashed off to get the Indian accreditation to cover the Indian election that by propitious timing was January 3 to 6. Indira Gandhi, having lost just 33 months earlier, stormed back to power with a majority. She was able to do it due to internal divisions in the ruling coalition and because of the Soviet invasion of Afghanistan. "The unspoken issue is 'Will the Russians come to India? And even if they don't, what price does India have to pay in the long run for the Americans arming Pakistan?'" Srikant Varma, a key Gandhi campaign coordinator, told me in what proved to be a perceptive observation. For Gandhi's part, she never condemned the Soviet invasion, and for playing India's cards well as a "non-aligned nation," got the biggest transfer of Soviet weaponry outside the Warsaw Pact.

* * *

In Kabul, the Ministry of Information provided a press pass with strict orders: "Do not leave the capital without permission. Do not interview anyone without official approval." At the hotel, which had an armoured personnel carrier in front, the management added its own instruction: "Do not venture out without a government-supplied guide." It was relatively easy to subvert both sets of instructions, being Indian and speaking Hindi/Urdu, which most Afghans understood. At a shop on well-known Chicken Street, the Sikh owner — his family had been there for generations — readily exchanged Indian rupees for afghanis. Yes, he knew a reliable driver and guide. That fellow gave me a surreptitious tour of the city. At a mosque, we met Wakil, one name only, a Pathan belonging to an insurgent group. "We have no hopes in Kabul," he said candidly. "The Russians have also got Herat [in the west] and other points on the northern highways. But beyond that, they haven't got anything…. Listen, brother, we'll kick the bastards out. I don't know when, but we will." A precursor, as it turned out, of the Taliban taunt a quarter-century later: "Americans have the clock, we have the time."

Resistance was already building, especially outside Kabul. Word filtered out that trouble was brewing in Kandahar, 500 kilometres south, and also in Herat, another 500 kilometres from there along the northwest border with Iran. Best way to get there, under the radar, was by bus.

Sure enough, Kandahar, the second-largest city in the country, had been shut for nearly a week. MiG-21s were flying low to terrorize the populace. Soldiers were shouting loudspeaker warnings from the safety of armoured personnel carriers that striking shopkeepers would face stiff fines. But no one was budging, except in the little cubbyhole chai and kebab shops. A charcoal barbecue up front, a samovar in the middle, and a raised platform at the back to sit down cross-legged on a rug to be served. The kebabs were better than the ones on Chicken Street. One came out smelling of charcoal and singed ground meat but satiated. At night, synchronized rallying cries of *"Allah o-Akbar,"* "God is great," were raised from mud-brick houses, copying the tactics employed during the Iranian Revolution.

The situation didn't portend well for the Soviets. Kandahar is the trading and cultural heartland of the Pashtun, the largest ethnic group in Afghanistan, with about 40 percent of the population. They spill over into neighbouring Pakistan across a border they don't recognize — the famous Durand Line, named after a British colonial officer, Sir Mortimer Durand, drawn in the 1890s as the northern line of British India. Most of the Pashtun resistance to the Soviet occupation was managed from the Pakistan side, as it was later by the Taliban against the United States and allies in the post-9/11 period. The West praised Pakistan for helping the anti-Soviet jihad, excoriated it for the anti-American resistance.

Heading for Herat, no sooner had the bus traversed the bend in the horseshoe highway and headed north than the driver suddenly pulled over to the shoulder, shut the engine down, and pronounced something in Pashto, frightened. Rumbling down the road in the other direction was yet another Soviet convoy. *"Roosi khabees, Roosi khabees"* ("Russian bastards, Russian bastards"), murmured some passengers. Those of us with a window seat on the left had a ringside view of a march past of Soviet armour: 61 armoured personnel carriers, 34 tanks, 20 heavy artillery pieces, 24 medium- and long-range guns, rocket launchers, and nearly 200 trucks and jeeps. It took nearly an hour for the armoured brigade to roll by. "Fear those who don't fear God," a bearded, turbaned man kept saying.

At a checkpoint, all vehicles were stopped, and passengers checked and grilled. What to tell him? That I was a fellow Muslim? That wouldn't do much good in a country crawling with Communists. Or that I was originally from India, their pro-Soviet ally? Still trying to figure out a response that would see me through, I got down. The soldier said something in Dari.

"Do you speak any Urdu or English?" I asked.

"Yes," he said. "Who are you?"

"Canada, Canada," I said instinctively, holding my passport.

"Ah, Kana-di, Kana-di." He smiled and waved me on.

I dodged the bullet in the middle of nowhere because of the good graces of Canada's reputation from several aid projects, including a well-known eye clinic in Kabul.

The bazaar in Herat was shut down, had been for 10 days, they said. But thousands had taken to the streets, chanting "Death to Russia," "Long live Islam," and a new twist, "Long live Iran." Handwritten posters and bills with Persian couplets were tagged or pasted to walls, Herat being mostly Persian-speaking, having once been part of a Persian empire.

Hotels were closed. A taxi driver knew the manager at one, who took me in. He opened a room. No heat. No running water. He handed me a couple of soda bottles for brushing teeth and ablutions. Said he and his wife would feed me. Dinner turned out to be a piping-hot lamb *shorba*, gravy, with rice. He advised against venturing out, even to see the city's famous minarets and mosques. The Russians were everywhere.

Official media were mum on the protests there and in Kandahar. There were no foreign newsmen, either, as far as I could determine. The fastest route back to Kabul was by a taxi. My host said he knew just the right person — "He has a Mercedes." It turned to be a beat-up relic with tires that had little or no tread. We left at dawn. The driver was a daredevil, like too many Afghans. He kept ignoring pleas to slow down. Suddenly, the car wobbled. He could barely manage a controlled stop on a narrow mountain ledge. A back tire had burst. He wasn't fazed — no problem, he had a spare. But he couldn't get the wrench to turn the rusted nuts. I tried to help, but the cold wind was unbearable, whipping through my flappy corduroy trench coat, in style for journalists then. He was even less warmly dressed than I was. We did manage to change the tire. No sooner had we resumed than another tire burst. He didn't have another spare.

"No problem," he said. "I'll hop on a truck to a nearby town and have the first tire fixed."

"No, thank you. Here's your money. Stand here and wave down a ride for me, please."

A bus driver was happy to add yet another passenger to his overload, the spillover bodies propped up on the cushiony raisin bags lining the long aisle.

In Kabul, I bought a thick blanket to wrap over my coat and also a Russian-style fur cap, Afghan-made, with side flaps that covered the ears and tied at the chin or flopped over and tied on top. Warm and beautiful. But I was told never to wear it, for fear of being mistaken as a Russian and shot. Forty years later, it's still as good as new.

In the bazaar, I saw a sight I'd never seen before — new handwoven carpets thrown onto the sidewalk or the road for people, donkeys, and carts to walk and drive on. Surface softened, the rugs were washed before being put on sale.

Trouble was brewing even in the Kabul Valley, home of timid civil servants and real or pretend Marxists. There were heavy Russian troop movements. I could hear the An-22 transport planes landing and taking off from Kabul's airport.

It was mid-February and time to leave. Young, fearless, and foolish, I'd stretched my luck enough for five weeks over 3,200 kilometres as the only Western correspondent to traverse the horseshoe highway. Gerry Utting, the legendary foreign correspondent at the *Star*, wasn't so lucky when he followed me later to Afghanistan, having flown into Kabul from Moscow. According to editor Pieri's notes, "Utting had a nightmarish experience. Stopped by Russian troops in a mountainous area, he was made to kneel and bow his head. After a terrifying silence, bursts of AK-47 machine-gun fire cratered the ground around him. It was a warning. He was ordered out of the combat zone."

"Frontier Gandhi"

Jalalabad was where a legendary figure lived — "Frontier Gandhi," a contemporary of Mahatma Gandhi in the non-violent, anti-colonial freedom movement. Khan Abdul Ghaffar Khan, a Pashtun tribal leader, had opposed the division of India, as had my ancestors. Like them, he was an observant Muslim, a *hajji*, and had established a madrasah of his own. But he'd opposed dividing India along religious lines. When India did get divided, Khan called for an independent entity for Pashtuns, Pashtunistan. When that got rejected, he pledged allegiance to Pakistan. But he was often at odds with it and just as frequently jailed or exiled to Jalalabad.

His bungalow wasn't too far from the dusty bus depot. Several people happily escorted me there. Khan was 91, frail and ailing. But he was welcoming. After ensuring that tea was served, he chatted for a long time, prostrate on his simple string cot. He was contemptuous of Soviet attempts at appeasing religious Afghans. "Everything in Afghanistan is done in the name of religion. But this is a political religion, not the religion of Islam and Allah and Muhammad. Our Afghan brethren, unfortunately, are illiterate. Communism has nothing to do with religion. It has to do with the stomach. The Russians know this, of course. But their calls to the Afghans have been in the name of religion."

As for his health, he said he'd become a political football between India, Pakistan, Afghanistan, and Russia as to who would treat him. In reality, none wanted to, certainly not the Russians. "An Afghan minister told me that the Russians had told him, 'We don't want to treat him because he's an old man. If he were to die on our soil, the Pashtuns would get angry and say that Russia has killed our leader.'" Khan eventually got to Peshawar, Pakistan, which was where he died under house arrest in 1988. His funeral procession attracted tens of thousands as his body was carried back north through the Khyber Pass to his house and buried metres from where he and I had talked.

I pressed on to the Khyber Pass, 80 kilometres south. It had been the route for a stream of invaders — Cyrus, Darius, Genghis Khan, Alexander the Great, the Mongols, and the Mughals. Echoing all that history, Mohammed Gul, a tribal chieftain near the pass, told me, "Afghans have been subdued but never conquered, and certainly never enslaved." His Pashtun tribe of 10,000 was gearing up for a new round with yet another set of foreigners. Bullet-studded bandolier shining across his chest, Gul added, "If the Iranians can knock off the Shah and the Americans, we certainly can kick out the Russians."

The message was about the same in different parts of Afghanistan. Even discounting traditional Afghan bravado and exaggeration, it was clear that resistance was beginning to jell within weeks of the Soviet occupation. It took a decade for the Soviets to depart.

The pattern repeated itself post-9/11, with the United States and allies, including Canada, taking double the time to conclude that Afghans have both the courage and patience to bleed any occupier dry.

Past the Pakistani border checkpoint at Torkham, I felt free and safe. It was another 50 kilometres to Peshawar, and I couldn't wait to get there — and to a phone.

Communications had been cut off in Afghanistan. With mobile phones still decades off, the only way to get in touch with the outside world was on a land line or telex, both of which were dead, been made dead. How to transmit copy? Mark Tully, the veteran India-born, Hindi-speaking BBC correspondent, suggested a solution. On the days that Indian Airlines came to Kabul, meet the crew and talk or tip them into taking copy and dropping it off at the Reuters news agency in Delhi for forwarding to Toronto. Done. But there was no way of knowing if the mission was being accomplished. To be doubly sure, I started making a carbon copy on the typewriter and going to the airport the day Pakistan International Airlines came and had its crew take the envelope to the Reuters office in Peshawar. When I finally got through to Pieri, he said, "Yes, the copy sent by the 'pigeons' reached me. Not once but sometimes twice."

10 Good to Go at a Moment's Notice

At the hotel in Peshawar, whom did I run into at breakfast? Sitting in a corner was Zbigniew Brzezinski, Jimmy Carter's national security adviser, an anti-Soviet hawk. But he wouldn't engage beyond pleasantries, not even after being nudged that I was, like him, a naturalized Canadian. I read later that he was in Islamabad to have Pakistan coordinate the anti-Soviet campaign in Afghanistan. Peshawar was where Afghan refugees were converging in the hundreds of thousands and where five anti-Soviet resistance groups were already operating. One rebel group was Hizb-e-Islami. Its spokesman, Mangal Hassan, brushed aside my skepticism about the prospects of nascent outfits like his taking on the mighty Soviets: "We are in for a long battle, and we cannot afford not to tell the truth."

On to Delhi, where a five-star hotel was a luxury after Afghanistan. The dinner was sumptuous, or felt so, served in proper china on a white linen tablecloth. I called for the chef, complimented him profusely, handed him and his crew a handsome tip, and went up and crashed for the night, exhausted. By 2:00 a.m., I was doubling up and running to the washroom. By 4:00 a.m., I was limp and calling for a doctor. One appeared soon enough.

"What did you eat?" he asked.

"Shrimps, jumbo shrimps."

"Do you know how far Delhi is from an ocean?"

"More than a thousand kilometres either east or west."

"There's your answer. This may be a fancy hotel, but refrigeration being what it is in India ..."

Then it was on to home in Hyderabad to recuperate from exhaustion, developing flu, and skin rashes. Pieri wired $500 and told me to stay as long as I needed to, even offered a job while there "as a specialist writer, with editing and travelling assignments." He also assured me that since the lease on my apartment in Toronto had ended, his assistant, Pat Wilson, a veteran administrator, had "sorted all that out for you," had the contents packed and put in storage.

"Where will I go when I return to Toronto?"

"We'll book you back at the Harbour Castle Hilton until you find yourself a new place."

Finally back in Toronto, it took days to do my expenses, which ran to several pages. Attached was a thick sheaf of receipts in six currencies

— American and Canadian dollars, Iranian rials, afghanis, and Indian and Pakistani rupees. Gus Morin, the assistant managing editor in charge of finances, was impressed: "This is how accounts should be done. Have you studied or done accounting?"

"Yes, at Abba's."

"What's that?" he asked.

I smiled.

11

In the Trenches

THE MORNING SHIFT BEGAN ROUTINELY AT 6:00. AS A COPY EDITOR ON THE foreign desk, I read the first three editions of the *Star* put out by the overnight shift. Our crew would do the next two, with a noon deadline for the final edition. That day, October 6, 1981, news flashed from Cairo that Anwar Sadat, the Egyptian president, had been shot. He was being rushed to hospital, fate unknown. We ripped up page 1, rejigged the inside pages, readied his obituary, and wrote alternate headlines: "Egypt's Sadat Survives Assassination Attempt," and a jumbo-sized screamer, "Egypt's Sadat Assassinated."

Deadline arrived and went. Every minute counted. If the paper wasn't out of the printing press on the second floor and into the trucks by a certain time, the highly synchronized distribution system would be thrown off. We on the news desk bore the burden of deciding whether to continue to hold the paper or let it go while the story hung in the balance. In frustration, I blurted, "Why doesn't the bugger just live or die?"

A few minutes later, a news flash confirmed the tragic news. The pages were released, the presses rolled, the trucks got to their destinations, the paper's standards were upheld.

I came out of the building to head home but was suddenly seized by deep disgust. A man sprayed with bullets had been fighting for his life, and all I could think of was our deadline. The joy and glory of journalism evaporated; its worst imperatives loomed large. It's said there's nothing worse as a reporter than having to ask a bereaved family for a picture of the dear departed — a task I'd been fortunate enough to avoid. But my callousness that morning was worse.

* * *

A year later, I was named a news editor. The news desk was the command centre of Canada's largest newspaper. But per the custom all my life, I was concurrently doing something else — writing spasmodically on India, Iran, Afghanistan, Pakistan, Sri Lanka, et cetera. The American hostages in Iran were released in 1981, but Iraq launched a war on Iran with the backing of the United States, Saudi Arabia, and several other autocratic Arab states afraid of popular uprisings in their own backyards. Afghan resistance to the Soviet occupation intensified, and I leaned back on sources I'd developed across the region. Some contributions proved prescient, others way off the mark — "Smuggled Afghan Note: We'll Beat the Soviets," "News Ban Can't Hide Soviets' Afghan Setbacks," and "Iran Sanctions Haven't a Hope," the last arguing that Iran wouldn't buckle under American economic sanctions, just as Cuba hadn't. Some whoppers: "Autonomy-Seeking Kurds and Azeris Could Split," which I should have known wasn't going to be permitted by the new regime; "Ayatollah's Fifth Column Threatens Oil" supplies across the Persian Gulf, a highly speculative piece with not much to back it up; and "War May Topple Khomeini," when, in fact, it helped him consolidate his rule.

In 1982, I travelled more than 700 kilometres along the Iran-Iraq border. The Iraqis had shelled a 30-kilometre swath from north to south, creating ghost towns and displacing as many as a million people. But contrary to Western media accounts, I found Iranian morale surprisingly high and local engineering ingenuity impressive — captured Iraqi weapons, including shot-up tanks, were being repaired and used. Iranians were deactivating mines, in some cases by cruelly marching volunteers, mostly teenagers, in kamikaze missions on a far bigger scale than the Japanese did during the Second World War. The kids were given keys to hang around their necks, ostensibly to open the doors to heaven as "martyrs." As in neighbouring Afghanistan,

11 In the Trenches

and earlier in Vietnam, the locals made do with very little against formidable and well-resourced invaders and occupiers.

My last stop was the most fiercely fought front at the Shatt al-Arab waterway at the mouth of the Persian Gulf. Slumped in the sandbagged fortifications of an Iranian bunker, we spotted through binoculars Iraqi snipers with their telescope-fitted guns aimed right at us. "Don't raise your head," warned Ismail Bakhtiari, the 25-year-old in charge of that patch of sandy bank. At our back were the bombed and shelled ruins of Abadan, once a thriving port city of 250,000. This war zone was punctured periodically by shots over the Shatt, often lobbed over the Iranian artillery fortifications into the city. The crew in our bunker took turns saying their late-afternoon prayers, leaving other colleagues to operate the long-range guns.

At a nearby airstrip, victims of Iraqi chemical weapons were brought from all over the front to be flown to Tehran hospitals. I could go with them in the air force C-130 Hercules transport, space permitting. With the wounded all aboard, word was passed down that there was one spot. The aircraft cabin was a nightmarish emergency ward: teenage soldiers on stretchers, faces disfigured, skin peeled off, noses connected to oxygen cylinders, veins to morphine drips. Most whined and wheezed. You could hear their agonized cries throughout the noisy flight.

There was little outrage in the West about Saddam's use of chemical weapons. He was our man then, backed by the United States and oil-rich monarchies that bankrolled his war on Iran. The chemical compounds were supplied by American, German, French, Dutch, Swiss, and Belgian companies. Satellite imagery was provided by the Pentagon.

Iran was fighting the war by itself, without borrowing a penny from the international money markets. "How is that possible?" I asked the chief of the Central Bank in Tehran.

"We help each other … I have 28 people living with me now, including three war widows in my family and their children."

That the war had galvanized Iran behind Khomeini didn't mean there was no internal opposition to him. He had plenty and was busy squelching it. His hitman was a sadistic prosecutor, Ayatollah Sadegh Khalkhali, "the hanging judge," whom I found very scary. Short and rotund, he took delight in describing, in his squeaky voice, gruesome details of how "the enemies of the state" had been or would be killed. He was gunning for Ayatollah Madari, the dissident cleric I interviewed two years before; Mehdi Bazargan, the eclectic former prime minister; and the bombastic former foreign minister, Sadegh Ghotbzadeh, who had studied in Canada in the 1960s at Notre Dame University College in Nelson, British Columbia. "They all should be shot," the hanging judge said. "If it was up to me, God knows, I'd have shot them already and invited the public to go to the coroner's office to see their bullet-ridden bodies."

Ghotbzadeh was shot dead. Ayatollah Madari was too important to be murdered, so he was kept under house arrest until his death in 1986. Another prominent revolutionary, Abol Hasan Bani Sadr, had already been impeached and fled the country. The suave Marxist professor from the Sorbonne in Paris had returned home after the 1979 revolution and become president, which is when I interviewed him and saw him sip hot tea through a lump of sugar in his mouth, seven or eight in the hour I was with him. But now he was gone — disguised as a woman in a chador on an Iran Air Force Boeing 707 piloted by a sympathizer who had flown him all the way to a French Air Force base west of Paris.

* * *

Upon my return to Toronto, a Canadian friend, also from Hyderabad, suggested I meet Yasmeen, also a Hyderabadi. She was revisiting Montreal to see her uncle and aunt. I didn't know that Yasmeen's family lived in the same neighbourhood in Hyderabad as my brother, Suleman. I met her in Montreal. There was chemistry. Yes, she was coming to Toronto to see a cousin. I could come and meet her there in Mississauga. I did. Proposed. She said she'd think about it, was going back home to her job in advertising. Letters ensued, me writing more than she. Tayabba approved, so did her parents, after her father, Lieutenant-Colonel Khusro Yar Khan, drove himself to get a reference from a former military colleague whose daughter lived in Toronto and who knew my family. The wedding in Hyderabad in 1983 was performed per our family tradition by Tayabba. Yasmeen's brother, Nader, was the designated driver to take the new couple to the groom's house. Midway, the car ran out of gas. Another family member following us completed the journey. For years, the family regaled itself at Nader's expense.

Back to Iran

The Iranian Revolution continued eating its children, and the war with Iraq went on unabated. I was back there in the spring of 1984. By then, the war was in its 42nd month and had left a quarter-million people dead and a similar number wounded or crippled. It had displaced two million people, mostly Iranians, and caused an estimated $200 billion in damage to both sides, mostly on the Iranian side.

The bigger geopolitical picture was even more depressing. The war, backed by the United States, prompted the Khomeini regime to resume a nuclear program that had been initiated under the shah with Western help.

My wife, Yasmeen.

The program had been shelved by the Islamic regime in its initial idealism, when it declared nuclear weapons to be un-Islamic. The United States, Israel, and Europe have since spent nearly 40 years trying to put the genie back in the bottle. The twists and turns of American foreign policy can be mind-boggling.

Later in 1984, Indira Gandhi was assassinated by her two Sikh bodyguards in the front yard of her house where I'd spent hours on several occasions waiting for her to emerge to greet supplicants and supporters with a *namaste*, folded hands raised to the chin, and a tight smile on her face.

She was killed in retaliation for ordering troops into the Golden Temple in Amritsar to flush out 1,000 or more militants holed up there for weeks, demanding a separate Sikh state of Khalistan. Their leader, the militant Jarnail Singh Bhindranwale, was also killed. The *Star* provided comprehensive coverage and analyses, prompting Ray Timson to put up a note lauding the collective effort, but adding: "I do want to identify and publicly thank Haroon Siddiqui. His analysis is a textbook example of quick, clear, concise expertise. Not only that, he reached back into his memory cells and gave the art department the info to draw the location map." More than my memory, he could have complimented my legs for doing long-standing stints on the Gandhi watch.

Outraged Gandhi supporters went on a rampage, with her ruling Congress Party stalwarts leading some of the murderous posses, killing about 2,800 Sikhs in Delhi and another 500 elsewhere — "a genocide," Sikhs called it.

Those events in India affected Canada more than any other country.

Covering Canada

A year later, Timson named me national editor. That meant being grounded in Toronto: "It's the Quiet Life Now for Haroon — No More International Travel," said a headline in *StarBeat*, the internal newsletter of the *Star*. Working long hours was a requisite for the job, as with several others at the *Star*. But I had my trick from the tropics — closing the door and napping in the afternoon. I also took to walking 182 metres to the docks on Lake Ontario, taking the 10-minute ferry ride to the Toronto Islands, and coming right back, standing in the aft, soaking up the sunlight and the wind and the spectacular view of downtown while going and of the islands coming back, returning refreshed and wide awake.

The national editor's remit was to provide full-bore national coverage and commentary. The *Star*'s bureaus in Ottawa and the provincial Legislative Assembly at Queen's Park were staffed by veteran reporters and columnists such as Carol Goar, Bob Hepburn, and Rosemary Speirs. The last was the first to ring alarm bells about climate change, which I was oblivious to, and I was duly scolded by her. Rosemary went on to be the founding chair of Equal Voice, which promoted the election of more women to public office. The *Star* had correspondents in Halifax, Montreal, Quebec City, and Vancouver, plus a string of freelancers across the country. The joy of having so much talent was that if I had an idea, my colleagues had better ones. The downside was that I had to deal with some prima donnas.

"No, you can't change *my* copy," they'd say.

To which my response was: "Sure, it's your copy, but the paper isn't yours and what you've written isn't getting into the paper."

That usually made them malleable, except for our man in Quebec City, Bob McKenzie, the former *Star* correspondent in France. He was so immersed in Quebec politics that he was thought to have "gone native" during the René Lévesque era. When Roch La Salle, a minister in Brian Mulroney's Cabinet, resigned after being charged with accepting a bribe, Bob refused to do a story on corruption and influence peddling in Quebec. "Corruption here is no worse than elsewhere," he said. "The difference is that in English Canada, you have lawyers do it for you."

My only travel was to the bureaus. Treks to Ottawa included the annual press gallery dinner where politicians and journalists poked fun at one another, along the lines of Washington's famed White House Correspondents' Association Dinner. Most media bureaus in Ottawa invited a Cabinet minister to their tables. One year we had Solicitor General Robert Kaplan. As his host for the evening, I went to his office from where we were walking to the dinner when he started waxing eloquently about his love for India and yoga but his dislike of Muslims! He assumed that being from India I could only be a Hindu.

We were joined by some others walking to the dinner. I didn't pursue the matter at the dinner table. It's one of those should-haves of my life.

The Sphinx

When prime ministers, federal Cabinet ministers, opposition leaders, premiers, and other prominent public policy figures came to the *Star* or were invited, the national editor was inevitably present. Usually off the record, the sessions with grizzled journalists questioning the guest could be very revealing: Does she or he have any depth? Knows the brief or was just winging it? Responds to the questions posed as opposed to giving stock answers?

Among those doing the questioning was publisher Beland Honderich. He was known as "the Mennonite Sphinx" for his stern demeanour. Or "the Beast" for his brusque, exacting, even ruthless ways. "Bee" for short — for both Beland and the Beast. He'd often host such meetings in a private dining room next to his office. At the first lunch I went to, he asked, "Who are you?"

"I'm your new national editor."

At the end of the meeting, he stood by the door saying goodbyes when he turned to me and said, "Thank you for coming, Abdullah."

Abdullah?

That probably was the only Muslim name he ever knew, perhaps from a book or a movie. I was steaming as we returned to the newsroom when colleague Steve Petherbridge said there was no need to get all riled up — "I'm his managing editor and he sometimes calls me David."

Liberal Party leader John Turner, having lost the 1984 federal election to Brian Mulroney, was searching for ideas and policy positions when he visited the *Star*'s editorial board. Bee, sitting next to Turner, kept hammering him on different issues. Turner tried to get chummy — "Bee, you can call me John, you know. Call me John."

Bee remained cold, detached: "You haven't answered my question, *Mister* Turner."

By the end of that session, Turner was turned into quivering jelly. As he was departing, Bee told him, "Come back when you have some policies."

Bee changed managing editors frequently. That was said to be his Stalinesque theory of management. In reality, he was forever seeking someone who could give him that elusive elixir of racy stories *and* serious public policy journalism. John Miller, head of the journalism department at Ryerson University (since renamed Toronto Metropolitan University) and a former deputy managing editor of the *Star*, said that Bee knew what he wanted but didn't know what he didn't. "He ran through 10 managing editors in 18 years."

Bee and I got along just fine. Partly because I was never in his direct line of fire, I didn't find him intimidating. I was also lucky to work with him when he had mellowed.

Bee wanted the paper to make money *and* make public opinion. The more money it made, the more freedom it had to hire and pamper the best columnists and writers such as Pierre Berton, Peter C. Newman, George Bains, Richard Gwyn, George Radwanski, Ian Urquhart, Val Sears, and others. And pursue the paper's agenda without having to mollify the powerful. "I've never fired anybody for spending too much money," Bee would say, "but I have fired people for not doing their jobs."

No one ever seemed to question the expenses. However, at times things could get out of hand, as in the oft-told tale of a long boozy lunch between city editor Bruce Garvey, business editor Alastair Dow, and senior editor Jim Rennie. They got into an argument over which pub was the best in London, England, so they had to go investigate immediately. Off they taxied to the airport, flashed their corporate American Express cards, bought tickets, and boarded a flight to London. Early the next morning, Timson got a call from a British immigration official at Heathrow, saying he was holding three passport-less drunks claiming to be big shots at the *Toronto Star*.

"Those men are vagabonds," barked Timson. "Send them back right away."

Upon return, the trio were given perfunctory reprimands and proudly dined out on the tale.

Bee was old-fashioned. When Margaret Trudeau penned a book, *Beyond Reason* (1979), after her separation from Pierre Trudeau, the *Star* paid $100,000 for excerpts, based on galley proofs. But when the galley arrived, some of the more salacious parts were missing. Informed, Bee said simply, "Let it be." He wasn't interested in splashing any more dirt about the prime minister and his estranged wife than was already being done.

That was in keeping with his personal inclination to keep private matters private. When Bee was divorcing his first wife, Florence, and marrying Agnes, John Bassett, publisher of the *Telegram*, was divorcing his wife and marrying a much younger and gorgeous Isabel Macdonald. Bassett suggested that the *Telegram* wouldn't report Bee's divorce if the *Star* didn't about Bassett's. Bee agreed. Years later, he said with much amusement and self-deprecation, "That was the worst deal I ever made" — Bassett being a larger-than-life social presence, while Bee was a recluse whose second marriage wasn't going to cause any great societal stir.

Bee was the proud keeper of the liberal flame and was unapologetic in having the newsroom pursue his social agenda. Other newspaper owners had their hobbyhorses, as well — the Thomsons at the *Globe*, the Bassetts at the *Telegram* and CTV, the Southams of the Southam chain of urban newspapers, and the Irvings out in the Maritimes. But Bee owned up to his crusades and didn't feel the need to pay perfunctory homage to journalistic objectivity: "Reporters and editors will strive to be as fair and accurate as possible, but the paper's value system — its point of view of society — will still prevail." The *Star* newsroom was under instructions to take its cue from the paper's editorials concerning what issues were near and dear to the paper, and therefore, had to be covered and explored thoroughly. That, however, didn't mean the *Star* was a left-of-centre version of what has become of Fox News, a font of partisan ideological poison and conspiracy theories.

Multicultural Canada

When Pierre Trudeau brought in his multiculturalism policy in 1971, he boldly declared that "Canada has no official culture, nor does any ethnic group take precedence over any other.... There's no such thing as a model or ideal Canadian. A society that emphasizes uniformity is one which creates intolerance and hate." All cultural communities would have "the right to preserve and develop their own cultures within Canadian society." His was a pioneering statement for Canada, indeed any Western nation. It reflected the old multicultural ethos of India, best articulated by a Gandhian activist, Shivaram Karanth. A prolific south Indian novelist and playwright in his native Kannada language, he had written, "There's no such thing as Indian culture. Indian culture is so varied as to be called cultures."

Now in Canada, too, individuals would have the sanction to do what I already was — not feeling pressured by the majority. Citizens wouldn't have to apologize for their faiths, ethnicities, or cultures, wouldn't have to negate their histories, their beings. As Trudeau put it, "National unity must be founded on confidence in one's own individual identity. Out of this can grow respect for that of others. A vigorous policy of multiculturalism will help create this initial confidence."

Where I grew up, multiculturalism was an established way of life, honed over thousands of years, with every people sure of their religious beliefs, customs, cultures, and multiple identities, while being proudly Indian. Once an Indian, always an Indian. They tend to be well anchored. Which is why immigrants from there — indeed the entire subcontinent, including Pakistan, Bangladesh, and Sri Lanka — have generally adapted well wherever they've gone: the Far East, Africa, or the Caribbean, without being overwhelmed by host cultures.

Having been a product of colonial India that won its freedom and became a republic, I was obviously delighted that Canada had at last patriated its constitution from London but disappointed that Trudeau had left the monarchy intact to reign over us. He had too many other battles to fight to get us where he had, under stiff opposition from the likes of Premier Sterling Lyon of Manitoba, the man who used to call me "Harry."

One area where the *Star* provided quick leadership was in exposing prejudice toward non-white immigrants. That was Bee's doing. In 1985, he commissioned pollster Martin Goldfarb to survey seven minority groups — Chinese, Italian, Portuguese, Jewish, Caribbean/Black, Anglo-Saxon, and Pakistani/East Indian. That last designation referred to people from the Indian subcontinent to distinguish them from West Indians. In subsequent years, they were referred to, first, as Indo-Canadians and then South Asians, a Statistics Canada definition for people from India, Pakistan, Bangladesh, Sri Lanka, Nepal, and the Indian diaspora from all over the world.

Based on the findings of the surveys, the *Star* produced a series of articles that ferreted out the bigotry that dared not speak its name at that time. From the Black community, Veronica Baptiste, Trinidad-born housewife and part-time cleaner, was quoted as saying: "You're always under suspicion. There are some stores you don't go to if you're Black. You know from the way they look at you. Like you're going to clear out the shelves and run away." Baptiste and others recounted their experiences at the airport when returning home. "It's usually a hassle. If you're Black, you can expect to have officers going through your stuff."[1]

The surveys also found the first signs of white backlash. One disgruntled white complained that "the city doesn't belong to real Canadians anymore." Another: "I don't care where people come from, they have to speak English in public."

The project was in keeping with a long-standing tradition of the *Star*, "a paper for the people." Started in 1892, it found its feet in the city of 180,000, especially under a young editor, 34-year-old Joseph Atkinson. He grew up in poverty, seeing his widowed mother take in boarders to support her eight children. After her death, he had to quit school at 14 and work in a mill, which burned down a few weeks later, forcing him to rely on private charity.

He never forgot those setbacks as he made his way up from being a clerk at a weekly to being editor of the new paper where he campaigned for economic and social reforms — strengthening labour unions and advocating for a minimum wage, worker compensation, unemployment insurance, disability and retirement pensions, and medical care. Atkinson was also well ahead of his time in decrying racial and religious bigotry. "Men who rob and maltreat Chinese laundrymen deserve severe punishment. The Chinese people are entitled to the fullest protection of the law" (1903). He argued for religious accommodation for Jews by easing the strict Sunday observance laws (1906). And he also decried the denigration of immigrants, who might "speak strange tongues and have ways that are not our ways" but deserved to be free from discrimination (1912).

Atkinson condemned the Orange Order's anti-Catholicism — "charges against Roman Catholics are by too many people greedily devoured and accepted without enquiry" (1918). He decried government crackdowns on immigrants/refugees: "At times an immigrant reaching a Canadian port is sent back to the ship in which he arrived. Sometimes, part of the family is allowed to land and part of the family is refused landing and is sent back again" (1932). During the Great Depression, when unemployed immigrants were being deported, the paper editorialized: "No man should be at risk of being banished from Canada by the police or a bureaucracy without right of appeal to the courts" (1933).

After Atkinson's death in 1948, and to ensure his views and values were continued by the paper, he bequeathed his shares to his Atkinson Foundation. One of the trustees was Beland Honderich, who had worked as reporter and business editor under Atkinson and in 1955 was named editor-in-chief. Honderich later emerged as a ferocious guardian of the Atkinson Principles.

Like Atkinson, the teetotaling Methodist, Honderich, the modest Mennonite, spent a lifetime championing the downtrodden and wrestling down religious bigotry. Bee's greatest quality was that he was incorruptible. He was beyond being schmoozed or lobbied. Power brokers couldn't corner him at tennis or golf or any social setting. If any tried to bend his ear, his usual response was: "Call my office and set up an appointment." He couldn't be schmoozed over lunch, either, for he mostly dined alone at a corner table at the low-key restaurant in the Toronto Port Authority building on Harbour Street, across from the *Star*. Those of us who also lunched there had to warn some of our guests not to be tempted to cozy up to him.

Free Trade

In 1985, Bee got a bee in his bonnet when a royal commission headed by former Liberal finance minister Donald Macdonald began looking into free trade with the United States. David Crane, business columnist and a former editorial page editor himself, was immediately pressed into service. He produced a five-part series, "Free Trade: Salvation or Sellout?," that was then compiled into a booklet, 500 copies of which were mailed to politicians in Ottawa and Queen's Park, while another 2,000 were grabbed by the public at $2 per copy. When the Macdonald Commission was ready with its report, recommending "a leap of faith" with a trade treaty with the United States, the *Star* got an advance copy. To ensure it didn't leak, David and I got holed up in his Rosedale apartment for days — him writing and me editing and organizing the copy into a special edition. Over on the editorial and opinion pages, editor Ian Urquhart was examining the issue critically: would free trade lead to the Americanization of Canada and the erosion of Canadian sovereignty?

Here again, the *Star* was in keeping with the legacy of Joseph Atkinson, who was no fan of the United States: "Uncle Sam bought Hawaii from her corrupt legislators. He bought the Filipinos at so much per head…. He set Cuba as free as any cat did a mouse. He stole Panama from little Colombia and his excuse is that he needed the isthmus in his business" (1904). Or "The United States is led by its evil genius to embark on an era of conquest and aggression" (1904). Not surprisingly, Atkinson argued against a free trade deal in 1911.

Similarly, Honderich's anti-free-trade campaign was relentless. We helped to set the agenda of the House of Commons Question Period as well as of most of the other media. For all that, we were accused of being one-sided. Our response was that we were asking pertinent questions about the deal that others were ignoring. Prime Minister Mulroney adopted the commission's recommendation despite his own initial reservations. The business establishment was all for the deal. So was the media establishment, including almost all the other daily newspapers in the country. Ian Urquhart recalled how CBC-TV's flagship evening program, *The Journal*, hosted by Barbara Frum, asked the *Star* to come and defend its coverage. Nate Laurie, an economist on the editorial board, was designated. Minutes before going live on the air, Frum went to Nate and told him, "I have always hated the *Star*." Poor soft-spoken Nate! He was thrown off balance and stumbled through the whole interview.

There was one part of the *Star* coverage, however, that I didn't relate to: the overwrought warnings about Canada being sucked dry of its fresh water by parched American states. Where I grew up, tap water was rationed daily — more so when we needed it the most in the summer. And here in Canada, blessed with a fifth of the world's fresh water supply, we were getting apoplectic about running out of it.

12

The Browning of Canada

THE *THEY* OF FAR-OFF LANDS WERE BECOMING PART OF *US* HERE. THEY WERE coming as immigrants or refugees fleeing upheavals. Foreign news was becoming increasingly local, befuddling many Canadians and much of the media, which couldn't distinguish between the *They* there and the non-white *They* here.

Some of the new arrivals were no doubt creating "old country" troubles here, but to a far less degree than had the French and the British. Yet white Canadian racism bubbled up, especially "Paki-bashing." A local chapter of the Ku Klux Klan was operating openly in Toronto, and landlords there were making up excuses to avoid renting to non-whites. Worse, a Tanzanian immigrant was pushed onto Toronto's subway tracks, crippling him. Author Bharati Mukherjee, an immigrant from India, quit Canada for the United States in protest: "I would have to board a bus last when I had been the first person in line. I was frequently taken for a prostitute or shoplifter. The physical assaults, the spitting, the name-calling, the bricks through the windows, the pushing and shoving on subways — it would be a very isolated Indian who has not experienced one or more of those reactions."

In response, Premier Bill Davis appointed a Cabinet committee on race relations headed by Attorney General Roy McMurtry, a Red Tory.

I didn't feel the hesitation that some journalists of colour did when assigned stories involving minorities. They feared being ghettoized into "ethnic" stories. To me, going into a defensive crouch about accounts of immigration or racism was to fall into the trap set by the majority. As journalists, we cover or supervise coverage of what needs to be, applying the same exacting standards as to any other topic while also ensuring that we aren't being used as an instrument of recycling majoritarian stereotypes of minorities. Immigrant integration and resisting racism were as much a mainstream issue as any other, more so. The *Star* put those issues front and centre of public debate and public policy. The paper also gave me a free hand in prodding colleagues to aim for news coverage and commentary of equal dignity for all groups — an adoption of McGill University philosopher Charles Taylor's dictum that multiculturalism would inevitably confer equal dignity on all citizens and groups.

Air India Bombing

Whereas the job of national editor was to provide full-bore coverage from Ottawa and Queen's Park, a torrent of foreign news was encroaching into national news.

The most explosive example was the assassination of Indira Gandhi, which prompted some jubilant Canadian Sikhs to distribute sweets on Gerrard Street East, then the "Little India" of Toronto. But the more lasting fallout came a year later when an Air India jet that had taken off from Toronto bound for Delhi was blown up over the Irish Sea, killing all 329 on board, a majority of whom were Hindus. In a Freudian faux pas, Prime Minister Brian Mulroney dashed off a note of condolence to Mrs. Gandhi's son, Rajiv Gandhi, who had succeeded her as prime minister. Mulroney had assumed that the victims were Indians. In fact, most were Canadians. Immigrants, especially non-whites, weren't considered Canadian even if they'd become citizens. That had me invoking Bob Dylan in a column:

> How long must a man live in Canada
> Before they call him a Canadian?

Matters were made worse by the RCMP with its lackadaisical investigation into the bombing, as though the murder of "Indians" didn't really matter. That even though the Mounties had followed the suspects into a forest and watched them do a practice run at blowing up a small bomb. The Mounties bungled further by destroying the evidence they'd gathered, as if covering their own tracks. A later commission of inquiry, headed by retired Supreme Court judge John Major, found a "cascading series of errors" by the RCMP, the Canadian Security Intelligence Service, and Transport Canada. The conclusions confirmed what Canadian Hindus had suspected all along — that our national institutions didn't much care about inter-minority violence.

However, one politician saw the dark clouds gathering over India and Canada: Roy McMurtry. He had knowledge of and experience with minority communities, especially South Asians. In the weeks before the Golden Temple raid, he happened to be leading a delegation to India when he made a courtesy call on Indira Gandhi. She asked to meet him alone. "What followed turned out to be one of the most memorable conversations I have ever had," McMurtry told me. Later, he recounted it in his book *Memoirs and Reflections*: "Mrs. Gandhi's principal concern was the amount of money coming from Sikh communities in the United Kingdom, the United States, and Canada to fund Sikh terrorism in the Punjab. She asked how involved Canadian Sikhs were in the movement." He replied that while there was "an active militant fringe," an overwhelming majority of Canadian Sikhs had little or nothing to do with it. He warned her that if the Indian Army entered the Golden Temple, it would "radicalize a significant percentage of the Sikh community in Canada…. The consequences in Canada would probably be very negative. An invasion would lead to a serious deterioration in relations between the Canadian Sikh and Hindu communities."[1]

Sikhs and Canada

A thicket of issues concerning India and Canada was thrown up all at once in the mid-1980s. Public fury at the biggest terrorist act in Canadian history. A blanket besmirching of the Sikh-Canadian community. Painful disappointment of Canadian Hindus with Ottawa and anger at Canadian Sikhs, almost all of them fellow Indians. White racism toward both Sikhs and Hindus. And strained Canada-India bilateral ties. This required knowledge of both Canada and India, as well as of the geopolitical, historical, social, cultural, and "ethnic" undercurrents feeding the multiple crises. While Canada's demography was changing rapidly, its full implications were yet to be grasped by policy-makers or the media.

As Roy McMurtry had predicted, Canadian Sikhs, about 200,000 at that time, got politicized almost overnight, including third- or fourth-generation Canadian descendants of pioneers who had come to British Columbia 100 years earlier. Many were in denial about the Air India bombing, convinced that it must have been an act of the Indian Secret Service to discredit Sikhs and the Khalistan movement. However, the majority was jolted into the realization that the future lay in the peaceful politics of Canada, not in some faraway homeland.

Thus began the remarkable involvement of Sikhs in federal and provincial politics in all three major parties, but mostly the Liberals because of anger at Brian Mulroney. He had befriended India's prime minister, Rajiv Gandhi, while working with him at a Commonwealth summit. Mulroney naively agreed to an intelligence-sharing agreement with India without the appropriate safeguards for Canadian citizens who happened to be Sikh.

Mulroney also paid the price for his handling of the boatload of Sikhs who waded ashore on the western tip of Nova Scotia in the summer of 1987. Fleeing the troubles in the Punjab, 174 Sikhs had bought passage on a freighter sailing from Rotterdam and ended up 19 days later at the fishing village of Charlesville. They were bused to Halifax and held in military detention at Canadian Forces Base Stadacona.

The prime minister called Parliament for an emergency session to pass draconian powers to turn back ships suspected of bringing bogus refugee claimants. The provision was later dropped due to public outrage from refugee advocates, churches, and humanitarian organizations. But Canadian Sikhs felt strongly that Mulroney was pandering to the growing anti-Sikh sentiments in Canada, fanned by many mainstream media. In one of the milder descriptions of the new arrivals, *Maclean's* wrote: "Men with the dark complexions of south Asia swarm ashore, risking the hazardous illegal landing to take advantage of Canada's well-known leniency toward anyone who manages to set foot on its soil and claim the status of a refugee."[2]

Some conservative commentators and academics were also in a state of dudgeon at the growing Sikh involvement in Canadian politics — they were "taking over" constituency associations and capturing Liberal nominations with "ethnic leaders" busing in gullible supporters. The argument was that "ethnics" getting politically organized amounted to undermining our political system whereas farmers, businesses, service club members, neighbours, and others doing it was an example of grassroots democracy. Yet another line of argument was that Sikhs and other minorities were drawn to the Liberal Party because it was under mostly Liberal governments that they'd been "let into Canada." By that logic, the record number of immigrants who have since come to Canada under both Mulroney in the 1980s and under Prime Minister Stephen Harper between 2005 and 2015 should have by now been voting in droves for the Conservatives.

After the 1993 federal election, Sikhs had the satisfaction of seeing more of them elected to the House of Commons than was the case for the Tories — three versus two. Sikhs went on to become the most politically engaged non-white community in Canada.

This was quite the journey for Canadian Sikhs since 1914, when the Japanese freighter *Komagata Maru* carrying 376 Indians, mostly Sikhs, was refused entry in Vancouver. For two months, they weren't allowed to disembark. As food and water dwindled and living conditions deteriorated aboard the ship, one passenger died and many became sick. Unmoved, Prime Minister Robert Borden ordered the cruiser HMC *Rainbow* to escort the *Komagata Maru* into the Pacific Ocean on July 23. The episode was movingly captured in a 2004 documentary, *Continuous Journey*, by Ali Kazimi of York University (a fellow Hyderabadi), and then in his book *Undesirables*.[3]

Today, Sikhs are in the forefront of minorities joining the Canadian Armed Forces, the RCMP, and municipal police forces. Their evolution in Canada also helped Canada evolve.

What has sustained this community of 22 million worldwide — a minority everywhere — is that its adherents are quintessential immigrants. They have a strong work ethic and belief in the dignity of labour. Almost all family members work, including women. Sikhs now control more than 50 percent of the truck transportation industry in Canada.

My Name Is Not Harry

* * *

In 2007, Prime Minister Stephen Harper unveiled a memorial to the Air India tragedy on a Toronto waterfront park, in my High Park neighbourhood where the Humber River empties into Lake Ontario. In 2010, on the 25th anniversary of the bombing, he offered an apology to the mostly Hindu families of the victims. He acknowledged that they were given "scant respect.... Your legitimate need for answers and indeed, for empathy, were treated with administrative disdain." He also noted that the national tragedy was treated as a foreign issue.[4]

Five years later, on the eve of the 2015 federal election, Harper offered an apology for the *Komagata Maru* incident in a bid for Sikh votes. But no sooner had he done so in Sikh-rich Surrey, British Columbia, than he was booed by the crowd. One of the organizers grabbed a mike and said that a drive-by apology wasn't acceptable and that the prime minister ought to do it from the floor of the House of Commons, as he'd done in 2006 to the Chinese-Canadian community for the 1904 head tax imposed on Chinese immigrants until 1923.

"Harper finished his remarks as quickly as he could and departed," according to Andrew Griffith, the senior federal multiculturalism bureaucrat who had accompanied Jason Kenney, his minister. "It was one of the most embarrassing moments" that Griffith had witnessed, he told me in a phone conversation in 2021. An upset Kenney refused the suggestion for a more appropriate official mea culpa: "The apology has been given and it won't be repeated." It was, though, by Prime Minister Justin Trudeau in the House of Commons in 2016, as some of the descendants of the *Komagata Maru* passengers looked on from the visitors' gallery.

A year earlier, Trudeau's election campaign was co-chaired by a Sikh, Navdeep Bains, whom Trudeau named to his Cabinet along with three other Sikhs, prompting the prime minister to boast that he had more Sikh ministers in his Cabinet than Indian prime minister Narendra Modi did in his — four to two. One appointee, Harjit Sajjan, became the first turbaned defence minister of a NATO nation.

In 2017, Jagmeet Singh, turbaned and bearded, became the first Sikh, indeed the first person of colour, to be elected leader of the New Democratic Party, or any other Canadian national party.

12 The Browning of Canada

* * *

Away from politics and conflicts, three simple events also conveyed Canada's progress concerning Sikhs. In 2000, the Royal Ontario Museum held a seminal exhibit, *Arts of the Sikh Kingdoms*, that included a model of the Golden Temple, which had been part of the royal collection in Britain but was sent to Toronto during the Second World War for safekeeping and was deemed on "extended loan." Other objects in the stunning collection were rare manuscripts and objects from the opulent court of Maharaja Ranjit Singh, whose reign from 1801 to 1839 in the Punjab marked the height of Sikh glory. My favourite was his octagonal golden throne, circa 1818.

The Canadian Sikh Centennial Foundation honoured two residents of Charlesville, Nova Scotia, who had extended a very Canadian welcome to the Sikh refugees in 1986. Janice Hines, a homemaker, made peanut butter sandwiches and Kool-Aid. Vernon Malone, a lobster fisherman, took many of the new arrivals to his brother's spacious front lawn and spread blankets for them to sit on: "It wasn't a big deal, since we were brought up that way," he said. When Hines and Malone were flown to Toronto to be feted, it was her first visit to the city — and to Niagara Falls.

In July 2004, about 70 of the Sikh boat people returned to Charlesville, some with wives and children, to thank the other villagers who had helped them. Vernon Malone's s response: "When you're a Nova Scotian, you help everybody who needs it."[5]

Tamil Boat People

A year before the arrival of Sikh refugees, 151 Tamils were plucked to safety off the coast of St. John's, Newfoundland and Labrador, by local fishermen. The Tamils had been adrift for days in two lifeboats. Fleeing the civil war in Sri Lanka, they'd come from West Germany after a 35-day voyage on a cargo ship that dumped them well short of the coast, about 300 kilometres by some estimates.

At the *Star*, we worked late into the night on the story, but I was back early the next morning — Atlantic time being 90 minutes ahead — to supervise further coverage, deploying resources and flying staffers in a chartered plane. Ray Timson, the managing editor, walked into my office, morning paper in hand. I thought he'd come to compliment our coverage, but he had something else on his mind.

"Have you found the captain yet?" he asked me.

"Who?"

"The captain of the ship who took off."

"We're in contact with the Coast Guard and Mounties."

"No, *you* find the captain."

I'm all at sea about boats and oceans. I don't like boating, sailing, or canoeing. Bobbing on water makes me queasy and getting scorched under the sun triggers Rudyard Kipling's sane observation that only mad dogs and Englishmen go out under the midday sun. I hadn't even been on a cruise — still haven't — and have no intention of doing so. Given this ignorance and aversion, I turned to an ace reporter, John Picton. He read the descriptions of the ship *Aurigae* provided by the refugees and guesstimated its speed and how far it could travel in the Atlantic before refuelling.

Meanwhile, another ace *Star* reporter, Bill Schiller, managed to speak by radio to Captain Wolfgang Bindel, who wouldn't disclose his location. Bindel denied any involvement with the refugees: "I never brought any Tamils to Canada." The break in the story came when Picton called the International Maritime Bureau in London. The ship had refuelled twice in recent months at Las Palmas in the Canary Islands, off the coast of Morocco. Picton called the port authority in Las Palmas, and sure enough, the ship was still there. Seventy-five minutes later, he was on an eastbound plane. Picton spotted the *Aurigae* 400 metres off a pier, the last of three ships tied by ropes. He mounted the gangplank onto the deck of the first, made his way across onto the second, and from there to the 425-tonne *Aurigae* and knocked on a door. Bindel at first refused comment, then said he'd already spoken to his lawyer in Germany, but finally admitted: "I did everything to save the lives of the people." With him was his wife, Anatte. The couple had reportedly made about $500,000 for transporting the Tamils. Picton won the National Newspaper Award for that story.

12 The Browning of Canada

* * *

Racist backlash in both Germany and Canada was severe, especially in Germany, which had seen an influx of 45,000 asylum seekers in the first six months of that year, a majority of them Sri Lankan Tamils. The public and the media associated the Tamils with the separatist and terrorist Tamil Tigers. In Helmstedt, a man in a market square screamed: "Gas them. Reopen Bergen-Belsen," a Nazi concentration camp. In Vilshofen, a town in Bavaria, the mayor said: "Today we are giving them bicycles and tomorrow we may have to give them our daughters."

The reaction was muffled in Canada but still clear: the refugees were queue jumpers gatecrashing into Canada. A genuine concern perhaps but suspect when invoked disproportionately in the case of non-white refugee claimants.[6] But Brian Mulroney was undeterred: "We don't want people jumping to the head of the line…. But if we err, we will always err on the side of justice and on the side of compassion."

That sentiment was in sync with the spirit of the Newfoundland fishermen who had rescued the Tamils, and of a St. John's resident who paraded outside the student residences at Memorial University where the refugee claimants were housed. He carried a placard in English *and* Tamil: WELCOME TO CANADA/HUMAN RIGHTS FOR TAMILS, TOO. That was Walter Davis, whom I got to know a few years later when he invited me to speak to the Newfoundland Human Rights Commission where he did stellar work.

Mulroney was also in consonance with Canadian history. If a graph is drawn with one line marking major famines, political upheavals, and persecutions around the world, and another line indicating the arrival of groups of refugees to Canada in the past 150 years, two lines roughly in parallel would be seen. There's no telling how many refugees might have lied their way in, but there's comfort in the greater truth that Canada always opened the door to genuine ones fleeing crises: the Jewish pogrom in Ukraine, the potato famine in Ireland, the upending of nations and peoples during the two world wars, the Soviet gulag and other atrocities behind the Iron Curtain, the Soviet invasions of Hungary and Czechoslovakia, the racist madness of Idi Amin's Uganda, the revolution in Iran, the return of Hong

Kong to China, the ethnic cleansing in the Balkans, the wars in Somalia and Sri Lanka, the Soviet occupation of Afghanistan, and the rule of the Taliban in Afghanistan, first 1996 to 2001, then since 2021.

Within weeks of the Tamils' arrival, the United Nations High Commissioner for Refugees awarded Canada its annual Nansen Refugee Award, the United Nations' highest distinction for helping refugees.

The Tamil diaspora in Canada is now the largest outside Sri Lanka. And like the Sikhs, the Tamils have also become engaged politically as councillors, as members of provincial assemblies, and as federal MPs. Concentrated in the Toronto suburb of Scarborough, they run thriving small businesses. My favourite, Embassy Restaurant, makes some of the best and cheapest veggie samosas in Canada.

Whenever Canadians have gone against this spirit, we've come to regret it, as in the cases of the *Komagata Maru* and MS *St. Louis* in 1939. The *St. Louis* was carrying 937 passengers, most of them Jews escaping Nazi Germany. It had come to Canada after being turned away from Cuba and the United States. Shamefully, Canada, too, refused. After the ship returned to Europe, 254 of the passengers were murdered in the Holocaust. In 2018, Prime Minister Justin Trudeau formally apologized for that anti-Semitic policy.

Yet Mulroney stumbled badly a year later, after the Tamils' arrival, in his handling of the Sikh refugees. His position in this case was out of character for him. He was a central player in helping the evolution of pluralistic Canada. He increased immigration to record levels, which meant waves of non-white immigrants. He set up the Immigration and Refugee Board, a pioneering initiative to process refugee claimants in a fair and transparent manner. He initiated an official apology to Japanese Canadians for their unjust internment during the Second World War, arranged compensation for survivors, and set up the Canadian Race Relations Board. Mulroney also supported the right of Sikhs to wear turbans in the RCMP. Then there was his heroic role in helping to end apartheid in South Africa.

I cite all these because, despite the *Star*'s many differences with several of Mulroney's policies, it must be said that he was no racist, notwithstanding his mistreatment of the Sikh refugees.

Global Village

Far less dramatically, other diaspora from the non-white world have settled in Canada, principally the Chinese, South Asians, and Filipinos — the top three immigrant groups attracted to Canada in the past three decades. The Chinese influx, starting with the well-to-do from Hong Kong, caused a minor kerfuffle in 1995 when the deputy mayor of the City of Markham, northeast of Toronto, said that too many Chinese were triggering a white flight. Carole Bell provided no figures concerning how many had actually left. She was also miffed that the Chinese weren't posting signs in English in their malls. Bell found little traction — in fact, her outburst was widely condemned, among others, by the *Star* and also a dozen mayors from the region.

Smaller non-white communities have become an integral part of Canada, some with spectacular success, such as the Aga Khan Ismaili Muslims, while others — Iranians, Afghans, Pakistanis, Somalis, Bangladeshis, Arabs from the Maghreb, et cetera — have made slow but steady progress. Of those, the Somalis suffered the most discrimination by immigration and security officials in Ottawa over the issue of identity papers. Somalis weren't the only refugees to come to Canada without proper documents, especially from war zones, yet were left in legal limbo for an unconscionably long time, thereby delaying the community's integration into Canada.[7]

The Iranian community is the second-largest Iranian diaspora after the one in the United States. If California has "Tehrangeles," Canada has "Tehronto." The Iranians who came to Canada fleeing the 1979 revolution had been beneficiaries of the shah's regime and brought their liquid assets with them. Others have arrived since, and the community encompasses the full range of the Iranian religious and ideological spectrum. Many don't want to be associated with the Iranian regime and Iran, preferring to call themselves "Persian," which prompts me to ask them, "Where's Persia, please?"

The more noteworthy development has been that Canada considers them as Canadian as anyone else — in 2020, when 55 Canadian citizens and 30 permanent residents of Iranian origins were killed in the shooting down of a civilian airliner after takeoff in Tehran, Prime Minister Justin Trudeau treated the incident as a Canadian tragedy, unlike Mulroney with the 1985 bombing of the Air India jet. Trudeau mourned with the community and kept up pressure on Iran to compensate the families of the victims.

Aga Khan Ismailis

The Ismailis came to Canada following the 1972 expulsion of Asians from Uganda by Idi Amin. Their entry to Canada was facilitated by Prime Minister Pierre Elliott Trudeau. As the Aga Khan once related to me, "Pierre and I were friends and there was an informal understanding that if there was a racial crisis," Canada would help. After Amin's edict, "I picked up the phone, and Trudeau affirmed then and there that Canada would wish to help. His response was magnificent."

Canada opened a special diplomatic mission in Kampala, operated from 6:00 a.m. to midnight, and within days, processed 6,000 Asians, including 5,000 Ismailis. Their properties and possessions confiscated, they left with one suitcase each. Later waves from Kenya, Tanzania, and elsewhere swelled their total in Canada to nearly 100,000. They proved to be a model minority — self-reliant, educated, organized, and entrepreneurial. Prime Minister Jean Chrétien became such an admirer that during the 1990s recession, he told me that what his hometown of Shawinigan needed was "a dozen Ismaili entrepreneurs."[8]

The Ismailis have more than paid back: the Aga Khan established a Global Centre for Pluralism to distill the Canadian wisdom on pluralism and export it to the world. His Aga Khan Development Network — a mini United Nations undertaking educational, health, environmental, architectural, and infrastructure projects around the world, transforming the lives of millions — became the biggest partner for Canada's international development work.

In Toronto, in 2014, the Aga Khan opened the Aga Khan Museum, the first in North America dedicated to Islamic arts and objects. American museums, such as the Metropolitan Museum of Art, the Morgan Library & Museum in New York City, the Library of Congress, and the Smithsonian Institution in Washington, D.C., have significant collections of Islamic arts and manuscripts. So do museums in London, St. Petersburg, Paris, and Berlin. But there was none that exclusively showcased the artistic, intellectual, and scientific contributions of Muslim civilizations. For that, one had to go to museums in Muslim cities such as Istanbul, Cairo, Kuala Lumpur, Doha, Kuwait City, and elsewhere. Canada was never thought of in that league until the Aga Khan opened his museum. He had originally planned it for London by the Thames River but ran into bureaucratic hurdles. He could have located it anywhere in Europe where he lives and works — France, Switzerland, Portugal — but opted for Canada to send a very Canadian message of pluralism to a world of rising bigotry, fundamentalisms, narrow nationalisms, and anti-globalization.

It was uplifting to hear Prime Minister Harper being unusually poetic the day the museum opened: "We celebrate today not only the harmonious meeting of green gardens and glass galleries, or of Italian marble and Canadian maple. We rejoice above all in the special spirit which fills this place and gives it its soul."

An architectural jewel, the $300 million museum didn't cost Canadian taxpayers a penny. It was significant that a Muslim built it — a European Muslim, at that, who's been unapologetic about his faith in the face of Muslim terrorism and unprecedented Western hostility to Islam. He, like Canada, is the perfect antidote to both.

Equally significant, though less noted, was the fact that, in the words of Farid Damji, a volunteer with the Ismaili community, it's "not an Ismaili Museum. It's a museum of Islamic and Muslim civilization meant to display that diversity," as well. On Canadian soil.

13

The Editorial Perch

IN 1990, JOHN HONDERICH NAMED ME EDITORIAL PAGE EDITOR, RESPON-sible for the editorial board, editorial policy, letters to the editor, and the op-ed page. That position at Canada's largest newspaper is one of the most influential journalistic jobs in the country. A good editor helps set the public policy agenda at local, provincial, and national levels. Before I could get into that august mission, however, I faced an immediate personal crisis.

Despite all the writing experience and knowledge of the issues, I couldn't write editorials. I'd gotten rusty as national editor, a job in which I suggested stories, directed reporters, and edited their copy, but rarely, if ever, wrote myself. Now words just wouldn't flow. Or when they did, they didn't cohere into an argument. I'd write a few hundred words, piling on information, background, and context, but no clear point of view emerged. That had Don Sellar, my predecessor who had stayed on the editorial board, pulling his nearly non-existent hair. "You're saying nothing here," he'd say. "Where's the reflection of the arguments and debates we had at the morning editorial board meeting?"

It took me weeks to get into the new groove, leading the reader through the pluses and minuses of an issue to convey a well-reasoned conclusion in 500 words or less. But my colleagues on the board more than picked up the slack. They were a formidable force. Besides Sellar, at various times there were Ian Urquhart, former managing editor and editorial page editor;

Carol Goar, former national affairs columnist and *Star* correspondent in Washington, D.C.; Bob Hepburn, former Ottawa bureau chief; Nate Laurie, who had worked for Pierre Trudeau, not as a partisan staffer but as an economist; Martin Cohn, foreign correspondent in the Middle East and Hong Kong; Royson James, an expert on Toronto city politics, a highly respected member of the Jamaican-Canadian community, and so decent and honest that he's seen as a moral beacon; and Laurie Monsebraaten, the other social conscience of our group. She almost singlehandedly persuaded us to support a controversial "rock garden" in the fashionable Yorkville area of downtown. Some of us, especially me, were highly skeptical of big boulders being hauled from the Canadian Shield to create an expensive bauble for urban yuppies. I'm glad she did — the half-hectare parkette has proved wildly popular.

The editorial board met in the morning. There being no internet in those days, I'd read at home all three Toronto dailies, and on most days, the *New York Times*, which also got delivered early. At the office, I had a glance at the various wire services for a quick update before the meeting. Everyone brought up a topic or two from their areas of expertise. We debated and developed a consensus within the framework of broad *Star* policies. Some issues needed time to research. The expectation was that editorial writers were also reporters who did their homework, made phone calls, and consulted experts. They weren't there merely to rewrite and garnish what had already been reported. Some editorials on major policy issues took days to formulate, sometimes a week or more. The final call was the editorial page editor's within the parameters of the paper's policies. Some publishers insisted on reading every editorial, others only those that constituted a shift in policy — or were likely to cause him or her grief.

We were a collegial bunch who debated vigorously, negotiated our differences in a civil manner, and cared for one another, as I experienced twice. First, when my younger sister, Syeda, came from Karachi for treatment of throat cancer, and a year later, when I developed heart trouble.

Syeda's difficulty swallowing solids began in 1988 in Harare, Zimbabwe, where her banker husband was posted. By the time the family returned to Pakistan, she had trouble even with liquids. At Princess Margaret Hospital in Toronto under the expert care and personal kindness of Dr.

13 The Editorial Perch

Brian O'Sullivan, Syeda underwent four weeks of radical radiation as an outpatient. At home we took turns caring for her — wife Yasmeen, sister Maryam and her daughter Sara from Montreal, brother Yousuf in Toronto, and me. Her forbearance through her pain and suffering was remarkable. When she left after three months in Canada, we were all reasonably hopeful for her recovery.

As for me, when I worked in my garden, I felt breathless. Putting the shovel aside, I sat down and felt fine. It happened again in subsequent days. And then suddenly, there was one cigarette puff too many. Inhaling it felt

With Yasmeen, 1992.

constrictive. So I went to the family doctor, to a cardiologist, and to a rehab centre and started a new routine of exercise, better eating, and giving up smoking cold turkey. I felt in control. I hadn't had a heart attack, only discomfort from two clogged arteries. The cardiologist, Dr. Bhiku Jethalal, an immigrant from South Africa, sent me to the top heart surgeon in the country, Dr. Tirone David, an immigrant from Brazil, at Toronto General Hospital for his opinion whether I needed a bypass. He said it would be advisable but he was booked up solid for months. However, his colleagues were just as good if not better. I said I'd wait.

A few months later, Dr. David's office called to say there was a cancellation and he could fit me in. After speaking to Yasmeen, I said I'd be there. I gathered the editorial board and broke the news. Someone noted that the *Star* had lately been critical of the medical profession over some festering fee issue and added, "I hope you haven't told them you're from the *Star*!"

I hadn't.

Double bypass done, I was back at work, feeling all fixed and thinking of my father who didn't get such advanced care because it wasn't available in the 1960s.

Strike at the *Star*

Office collegiality was tested but not found wanting during a month-long 1992 strike over cost-cutting and outsourcing of circulation delivery. Senior editors lived and worked inside the building nearly 24/7. I wrote the editorials, edited all the columns and letters, and laid out the pages with the help of Denise Morrison, the editorial secretary. Then, in walked Beland Honderich. He'd retired as both publisher and chair of the Torstar board and had moved into a small office to sort through his and the newspaper's records.

Bee was painstakingly scanning 100 years of editorials. We'd run into each other in the washroom where he had questions and suggestions.

"Your editorial today was too convoluted," he would say. "Keep it simple. The one yesterday tried to make too many points. Drive home one message. And why aren't you writing about so-and-so issue? Oh, you did. Then say it again. You have to keep hammering away to move public opinion." While he was holding court in the confined space of the washroom — five minutes or more — others who wanted in had to scoot right back out.

Now Bee had come to help. "What can I do for you? I think I can still write."

Delighted, I asked, "Can you pen an editorial whenever you can?"

Sure enough, he started turning up most mornings, discussed a topic, and returned in the afternoon, well ahead of the deadline, with a neatly typed editorial. His writing was old-fashioned and had also gotten stultified for being out of service, but it was serviceable. One editorial he wrote was on the monarchy. Canada should become a republic, *but* Her Majesty Queen Elizabeth II has been terrific, so let's not change that during her lifetime, et cetera. It was too namby-pamby for my republican tastes, but I wasn't going to argue with something that was perfectly adequate to fill the empty space staring at me. Unfortunately, that became the standard *Star* editorial stance on the issue for the next three decades — the *Star* never did confront the fact that to terminate this royal connection, we needed to have a national debate and a parliamentary vote *during* her lifetime to execute the plan upon her passing. When she did depart in 2022 at age 96 and Charles donned the crown, Canada had little or nothing to say except to fall in line.

Constitutional Saga

Just as with free trade, the *Star* was deeply engaged with Brian Mulroney's 1987–92 marathon effort to bring Quebec into the constitutional fold. The province had refused to sign the 1982 Constitution under the then separatist government of Premier René Lévesque. Mulroney made valiant efforts to align the province's new premier, Robert Bourassa — a federalist Liberal but still a Quebec nationalist — with the other premiers. Their first agreement — the Meech Lake Accord, hammered out at a federal heritage estate in the Gatineau Hills — was signed in June 1987 at 4:45 a.m. to the relief of not only the first ministers but also the journalists on the scene and their editors back in our offices keeping a round-the-clock vigil.

The deal soon ran into several setbacks, the biggest of which turned out to be Pierre Trudeau, who came out of retirement to oppose it. The *Star* and *La Presse* carried a bylined article by the former prime minister critiquing it, the *Star* on its front page. The new Constitution would hand over too much power to the premiers, including naming senators; empower the Senate at the expense of the elected House of Commons; emasculate the federal government; and spell the end of Canada as we knew it, et cetera.

But John Honderich, who had taken over as the *Star*'s publisher, tried to be more accommodating of Quebec than his father or Trudeau. Canadians, too, were feeling drained by the constitutional marathon. When the package was put to a vote in a national referendum, the *Star* endorsed it in a page 1 editorial: "Yes for Canada." We'd given up after putting up a long fight, only to see Canadians reject the deal — in Quebec because the package didn't offer the province enough powers, and in English Canada because it gave away too much to Quebec.

Ian Urquhart, who as managing editor had done so much to spark a national discussion on the constitutional package, which he'd initially opposed but also eventually supported, told me in 2021 with the hindsight of 30 years: "I am glad it went down to defeat, even though I voted for it. Imagine Jacques Parizeau and Ralph Klein naming senators!"

Such had been the yin-yang of the constitutional package — we could talk ourselves either way at that time to accommodate Quebec or accommodate the West but not both.

* * *

Mulroney was so miffed at the *Star* over free trade, the Constitution, and several other issues that he refused to meet the paper's editorial board despite several invitations, both informal and formal. I mentioned that to Bill Davis, the genial former premier of Ontario. "I'll see what I can do," was his typical response. Sure enough, word came from the Prime Minister's Office that he would visit us. What did Mr. Davis do? "Oh, I told him, 'There is only one prime minister and there is only one *Toronto Star*.'"

The prime minister sailed through the editorial board — solid on content, smooth in delivery, attentive to everyone, at the end of which he was also happy to take up city editor Lou Clancy's suggestion for a tour of the newsroom. During that, he charmed the pants off even grizzled veterans. As word spread to the advertising, circulation, and other departments on other floors, staffers came down to the mezzanine and ground floor to see him depart. Mulroney was at his gregarious best — chatting people up, posing for pictures, waving. As I escorted him to his car, I said, "Prime Minister, it wasn't so bad, was it?"

"No, it was wonderful. Thank you."

* * *

In a bid to understand Quebeckers better, John Honderich started an exchange of letters with Alain Dubuc of *La Presse*, the Montreal daily, which were published simultaneously in both papers on Saturday, the biggest paper of the week.

As we approached the 1995 referendum on Quebec sovereignty, polls showed the separatist side losing. English Canada was relaxed, even more so than it had been during the 1980 referendum, in which Quebeckers were asked whether the province should negotiate a sovereignty-association agreement with Ottawa. The national mood then was encapsulated by Charles Dubin, chief justice of Ontario, who told me how on the day of that first referendum, he happened to be holding a hearing in Vancouver as head of a commission on aviation safety. He adjourned the hearing early, around 4:00 p.m., 7:00 p.m. in Quebec — "given the event of national importance tonight." As he was leaving, one of the senior lawyers asked him, "Your Honour, what event were you referring to?"

But in 1995, the separatist cause kept gathering momentum. The stock market shuddered, and English Canada panicked. The *Star* sent a special insert for *La Presse* with letters from *Star* readers addressed to Quebeckers. *La Presse* didn't run it, for fear of running afoul of a provincial law restricting outside funding. In any case, Dubuc was dismissive: "Quebeckers find these love letters a bit ridiculous and, above all, irrelevant." Honderich was "enraged" and crossed a journalistic line into political activism by hiring six buses to transport Torontonians to Montreal to join what was dubbed a Unity Rally on the eve of the referendum, attended by nearly 100,000 people.

The vote was terrifyingly close — 50.58 percent No and 49.42 percent Yes out of five million votes cast. Premier Jacques Parizeau (in)famously blamed the loss on "the ethnics" — anglophones and the allophones, immigrants whose mother tongue was neither English nor French. Parizeau said: "Three-fifths of us who are what we are, voted yes…. We have been defeated. But by whom? By money and by the ethnic vote." His reference to "money" was seen as his euphemism for Quebec's Jewish community. A year earlier, Parizeau had boasted that he'd win the provincial election "with exclusively Quebeckers of the old stock." Another stalwart of the separatist movement, Lucien Bouchard, lamented that white Quebec women "weren't making enough babies." The ethnocentricity of the separatists had been laid bare.

Multiculturalism was meant to get Canada away from just such regional, linguistic, or racial tribalism. But Quebec didn't feel bound to a Constitution it hadn't signed. The province also rejected the Multiculturalism Act. Instead, Quebec floated its own policy of *interculturalisme*, which expected immigrants to bow to Quebec's communal values and develop a feeling of belonging — nebulous ideas with no measuring yardstick. In effect, the law expected immigrants to know their places as second-class citizens: Be grateful, be subservient, be like us, consider our enemies as your enemies, vote the way we do. But most immigrants don't relate to separatism. Their instincts, acquired abroad, tell them that nationalism, ethnic or otherwise, is bad news. "Demographics would kill the separatist cause," I wrote. It has — combined with other typically Canadian solutions. We pay elected Quebec separatists to sit in our national Parliament, berate Canada, and after six years of such (dis)service, qualify themselves for good Canadian pensions. The bribery works.

A Richard Burton Diversion

Bay Street financier Sir Christopher Ondaatje came calling. He was obsessed with the Victorian British explorer Sir Richard Burton, a chameleon rascal of many talents who explored the source of the Nile River, measured men's penises in Africa, performed the holy pilgrimage to Mecca and Medina in the guise of a Muslim, and visited my hometown of Hyderabad to see if he could make a quick buck out of the famous Golkonda diamond mines, the

13 The Editorial Perch

same pit that produced the legendary Koh-i-noor diamond. Burton, a prolific writer, translated the *Arabian Nights* as well as the *Kama Sutra*, the Indian sex manual, and penned 40 or so books, including a "report" on the brothels of boys and eunuchs in Karachi, the port city of Sindh in the northwestern corner of colonial India.

Ondaatje had already retraced Burton's steps to Lake Victoria and produced a tabletop book. Now he wanted to retrace Burton's years in India (1842–49). Burton had served the East India Company, acted as an adviser to the maharajah of Baroda, and worked as a spy in Sindh. Chris, a Burgher from Sri Lanka, didn't know India and even less Pakistan. He wanted me to go with him.

"Getting Haroon was like stalking a leopard," Chris wrote in *Sindh Revisited*, his travelogue of that memorable six-week journey to Bombay, Baroda, Surat, Karachi, and the interior of Sindh along the great Indus River Basin. Chris took stunning photographs that only a locale like India and Pakistan can offer: a riot of colour, both in landscapes and people such as rajahs, nawabs, mendicants, hookers; village fairs, temples, mosques; Sufi shrines and the ancient ruins of Mohenjo-daro.

I have vivid memories of that great journey. I'll share three here.

Before going, I'd written to Maharajah Fateh Singh Rao Gaekwad, a descendant of the maharajah of Baroda, for whom Burton had worked. Fateh Singh was president of the Board of Control for Cricket in Bombay when I worked there as a junior reporter in the 1960s. The reply was prompt — yes, of course, we'd be welcome to see him and the family palace.

In Baroda, we were ushered into the grand Laxmi Vilas Palace. I was stunned to see how the rotund rajah had thinned out, and, in fact, no longer looked anything like what I remembered of him. Noticing my puzzlement, the host said, "I am his younger brother. He died seven years ago." Maharajah Ranjit Singh Gaekwad, now the titular head of Baroda, had the grace not to inform me about the change of guard, lest it signalled any reluctance on his part to welcome us. His brother's friend was his.

In Sindh, we flew from Karachi into the interior as a guest of Hamid Haroon, owner of *Dawn*, Pakistan's largest English daily. We went to the small town of Bhit, the locale of the shrine of Shah Abdul Latif Bhitai, the greatest Sufi poet of the Sindhi language, whose collection *Risalo* has been compared to the *Masnavi*, Rumi's classic. Every Tuesday evening at his shrine, there's a recital of his poems. But Haroon had arranged a special post-lunch session on the lawns of the Bhit dak bungalow. A cavalcade of singers performed for us. The last was the best — Sohrab Fakir, the greatest living singer of Sindhi Sufi poetry, about whom I knew nothing.

At work in India, following in the footsteps of Sir Richard Burton, 1996.

13 The Editorial Perch

Quite a character he was — wiry thin, turbaned, beard and moustache glowing with red henna, fingers glinting with silver rings, wrists adorned with bead bracelets. He sang to the tune of his harmonium. His accompanying musicians sang and played either the *ektara*, a single-string instrument, or clapped in unison, as in a *qawwali*, the group singing that the great Pakistani singer Nusrat Fateh Ali Khan popularized in the West. Midway, Sohrab Fakir got up and danced, grabbing the ends of the long scarf hanging from his neck — the *ajrak*, the block-printed red-and-black cotton cloth that's a trademark of Sindh. He cast a spell that was to outlast that trip.

The third memory is of Chris insisting on checking out Burton's favourite haunt, the red-light district of Karachi. A line of "sex shops" offered aphrodisiacs and "cures" with signs in English and Urdu: CURE FOR UNMANLINESS, CURE FOR IMPOTENCY, CURE GUARANTEED TO HAVE CHILDREN, MANLY WEAKNESS FIXED, YOUTH RETURNED, SEX PROBLEM — HELP AVAILABLE, ENJOY LIFE TO THE FULL.

Chris went into one shop where the specialist inquired about his sex life and talked him into having his penis tested in a dirty glass tube connected to a little air pump. "Master problem," the quack concluded. But he could fix it, of course, with a 14-day treatment of ointment, pills, and potions — only 5,500 rupees (about $50 then). I suggested Chris should think about it overnight. We escaped paying only the consulting fee of 50 rupees ($1). The episode provided Chris three of the most readable pages in *Sindh Revisited*.[1] In retrospect, the quack deserved far more.

During the trip, Ondaatje weighed a request from the Royal Ontario Museum and the South Asian community to set up a South Asian gallery. He asked what I thought of it. I said that as a journalist I refrained from asking anyone for money for anything. But it was a good idea as long it was truly South Asian — Indian, Pakistani, Sri Lankan, Bangladeshi, and Nepali. That would ensure that Canada would bring the quarrelling communities of South Asia together. Ondaatje ended up matching the $1 million raised by the community, and the gallery did open in 2000.

Afghanistanism

Foreign issues kept demanding attention: Saddam Hussein's 1990 invasion of Kuwait, the retaliatory 1991 First Gulf War, the collapse of the Soviet Union, the breakup of Yugoslavia that led to the worst genocide in Europe since the Second World War, the end of apartheid in South Africa, and the two Chechen wars (1994–96 and 1999).

Each had varying degrees of echoes in the new Canada of internationally attuned Canadians. They expected more informed coverage and commentary on geopolitical developments rather than the black-and-white portrayal of good guys versus bad. Most new immigrants tended to be savvier about world events and expected the media to be less ignorant. That meant the end of the old journalistic formula of taking greater liberties with the truth the farther away from home. Gone, too, was what we used to call Afghanistanism — when out of ideas for an editorial, the easiest way out was to write something about a faraway land, knowing we could get away with any clichéd content. But now if we got a fact or the context wrong, there would always be a reader or two who'd write or phone to pour disdain into our ears.

One near-constant was the Jewish community's unhappiness with the *Star*'s coverage and commentary on Israel — anything less than full-throated support drew complaints. However, in 1988, one *Star* editorial did cross the line into the canard of dual loyalty. When Foreign Minister Joe Clark was booed off the stage in Ottawa for recognizing the Palestine Liberation Organization, and the mostly Jewish audience broke into the Israeli national anthem, an editorial reminded "the Jewish community in Canada that they are citizens of Canada, not Israel." That was before my time as editor. Relations were still frosty when I took over. Without compromising the paper's balanced approach to the Israeli-Palestinian conflict, I reached out to the community, addressing conferences and meetings of the Canadian Jewish Congress, B'nai Brith Canada, the York University Centre for Jewish Studies, International Association of Jewish Lawyers and Jurists, etc., for which Irving Abella, Frank Dimant, and other community leaders were generous enough to acknowledge in letters to myself and Honderich. That, however, didn't mean that there were no more differences of opinion — there were plenty.

In the case of Saddam's brazen invasion of neighbouring Kuwait, which was quickly overturned by a U.S.-led coalition that included Canada, both Western governments and the media seemed at sea concerning why so many ordinary Arabs were cheering him on. Drawing the wrong conclusion, Mulroney and Foreign Affairs Minister Clark floated a naive proposal for redistributing wealth between rich and poor Arabs. Ottawa wasn't going to contribute one cent to this Mideast version of our equalization payments. Instead, such transfer payments would come from oil-rich, thinly populated Saudi Arabia, Kuwait, the United Arab Emirates, and Qatar. While the poorer Arabs did resent rich Arab shaykhs, that wasn't what was driving them and Muslims elsewhere into supporting Saddam. They were, and still are, angry at the West's double standards — defending and courting oil-rich Arabs but not poor Palestinians. And they were upset that Iraq's industrial, medical, and social infrastructure was being bombed out. The U.S.-led coalition had flown about 50,000 sorties, some escorted by Canadian CF-18s, and dropped 95,000 tonnes of explosives. That's more TNT than five Hiroshimas. The war left 100,000 Iraqi soldiers and civilians dead, 72,000 homeless.

Azerbaijan to Ukraine

When the Soviet Union collapsed, the *Star* led the way in backing the independence of Ukraine, Armenia, Azerbaijan, the Baltic states (Estonia, Latvia, Lithuania), and others. But while 15 Soviet republics were allowed to become independent, Chechnya wasn't. Many of the other states were smaller and with lesser claims to national identity and history than Chechnya. The Chechen crime? Being independent-minded Muslims with a defined culture and geography who had long resisted Russian imperialism, both under the tsars and Stalin. For their courage, they were attacked by Moscow but lionized by Leo Tolstoy, Karl Marx, and Alexander Solzhenitsyn, who wrote in *The Gulag Archipelago*, "there was one nation that would not give in…. These were the Chechens."

In 1944, Stalin had deported all 387,229 Chechens to barren central Asia where about 100,000 died of starvation and sickness. It wasn't until the late 1950s that the survivors were allowed to return. After the collapse of communism in 1991, the Chechens voted for independence. But the 1.2

million Chechens were attacked instead. The war lasted three years, killed about 80,000, and reduced the capital Grozny to rubble. The United States let the Chechens become collateral damage in its policy of having Boris Yeltsin deactivate much of the Soviet nuclear stockpile.

Olivia Ward, the *Toronto Star*'s Moscow correspondent, covered that war and won a National Newspaper Award for her reporting. I was there the night in Toronto when she dedicated the award to "the forgotten people of a society that's truly devastated." Characterizing her own work as "a failure," she said: "In Chechnya, people come up and say, 'Tell the truth.' They hope the world would step in and help."

The world didn't.

* * *

As Yugoslavia began to break up in the 1990s, the *Star* was the first to respect the wishes of the people of Slovenia, Croatia, Montenegro, Bosnia and Herzegovina, Kosovo, and Macedonia to break off from Serbia, the successor state of Yugoslavia. When Serbia drew the line against Muslim Bosnia rather than let it secede, the European Community, NATO, and the United Nations prevaricated. The *Star* was the leading voice for effective international intervention: "Stop the killing"; "End this racist barbarism"; "Mere appeals for restraint are wasted words"; "George Bush, John Major, François Mitterrand, and Boris Yeltsin sound very much like Neville Chamberlain"; and "Bring war criminals to trial, collect evidence against Slobodan Milošević and his henchmen in Bosnia."

Mulroney felt the same way, and not necessarily because his wife, Mila, was born in Sarajevo — in fact, despite it. She hailed from Serbia, a point raised at the *Star* editorial board by a group of Croats who had come to lobby us. They kept referring to Mulroney as "the Serb's husband."

"I found that chilling," recalled a colleague who was at that meeting.

Diversifying Content

The *Toronto Star* diversified both content and authors, broadening the stable of columnists by incorporating women and visible minorities, including

13 The Editorial Perch

North America's first bearded, turbaned Sikh columnist, as well as the first vegetarian columnist, long before veganism was in vogue. We expanded the topics to include issues of immigration, integration, equality, and geopolitical news developments of interest to diaspora communities in Canada. Additionally, we doubled letters to the editor to allow newer voices, especially about overseas issues. The *Star* became the biggest forum in North America for international issues. During the 1991 Gulf War, we devoted extra pages to accommodate a representative sample of the 300 to 350 letters per day we were getting, representing the Canadian echoes of the full panoply of views heard at the United Nations. Even when there was no international crisis, we received an average of 125 letters per day, second only to 300 per day for the *New York Times*. But we were publishing, on average, 16 per day versus 15 for the *Los Angeles Times*, 13 for the *New York Times*, and 11 for the *Globe and Mail*.

While we were attracting new readers, or at least engaging existing ones, not everyone was happy. One letter to the editor, published in 1993, from Eileen Hunter of Hamilton, echoed the increasing resentment: "Am I living in Canada and buying a Canadian newspaper? Out of 26 letters to the editor published in a two-day period, 24 were about fighting between Bosnians, Serbians, Israelis, Palestinians, Greeks, Macedonians, Sri Lankans, and so on."

That was the reality of the new Canada.

Another was the pushback from — what's the right term? — the "old Canada." It manifested itself in ferocious opposition to employment equity. Just as the introduction of official bilingualism in 1969 had let loose a fear of job losses among English Canadians and brought out anti-French bigotry, employment equity unleashed animosity toward visible minorities. Ottawa had already decreed in 1986 that the federal service as well as federally regulated sectors — banking, transportation, broadcasting, and the post office — should hire Indigenous people, women, visible minorities, and the disabled commensurate with available skills in those groups. The Ontario New Democratic Party government of Bob Rae followed with an employment equity act of its own in 1993, covering both the public and private sector — with strong support from the *Star*. But the policy ran into opposition, with the most visceral reaction against minorities, as expressed in this gem in a *Globe and Mail* editorial: "Unemployed Ontarians would be well advised to ferret out the ancestor who claimed native roots or a history on an African slave ship."

The Ontario Conservatives under Mike Harris were getting ready for the 1995 provincial election. In focus groups, they found that "nothing

An Aislin cartoon, with me in mind, when he was part of the editorial board at the *Toronto Star*.

moved the needle as much as the topic of reverse discrimination against white males," I was told by a person who was part of those preparations. Tom Long, Conservative Party president, conceded: "This issue turns normally mild-mannered voters into table-thumping partisans."

The Tories fully exploited the issue. The party propaganda entailed such sweeping distortions as that the equity act is "a quota law," that it breeds "mediocrity," "ignores merit," and "compromises excellence."

Yet there had always been quotas in Canada.

Atlantic Canada gets more seats in the House of Commons than its population warrants, especially Prince Edward Island, which gets four seats for a population that can be fitted into one of several Toronto federal ridings. That was its condition for joining Confederation. Atlantic Canada is over-represented because of a 1915 formula guaranteeing that no province would have fewer seats than it had senators. It gets 32 seats compared to Alberta's 34, with only half its population. Quebec has had a quarter of the seats in the House of Commons, regardless of the size of its population. An unequal franchise all round.

By tradition, the federal Cabinet has a minister from every province, regardless of the population or the small number of the governing party's MPs from that province. This works against MPs from urban centres, especially Toronto and Vancouver, where some highly talented MPs never make it to the Cabinet, victims of reverse discrimination, if you will.

Canadians have long accepted such anomalies, yet many got into a tizzy when it was decreed that qualified women and visible minorities be not discriminated against because of their gender and skin colour.

All those neatly argued points made no difference. Harris and the Conservatives won handily. The new government proceeded quickly to kill the employment equity act and rubbed it in by calling its legislation "An Act to Repeal Job Quotas and to Restore Merit-Based Employment Practices."

* * *

What Harris and the *Star* did agree on was the paper's campaign for amalgamating Toronto and its five surrounding boroughs into one megacity. The issue proved highly divisive. Most residents, especially of Toronto, identified strongly with their municipalities. One day, Yasmeen and I were out walking in our neighbourhood in High Park when a man coming from the opposite direction recognized me, instantly raised his hand to point his index finger straight at my face, shouted, *"Et tu, Brute,"* and kept going.

Startled, I tried to figure out what that was all about when Yasmeen smiled and said, "Amalgamation!"

Bosnia, Kosovo, Macedonia

President Bill Clinton finally stirred into action in 1995, and NATO bombed Serbia and forced Milošević and his henchmen to the negotiating table in Dayton, Ohio. The *Star* welcomed the development, but we were dubious because the deal brokered by American envoy Richard Holbrooke was a bad compromise, entrenching three separate entities — the Bosnians, Croats, and Serb minority — in a way that wouldn't allow a democratic state to emerge. Unfortunately, that proved prescient.

Serbia also drew the line against the Muslim Kosovars, who, too, had voted in a referendum to secede. Again, the *Star* led the way in calling on the new Liberal government of Jean Chrétien to mobilize international action.

Toronto's Kosovar/Albanian community of about 5,000 pleaded with Ottawa to try for "an immediate, internationally enforced end to the conflict." They wrote to Foreign Minister Lloyd Axworthy: "We are certain you share our fear that the torture and the massacres are but the beginning of another ethnic cleansing in the Balkans." But he didn't seem to care, much to my disappointment. I had known him from Winnipeg where he had a reputation as a humanitarian — and would prove so in later years with his initiatives on the United Nations–approved principle of humanitarian intervention, R2P, Responsibility to Protect. But on Kosovo, he was insensitive.

The *Star* had an unlikely ally on Kosovo: the Nobel laureate John Polanyi, professor of chemistry at the University of Toronto. A long-time peace advocate, he had been to Bosnia and Croatia twice to work with fellow scientists and academics there to heal the wounds of ethnic cleansing. He warned about the coming conflagration in Kosovo, though he didn't support its secession. When Ottawa hosted a Balkans round table, he warned: "We can't just deplore these crimes against humanity but stop them." Canada and its allies were in danger, once again, of becoming appeasers of the man responsible for some of the worst massacres since the Holocaust.

In my own periodic bylined columns, I called for the independence of Kosovo, something it didn't achieve until 2008 after NATO's military intervention in 1999.[2] Macedonia faced a crisis of a different sort after declaring itself independent in 1991. Greece was laying sole claim to the name Macedonia and was doing so with Europe's indulgence. The *Star* was blunt: "It's irrational of Athens to lay sole claim to that name, history, and culture. Greece cannot appropriate the name.... Ottawa has to shake itself loose from Greek pressure and the Greek-Canadian lobby and recognize Macedonia. Better still, the 300,000-strong Greek-Canadian community should start disassociating itself from this Athenian absurdity." The Greek-Canadian community had choice words for us.

* * *

Unbeknownst to us at the time, a young Canadian lawyer, Payam Akhavan, who had come to Canada as a child from Iran, was working for the United Nations and initiating the proposal for the International Criminal Tribunal for the former Yugoslavia, leading to the first-ever war crimes prosecutions since the Nuremberg Tribunal. In 1993–94, he investigated ethnic cleansing in Croatia as well as in Bosnia and Herzegovina for the United Nations. He helped the Office of the Prosecutor prosecute Slobodan Milošević, Radovan Karadžić, and Ratko Mladić, the "Butcher of Bosnia." Payam was a Canadian Bahá'í whose family had fled a Muslim country because of religious persecution there and was now bringing to justice persecutors of Muslims in a third land — a personification of the miracle of Canada.

The myriad of foreign issues showed how both sides of every conflict in the world were present in Canada — Russians versus Ukrainians and others from the former Soviet Union; Serbs versus Croats, Bosnians, Kosovars, and Macedonians; Armenians versus Turks; Sikhs versus Hindus; Tamils versus Sinhalese; Indians versus Pakistanis; Arabs versus Jews; Coptic Christians versus Muslims; and all the factions of highly divided societies such as the

Iranians divided between pro-shah and pro-ayatollahs, Marxists and believers, majority Shias and minority Kurds, Azeris and Bahá'ís. It was a tribute to Canada and the *Toronto Star* that I was welcome in all groups, including those that did not talk to each other.

They all call Canada home, and for the most part, keep their differences peaceful.

Twists of Fate

The dreaded phone call came.

Syeda's cancer had resurfaced more than five years after her treatment in Toronto. She was sinking. I emerged at the Karachi airport to the news that she'd already passed away. She was all of 50. A noble soul. Like Amma, she never spoke ill of anyone, never complained. I never heard her raise her voice.

A few hours later, Maryam arrived from Montreal and Yousuf from Toronto. But Suleman, from neighbouring India, couldn't, a victim yet again of the cruelties of the hard border.

We took turns reciting the Qur'an by Syeda's body throughout the night, sobbing, crying. In the morning, she was given the ritual bath by Maryam and other women of the family — the progeny of the exiles from post-1947 India who had settled in Karachi. Syeda had re-established family connections with those lost cousins and their children. They adored her — "Syeda *apa*" (sister), "Syeda *khala*" (maternal aunt), "Syeda *phoopi*" (paternal aunt).

The males took turns carrying her bier to the mosque for the last prayer for the dead and on to the cemetery on the hill overlooking her neighbourhood.

Can there be anything crueller than a younger sibling predeceasing you? God sure tests you in a million ways.

14

Multicultiphobia

THE CANADIAN CHARTER OF RIGHTS AND FREEDOMS CONSTITUTED A "REVO-lution on the scale of the metric system, the great medical discoveries of Louis Pasteur, and the invention of penicillin and the laser." That was Chief Justice Antonio Lamer speaking in 1992 on the 10th anniversary of the charter. Yet there was increasing resistance, even among liberals, to what the charter was ushering in — an era of multicultural rights.

For example, Keith Spicer, a former commissioner of official languages, ostensibly a liberal, was propagating decidedly illiberal views in the nation's capital as editor of the *Ottawa Citizen*. Using that pulpit, he fulminated against "the multiculturalism zoo" that was undermining the "shared solidarity" of the nation; "tribalizing Canadian society;" and encouraging "Balkanization, ghetto mentalities, fiscal Bantustans." Of the Multiculturalism Act, he wrote: "We're about to legislate ethnicity as a feature of Canadian life. With similar incitement from the 1982 Constitution, we are going to pay in perpetuity to ensure that Canadians will never feel they are a single, distinctive people."

Despite such intemperate views, Prime Minister Mulroney in 1990 named Spicer head of the Citizens' Forum on Canada's Future. The commission was meant to pave the way for the prime minister's high-stakes quest to get Quebec to sign on to the Constitution, which it had boycotted. What the commission found in cross-country hearings was "fury in the land" against Mulroney himself, against bilingualism, against concessions to Quebec, and against multiculturalism, in that order. Yet Spicer spun it cleverly, highlighting the last. I condemned him for being "intellectually dishonest — beating up on the most vulnerable segment of the population, in order to protect the prime minister, Quebec, and bilingualism."

Even the Economic Council of Canada, which could usually be counted on to present sound studies and sensible ideas, issued a highly inflammatory report, *New Faces in the Crowd*. It suggested that newcomers relinquish such traditional practices as "treatment of women as intrinsically inferior," as though some Canadian-born also didn't think that way. The council was obviously oblivious to our national disease of wife battering and violence against women by full-blooded Canadians. As for its hare-brained idea of a "moral contract" between newcomers and the host society, it was showing an amnesia about the generations of immigrants who had brought seemingly strange customs, faiths, and habits, yet weren't asked to sign any "moral contracts." Why the sudden demand on new immigrants? Because many were non-white? Of course.

Quebec, too, flirted with just such a "social contract." But we already have a social contract — the rule of law, which codifies the limits of what people can or cannot do. The law is our holy parchment, the covenant by which we, both the foreign-born and the native-born, live. This is not a negative assertion. Rather, it is an affirmation of one of our core beliefs: The strong shall not dictate to the weak over what is, or is not, acceptable. That power rests only with the people's parliaments.

On the Prairies, the Reform Party under Preston Manning was making headway advocating the repeal of the Multiculturalism Act. He was openly calling for a return to immigration from Europe, so as not to "radically or suddenly alter the ethnic makeup of Canada." Translation: slow down the Brown Express. Manning's followers bemoaned hyphenated Canadianism as though they themselves weren't hyphenated. They demanded that immigrants be fully "integrated into the mainstream of Canadian life" without ever defining what that would entail.

In the 1993 election — that the Liberals under Jean Chrétien won — Reform made a breakthrough with 52 seats in Parliament. Much of the liberal establishment was apoplectic. But I welcomed the Reformers. It was better to have their views tested in Parliament than left festering in the Royal Canadian Legion halls of the Prairies or on the streets.

Many in the media and academia were also turning against multiculturalism. Some were quite brazen about their antipathy to non-whites, such as Doug Fisher, a former Member of Parliament for the left-of-centre New Democratic Party who had become a columnist for the *Toronto Sun*, the unabashedly right-wing tabloid. This was Fisher's response to Ottawa's 1994 decision to cut back on family-class immigrants: "Will the majority of entrants continue to be ... from Asia?" He dreaded that "the bulk of our immigrants will be from Asia and increasingly of Chinese stock."[1]

Uncharacteristically, the *Star* added to the hysteria. At that time, we had an annual Atkinson Fellowship in Public Policy to further liberal journalism in Canada. In 1992, the year-long study explored immigration. A five-part series by Daniel Stoffman ensued on the pluses and minuses of the immigration and refugee system, with a view to "striking a balance." It was anything but balanced, in my opinion.

"Why Canada Must Reassess Its Wide-Open Immigration" verged on the sensational. It over-relied on critics and contained assertions that have proven to be false. A "swelling tide of humanity" was pounding at the gates of the West. Canada was already taking too many — there were no economic or demographic reasons to justify admitting 1.2 million immigrants every five years. "What's in it for us? Why do we want to cram so many new people, half of whom cannot speak either official language, in our largest cities every year?" "There is no evidence" that immigration is essential to the economy. Nor did we need immigrants to fill jobs — "Because we have so many women of child-bearing age, our population would be growing even without any immigration."[2]

The more dangerous were those who couched their anxieties in more sophisticated arguments, such as Richard Gwyn, the *Star*'s own star columnist. When he returned home in 1992 after a seven-year overseas stint in London, he and his wife were spooked by the demographic changes. He wrote: "A good deal of Canada that we had left behind in 1985 had evaporated."[3]

In his *Star* columns, he wrote:

> One of the most troubling aspects of contemporary Canada is that our multiculturalism may be turning into multinationalism. It becomes easier for individuals to live in this country while remaining outsiders, emotionally and psychically.... Return trips "home" to find a bride or groom are increasingly common.... More and more Canadians care more passionately about events in their "home" country than in their "adopted" one.... Outside of Quebec, our central notion, or national glue, has always been the culture of Anglo Canadians. But Anglo Canadians are progressively losing their self-confidence and their self-esteem.... We risk becoming a fragmented multinational mosaic.[4]

As his editor, I defended his right to his opinions while disagreeing wholeheartedly. He went on to write a book, *Nationalism Without Walls*, a long lament on the decline of English Canada *and* "English-Canadian values and myths" under multiculturalism that "permits, almost encourages infinite diversity."[5] He also floated a strange conspiracy theory: "It cannot be a coincidence that the higher the various cultural walls have gone up inside Canada, the stronger the popular resistance to paying taxes has become."[6]

A more poisonous book was Neil Bissoondath's *Selling Illusions*. Multiculturalism was encouraging multiple solitudes. People were "sticking with their own," as in what he witnessed at York University: "Chinese students congregated behind a wall of Cantonese."[7] Ethnics were being encouraged to keep their identities and connections to their homelands. "*There* is more important than *Here*." It was the same charge of dual loyalty that had long been hurled at the Jewish diaspora, that their attachment to Israel made them less loyal to the nations where they lived.

Bissoondath was following in the footsteps of uncle V.S. Naipaul, who made his name mostly by deriding his own people in the Caribbean and in India. As great a writer as Naipaul was, and as serviceable as Bissoondath's prose is, both served the same purpose: brown men giving whites the licence to let it rip against minorities. No surprise, then, that many a liberal pundit, including Richard Gwyn, quoted Bissoondath extensively.

In 1998, historian J.L. Granatstein published *Who Killed Canadian History?*[8] Advocates of multiculturalism, that's who, he said. This was absurd. The subject had been dead long before diversity became official.

As entitled as such critics of multiculturalism were to their opinions, others had a right to critique them. Did these highly educated men, especially the historian, not know Canadian history? Or were they being wilfully blind? Canadians had always been a people of multiple identities and competing loyalties. University of Toronto historian Desmond Morton wrote: "Canadian citizenship has always had to co-exist with old homelands, newer provinces, or nations within, and protected by the federal state, especially *la nation canadienne française*."[9] John Porter in his highly valued book *Vertical Mosaic* noted that "in Canada, ethnic segregation and intense ethnic loyalties had their origins in French, Scottish, and Irish separateness from the English."[10]

Modern immigrants can no more be expected to develop amnesia the moment they land here than previous generations. All we can insist on, and do, is that newcomers keep their ancient hatreds peaceful, which they largely do. Those who don't run afoul of the law and face appropriate consequences.

Also, it's absurd to mischaracterize multiculturalism as multinationalism. As our two leading political and constitutional experts, Will Kymlicka of Queen's University and Alan Cairns at the University of British Columbia, have noted, multiculturalism didn't create new nationalities with ethnic-specific linguistic, educational, or self-governing rights. Nor are modern immigrants secessionists; in fact, in Quebec, immigrants proved decisive in thwarting separatism. Immigrants weren't regionalists, either, like many Albertans. Immigrants were very much for national unity; they identified with Pierre Trudeau precisely because of his pan-Canadian vision, not as some shoddy commentaries had it because he "let them" into Canada.

Newer immigrants weren't creating any more "ethnic ghettoes" than earlier waves of immigrants — in fact, far fewer. Besides, was Toronto's predominantly Anglo-Saxon Rosedale neighbourhood an ethnic ghetto? Were

Montreal's Westmount and the Town of Mount Royal English and Jewish ghettoes? Canadians have mobility rights and may live where they wish.

Religion and Gender Equity

Multiculturalism also wasn't responsible for controversial religious or cultural mores. The Hasidic, Hutterite, and Mennonite communities, for example, have long been part of Canada. Discrimination against women is part of several religions. Catholic women must remain in the pews and not be elevated to the pulpit. Jewish women are skipped over by the rabbi as he counts to the 10 men required to begin the communal service. Among the newer faiths to Canada, Hindu women aren't allowed on the same elevated rung as male Brahmin priests. Muslim women are relegated to the back of the congregation in the mosque or in dingy basements or hot mezzanine enclaves. All are told they have the option of quitting such faiths or finding more liberal congregations within their religions, if any. Such are the uneasy democratic compromises when fundamental rights clash, such as the right to religious freedom and the right to gender equality. The courts have refused to be drawn into creating a hierarchy of rights between competing constitutional values. Such tensions have nothing to do with multiculturalism.

The plethora of false charges levelled at multiculturalism were refuted by academics and others. The best such forensic examination was by Phil Ryan of Carleton University in his book *Multicultiphobia*.[11] But such effective critiques took years to appear, in Ryan's case even longer, because he initially thought that Bissoondath's hypothesis was so patently false that no one would pay much heed. When I reached out to him in 2021, he recalled that in the 1990s he was assigning parts of the Bissoondath book in his courses to show students the absurdity of some of the book's propositions. "I assumed that the points I was making were so obvious that the book would sink below the waves," and that his own notes were "nothing publishable. How naive of me."

The need of the hour clearly was to debunk, in a timely fashion and at every turn, the narrative that Canadian greatness and glory were in danger because of an influx of brown and black people. Public opinion was where the battle was going to be won or lost. While the courts were beginning to enforce equality, getting broad social acceptance was the key.

14 Multicultiphobia

That's where the *Star* provided the leadership in news columns, editorials, and bylined columns. Several people helped me: Charles Taylor of McGill University, Canada's foremost philosopher; Max Yalden, a suave federal bureaucrat who was one of the architects of multiculturalism under Pierre Trudeau; two academic activists in Toronto, Frances Henry and Carol Tator, both white, who emerged as among the most trenchant critics of Canadian racism; Ratna Omidvar of the Maytree Foundation, a pro-immigration think tank in Toronto, herself an immigrant from India via Iran who came up with the memorable line that "Canadians want immigration without immigrants"; and Naomi Alboim, an Ontario deputy minister and later professor at Queen's University in Kingston and Toronto Metropolitan University. She could critique any component of the complex and intertwined immigration-multicultural policies so crisply that even a journalist could understand.

My relationship with Taylor, though, got off to a disastrous start. Having interviewed him on the phone, I was keen on an in-person meeting. We met at Il Posto Nuovo, the high-end eatery in posh Yorkville. The food was excellent, the conversation exhilarating, his range and erudition breathtaking. On the way back to the office going over my scribbled notes, it was obvious that paraphrasing wouldn't do justice to his eloquence. I'd merely introduce an idea and let the transcript do the talking. Closing the office door to my office, I cleared the desk, laid out the notes, and turned on the tape recorder. Nothing. Panicky fiddling with the machine still produced nothing. I literally cried.

Yalden was a former diplomat who had served in Moscow, Paris, and Brussels. He was official languages commissioner (1977–84) before heading the federal Human Rights Commission (1987–96), good listening posts for all the bigotry spouted against the French minority and other minorities. He could write, too. When the Reform Party started attacking multiculturalism, he dismissed it initially without naming the party, of course, as "garden variety chauvinism." But as the party gathered force, he was forthright about "the persistent undertow of opposition to allegedly uncontrolled immigration from countries with 'different traditions,' a code phrase, one suspects, for different racial make-up." And on why some people had gone sour on multiculturalism, he minced no words: "The difference, let's be honest with ourselves, relates largely to race and non-Judeo-Christian religions."

The Colour Line

What was bothering some Canadians was that the Great White North wasn't so white anymore. That needed to be brought out in the open and confronted.

As the historian Irving Abella said, Canada was a nation of immigrants that hated immigrants. The last one in wanted the door shut right behind him or her. Older immigrants dismissed the latest arrivals as unfit for entry. They scapegoated immigrants for unemployment, welfare rolls, and crime, when facts proved otherwise. They simply knew they'd suffered when they came, so new immigrants should, too. They'd "adjusted," so should new immigrants. They were once at the bottom of the totem pole and had crawled up, so newcomers should, as well. Those demanding equality from day one threatened that long-standing pecking order.

But Canada was bringing in immigrants not as a favour to the newcomers but to fulfill our own needs. Canada's fertility rate was too low for the population to replace itself. Canadians were aging. We needed immigrants of working age to add to our gross domestic product and pay for our pensions and medicare. The only immigrants available were from the Third World, not Europe, which itself was aging. And unlike the immigrants of the past, the new arrivals were better educated than the native-born, possessed above-average skills, and many had money. In the 1990s, immigrants from Hong Kong invested an average of $1.5 billion per year in Vancouver, shielding British Columbia from the recession. Such immigrants weren't likely to be the obedient kind but rather confident and assertive of their rights. The days of minorities of wavering self-esteem apologizing for their identities were coming to an end. Only refugees would have a sense of gratitude but they, too, had rights under both Canada's obligations to international norms and our own laws.

Enlightened self-interest demanded that we celebrate immigrants, not decry them.

As obvious as all this seems today, it wasn't in the 1990s and early 2000s. Or it was but wasn't accepted by sizable portions of the population. Such home truths had to be hammered home as forcefully and as often as possible.

Diversity in the Media

Newspapers, television, and radio didn't read, look, or sound like the people on a subway. New minorities were agitating against their underrepresentation and misrepresentation in both news and advertising. Being the only non-white in a senior management position, the only Indo-Canadian, and the only prominent Muslim in the media, I was often asked to speak at conferences that turned into gripe sessions.

As early as 1981, a gathering of Italian, Chinese, Japanese, Indian, Pakistani, and Black Canadians in Toronto called for eliminating racial and other stereotyping. Several of the attendees later emerged as stalwarts of the equity movement. Jean Augustine became the first African-Canadian woman elected to the House of Commons. Susan Eng was the first visible minority chair of the Metro Toronto Police Services Board, only to be stymied at every turn trying to put rules around gun use by police. And there was the above-mentioned dynamic duo of Frances Henry and Carol Tator from the Urban Alliance on Race Relations.

I soon found myself chairing the InterCultural Media Committee and being secretary of the Canadian Asian Artists' Association to help racialized writers and artists break into the mainstream Canadian artistic market. We achieved little.

In 1983, the House of Commons struck the Special Parliamentary Committee on Participation of Visible Minorities in Canadian Society. As a witness, I was thrilled to follow Victor Goldbloom, a pediatrician who had served as a Quebec Cabinet minister under Premier Robert Bourassa. Dr. Goldbloom appeared as president and chief executive officer of the Canadian Council of Christians and Jews; his son, Michael, later become my boss as publisher of the *Toronto Star* (2004–6) and a friend. The senior Goldbloom called on the media to improve "the portrayal and participation of members of visible minorities." I followed him with: "Let's be frank — the media, by and large, reflect a white man's world."

In its report *Equality Now*, the committee urged the media to create better awareness of the demographic changes and to include non-whites in television programming as well as in advertising. The advice fell on deaf ears. However, in 1989, the Canadian Daily Newspaper Association did carry out a census of newsrooms. It showed that minorities made up just 2 percent of the staff at 48 newspapers.

In 1989, when Cecil Foster left the *Globe and Mail*, he observed that "100 percent of the Black editorial staff went with me." The next year, the *Ottawa Citizen* explored the subject in a report titled "Why Are the Newsrooms of the Nation White Enclaves?"[12]

Hiring minorities was "like visiting sick friends in hospital. We all know we should do it, but we don't get around to it nearly as often as we should," said Kerry Lambie, executive vice-president for Thomson Newspapers, then Canada's biggest chain with 50 newspapers. Getting closer to the truth, the *Globe*'s managing editor, Tim Pritchard, said: "One does not hire just to hire visible minorities. We have other priorities that have to be met. We have to hire the best reporters and editors we can find."

I'd imagined my colleagues would be more enlightened.

Tony Westell, head of the Department of Journalism at Carleton University and a former national affairs columnist and Ottawa editor for the *Toronto Star*, invoked the reverse-discrimination argument: "Why should we? If we go out and persuade visible minorities to come and give them preference, then we are excluding people in the majority and we are penalizing them."

"That's total bullshit," retorted Sat Kumar, head of the University of Regina's School of Journalism. "What little has been achieved by women in the workforce, for example, would never have happened with that attitude."

White World of Ads

By 1990, some of us had persuaded the Canadian Advertising Foundation to form a Race Relations Advisory Council on Advertising, with representatives from the advertising industry, the media, and the public. Our initial discussions were led by Wilson Head, an African-American immigrant to Canada who was a respected human-rights activist. After one of the first sessions, I told him I thought he was too tough on the attendees who were, after all, people of goodwill who were hearing us out. He shot back: "In the struggle for equality, you can't call your adversaries half-racist. Either they or their organizations are racist, or they are not." With a man of his age and stature — 28 years my senior — I wasn't going to argue. I told him, respectfully, that as a newspaper man, I wasn't an activist. He would do his thing, and I mine.

In 1980, Wilson was hit on the head from behind as he was going up the steps to the office of the Urban Alliance on Race Relations. The police took 40 minutes to respond and never did find his assailant. The incident was behind him by the time I had the privilege to meet him. I never heard him mention it once.

What really helped change industry attitudes was the pioneering multi-racial advertising campaign, the United Colors of Benetton, by the Italian clothier with its big billboards showing a rainbow of models.

Recalcitrant News Media

The advertising sector was a minor culprit compared to the news media. There had been mounting complaints by minorities that they were missing on both payroll and content. There was the 1979 scandal of an ostensible exposé of foreign Chinese students taking up spots in Canadian university faculties such as medicine, dentistry, and pharmacy. "Campus Giveaway" was a racist segment in CTV's flagship program *W5*. The students were Canadians. But to CTV, anyone of Chinese origin had to be a foreigner. There was the incongruity of CBC-TV going live to South Africa in 1990 for the release of Nelson Mandela and the dawn of a new day for Blacks and having a white South African Canadian as the expert commentator in Toronto. Or having only non-Muslim experts pontificating about Islam and Muslim Canadians during the Salman Rushdie affair. Or featuring the reaction of only whites to federal and provincial budgets as though non-whites weren't impacted.

Buffeted by such criticism, the Canadian Daily Newspaper Association formed a diversity committee in 1993. I spoke at its first meeting: "It was two decades ago that the editorial division of the then CDNPA [Canadian

Daily Newspaper Publishers Association] held a seminar in Winnipeg on 'Women and the News,' a gathering at which there were hardly any women. Today, at this gathering on diversity, there are hardly any visible minorities. In Winnipeg, some of us had evoked the spirit of Nellie McClung, Agnes Macphail, June Callwood, Lotta Dempsey, and others. Today, there are hardly any parallel names to invoke."

Our committee was chaired by John Miller, head of the Department of Journalism at Ryerson University (now Toronto Metropolitan University) and a former colleague at the *Star*. When Miller polled publishers in 1994, he found that diversity ranked as 19th on a list of 21 issues facing newspapers: "There's denial. They just don't get it."

Focus groups of Chinese, South Asians, Muslims, and Blacks in Vancouver, Toronto, and Hamilton showed, not surprisingly, that more than half said visible minorities were treated like foreigners by daily newspapers.

My friend Hyder in the Rocky Mountains after he moved to Canada in 1974.

In 2004, Miller did a census of Canadian newspaper newsrooms. Of the 2,119 journalists working at 37 papers, only 3.4 percent weren't white at a time when non-whites were a fifth of the population. "The typical Canadian newspaper in 2004 was staffed by journalists who were almost as white as the paper they were printed on," he wrote.

"They Don't Speak English"

Far too many editors paid lip service to diversity. Some weren't convinced it was worth investing in "the ethnics" — "they don't speak English, anyway," "they don't read newspapers." These were stereotypes retained from the old days of peasant immigrants from non-English-speaking nations.

The simplest of suggestions got little traction, such as calendar journalism — today is Hannukah, or Diwali, or Eid, or Orthodox Christmas … I didn't mind tokenism to get things going. Even when individual editors and reporters were sincere in wanting to make changes, institutional barriers got in the way.

Journalists are on the frontiers of news, yet they're rarely on the cusp of social change. In fact, they're usually the last people to know the sociological pulse of Canada. Pretensions notwithstanding, the media are part of the establishment. They cover institutions, not people. They mostly talk to the rich, the well heeled, and the well entrenched. They don't talk to immigrants, don't understand immigrant issues or immigrants.

The outrageous and the weird are what journalists are drawn to, but immigrants don't do weird. They don't join too many public protests, let alone jump barricades or climb fences for the cameras. Usually, they're busy being hard-working, taxpaying citizens. They don't bare their souls in televised confessionals, either — when in grief, they go private.

What *Show Boat* Showed

That the media and the Toronto establishment were out of touch came to the fore with two cultural events. In 1989, the Royal Ontario Museum (ROM) mounted an exhibit called *Into the Heart of Africa*, featuring objects and imagery collected by colonial soldiers and missionaries, including a grotesque magazine cover of a British soldier plunging a sword into a Zulu warrior.

The museum, and the media, dug in their heels when the Black community protested. The community called it racist; the ROM invoked free speech, as powerful institutions and individuals do, especially when bashing and belittling institutions and people of colour. Nourbese Philip, one trenchant critic, said: "Freedom of expression in this society is underwritten not by the free flow of information but by the fact that there are those who are powerful enough in society to make their voices, their version of history, and their perspectives heard."[13]

In 1993 came an announcement of the revival of the 1928 American musical *Show Boat*. It was to be the opening act of a new $51 million Centre for Performing Arts built by the Toronto suburban municipality of North York. The *Star* was a sponsor, one of those anodyne promotion deals that marketing and circulation departments often strike. But this one came back to bite us when protests erupted: "Stop This Racist Play," "*Show Boat* Hurts," "Terrible Use of Taxpayers' Money." A quickly formed Coalition to Stop *Show Boat* declared that "the entire play, its plot and characterizations, demean black life and culture," said Angela Lee, manager of Black Artists in Action. "*Show Boat* was created by white people for white people," said Jeff Henry, a York University professor of drama and founder of Black theatres in Toronto and Montreal.

The United Way, which had arranged a benefit performance, had a revolt on its hands. Nearly its entire Black and Caribbean Fund-Raising Committee quit. The charity organization tried to finesse its way by saying the show wasn't racist but rather "about racism." That sophistry didn't fool the Black community. The United Way pulled out. The *Star*, however, didn't. A tame editorial followed, "Compromise on *Show Boat*": "With no compromise palatable to the objectors, the *Star* has decided to honour a promotional agreement with the show's producer, Garth Drabinsky." The editorial also parroted his defence: "The musical draws little controversy among American blacks."

"We Are Not Racists"

Frances Henry and Carol Tator kept up their condemnation of newspapers, especially "the criminalization of immigrants and the racialization of crimes." In their 1995 book *The Colour of Democracy: Racism in Canadian Society*, they wrote: "Canadian media industries marginalize people of colour, reduce them to invisible status and devalue their images in and contributions to Canadian society. Media reinforce the 'rightness of whiteness.'"[14]

The book was a broader indictment of Canadian racism, which was at the heart of the opposition to immigration and multiculturalism: "In a society that espouses equality, tolerance, social harmony and respect for individual rights, the existence of racial prejudice, discrimination and disadvantage is difficult to acknowledge and remedy."[15]

Tator and Henry cracked the code of Canadian denialism:

> *I am not a racist. She/he is not a racist. This is not a racist institution. Canada is not a racist society.*
>
> These mantras cast an illusory spell that has allowed Canadians to ignore the harsh reality of a society divided by colour and ethnicity. Canada suffers from historical amnesia. Its citizens and institutions function in a state of collective denial.
>
> Canadians appear deeply ambivalent about the public recognition of other cultures, the freedom of non-White racial and non-European cultural groups to maintain their unique identities, and the right of minorities to function in a society free of racism.[16]

Henry released a major media audit in 1999. She analyzed crime stories, 2,622 of them in the *Toronto Star*, *Globe and Mail*, and *Toronto Sun*. She saw "a racist discourse that unjustly stereotyped" Vietnamese and Blacks, especially Jamaicans, as criminals and as "problem people." How so? In three ways:

- By overreporting the two groups' alleged criminality and underreporting their contributions to society, except Blacks in sports and entertainment.
- By "racializing crime" — identifying Blacks twice as often as whites in crime stories. Whereas Blacks constituted only 7 percent of the population of Metropolitan Toronto, they were featured in 44 percent of the pictures of minorities

used, more than 50 percent by the *Sun*. By any measure, Blacks don't commit crimes at anywhere close to that rate.

- By "criminalizing immigration," depicting, wrongly, the foreign-born as more prone to crime.

The indictment would have been "far worse" had she included the *National Post*, which hadn't been launched when the research began.

The *Star* stopped identifying alleged culprits by race, which upset the *Toronto Sun* and provided grist for talk radio.

Diversity at the *Star*

Of the three battles waged through the 1990s — multiculturalism, nudging the advertising industry to better reflect the changing demography, and the news media's portrayal of minorities — we made the least progress on the last. But at least the *Star* was conscious of the need for change.

An internal content committee report in 1992 said: "The paper is increasingly, and dangerously, irrelevant to a growing number of our readers. We don't write about what concerns them because we often don't know what that is. We think of ourselves as the paper that speaks to the average citizen, yet we haven't come to grips with the fact that the average citizen has changed dramatically."

A newsroom diversity committee report in 1995 stated: "For years, we at the *Star* have talked about, sometimes in terms bordering on despair, the need to reflect the changing nature of the city.... Our coverage does not reflect this new reality, even though we've done a better job than any other paper in Canada."

While the day-to-day coverage of minorities remained poor, one-off specials were spectacular. For the *Star*'s centennial in 1992, we did something no other newspaper in North America or Europe had ever done — special sections, beautifully designed and well written, on Toronto's Chinese, South Asian, Jewish, Portuguese, Black, Filipino, Japanese, and Italian communities, telling stories that otherwise wouldn't have been told. The pioneering effort was the brainchild of Mike Pieri, my former foreign editor, who never did anything half-hearted. He set up separate committees in each of those communities and spent weeks hearing them, their stories, their challenges, and their hopes. It showed in the content.

In 1997, Pieri organized a special edition for the 50th anniversary of the independence of India and Pakistan, and another one a year later on the 50th anniversary of Israel. The *Star* was again the only paper in North America to mark those milestones in such an editorial product.

As an outreach to minorities, the *Star* brought the *Sing Tao Daily* newspaper to Canada in an agreement with the Hong Kong–based Sing Tao News Corporation.

My own idea of forging a partnership with a daily in India came to naught. After scouring several possible partnerships in India, I worked out an agreement with the largest media conglomerate, the Bennett Coleman Company, publisher of the *Times of India*, for a joint publication in Toronto. But the project was abandoned due to the 2008 economic collapse and the parallel precipitous drop in the North American newspaper revenue model. The *Star* did buy out two publications in Toronto started by immigrants from India — the fashion magazine *Suhaag* and *Canadian Immigrant* magazine.

Police Versus the *Star*

The *Toronto Star*'s most substantial contributions to advancing equality for Blacks came from the newsroom, starting in 1989 with a series, "Black and White," followed in 1994 by a special section, "Young, Black and Male." The big breakthrough came in 2002, almost by accident. Reporter Jim Rankin was intrigued by a police bulletin describing a suspect as yellow. He filed a freedom-of-information request for the police database of racial information on suspects. It took two years to negotiate access. Rankin and his colleagues got what they suspected all along: justice was different for Blacks and whites. Their groundbreaking story, "Race and Crime," nailed it:

> Blacks arrested by Toronto police are treated more harshly than whites, a *Toronto Star* analysis of crime data shows.
>
> Black people, charged with simple drug possession, are taken to police stations more often than whites facing the same charge.

> Once at the station, accused blacks are held overnight, for a bail hearing, at twice the rate of whites.
>
> A disproportionate number of black motorists are ticketed for violations that only surface following a traffic stop. This … suggests police use racial profiling in deciding whom to pull over.
>
> The evidence is contained in a massive police database recording more than 800,000 charges dating back to 1996.

Exposing police and other institutional racism became a *Star* staple. By 2014, the police board under progressive chair Alok Mukherjee restricted carding. But that was stalled by Bill Blair, the police chief then, and undermined by newly elected mayor John Tory, who talked a good game of inclusive politics but sided with the police. That prompted Royson James, the *Star*'s city columnist, to declare that "citizens no longer wanted to hear from Tory. He symbolizes the problem."

Blair did abandon carding in 2015, and the Ontario government of Premier Kathleen Wynne ushered in regulations forbidding random stopping and laid down rules to make non-criminal police interactions with the public more transparent. The use of the practice plummeted across the province and the country, though it hasn't been eliminated entirely for Black and certain racialized groups.

Here was the paradox: a newspaper with a history of progressive ideas and brave campaigns on behalf of minorities couldn't change its newsgathering methodology to portray minorities in a consistently fair manner. When the Canadian Association of Journalists, a volunteer organization, conducted a national census of newsrooms in 2021, the *Star* fudged the answer. It estimated that its newsroom had between one and four journalists who were Middle Eastern, Black, or Latin. And it didn't have a single Indigenous journalist on staff.[17]

Only in Canada, Eh?

One sign that Canada was changing came when the Reform Party dropped its proposal to control non-European immigration. Preston Manning appeared at a Chinese New Year rally in Toronto in 2000 and wished the audience happy new year in broken Cantonese. That was testimony to the power of demographics *and* the new consciousness of the nation. I was there that night and thought: *Only in Canada, eh?* Would the chancellor of Germany, let alone the leader of a right-wing party there, or a Geert Wilders in the Netherlands, appear before German and Dutch Turkish audiences to greet them in Turkish? Or the president of France, let alone the Islamophobic Marine Le Pen, bring Eid greetings to French Muslims in Arabic?

Canadians are now the only people in the Western world with a national consensus in favour of immigration and multiculturalism. They rate pluralism as the defining value of the nation, even ahead of such traditional unifying symbols as the national anthem, the national flag, hockey, or the beaver. Immigrants, especially visible minorities, who were stigmatized and denigrated as deviant from the Canadian norm and incompatible with Canadian values, are now among its most innovative, productive, and loyal citizens.

With *Toronto Star* publisher John Honderich; Nelson Mandela; his wife, Graça Machel; and *Star* foreign editor Jimmy Atkins, 1998.

This is all the more remarkable at a time when skin colour has emerged as a major fault line of the West, with white nationalists and their xenophobic anger catered to and fanned by populists and demagogues. Canada's unique history and contemporary multiculturalism, constitutional as well as a lived reality, have provided the ballast. No overtly anti-immigrant party can find success in Canada. The few politicians who have tried have failed to win a seat in Parliament. We have, indeed, fashioned Marshall McLuhan's global village in Canada.

Phil Ryan, the author of *Multicultiphobia*, agrees. I spoke to him for this book and he told me this:

> The conservative critics that I examined in *Multicultiphobia* regularly predicted that multiculturalism would lead to the splintering of Canada. It seems instead to have led many Canadians to a more relaxed, less brittle, sense of Canadian identity. This process is certainly incomplete and uneven. But we should acknowledge and cherish the change, especially as we watch in horror as the nation to our south shatters, in part because of the influence of rigid nativist conceptions of America.

15

Becoming a Columnist

IN 1998, AFTER EIGHT GRUELLING YEARS AS EDITORIAL PAGE EDITOR, JOHN Honderich, the *Toronto Star*'s publisher, offered me a column. My status as part of the senior management team that set the strategic direction of the paper wouldn't be affected, including leading diversity initiatives to better reflect the new demographic realities of Canada. He provided no reason for the change. Kings don't have to explain. That's their prerogative. Ours is to stand up to them when conscience calls. I'd done more than my share of disobeying. John, to his credit, had let me be. He may have had more than his share of backing off. Now we could shake hands on a fair draw, as in cricket.

An editorial page editor toils mostly in anonymity, given the *Star*'s sound policy of unsigned editorials. Readers aren't distracted by the writer's name and the baggage it might carry, positive or negative. They get to weigh the opinion of the newspaper on its merit.

As a columnist, it's liberating to express your own opinions. You aren't tied to the consensus arrived at by the editorial board within the newspaper's ideological orientation. However, you lose the collective wisdom of your colleagues, though you may consult them individually, as I kept doing. Another luxury is the comparatively leisurely pace — in my case, twice a week — which provided time to do interviews, develop ideas, think.

A columnist's logo — byline with a photo — is an ego booster. But I'd had my fill of it, often from page 1 at that, when reporting from abroad.

Sorry, that's not quite true. A front-page byline is like a fix; one never has enough of it. I've known colleagues who suffered withdrawal symptoms after the hot stories they were on fell off the front page.

Unlike columnists tethered to a news beat or a genre, I was allowed to graze far and wide. John gave me the freedom to write on any subject from anywhere on the *Star's* dime or at times mine. My beat was anything and everything in Toronto, Ontario, Canada, and the world. I could take advantage of travel anywhere — holidays, speaking engagements, meetings of PEN International on different continents. That was how I got to write from dozens of countries. That also meant I was never not working — multitasking more than ever before.

But why would anyone read what I'd write? There's never a shortage of pontificators in the world, their voices magnified with the dawn of the digital age. Readers need reasons to read you. Great writing? Sure. But most journalistic prose tends to be pedestrian — mine doesn't sing, for sure. Humour? Few can pull it off. Bombast? Barkers on radio and TV had the market cornered. Me-me-me journalism? No.

Knowledge is what gives gravitas to writing. Even when you think you know, you don't know enough. The most important thing to know is what you don't know. As author Eric Nicol of Vancouver once famously put it, a specialist is one who knows more and more about less and less until he knows everything there is to know about something, while a journalist is a generalist who knows less and less about more and more until he knows nothing about everything. I limited myself to subjects I was familiar with. There was no point in rewriting news clippings.

Read up. Learn. Talk to the experts. Take the reader along on your journey of discovery. Add analysis, insight, argument. Avoid overwrought adjectives. Eschew exaggeration, melodrama. Don't climb on your high horse. Or soapbox. On emotionally charged topics, lower the temperature — go into the passive voice, let the facts to do the talking. Pray that the penny drops in the reader's head. Or he or she says, "I didn't agree with a damn thing you said, but I learned something." Or "you made me think."

Follow the *Star's* Atkinson principles — economic and social justice, equality of citizens, and independent Canadian economic and foreign policies.

15 Becoming a Columnist

Add contemporary subjects, especially those not being addressed or being addressed badly: the remarkable transformation of Canada into the most heterogeneous society in the history of humanity. The concomitant imperatives to defend the Charter of Rights and Freedoms, minority rights, and multiculturalism; to battle racism and bigotry; to give voice to new Canadians; to tether public policy, including foreign policy, to the emerging new Canadian cosmopolitan sensibility; and to bring an international perspective to Canadian affairs and a Canadian perspective to international issues.

Rather than follow public opinion, lead it, without getting too far ahead of it. If lucky, you may be proven prescient.

In catering to the mass market, which is what big-circulation dailies do, resist pandering to the lowest common denominator; try to reach for the highest common factor.

Foreign issues, even the most controversial ones, I found easy to deal with. I had some knowledge of parts of the world I was writing about, and a perspective that was often different than the prevalent one.

It wasn't a case of being contrarian for the sake of it. Rather, I found myself repeatedly challenging the dominant narratives on the Third World, on Muslims and the Muslim world, and on new minorities of Canada. News coverage and commentary on most of those seemed to me to be riddled with double standards and blind spots.

I found myself atop several fault lines — First versus Third World, pro-America versus anti-America, Muslim versus non-Muslim, white versus non-white, majority versus minorities, media versus their critics. Whose side was I on? Nobody's. Which of those were "my people?" None. I was a reporter-columnist with a point of view, for sure, but one based on what I saw, which others either didn't or had chosen not to. I wasn't peddling any ideology. I wasn't out to make friends or enemies. I was doing my job.

I didn't think about it at the time, but I avoided the pitfalls that can befall a journalist hailing from a minority community — going along to get along with newsroom clichés and prejudices, hidden and not-so hidden; avoiding reporting or commenting altogether on issues affecting minorities for fear of being pigeonholed; or, alternatively, becoming their strident mouthpiece. I never thought of not writing about Muslims or other minorities, or about

India and the rest of the Third World, for fear of being typecast. I wrote what I thought needed to be written based on my journalistic judgment. By chance, the domestic and international issues that popped up were to define our times. In that sense, I got lucky.

Still, there was no such thing as an easy column — not for me. Nor inspired writing — maybe there is, but I've not known it. Nor stream-of-consciousness writing, whatever that is. Writing is hard work. Every piece of writing is a production, or at least I manage to make it so. There was no news report, no analysis, no editorial, no column, no essay of mine that couldn't have been rewritten and improved. Deadlines saved me from myself, prying the copy out of my clutches.

Tumultuous 1990s

For Muslims, the 1990s were to prove a prelude to 9/11 and what followed: the Salman Rushdie affair; the continued brutal Israeli occupation of Palestinians, which led to a second intifada; the ethnic cleansing of Muslims in the Balkans; the rise of the Taliban and the American-led sanctions on Afghanistan; and the crippling sanctions on and the Anglo-American bombing of Iraq.

With my wife, Yasmeen, and sons, Faisal and Fahad, 1990s.

15 Becoming a Columnist

To me, too much of the media coverage and commentary smelled of American propaganda. My take was that the United States and its allies were inflicting too many horrors on Muslims and Muslim lands, that American credibility was taking a big hit despite its intervention on behalf of Muslims in Bosnia and Kosovo, and that the West was hurtling toward cultural warfare on Muslims. As for Muslims, they were getting angrier at their impotency to stop any of the many onslaughts on their lands, their sovereignty, their freedom, their dignity.

It was this milieu that made Osama bin Laden. He'd been agitating against his native Saudi Arabia for hosting an American military base, but he pierced Western consciousness only in 1998 with terrorist attacks on American embassies in Kenya and Tanzania. "Carried out in the name of Islam and Muslims, such acts are totally un-Islamic," I wrote. "No religion condones the killing of civilians, and Islam specifically forbids suicide."

However, the American response was botched. Cruise missiles destroyed a pharmaceutical factory in Sudan on the false claim that it was financed by bin Laden and making chemical weapons. The United States didn't bother to apologize, let alone help rebuild the facility that was making desperately needed antibiotics for the Sudanese. The Americans also slammed cruise missiles into what was said to be bin Laden's Afghan "headquarters," calling it "the largest terrorist training facility in the world," which on that very day was ostensibly hosting "literally thousands of terrorists from around the globe." It turned out to be an empty shed with a few animals that got vaporized — at a cost of about $45 million ($750,000 per missile times the 60 fired).

Americans couldn't seem to get things right and didn't care that they didn't, what they destroyed, whom they killed. In 1988, an American warship, the *Vincennes*, in the Persian Gulf mistook an Iranian civilian airliner for a fighter jet and killed all 290 people aboard, prompting President George H.W. Bush to boast: "I will never apologize for the United States. I don't care what the facts are." Instead, Washington awarded medals to the captain and crew of the *Vincennes*.

Where was all this going? What would be the consequences?

Chechnya, Again

Having failed to crush the Chechens in 1994–95, Russia launched a second war in 1999, this time under Vladimir Putin, following mysterious bomb blasts in Moscow attributed to Chechen jihadists. Most of the West fell for the bogey of Islamic fundamentalism, including Lloyd Axworthy, Canada's foreign minister. Indeed, in 2000, Ottawa rolled out the red carpet for Putin, whose war had killed 4,000 Chechen civilians and displaced 200,000. His crimes were far worse than what the Chinese did to their dissidents in Tiananmen Square, or the Indonesians to the East Timorese.

The Canadian media, too, was solicitous of Putin. As a prelude to his arrival in Ottawa, he granted interviews in Moscow to Canadian media outlets. The resulting propaganda let him portray himself as an ice-hockey-loving democrat taming corrupt capitalism, introducing rules to a lawless society, and curbing jihadism. The old *Pravda* would have been proud of the Canadian coverage given this war criminal.

By contrast, Anna Politkovskaya of the Russian biweekly *Novaya Gazeta* was brave in exposing Putin's horrors. Her dispatches were published in their English translation, *A Dirty War*, in 2001.[1] During a visit to Toronto, she was emphatic in telling me that those 1999 bomb blasts in Moscow were the work of the Russian Federal Security Service, the successor agency to the KGB.

When she returned to Russia, she received multiple death threats. In 2004, she was poisoned but survived. In 2006, she was murdered in the elevator of her Moscow apartment building.

Muslims and America

The U.S.-led economic sanctions on Iraq caused the slow death of about a million Iraqis, half of them children under the age of five. In 1996, Madeleine Albright, the U.S. secretary of state, was asked if such a high price was worth the American goal of regime change in Baghdad. Her chilling reply was: "We think the price is worth it." That was widely viewed as yet another proof of America's malevolence toward Muslims.

The Foreign Affairs Committee of the House of Commons, chaired by Toronto MP Bill Graham, called for an end to the sanctions. So did the

Canadian Mennonite Central Committee and the Canadian Council of Churches. Yet that had little impact on Ottawa, mostly because Canada at the time held a seat on the U.N. Security Council and the bureaucracy at the foreign ministry was working with Americans on several issues.

The United States also imposed sanctions on the Taliban after failing to kill or capture Osama bin Laden. It was instructive that the sanctions had the backing of Russia. Afghanistan had the largest number of land mines after 21 years of war; the highest rate of infant, child, and maternal mortality; and the highest rate of hunger after two years of drought. A million people faced starvation. Half a million had been displaced. Yet urgent U.N. appeals elicited little response.

I went out on a limb and advocated for Canada to take Afghan refugees, perhaps 25,000. That wasn't a big number, considering we'd provided a haven for victims of various crises: 37,000 Hungarians, 12,000 Czechs, 7,500 Ugandans, 200,000 U.S. Vietnam War draft dodgers and deserters, 160,000 Indo-Chinese boat people after the Vietnam War, and 25,000 from the former Yugoslavia, among others. The appeal was met by deafening silence, both by the government and the public.

Muslims weren't the only ones upset with the United States and its allies. Kishore Mahbubani, "Asia's Toynbee," the Canadian-educated ambassador of Singapore to the United Nations and concurrently high commissioner to Canada, said: "The West has abrogated unto itself the moral high ground from which it lectures the world, except that the people being hectored see no high ground, only double standards on democracy, human rights and globalization…. Inconsistencies are more pronounced in the Middle East. There's total disregard for human rights in Israel and the occupied territories and, to a lesser degree, in oil-rich Arab states." He was talking to me in the spring of 2001 at the release of his book *Can Asians Think?*[2]

Babu Clinton in India

In the spring of 2000, Bill Clinton was going to India, Pakistan, and Bangladesh — the first American president in the subcontinent in more than two decades. The trip was bound to produce good copy, which I could enrich with insights into the politics and people of the region. So, I got

My Name Is Not Harry

accredited with the White House, the only Canadian in the media contingent of about 250.

The United States was courting democratic India as a counterweight to China. India was emerging from its "permit raj," overbearing socialist control in which most economic activities required a government permit. Starting in 1991, Manmohan Singh, India's finance minister and later prime minister, was liberalizing the economy. I'd been writing editorials urging better Canada-India trade, which prompted David Galloway, the CEO of Torstar (owner of the *Toronto Star*) and a Harvard MBA with great business acumen, to say: "Not likely to happen — too far, too little returns."

Clinton was on a charm offensive in India. Hillary Clinton and daughter, Chelsea, were already Indophiles, having basked in a 1995 visit lavishly choreographed by India. For this trip, Clinton was at his best and American hypocrisy at its worst. But for me the more enjoyable parts of his visit were social.

Within minutes of checking into his Delhi hotel late in the evening, Clinton was down in the lobby restaurant Bukhara that specialized in tandoori. He polished off two plates of kebabs and a double order of a rich dessert. Those were his pre–heart operation days, but he'd already sworn off cheeseburgers and was ostensibly on a low-fat diet. However, he wasn't going to let that get in the way of devouring some real Indian food as opposed to what often passed for it in North America, mostly peasant food from the Punjab.

The first official day of Clinton's visit began with a horror: front pages splayed with headlines and gruesome photos of 35 Sikhs massacred overnight in Kashmir, the disputed Muslim-majority state between India and Pakistan. India promptly blamed Pakistani terrorism. Pakistan and a Muslim group in Kashmir blamed India for staging the massacre with impeccable timing for the morning of Clinton's meeting with Atal Bihari Vajpayee, India's prime minister. The massacre set the agenda and coverage of that meeting and much else.

That bilateral meeting was held at Hyderabad House, with which I had a long affinity. It was the grand palace of the nizam of Hyderabad for his stay in Delhi. But he never did use it. Built by the British architect Edwin Lutyens, it was second in size only to the Viceroy's House. After the Indian

15 Becoming a Columnist

takeover of Hyderabad in 1948, the 36-room palace on nearly 3.6 hectares of prime real estate in the area called Lutyens' Delhi was taken over by the federal government. I was there earlier as a tourist, checking out my heritage.

Clinton gave a well-crafted speech to Parliament, balancing praise with gentle admonitions about India's nuclear ambitions:

> Is it atomic weapons or ahimsa [non-violence]? A land struggling against poverty and inequality, or the world's largest middle-class society? Is it Bollywood or Satyajit Ray? Only India can decide.
>
> The greatest of India's many gifts to the world is the example its people have set: virtually every challenge humanity knows can be found here; and every solution to every challenge can be found here, as well.

He lauded Mahatma Gandhi's philosophy of non-violence "without which the great civil-rights revolution in the United States would never have succeeded on a peaceful plane." His fulsome praise for India's pluralism rang a bell for this Canadian: "Far from washing away the uniqueness of your culture, your democracy has brought out the richness of its tapestry and given you the knot that holds it together."

Arrayed in front of him in the jam-packed chamber was India's rich diversity: light-skinned blueblood Brahmins from the north, dark-skinned Dravidians from the south, tribal representatives from the northeast, politicians of modest backgrounds or from the Dalit community (formerly called untouchables) sitting next to old royalty — a riot of colourful turbans, knitted caps, saris, Western-styled suits, Indian *sherwanis* and vests, and crisp white *kurtas* and pyjama. He held the audience to rapt attention, and when he was done, they rose to a man to cheer him, hooting and hollering like kids at a rock concert. As he walked out through the aisles to a crescendo of applause, old men climbed on chairs and desks, extending their hands to touch him. A South Indian parliamentarian pulled out his *angavastra*, the white scarf around his neck, and tossed it at the president. It was a lovefest across cultures and races.

That, however, was the only display of spontaneity in the six-day trip. Wrapped in a sterile security cocoon, Clinton was kept away from a people who were among the world's most hospitable and tactile. The overbearing U.S. Secret Service seemed twitchier than usual, operating in an unfamiliar culture that thrived on exuberance.

At first the public was amused. It was reported there were 40 landings of the giant C-130 Hercules transport planes unloading not only bulletproof presidential limousines and helicopters, FBI vehicles, guns, and electronic gadgetry, but also water bottles, pop, and packaged food. That prompted a patron at a café in old Delhi to crack: "They're coming to India to eat American chips?"

But the public mood turned sour as roads were closed, trains diverted, rallies and demonstrations banned, vendors — the most visible symbol of commerce in this culture — ordered out, and shops locked shut.

As Clinton rolled into Agra to see the Taj Mahal, the 15-kilometre route from the airport was eerily empty, as if hit by a bomb that killed people but left buildings intact. Invoking security, the Secret Service and local authorities swept the people right out. We didn't see a soul for long stretches — not in the streets, not in school playgrounds, not even in apartment buildings, where doors and windows were shut tight. Were the occupants holed up inside? Or ordered right out of their poor neighbourhoods?

To My Hometown

Then it was on to Hyderabad, by then an emerging centre of high tech under a dynamic new chief minister of the state of Andhra Pradesh, of which my hometown was the capital. Chandra Babu Naidu, in power only since 1995, had zero charisma but a strong work ethic. He got up at four in the morning, did yoga, fired up his laptop, looked at progress reports from various departments, tapped out orders, and got into his car for spot checks on whether roads were being cleaned, garbage was being picked up, and water in the public taps had enough pressure. My father-in-law, Colonel Khusro Yar Khan, was mighty pleased that the young premier was making public services and public servants shipshape.

Naidu also had a vision of dragging the agricultural state of 76 million into the high tech age and turning Hyderabad into *Cyberabad*, along the lines of Bangalore, 650 kilometres south. Indian software engineers had just made a mark on the world working out the "millennium bug," the feared havoc when computers changed from 1999 to 2000. Naidu made pilgrimages to Davos, toured the United States, tapped the World Bank for a $3 billion loan for infrastructure improvements, and got Bill Gates to set up Microsoft's first research facility outside America in Hyderabad.

On a subsequent visit, Naidu told me how he'd cornered Gates at the residence of the U.S. ambassador in Delhi and asked for 10 minutes. After a 40-minute PowerPoint presentation, Gates was committed. Naidu also convinced IBM, Oracle, Motorola, and others to come to Hyderabad. And he set up community portals in all 20,000 local governments, "one window service." People could pay their utility bills and property taxes, do land transfers, get birth and death certificates, and apply for microloans. Clinton was so taken with those internet community stations in villages that he couldn't stop talking about duplicating them in rural America. Hyderabad also went on to produce software engineers, tens of thousands of whom ended up in the United States and Canada on contract work or as immigrants.

The Clinton entourage in Hyderabad stayed only a few hours, during which I got out of the security cordon for 45 minutes to see my two families, mine and Yasmeen's. That felt strange — an Indian coming back from North America and not prioritizing family because of some big-shot politician! But I had no choice. It was back to the plane, this time to Mumbai, where I had my first job in 1963.

The Security Dodge

In Mumbai, security concerns reached paranoid levels as the president prepared for his trip to Pakistan. At Mumbai's airport, we were hustled onto a Hercules cargo plane. From one of its narrow windows, I watched the proceedings outside. Air Force One was nowhere in sight. Instead, there were two small Gulfstream jets. The presidential motorcade arrived at the staircase of one, Clinton got out, and instead of climbing up, darted sideways and disappeared. He did the dodge to get into the other jet.

As we approached the Pakistani capital of Islamabad, our plane went into a holding pattern, circling for a good three-quarters of an hour. It obviously wasn't queueing up in heavy traffic, airspace having been closed for Clinton's arrival. Why wasn't it landing? But there was no crew to explain. I surmised that the plane was doing some sort of reconnaissance. I told the nervous guy next to me to relax, do some deep breathing, or say his prayers, while I went into my usual low-key recitation of the Qur'an.

When we finally landed, the plane taxied to a remote offshoot of the runway, with nothing else in sight, except the buses to ferry us.

Where was Clinton? No answer.

After we got to the hall where there was supposed to be a briefing, and hopefully, a presidential presser, TV screens showed Clinton's arrival back at the airport. He'd flown in his decoy plane, fooling the welcoming party and the live cameras into focusing on the wrong aircraft.

Clinton spent only five hours in Pakistan. He met Pervez Musharraf in private so as not to be photographed with the general who had toppled a civilian government five months earlier. Clinton demanded airtime on the national TV network, which he used to lecture Pakistanis about democracy — a sermon to the sinners. He told them to forget about Kashmir and refused to meet the Kashmiris. They didn't count, as hadn't the Chechens, the Palestinians, the Iraqis, the Afghans ...

The president framed the new American policy as standing with democratic India and shunning militarily ruled Pakistan. That was good spin but nonetheless spin. Long-standing American relations with dictators in the Middle East and Latin America were inconvenient reminders of American hypocrisy. Having insulted Musharraf on his home turf, Clinton left. I stayed behind.

The general salvaged some of his and his nation's dignity with an unassuming performance at a televised news conference hours later. Contrary to how he was being portrayed by the Americans, he didn't have horns. In fact, his military junta might have been the most civil government in Pakistan in years. As for Musharraf being an Islamic fundamentalist, as some Western media had it, how "fundamentalist" could he be if, in his first photo op after the coup, he showed up with his hijab-less wife and daughter, happily holding the leash of a dog, among the lowest of the low in Islamic cosmology.

As overdue as the American tilt to India was, ditching Pakistan meant that the decades-long special relationship between the United States and

Pakistan was going up in flames. It was from Pakistan that Gary Powers had flown his ill-fated 1960 U-2 mission to the Soviet Union; that Henry Kissinger had launched his 1971 secret trip to Beijing to pave the way for Richard Nixon's opening of relations with China; and that the Central Intelligence Agency and the Afghan mujahideen had waged their 1979–89 guerrilla war to overturn the Soviet occupation of Afghanistan.

But I was proven wrong. It took only a few days after 9/11 for the United States to re-embrace Musharraf and pronounce Pakistan "an indispensable ally," as George W. Bush put it. And then, just as suddenly, the United States, with Canada and others in dutiful tow, soured on Pakistan, blaming it for their self-made quagmire in Afghanistan.

Priceless Pierre

At Pierre Elliott Trudeau's death in 2000 at the age of 81, I felt as though a member of my own family had died. I'd known him only professionally, not personally, yet the Canada he created recognized that monoculturalism was no longer sustainable in increasingly globalized democracies. Non-Christians and non-whites loved him for that. But they weren't the only ones. His vision of Canada had broad appeal. The unparalleled outpouring of public sentiment, including in Quebec, was a celebration of his Canada: a bilingual, multicultural, just society.

While politicians were pedantic in their tributes to Trudeau, ordinary Canadians were poetic and eloquent. Who could forget the man from Sault Ste. Marie who said that his vigil at Trudeau's casket was his way of atoning for the sins of his city fathers for passing an English-only resolution during the 1995 Quebec referendum? Or the Anglo woman from Toronto who said she came to thank him for the gift of bilingual education for her four grandchildren in a public school system free of charge? Or the immigrant from the Caribbean who said she'd come "to say farewell to my brother"? Or the woman who held aloft a canoe over her head as the Trudeau train passed from Ottawa to Montreal? At the funeral at Notre-Dame Basilica in Montreal, Justin Trudeau's eulogy was moving, despite his overwrought, Shakespearean opening, "Friends, Romans, countrymen."

It was a week that made many of us more Canadian. It also provided a moment of reflection: would his vision outlast him?

Whereas the need for immigrants was officially well understood, public acceptance of them wasn't. Immigrant economic integration wasn't going well, either. It was taking immigrants longer than previous cohorts to find jobs or to make a decent living. Those mired in dead-end jobs and poverty were overwhelmingly non-white. "The more visible you are, the more difficulties you have," reported Michael Ornstein of York University, based on his research. A University of Toronto study showed a discernible disparity in the welcome extended to Europeans and to non-whites, despite similar qualifications and experiences.

Yet the blame was being shifted to the immigrants themselves by many people and by much of the media, suggesting that the qualifications of the new immigrants must be phoney, or their experience wasn't up to snuff, or their social skills were negligent ...

The squeaky whine of prejudice had to be challenged column after column, speech after speech, educating, persuading, admonishing, as in the cheeky column that Canada should freeze immigration for five years and see what happens.

The Toppled Buddhas

In the spring of 2001, the Taliban destroyed the sixth-century statues carved into the sandstone cliffs of Bamiyan Valley north of Kabul, including two giant-sized Buddhas. There was worldwide outrage, justifiably so. Still, a question hung in the air. Would the Taliban have destroyed the priceless pre-Islamic treasures had they not been isolated from the world by the economic sanctions, starved of resources of which they had few to begin with, rendered too helpless to do anything for their internally displaced people, reduced to being mute witnesses to the death of starving and shivering children in winter refugee camps? Perhaps, perhaps not. But of this I had little doubt: we would have had greater credibility trying to save Afghanistan's historic treasures had we been more helpful saving its human beings.

Given that the Taliban rationalized their dastardly deed in the name of Islam, there followed another round of Islam-bashing in the West, ignoring that Muslims everywhere had joined the chorus of condemnation. Most Muslims knew that the philistine Taliban were ignorant of the theology they invoked. Theirs was not so much an austere interpretation of Islam as one that violated the words and spirit of the faith.

Next Up, Crimea

Having gotten away with Chechnya, Vladimir Putin grabbed the Georgian territories of South Ossetia and Abkhazia in 2008, doling out Russian citizenship to Russian-speaking residents. Next, he set his eyes on Crimea, the traditional home of the Muslim Tatars, not to be confused with the Tatars of Tatarstan, the Soviet republic in the east. The Crimean Peninsula on the Black Sea was first annexed by the tsars in 1783. In 1944, Joseph Stalin deported all 200,000 Tatars to Central Asia. The survivors returned only after the collapse of the Soviet Union when Crimea was incorporated into independent Ukraine. They found their ancestral homes and lands occupied by Russian-speaking people who by then constituted 80 percent of the population.

Among the returnees was Mustafa Dzhemilev, known as the Mahatma Gandhi of Crimea for his lifelong commitment to non-violence. I interviewed him in 2010 in Toronto when he came at the invitation of the Canadian-Ukrainian community. A small man with a leathery face, he spoke softly but commanded attention.

His was a remarkable story, not known to most people in the West, not known to me. Growing up in India, we were never told the horror stories of the Soviet Union, India being a close ally.

Dzhemilev was six months old when his parents were deported. At age 18, he refused to serve in the Soviet army and was jailed for three years. He was imprisoned six more times, often in solitary confinement, and was malnourished, all the worse for his frequent hunger strikes. The longest lasted 303 days, which he survived only because he was force-fed.

In the post-Soviet era, he began rebuilding Tatar culture and language and regaining territorial autonomy "within an independent, democratic, and stable Ukraine." But Moscow kept undermining him. There was an assassination attempt on his life, but he remained committed to non-violence: "We are proud that not a single opponent of ours has been killed by us," he told me. He called for the dismantling of the Russian naval base at Sevastopol, and for Ukraine to be admitted to the North Atlantic Treaty Organization. That was the only way to guarantee the future for Crimea and Ukraine.

His words went unheeded. In 2014, Putin seized Crimea and used it as a base for his 2022 invasion of Ukraine.

Bouquets and Brickbats

My columns rattled a whole lot of people, mostly in the establishment, particularly in the media.

A prime specimen of the old generation of journalists was Robert Fulford, a former editor of *Saturday Night*. Fulford wrote a 4,300-word feature on me in *Toronto Life*. He accused me, among a series of sins, of Third Worldism:

> Siddiqui makes the most strenuous effort to bathe Third World countries in a soft light. No matter how outrageous its actions, a non-Western government can usually count on him for a little sympathy. He found a way to look with a degree of tolerance even on the Taliban's destruction of ancient Buddhist sculptures....
>
> Whatever goes wrong, the West is at fault. If government in Africa doesn't work, it's the legacy of colonialism. If people starve in Indonesia, if forests burn in Brazil, if Iraqi children die for lack of medicine, it's all because the policies of the West are callous, insensitive or selfish.[3]

Fulford had ignored my criticisms of the Taliban as obscurantist and uneducated, indeed, un-Islamic, and also of the growing fundamentalism in Pakistan, the jingoism in India, the military or monarchial dictatorships in the Arab world.

He also faulted me for my public-speaking engagements, especially to minority groups:

> Siddiqui is a former editor of the editorial page but he's no ordinary ex-editor; he is editorial page editor emeritus....

15 Becoming a Columnist

> In recent years, he's emerged as both an articulate symbol of the new Toronto and the human embodiment of our media's earnest but not always rational ways of dealing with multicultural reality. Siddiqui is a newspaperman of unusual intelligence, charm and experience but what sets him apart is the way he has made multiculturalism his special subject. He lectures to such organizations as the Sikh Centennial Foundation, the Chinese Canadian National Council, the Canadian Arab Federation and the Jamaican Canadian Association.... He's a figure. He's a statesman. And this is terribly crippling for a journalist. Whatever he does is a significant statement of something or other. There's a spotlight on him that isn't on other people, because he's spent so much time on this one set of issues.[4]

Would Fulford have accused a financial columnist of placing herself in a "terribly crippling" circumstance by speaking to the Chamber of Commerce or the Board of Trade? Or a political analyst for speaking to a gathering of parliamentarians? Or a religion reporter speaking to the Canadian Council of Churches, the Canadian Jewish Congress, or B'nai Brith?

It so happened that I'd spoken to each one of those groups, as well. But what really seemed to bother Fulford was that this brown immigrant from the Third World was addressing immigrant, non-white groups — clearly a suspicious activity. Plus, that I had the temerity to insist that issues concerning the non-Western world might not be as black and white as people like him were used to portraying. And worse, that I was advancing my arguments from Canada's largest newspaper, rather than from the ignored margins of society.

That really was his source of anger, as well as I could decipher him.

Lieutenant Governor Hilary Weston conferring the Order of Ontario, 2000.

16

Post-9/11 Canada

SEPTEMBER 11, 2001, CHANGED THE UNITED STATES AND THE WORLD IN ways that could only have been dreamed of by Osama bin Laden and his 19 flying terrorists. The West was knocked off its moorings; the United States and its allies, including Canada, went charging into their longest and most expensive wars in history with little or nothing to show at the end. The U.S. Treasury was drained by about $8 trillion,[1] the country's public discourse was coarsened, and American public policy priorities were distorted at the expense of much-needed ones for ordinary citizens — all making the perfect breeding ground for demagoguery, authoritarianism, majoritarianism, nativism, xenophobia, and white nationalism. Nor could bin Laden and company have imagined that nearly 900,000 Muslims would be killed and almost 37 million Muslims displaced by the forever war on terrorism waged overtly and covertly in more than 80 countries. That was more people killed than in the Rwandan genocide.

The Green Scare turned out to be worse than the Red Scare of the 1950s. It had a bigger footprint, extending beyond the United States to Canada, Europe, Australia, and elsewhere; it lasted much longer; and it impacted, besides the Muslim world, the 30 million Muslim minorities across the West.

* * *

From a journalist who happened to be Muslim, I was deemed a Muslim journalist, told to denounce Islam and fellow Muslims for the acts of a handful of Muslim terrorists. I refused.

A twin political and sociological phenomenon emerged: 9/11 made most Canadians more Canadian, but it made a minority of Canadians ardently pro-American and virulently anti-Muslim. While a great majority of Canadians felt that Canada had less and less in common with the United States and its hegemonic behaviour in the world, their voices were drowned out by a loud minority whose point of view was amplified by the conservative newspapers that dominated urban Canada — more on that later. Even in Toronto, where there was a choice of four dailies, only the *Toronto Star* offered an alternate point of view to the *Globe and Mail*, the *National Post*, and the *Toronto Sun*. In the *Star*, too, the pro-American, more accurately, anti-Muslim, voice wasn't missing.

I had a unique preview of the pulse of the nation after 9/11. Almost overnight, reader responses to my column shot through the roof, and they turned out to be a near-perfect barometer of where public opinion would settle. This is best illustrated in the raw reactions to my columns in the immediate aftermath of 9/11.

The First Shots

My first column after the tragedy, "A Letter to Our American Friends," began: "Dear Neighbours: In your darkest hour of shock, grief, and outrage, we walk with you in your collective mourning." But it quickly warned that while President George W. Bush was claiming America was targeted because it was "the brightest beacon of freedom and the best hope for humanity," it was, in fact, attacked because it no longer lived up to those ideals. It had become indifferent to the suffering of too many Muslims from Afghanistan, to Chechnya, to the Middle East, driving the ordinary folk there to seethe in silence against America and the crazed ones into fanatical acts. Still, the terrorists were no more representatives of all Arabs or Muslims than Baruch Goldstein was of all Jews or Irish Republican Army members were of all Catholics. "So, dear Americans," I wrote, "hit the terrorists hard. Be merciless in going after them. But spare the innocents, both abroad and at home."

The second column, "Don't Scapegoat Canada for Terrorism in America," shot down suggestions already afloat that the 9/11 terrorists might have infiltrated the United States from Canada. The allegations of a possible Canadian link were being levelled with greater vigour by Canadian right wingers than by Americans.

What caused the biggest stir was the third column, "It's the U.S. Foreign Policy, Stupid." It said that the United States wasn't attacked because Islamic fundamentalists hated American democratic ideals of freedom, liberty, and "all that we stand for," as Bush claimed. The suicide bombers didn't fit the mould of the pious seeking martyrdom. One who had come from Germany liked to dance with his live-in girlfriend whom he had ditched before crossing the Atlantic. Nor had the bombers come from impoverished hellholes, the breeding grounds of zealots and recruits for extremist causes. They were educated products of privilege, sons of affluent families from Arab nations that were among America's strongest allies:

> This was scarier than we thought. Either out of ignorance or calculation, the theories on the motives for last week's attacks avoid the most obvious: America has many enemies due to American complicity in injustice, lethal and measurable, on several fronts:
>
> The Israeli-Palestinian conflict ...
>
> The decade-long American-led economic sanctions on Iraq that have killed 500,000 children under the age of five ...
>
> The mess in Afghanistan where the CIA recruited and trained the likes of Osama bin Laden to overturn the Soviet occupation but dumped them once that mission impossible was accomplished ...
>
> American strategic alliances with the military and monarchical dictatorships of Algeria, Turkey and Egypt, as well as the oil-rich Arab states, all of whom crush even the smallest steps towards democratization ...

> America needs, beyond any tactical strikes or smart bombs it might deploy, a more humane and even-handed approach to the world.

The column left the political, business, and media establishment aghast. It had said the unsayable within days of the tragedy. But as a journalist, it wasn't my job to be a therapist for the injured American psyche.

Globe and Mail columnist Marcus Gee was to fume: "Anti-Americanism of that kind I think is silly at any time, but at a time like that I just thought it was in terrible taste."[2] Another *Globe* columnist, Margaret Wente, characterized the column as an example of blaming the victim for the crime. "He, of all people, should have been alert to the critical problems posed by Muslim fundamentalism, by failed Muslim states, and by the poisonous public discourse of anti-Americanism and anti-Semitism that pervade much of the Arab world."[3] That was the sum total of her take on the terrorist attack.

My *Star* colleague, editorial writer Nate Laurie, responded that "when someone named Haroon Siddiqui says it, it seems to carry a different message. Many people read the column as America got what it deserved. He said, how did we get here? But if your name is Haroon Siddiqui, you are defending all Muslims, be they terrorists or not."[4]

A majority of the 450 or so immediate reader responses said: "Thank you for saying it." The praise was uplifting, but the backlash was more instructive:

- Your column was either brilliant satire or the worst case of Third World thinking I have ever encountered.
- Blame the victim, stupid.
- As Dan Aykroyd used to say to Jane Curtin, "Jane you ignorant slut."
- You are in the payroll of Bin Laden.
- Go to hell…. Thanks for the advice about a more humane approach to the world. You can kiss our collective asses when you need help in the future. Ungrateful bastards.

- Why in the hell can't trash like you go back to the country you came from. It's clear from your name where your sympathies are.
- Scumsucking piece of s--t. Which one of those islamic rat hole countries are you from?
- What you said was disgusting.... I will just give you a hearty Fuck You.
- islam is a pagan religion and it existed before mohammid ever even came along ... mohammid exhibited the symptoms and side effects of a demonically possessed human being. muslims are nothing more than pagans.

Those who agreed with the column included ex-pat Canadians and also Americans, many of whom bemoaned the absence of critical thinking at a time when it was most needed:

- You have calmly summarized many, if not most, of the thoughts and worries that have been filling my head for the past two and a half days.
- The most lucid and forthright article I have read since Sept. 11.
- Thank you for articulating so well what a lot of us ex-pats here (in Beijing) have been discussing. Many of us Canadians, Africans, Arabs, Europeans, Brits, Aussies, and even some Americans wholeheartedly agree with your views.
- Thank you for expressing the feelings I've had since the WTC disaster. Your comments are wise, especially in this time of overwhelming, yet shallow, coverage by the U.S. media.
- A voice of reason in the world of CNN-ic media.
- I only wish the American media printed such a point of view. The more measured perspectives are being intimidated into silence, a nouveau McCarthyism.

- There's a conspiracy of silence surrounding this subject, and you say clearly what most others are only willing to allude to.
- Word has been that we should keep our sentiments to ourselves, avoid rational expression and just say what people want to hear. It has been depressing. I was glad to read your column, and I thank God that He gave you all this courage.
- Siddiqui has taken the most dangerous path a writer can take at a time of war — he has told the truth. It takes courage.

At the old Linotype machine in the lobby of the *Toronto Star*, 2001.

Such reactions continued, indeed intensified as the war on terror became the war on Afghanistan, the war on Iraq, the war on the Geneva Conventions, the war on liberal democracy, the war on common sense, and an endless cultural warfare on Muslims.

The nasty tenor of some of the reader feedback was also a precursor of the debased discourse that became the common currency of social media.

Life of In-Betweens

For all the kerfuffle the columns were causing and continued to for years, I wasn't writing anything different than what I had been prior to 9/11. But the message obviously hit a nerve in some people during that highly charged time.

I was told numerous times, including by many well-wishers, Muslims and non-Muslims, that it was decidedly not good for my career to be writing what I was. Life would be much easier and I more popular were I not to question the mainstream post-9/11 narrative on Islam and Muslims. My response was that, as with any other subject, I wrote what I thought needed to be.

Much to the credit of the *Star*, I wasn't told what to write or not to, except once when publisher John Honderich tried to nudge me in a certain direction. Returning from a holiday in Florida, he handed me a clipping from a U.S. paper by an Egyptian American who was spreading collective guilt on Islam and all Muslims for the action of a few Muslim terrorists. "You should consider this," or words to that effect, he said. I didn't oblige. Much to his credit, he didn't come back.

John was often pestered by those clamouring for my blood: "What are you doing about that Siddiqui?" Nothing.

Such institutional backing is priceless in journalism and was especially so when I was going against the dominant American narrative, which was adopted holus-bolus by too many in the Canadian media.

A different burden came from being among a handful of non-whites in North America, indeed the entire West, and the only dissident Muslim to hold senior journalistic positions in a major daily newspaper. Pre-9/11, representational responsibilities were thrust on me by BIPOC communities,

My Name Is Not Harry

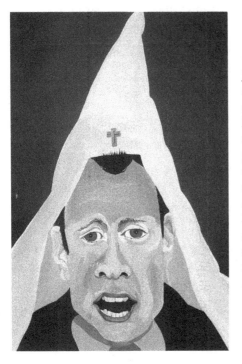

Joe Mendelson — singer, songwriter, author, painter — kept my spirits up with uplifting missives. From his home in Emsdale township in the Ontario Highlands, he'd send postcards — with a photo of one of his paintings on one side and his cursive scribbles on the other, using every centimetre of available space. In February 2023 came the sad news that he had died. He had been suffering from Parkinson's disease for five years, and opted for medical assistance in dying, signing off with his usual flourish: "To be born Canadian is a great blessing. We have free speech. We have healthcare. We have MAID. Thank you, Canada."

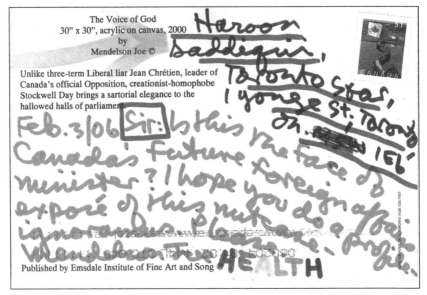

especially South Asians — Indians, Pakistanis, Bangladeshis, and Sri Lankans. Post-9/11, by Muslims mostly.

They all felt I was their voice. But I wasn't. I valued their concerns and feelings instead of dismissing them as the media had historically done with minority viewpoints. My views often coincided with theirs, but not always. Nor was I a defender of or an apologist for Islam as supporters and critics had it. I tried to correct distortions and provide the context. I criticized Muslims, especially Muslim regimes when they needed to be, which was often. My knowledge of Islam and Muslims proved invaluable, though mostly because I had so little competition. I had lucked on to a topic that too many were either ignorant of or malevolent about.

I saw things from my Indian eyes, Third World eyes, southern eyes, and Muslim eyes, which were now Canadian eyes. But for many critics, those were illegitimate lenses, particularly the Muslim one. A Christian could write about the Christian-majority West, a Jew about Israel, a Hindu about India, but not a Muslim about Islam or Muslims without raising suspicion. That, however, was their problem, not mine.

The Muslim/non-Muslim divide was only one of several that emerged in a world of absolutes: pro-American/anti-American, booster/saboteur of the war on terror, comforter of the anxieties of the (white) majority/defender of the rights of (non-white) minorities. But I was more used to a life of in-betweens.

Nevertheless, I found my post-9/11 voice right away. Still, the work was exhausting — all that reading, researching, and interviewing multiple experts across continents, many off the record, to get the judgments and balance of the columns right. At times I was doing my own reporting because many unsavoury aspects of the war on terror were being ignored. In the middle of this hectic schedule, I got a call from travel agent Sadat Khan, a cousin of Yasmeen, reminding me to book the tickets for our Christmas holiday visit to India. I said I was busy but figured that finding seats shouldn't be an issue given that international travel had dried up post-9/11.

"What are you talking about? Only the white man is not flying."

Blaming Muslims and Islam

George W. Bush insisted, and the anti-terrorism alliance agreed, that they were at war with Muslim terrorists, not Muslims, let alone Islam. Yet the drive to demonize Islam and Muslims kept gathering pace, the main theme being that the West was confronted with a clash of civilizations. Ironically, this is exactly what Osama bin Laden was saying, as well. The world, according to him, was "divided in two camps, the camp of the faithful and the camp of the infidels."

Within his "camp of the faithful," he had two constituencies — the few who joined his terrorist campaigns and the many who merely identified with his articulation of Muslim grievances. Western commentators analyzed his Islamic theology and ignored his political message. Muslims did the opposite. Neither side made much effort to understand the other.

The conflation of Muslim terrorists and Muslims led to laying collective guilt on law-abiding Muslims. Disproportionate pressure, overt and subtle, was put on Muslim citizens of North America, Europe, and Australia to not only condemn the attack but to "own up to it" and "take responsibility." I was routinely asked after any atrocity by a Muslim anywhere: "What do *you* have to say about this?"

I decided early not to be baited. But most Muslims and Muslim groups didn't have that luxury. They felt obliged to respond to incessant political, public, and media demands to condemn terrorism. That they did, frequently and forcefully, but got little or no coverage. They learned to issue news releases, develop websites and social media platforms, and hold press conferences, only to be ignored or mocked. That placed them in a no-win situation: "Why don't Muslims condemn terrorism?"

Muslims were deemed fifth columnists, as about 22,000 Japanese Canadians and 120,000 Japanese Americans had been during the Second World War and interned. Muslims weren't detained en masse, but they felt psychologically interned — subjected to suspicion, surveillance, and siege by the security agencies *and* also by the media.

I asked Bishop Desmond Tutu of South Africa what he thought of this guilt by association. In that 2002 conversation, he was characteristically passionate and to the point:

Christians would resent it very, very deeply if they were characterized by some of the weird fundamentalists in our camp. They would resent it very deeply if it is said that we are like the people in Northern Ireland who have been at each other's throats seemingly forever.

The Crusaders were Christians. Is that a justification for saying that Christianity is an aggressive religion?

Who was responsible for the Holocaust? Because some Christians did that, would we then say that Christianity is a violent religion?

Fascism — where did that come from? Europe.

Nazism? Europe.

Colonialism? Europe.

Does that justify our saying that all of that was due to Christianity?

Apartheid was supported by one of the major Christian churches in South Africa. Do you then say, "Ah, Christianity is responsible for all this racism?"[5]

* * *

Was jihadi terrorism the result of Western wars on Muslims? Or was it an integral part of the Islamic ethos? That was a hot topic for years.

If Islam was a violent religion, what explained the fact that the phenomenon of contemporary Muslim terrorism exploded only in recent years? The first generation of Muslim immigrants to the West weren't terrorists. It was the second generation, born or raised here, highly assimilated in the language, education, and pop culture of the West, who turned up as jihadists, as in the 2005 bombings of the London subway system, killing 56, and the year earlier the bombings of Madrid commuter trains, killing 195. Elizabeth Manningham-Buller, former head of Britain's MI5, said: "Our involvement in Iraq has radicalized a whole generation of young people." About the same message was conveyed by most Western intelligence services, namely, that the radicalization of young Muslims in the West was largely a result of U.S. foreign policy.

But we weren't supposed to probe this link. "To question this is almost to be terrorist oneself," noted British author Tariq Ali. The link between Western wars on Muslim nations and Muslim terrorism remained a taboo topic with much of the media, which proffered dozens of reasons for terrorism except the most obvious one.

The Arab Suspects

Here at home some innocent Canadians were caught in the large American anti-terrorism net with the assistance of Canadian security agencies. The most high-profile case was that of Maher Arar, a Syrian-born engineer in Ottawa. In the fall of 2002, he was returning from a vacation via New York, where on information provided by Canadian security agencies he was picked up and packed off to Syria. There he was detained for a year and tortured.

I was shamefully late in picking up his case — it seemed too complicated, too time-consuming. I didn't have the right contacts to credibly counter all the damaging allegations being floated by security services to cover their own tracks in his abduction and torture. It kept nagging me that I was ignoring what seemed like a clear case of injustice against a fellow Canadian whose case was being championed by an American non-governmental organization, the New York–based Center for Constitutional Rights, but not by Canadians. When I finally got around to it, I noted the many discrepancies in federal statements and called for the resignation of Solicitor General Wayne Easter and for a judicial probe into the scandal. Canadians needed to know what roles the Royal Canadian Mounted Police and the Canadian Security Intelligence Service played in Arar's arrest. What were they hiding?

Arar's supportive and indefatigable spouse, Monia Mazigh, had been lobbying human-rights groups and federal politicians. She was getting nowhere when out of the blue she was called by Alexa McDonough, federal leader of the New Democratic Party (NDP), who offered to take up her battle. McDonough raised the issue in Parliament and kept badgering the Liberal government, which didn't seem to want anything to do with the case. The NDP leader told me that she was often asked, "How do you know Arar isn't a terrorist?"

Her standard response was: "I don't. The justice system gets to decide that. But where's the justice in what's happening? For a lot of Canadians, that has been enough of an answer and caused them to wonder, 'What are we doing to this guy?'"[6]

I did a profile of Mazigh, a Ph.D. in economics from McGill University, about whom McDonough said: "She's highly intelligent and focused. She has an intensity about her. She has a sense of humour. She's humble and unassuming. She's extremely articulate [French, English, and Arabic]. At a meeting when we were discussing the Arar case, a lawyer in the room said, 'This woman belongs on the Supreme Court of Canada. She has a wisdom beyond her years, and an impeccable sense of justice and how it is supposed to work.'"

Mazigh told me that besides her love for her husband, what kept her going were their two children — daughter Baraa, six, and son Houd, 20 months — plus her faith. "I did not want them to be treated like second-class citizens. I did not want them to be accused or suspected of being a terrorist because of their origin, because they are Muslim, and they bear a name that has an Arabic sound. I had many spiritual discussions with myself. I felt closer to my Creator."

Told that she was being hailed as a new Canadian heroine, she said, "Oh, my goodness," and after a long moment of silence, added that she was forced by circumstances to play a public role. She urged Muslim men to "encourage their wives and daughters to raise their voices and be outspoken. Muslim attitudes here must change. We have to take the wonderful opportunity of democratic Canada to get educated and protect our rights."

The Man from Kingston

Arar's plight was put into context with the 2004 revelations about American torture at Abu Ghraib Prison in Iraq and of the Central Intelligence Agency (CIA)'s kidnapping of suspects and transfer to "black sites," secret torture chambers around the world, including the Bagram base north of Kabul. Shining a light on these dark deeds weren't the mainstream media, which were still in thrall of the virtuous war on terror. However, the Red Cross and human-rights organizations such as the New York–based Human Rights Watch and the American Civil Liberties Union (ACLU) did. In particular, an unknown young Canadian lawyer with the ACLU, Jameel Jaffer, challenged the many tentacles of the American juggernaut, from the White House to the Pentagon to the CIA.

The Canadian Club in Toronto, of which I was a director, invited the counsel for Human Rights Watch, Reed Brody, to speak. That was in 2004, and Maher Arar, now back in Canada, was asked to sit at the head table. Brody explained to a stunned audience "the globalization of abuse" and of "cross-border arrests that verge on kidnappings. Nationals of second or even third countries are being handed over and transferred from one country to another without due process, without resort to regular extradition proceedings and often in situations where they may face torture, cruel, inhumane, and degrading treatment, unfair trials, or even the death penalty." The U.S. had "rendered" suspects to Uzbekistan, Pakistan, Egypt, Saudi Arabia, and Morocco where they were tortured or mistreated, as Arar had been in Syria. This was the backdrop of the folly of Canadian soldiers in Afghanistan handing over detainees to Afghan and American custody where many were tortured.[7]

Jaffer, 34, was at the centre of many of the hundreds of ACLU lawsuits against the Bush administration, especially the Orwellian manifestations of the Patriot Act. The Federal Bureau of Investigation swooped down on libraries, bookstores, and universities to scoop up their lists of clients *and* slap them with gag orders to prohibit the institutions from breathing a word about the visits. Born in Kingston to immigrants from Tanzania, Jaffer studied in Toronto at Upper Canada College (UCC); graduated from Williams College, the prestigious American liberal arts institution; trained as an investment banker in Manhattan; abandoned the profession; did a master's degree at the University of Cambridge; and went to Harvard Law School. After that he clerked at the Supreme Court of Canada under Chief Justice Beverley McLachlin.

I knew nothing about Jaffer until I heard him speak at UCC, his alma mater. He was impressive — highly knowledgeable, precise, modest, calm. Yet no Canadian media said a word about this remarkable young Canadian doing prodigious work of historic importance at the heart of the war on terror.

Litigating under the Freedom of Information Act, Jaffer helped unearth 100,000 pages of secret documents — autopsy reports, interrogation orders, memos, emails, et cetera. Among them was the 2003 memo endorsing torture, written by the infamous John Yoo — a U.S. Department of Justice lawyer, aka Dr. Yes. They revealed, among other crimes, details of waterboarding, the simulated drowning technique employed by the Japanese during the Second World War. Contrary to Bush's claim that the abuses were an aberration by a few bad apples, the documents proved that torture was systemic and had been tried out first at Guantanamo. Abu Ghraib was, in fact, being Gitmo-ized when the horrible pictures were leaked.

Jaffer compiled the trove into a book, *Administration of Torture: A Documentary Record from Washington to Abu Ghraib and Beyond*,[8] the first such account. His co-author was a fellow lawyer at the ACLU, Amrit Singh, also of Indian origin. Daughter of India's then prime minister, Manmohan Singh, she skewered Bush while her father worked closely with the president to promote Indo-American bilateral relations. She felt no awkwardness — her father had brought her up to think independently.

Jaffer became my guide through the thicket of several aspects of the American war on terror, and thus, also some Canadian policies. In later years, I came to think of Jaffer as Canada's potential Barack Obama.

On the Arar case, a commission of inquiry was eventually set up. Justice Dennis O'Connor reported in 2006 that he found "no evidence to indicate that Mr. Arar committed any offence or that his activities constituted a threat to the security of Canada." He said Canadian officials had provided inaccurate and unfair information to the Americans. The Canadian federal government apologized to Arar and paid him $10 million compensation.

In 2007, on a trip to Halifax, I paid a courtesy call on Alexa McDonough, by then retired as NDP leader. I thanked her, as a Canadian, for having had the courage to take up the Arar case when no politician or journalist was willing to. "You embodied the best of Canada," I told her.

She replied with a simple thank you, then segued into "You take milk with your tea?"

The Other Tortured

Canadian security officials were also complicit in the torture of three other Muslim Arab Canadians in Syria. This came to light after a 2008 judicial inquiry, which I, among others, had called for. To head the inquiry, Ottawa chose Frank Iacobucci, a distinguished former judge of the Supreme Court of Canada.

Iacobucci concluded that Canadian officials were complicit in the torture of Abdullah Almalki, held for 22 months in a Damascus dungeon; Ahmad El Maati, imprisoned there for two months and for 24 months in Egypt; and Muayyed Nureddin, jailed for 33 days in Syria. The former judge found the allegations against the three — that they were potential terrorists and a danger to society — to be "misleading, inflammatory, and lacking interrogative foundation."

At the time of the inquiry, Iacobucci was chair of Torstar Corporation, owner of the *Toronto Star*. He often helped me understand complex public policy issues, especially related to national security. We, of course, refrained from talking about his inquiry until well after the release of his report.

Despite all of Iacobucci's legal brilliance — he'd been dean of law at the University of Toronto — he's an unassuming man with an immigrant sensibility. He'd often tell the story of how growing up in Vancouver in the 1940s he used to be embarrassed by his Italian mother's panini sandwiches, "brimming with a combination of egg, tomatoes, cheese, peppers, and prosciutto, whereas most of my Anglo-Saxon classmates had neat and tidy store-bought white bread with slim fillings. It was an awkward feeling: my sandwich being out of step with the 'majority sandwich' gave me a sense of not belonging."

The Iacobucci and O'Connor inquiries demonstrated two welcome developments of contemporary Canada: there was no longer an impunity for treating immigrants and non-whites differently than others, as had been the case throughout the country's history; and Canada was the only country in the world to have the moral compass and self-confidence to conduct two judicial reviews of post-9/11 wrongs. This was also evident in the case of five Canadian residents of Arab origins who had been held on secret evidence under what were called "security certificates." The Supreme Court of Canada ruled the practice unconstitutional.

My Man "Bee"

In the aftermath of 9/11, I missed Beland Honderich, the old publisher. Despite his reputation as a tough guy, I'd found him to be a reassuring presence and rather liked him. And dare I say, he used to reciprocate, albeit in the limited way he was capable of emotionally. But he'd retired to Vancouver. On a trip there, I met him for lunch in Stanley Park to apprise him of some of the pressures I'd been subjected to. He said telling the truth was always risky, but "the worst they can do is fire you — keep writing."

Easy enough for him to say. But he did make me realize that getting fired need not be the end of life.

Bee came to Toronto in 2004 to celebrate his son, John, receiving the Order of Canada. John had succeeded him not only as publisher but also as chair of Torstar's board. As soon as I entered John's crowded living room that day, Bee signalled me over from the sofa he was slumped on. As I leaned in, he said, "You're doing a good job. Keep writing." That was as big a compliment as I ever heard him extend anyone.

Toronto Star publisher Beland Honderich.

I didn't realize it then, but he had traits of some of my ancestors — unflashy, steady, steadfast in his beliefs, and unafraid of the sultan of the day or the received wisdom of the age. His conscience was his guide.

17

Afghanistan and Iraq Wars

In the Beginning

I SUPPORTED THE AMERICAN INVASION OF AFGHANISTAN, GIVEN THAT THE Taliban were hosting Osama bin Laden, even though it emerged later that they were more open to negotiating his surrender than the Americans admitted at the time. It didn't take long for the U.S. mission to start losing its moral high ground. The bombing campaign the Americans opened the war with showed little or no regard for civilian lives. U.S. troops also violated deeply rooted Afghan cultural norms such as stripping the privacy of Afghan households with nighttime raids on ostensibly suspected militants. No Afghan, man or woman, was ever going to forget and forgive. As a non-Afghan sitting in Canada, I cringed — "What are you doing, you idiots?"

Months passed before American general Tommy Franks admitted, "We don't do body counts." But that was already evident. Within a month, the death toll from the American bombing was already double that of the 9/11 murders.

The Americans were waging war on a people who had nothing to do with 9/11, just as they had with their sanctions on Afghanistan in the 1990s in retaliation for Osama bin Laden's bombs in Africa, which the Afghans weren't responsible for, either.

In my increasing doubts about the advisability of the Canadian military presence in Afghanistan, I found a venerable ally in Dalton Camp, fellow columnist at the *Toronto Star*. In a scathing column on January 13, 2002, lamenting "Ottawa's unbecoming frenzy to support this American war," he declared with succinct but thundering clarity: "Why are we in Afghanistan? What are we doing there? When and how do we get out?"

Camp, a former guru of the Conservative Party, had been a national figure for decades ever since he engineered the 1967 downfall of John Diefenbaker and the rise of Robert Stanfield. For that he won the everlasting enmity of the populist Dief's loyal followers in the Prairies. This I was made aware of in Manitoba, given that the *Brandon Sun* used to carry Camp's column. At the *Toronto Star*, as editorial page editor, I inherited him and found that Canada's most perceptive commentator and erudite columnist was also a decent and kind man. I took to calling him often for guidance on the thorniest of issues and found him always forthcoming, especially over lunches on his periodic visits to Toronto from his retirement home in Jemseg, New Brunswick.

He might have been a Conservative, but he was a Canadian first. He particularly disdained those who kowtowed to Washington — my kind of Canadian.

As if to confirm Camp's doubts, Canadian troops in Afghanistan acted as assistants to the GIs. By February 2002, they were handing over Al Qaeda prisoners into the eager hands of Americans, obviously without realizing they might be violating Canada's international and domestic obligations under the Geneva Conventions.

In July, Americans killed four Canadian soldiers in Afghanistan in "friendly fire." The gang clearly couldn't shoot straight, mistaking friends for foes.

The Americans also routinely lied about civilian casualties, claiming they killed "militants" and not admitting mistakes until confronted with incontrovertible facts. This was also the case with the U.S. bombing of wedding parties, slaughtering dozens of civilians. America, drunk with power, no longer had a moral core to its conduct.

War in Iraq

Even while the Afghan mission was floundering, the United States was hell-bent on invading Iraq, though Saddam Hussein had nothing to do with 9/11. Despite the many obvious lies told to rationalize the invasion, Canada's political and media right wingers dutifully lined up and berated Prime Minister Jean Chrétien for resisting. Opposition leader Stephen Harper, sounding more pro-American than the Americans, seemed less concerned about whether joining the war would be in Canada's interest but more about Ottawa obeying Washington's orders, even though public opposition to the conflict grew by the day.

In January 2003, I was in India and spoke to Inder Gujral, the country's former prime minister and easily the most thoughtful and moderate Indian leader since Jawaharlal Nehru. An intellectual in the mould of Václav Havel, the Czech playwright and president, Gujral told me: "It would be a great tragedy for the world if there was to be a war on Iraq. It would be particularly calamitous for our region. The main American aim seems to be to gain control of the world's second-largest oil reserves and to dictate the flow of oil to the world market. This has, in fact, long been the objective of American diplomacy in oil-rich West Asia." Gujral recalled a 1990 meeting with U.S. secretary of state James Baker. "He minced no words when he told me: 'Oil is our civilization, and we will never permit any demon to sit over it.' That still seems to be the main objective of the American policy."

* * *

On the way back from India, I went to an anti-war demonstration in London and was surprised by its size and intensity. The million-strong anti-war march was the biggest public protest in modern British history. The first thing that struck me was how un-British it was, despite the very British orderliness of the human tide that kept rolling patiently along central London all Saturday afternoon before converging on Hyde Park. The rally was to British politics what the communal mourning at Princess Diana's 1997 funeral had been to its sociology — a sudden and sharp break from tradition. More people turned up than anyone imagined possible. Most shed their British reserve for banter with strangers. Their diversity — young and old, white and visible minorities, poor and middle class, grunge and Gucci, veteran protesters and first-time marchers — constituted a rainbow coalition of the North American kind.

The anti-war movement worldwide offered an interesting insight. In the 60 nations where protests were held, the biggest turnouts were where governments bucked their electorates to back the American march toward war — Italy (two million), Spain (two million), and Australia (500,000, the biggest political protest in Aussie history).

An overwhelming majority of Canadians were opposed, as well. On the eve of a visit to the White House, Prime Minister Jean Chrétien phoned me at home to ask what he should be telling the president. "Far be it from me to advise a prime minister," I replied, "but I've been hearing growing opposition to our involvement."

"Yes, that's what I hear, especially from immigrants," he agreed.

His antenna was up: the new Canada of the more recently arrived people from around the world, innately skeptical of the United States, didn't want to be dragged into the war. The democratization of the Canadian perspective on the world has been one of the biggest but least understood by-products of our pluralism, which Chrétien clearly understood.

War Whoops

Yet there was no let-up from the pro-war lobby, now joined by Brian Mulroney, king of schmooze to the Americans. As prime minister he'd lined up Canada's participation in the 1991 Gulf War within hours of a phone call from President George H.W. Bush. He had since developed extensive personal corporate interests in America. Now he was echoing business and right-wing circles in advocating an axis of convenience between Ottawa and Washington. Their case was simple: being a courtier to the White House would earn Canada brownie points, cashable later for valuable contacts and lucrative contracts. There was a rather unusual pro-war demonstration at Toronto City Hall where Ontario premier Ernie Eves and Bay Street mavens arrived in limousines. The text of his speech, released to the media in advance, had him calling Prime Minister Chrétien "a coward" for not jumping on the war bandwagon, though Eves had the good sense to drop that line when speaking. Some in the well-heeled crowd even carried placards calling for regime change in Ottawa. Eves's predecessor as premier, Mike Harris, also made himself clear: "If it comes down to Jean Chrétien or Don Cherry speaking for Canada, I'd take Don Cherry."

* * *

I wrote a stream of columns on the Iraq war, among them: "Tony Blair, Chief Spin Doctor for George Bush"; "World Wary of Bush War Case"; "Imperial War Machine on the Move"; "The Case Against the War"; "Keep Leash on Dogs of War"; "Canada Should Sit Out This War."

While most readers agreed, those who didn't made themselves clear:

- If you like Iraq that much why don't you move there?
- My dear sir: I believe you are an unhappy man.
- I understand your loyalties are to the Muslim world judging by your name.
- No one wants Muslims in this country. Do us all a favor and go home to Pakistan.
- You're a sick demagogue, spreading your Islamist lies. The Iraqi people want to be free, you wish to keep them enslaved. You should live in Iran.
- When do you retire?
- You bloody terrorist lover.
- You have mad cow disease.
- My greatest wish is to meet you alone and rearrange your pukey little face.

Busy Blowing It

Within a month of the invasion, it was apparent that, as in Afghanistan, the United States had little or no clue what was happening on the ground. The straws in the wind were social and religious, which the Americans almost always read wrong or didn't read at all.

Following the fall of the Taliban, Afghans started shaving their beards. After the fall of Saddam, Iraqis grew theirs. That was the unmistakable assertion of majority Shia religious and political identity. If there was any doubt, it was dispelled by a million pilgrims, including women, turning up at the holy cities of Najaf and Karbala, pilgrimages that Saddam had banned. That turnout was of far greater import than the photo-op toppling of Saddam's statue in Baghdad. What made the pilgrimages even more potent were the anti-American slogans. Their message was clear: "Thank you for freeing us from Saddam, but now please go home." Can anyone recall a time in history when the liberators of an oppressed people outlived their welcome in so short a period?

Iraqis knew that their country wouldn't have been targeted had it been a major producer of, say, corn rather than oil. What they saw, they liked even less — sufficient troops and tanks protecting the oil fields of the south and north, even the oil ministry in Baghdad, but none to guard the national museum and library, both of which got looted and destroyed.

"All it'd have taken was two soldiers and a tank" to safeguard those great treasures, said Reza Baraheni, Canadian-Iranian poet, human-rights activist, and my predecessor as president of PEN Canada. He had escaped to Canada in 1998, and, unlike many other victims and critics of the Islamic regime, didn't become an apologist for Iran's adversaries, including the United States. He was so agitated by the twin disasters in Baghdad that, distraught, he phoned me. I said I could quote him in my column but that preferably he'd write down his thoughts for publication in the *Toronto Star*. He obliged with the most learned lament that I was to read on the cultural tragedy:

> The Museum was the cradle of Eastern and Western civilizations and cultures. The library held the collective memory of many peoples who lived in the Middle East or passed through it. The list of these civilizations is long: Assyrians, Akkadians, Sumerians, Babylonians, Arabs, Jews, Medes, Persians, Parthians, Turks, and Mongols.
>
> Baghdad, one of the most ancient cities of the world, means God-given. It seems that God gave the people of

17 Afghanistan and Iraq Wars

Iraq two things: oil, and a collective memory, with its books and artefacts gathered in their library and museum. But the world's greatest power, the U.S., was careful to secure Iraq's oil wells but did nothing to protect the cultural sites, the patrimony of all humanity.[1]

Much of Baghdad — the birthplace of Sufism, whence my ancestors had gone to India in the 14th century — was destroyed, as it had been by the Mongols in the 13th century.

* * *

Another internal dynamic the Americans didn't understand was the powerful hold of the religious class on Iraqis. Unlike the mostly illiterate Taliban in Afghanistan, the clergy in Iraq, as in Iran, are highly learned. Shia Iranians and Iraqis defer to their ayatollahs, the most respected of whom in Iraq was Grand Ayatollah Syed Ali Sistani, with followers all over the world, including North America and Europe. While Ayatollah Khomeini in Iran had evolved into a political firebrand, Sistani was a "quietist," keeping away from politics. Yet he had blessed the American invasion, given Saddam's murderous rule. However, the Americans managed to alienate even him by their heavy-handed tactics and lack of respect for Iraqi lives. He refused to take a call from George W. Bush and wouldn't countenance a visit by Paul Bremer, the American administrator of Iraq.

I could relate to that — the reverence for the religiously learned — and to the eternal tussle between church and state, not in the sense understood in the West, as keeping the two apart, but rather as rival forces of power forever in a delicate dance. What was happening in Iraq was a replay of the classic standoff of Islamic history: the ruler versus the saint, with the former desperate for the blessing of the latter but being denied. Bush, commander of the biggest military power in history, was snubbed by an aging cleric living in a modest home in a dusty alley in a small town. And Bremer, the interim ruler of conquered Iraq, was denied an audience and the legitimacy of a holy handshake. The Americans never recovered from the brush-off.

As in Afghanistan, the Americans blamed a neighbour — in this case, Iran. But Pakistan and Iran, trying to safeguard their interests, had more reasons to interfere in their neighbouring nations than did America, having come from halfway around the world. Iran and Iraq had long-standing and even deeper ties with each other than Afghanistan and Pakistan ever did. Scapegoating Iran wasn't going to help manage postwar Iraq, just as blaming Pakistan wasn't helping the botched mission in Afghanistan.

Becoming the Enemy

You know you've descended into depravity when you begin doing what you despise your enemies for. American troops killed Saddam's two sons, Uday and Qusay, instead of capturing them and putting them on trial for their many heinous crimes. Worse, the U.S. troops made a macabre display of the brothers' shattered bodies. Defense Secretary Donald Rumsfeld said he was "glad" that he authorized the release of grisly photos: "I honestly believe that these two are particularly bad characters and it is important for the Iraqi people to know they are not coming back." That was the same logic Saddam used after eliminating his enemies, as did the Taliban. Upon conquering Kabul in 1994, they strung up the mangled body of the toppled president by a traffic control post to let the citizenry know the evil ruler was gone forever.

In 2006, Saddam was sentenced to death. Bush called it "an important milestone in Iraq becoming a democracy." But much of the non-Western world saw it as jungle justice. In a sham trial, he was found guilty of ordering the killing of 148 Shias in 1982. But he had committed far worse crimes, most when he was a close ally of the United States. He had been ours until he wasn't. Just like bin Laden. Just like the Taliban/mujahideen. Just like Muammar Gaddafi — a bad guy who was deemed a good guy, then a bad guy again. After being toppled in 2011, he was cornered, beaten, sodomized with a bayonet, and shot several times by a mob aligned with the West. So much for the rule of law.

War in Afghanistan

In 2005, Prime Minister Paul Martin and General Rick Hillier, the chief of the defence staff, quietly committed Canadian soldiers to a combat mission in Kandahar Province where the Taliban insurgency was well underway.

17 Afghanistan and Iraq Wars

Trigger-happy Hillier drank the American Kool-Aid. He was going to "squish" the Taliban, those "detestable murderers and scumbags," who, if not vanquished there, would come to Canada to spread their "venom" here. Martin wanted to placate the Americans by doing penance for Canada not joining the Iraq war. In agreeing to have Canadian troops replace Americans in Kandahar, he committed them to a mission impossible: battle the Taliban, provide security to the populace, *and* lead reconstruction teams to win the battle of hearts and minds. Kiss and kill at the same time. Wage war and make peace. In reality, they were there merely for Ottawa to score brownie points in Washington.

When Martin lost the 2006 election to Stephen Harper, the new government was even more gung-ho about the war, as were most of the media and the growing army of military and security experts parading on TV networks. Yet anyone familiar with the region and its history could tell that the war was going nowhere.

The one person in the world likely to have the clearest and least biased view of Afghanistan was Lakdhar Brahimi. He'd been the U.N. special envoy to Afghanistan twice during the 1990s and after 9/11. I met him at a conference in Saudi Arabia and spoke to him again in the post-Taliban era. He was the one who organized the 2001 Bonn conference and then the *loya jirga*, the traditional gathering of tribes, that legitimized Hamid Karzai as president. Since then, he'd been the special envoy to Iraq and Darfur. I reached him in his Paris apartment. He told me:

> We have expected miracles in Afghanistan, but miracles don't happen very often on earth. A country that has systematically been destroyed for 25 years is not going to become paradise in 25 or 35 months.
>
> The Taliban had never been defeated. They had only been pushed out of Kabul, were scattered all over, and demoralized, but now some of them have regrouped and are reminding the world that they exist.
>
> One of my own biggest mistakes was not to speak to the Taliban in 2002 and 2003. It was not possible to get them in the tent of the Bonn conference because of 9/11 and they

themselves were not eager. But immediately after that, we should have spoken to those who were willing to speak to us.

That I consider to be my mistake — a very big mistake.

What other mistakes had he made?

The international force should have gone out of Kabul when people outside Kabul were begging to have them. All we were asking for is 3,000 to 5,000 more troops. But we never got them. If we had, we'd have done much better. But the Americans — Donald Rumsfeld, in particular — were not interested in nation-building. The Americans did come around by 2003, but by that time, we had lost a hell of a lot of time.

What should Canada do? "You have to be there to help contain terrorism — not by killing terrorists, which is what's happening now, but by preventing people from becoming terrorists. Fight drug production better, fight corruption better. And get along better with Pakistan."[2]

I went to Pakistan.

The Wild West

In both Islamabad, the capital, and in the northern Pakistani province of Baluchistan along the border from Kandahar Province, I got blanket denials on Pakistani complicity. General Pervez Musharraf, Pakistan's president, responding to charges that he was letting Taliban leaders operate freely from Pakistan said: "Tell me, how many Taliban leaders have been caught in Afghanistan. Name me one."

Shaukat Sultan, his spokesperson, was less belligerent: "We don't deny that Taliban come and go, but that's not the entire truth. If 25 percent of the problem lies on our side, 75 percent lies on that side."

Information Minister Tariq Azim told me: "If the U.S. cannot stop infiltration from Mexico, how do you expect us to control our border with Afghanistan that's mostly desolate and mountainous?"

For me, it was best to go to the Wild West border — the Durand Line, drawn in 1890–95 by the colonial British, 2,400 kilometres of it from Iran to China through what was still mostly uninhabited terrain. Kabul had never accepted the demarcation line. Nor did the tribal Pashtuns who lived on either side of the border, at least 15 million on either side.

In Quetta, the capital of the rugged Pakistani province of Baluchistan, I met Owais Ahmad Ghani, the governor. Why wasn't he controlling the comings and goings of the Taliban? He snapped: "Suppose we are letting the Taliban cross the border to Afghanistan. Why aren't they being picked up when they step onto the Afghan side? American troops are there, Canadian troops are there, other NATO troops are there."

But the International Security Assistance Force wasn't in the business of controlling the border. "They are in the business of controlling terrorism, aren't they?" he shot back.

It was noon Friday and time for the communal afternoon prayer. "No need to go anywhere," Ghani told me. "There is a small mosque in my compound." Built in 1876 for the British resident, his elegant residence had high ceilings and lots of teak wood.

When our prayers were done, I commented, "The imam's sermon was short and sweet."

"He's been told to keep it brief. That's one order of mine that's carried out faithfully."[3]

Good for you, Guv, I thought.

The Afghan-Pakistani Border

The next day, I left at 3:00 a.m. for a 138-kilometre journey to the border post of Chaman, abutting Kandahar Province, not far from where Canadian troops were deployed. I suggested to the driver that he avoid the bone-rattling ride by driving on what looked like the smoother shoulder.

"No," he said, "it may have mines."

The driver wouldn't even stop for the pre-dawn prayers until he got to a military post and the relative safety of its sandbagged compound.

Soon, we were climbing the hair-raising bends of a high mountain. The rising sun exposed the roadkill — three turned-over vehicles by the roadside and one truck rolled down into the valley below. Mercifully, we were slowed down to a crawl behind a line of trucks, belching black smoke from their heavily leaded gasoline, or perhaps, kerosene.

At the border post of Chaman, clouds of dust rose from the traffic already underway early in the morning. As in most Muslim nations, the day began soon after pre-dawn prayers. A sea of humanity flowed through in both directions, mostly on foot, bikes, or donkey carts. They were mainly Pashtun, as were the Taliban. And many or all those at this crossing could be Taliban.

Chaman was the transit point for bilateral trade, the focal point of which was an Afghan bazaar just north. Most of the vehicles were headed there, carrying consumer goods. But the most arresting sight was a long line of flat-bed donkey carts coming south, bringing scrap metal. The Afghans, of necessity, had become environmentalists — experts at squeezing the most out of captured tanks, vehicles, and machines, then recycling the dead heaps.

Opium might have been coming, too, to be smuggled through Baluchistan's western desert region, some to Iran but most to ports on the Arabian Sea, bound for Europe and beyond. Besides the traders, the human tide at the crossing consisted of day labourers and family visitors, in both directions, plus the sick seeking treatment in Quetta.

The Pakistani officer in charge, Lieutenant-Colonel Nasir Rehman, had one of his clerks read me the statistics from the day before: pedestrians, 21,193; vehicles, 1,563; bicycles and motorcycles, 6,792; donkey carts, 1,262.

Everyone crossing the border had to have identity cards. But given the male Pashtun norm — beard and turban — the cards couldn't be all that conclusive at a cursory glance, which was all the time the guards had before doing a quick body check. And women's ID cards didn't have photos, following a protest against invasion of their privacy.

Under American pressure, Pakistan had installed six biometric scanners for retina readings and fingerprints. No sooner was that done than the resistance began. A fee of 150 rupees for the new card didn't help. While the Pashtuns historically resisted control over their free movement, there was another factor at work — an estimated one million phony IDs in circulation, bought and sold on the black market. The machines were destroyed. By the time I saw them in their aluminum-roofed shed, they were coated in dust.

17 Afghanistan and Iraq Wars

Colonel Rehman took me up the 36 steps to the top of the Friendship Gate to survey the scene below. Unlike many international border posts, this one didn't have a no man's land. The border straddled a village. "If you draw an imaginary line through the village," he told me, "you can see the living room is in Pakistan and the kitchen in Afghanistan."

Those who thought Pakistan should do more to control the Taliban traffic should have come to this bustling post. Or any of the other five along the Durand Line. Or the numerous illegal pathways through the mountains and valleys.

* * *

One Canadian who did understand the complicated relationship between Pakistan and Afghanistan was Bill Graham, chair of the House of Commons Committee on Foreign Affairs and later foreign minister, then defence minister. But he understood it too late, as he put it forthrightly in his 2016 memoir, *The Call of the World*:

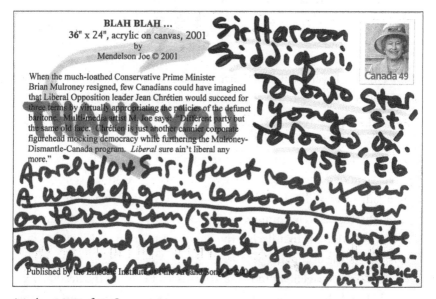

Another missive from Joe.

More knowledge of Afghanistan's porous borders and a better understanding of its tribal conflicts would have been useful when I became defence minister. They would have given me the context to appreciate what President Musharraf meant when he spoke of Pakistan's inability to control the Northwest Frontier. And I might have raised more concerns when assessing Canada's commitment to send our soldiers into an environment that was unlike anything they had encountered before.[4]

Bill, who died in 2022, was as Canadian as they make them — modest, decent, pleasant, kind, humane, straightforward, uncomplicated, generous, giving, loving. He carried those attributes into politics and maintained them even as Canadian politics got nasty with the importation of U.S. tactics of treating opponents as enemies to be destroyed, not adversaries to debate.

As a columnist, I was highly critical of his policies as defence minister, especially the mission to Kandahar Province. Yet he remained gracious whenever we talked. In retirement, we became friends.

* * *

From Quetta, I went 800 kilometres northeast to Peshawar and beyond to Jalozai, a refugee camp I first visited in 1980 when it sprang up after the Soviet invasion of Afghanistan. At that time, it had a few tents and a few hundred refugees. Now Jalozai was a semi-permanent ghetto of 54,000 people in mud houses abutting narrow lanes with open sewers. It was one of nearly 50 camps across Pakistan. Between them and the urban centres, there were about three million Afghan refugees still in Pakistan, and yet more batches of refugees were coming, fleeing the chaos of southern Afghanistan. The irony of Afghans first fleeing the Soviet occupation and then NATO's wasn't lost on the occupants of Jalozai.

A speaking engagement took me to Brussels, Belgium, the headquarters of NATO and the European Commission. The consensus there was that allied troops could hold off the Taliban in Afghanistan to buy the time needed to establish the security to do the development work to win over the Afghans in the troubled south. More hope than policy.

Bad to Worse

The Iraqification of Afghanistan became clearer by the month. A spreading insurgency with roadside bombs and suicide bombers. Widespread public insecurity, civilian deaths, joblessness, homelessness, and hunger. A weak and highly partisan central government confined to barricaded compounds in the capital, not unlike the Green Zone in Baghdad.

The Afghan situation was bleaker, given the higher level of corruption, record opium production, and mountainous topography. The Canadian mission had veered off into American-style warfare at the expense of reconstruction and development. Yet it had failed to control the insurgency and might be feeding it. The quandary was the same as in Iraq: couldn't win, couldn't quite quit. We were there because we were there.

In 2008, Harper named John Manley, the hawkish former Liberal deputy prime minister under Jean Chrétien, to assess the Canadian mission. Manley came back with an honest enumeration of the many failures of the mission yet recommended its continuation. But he urged shifting from combat to construction; promoting a "negotiated political and social reconciliation"; and getting Pakistan onside. That was what Lakdhar Brahimi had said, more or less, two years earlier.

Harper ignored most of the advice except to extend the Afghan mission. But he did come to the realization that "we are not ever going to defeat the insurgency." Two years later, he did "cut and run" and wound down the combat mission, opting instead for a small contingent in Kabul to train Afghan forces, an assignment that ended in 2014. To mark the occasion, he organized "a day of honour," paid for with handouts by corporate Canada. He wanted his photo op but didn't want to pay for it, though he'd just shelled out for a state funeral for Jim Flaherty, his former finance minister — a brazen breach of protocol to canonize his and the Conservative government's management of the economy.

Killing Bin Laden

In 2011, the Americans assassinated Osama bin Laden, who was hiding in Pakistan. His bullet-riddled body was flown to Afghanistan and then 1,287 kilometres west for a water burial in the Arabian Sea. The Americans seemed afraid of him even in death, holding back the news until the deed was done and leaving no trace of him for a potential monument on earth. Former Republican vice-presidential candidate Sarah Palin and others demanded the grisly photo of his gunshot face — "Show photo ... it's part of the mission." She echoed Donald Rumsfeld's rationale for the display of the mangled bodies of Saddam's sons.

Since the 1970s, there had been a ban on assassinations by American personnel. The Central Intelligence Agency (CIA) had tried to eliminate the leaders of Cuba and the Congo and were also involved in assassination plots in the Dominican Republic, Chile, and Vietnam. But after 9/11, assassinations were rebranded as "targeted killings," and the United States joined Israel and others in the assassination business.

Part of the intelligence on bin Laden's whereabouts had come from waterboarding at Guantanamo Bay that Obama had long opposed. However, Bin Laden's killing was cheered by Obama — "We got him" — and by flag-waving crowds near the White House and Ground Zero and in sports arenas with shouts of "U.S.A., U.S.A!" That prompted *Toronto Star* sports columnist Cathal Kelly to write: "By American lights, it was an emotional, patriotic spectacle. To this outsider, it had an unseemly aspect. A celebration of death smacks of a barbecue held outside the gates to the gas chamber."

The Verdict

Nearly 41,000 members of the Canadian Armed Forces participated in the 13-year Afghan mission, Canada's longest war, at a cost of $18 billion and the loss of 158 soldiers and seven civilians. For the price of a paint job, Harper renamed the Trans-Canada as the Highway of Heroes, rather than look after the returning soldiers suffering from post-traumatic stress disorder, as many as 3,500 of them, of whom 175 committed suicide.

I had my share of regrets. Instead of critiquing nearly every aspect of the mission, I should have clearly and more forcefully called for quitting

17 Afghanistan and Iraq Wars

Afghanistan once the job of toppling the Taliban was done. In retrospect, many of my columns read like someone taking potshots without offering a clarion call to rally public opinion against the folly of the Afghan mission.

Canada did well to get out when it did; the United States lingered for another decade. With each passing month, one could see the wisdom of the Taliban, whatever one thought of them: "You have the clock, we have the time."

Obama could have ended the war as Vice President Joe Biden kept telling him to. But the president didn't have the courage to admit he was wrong to call it a good war as opposed to the bad war in Iraq, which he opposed and which did wind down by 2011. Having boxed himself in, he extended the Afghan mission under pressure from the Pentagon, for which Afghanistan served several purposes: a theatre rich in career advancement opportunities, a training ground for troops, a testing ground for the latest drones and bunker-busting bombs, and a strategic locale for bases close to China, Russia, and Iran.

Donald Trump tried, in his clumsy way, to extricate the United States from Afghanistan on any terms dictated by the Taliban. But it wasn't until

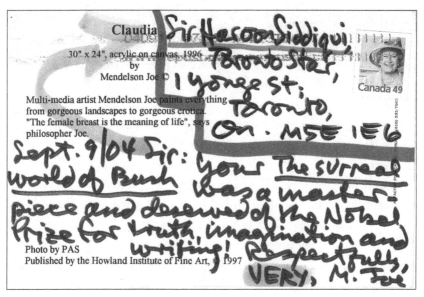

One more from Joe.

Biden assumed the presidency that the venture ended disastrously in 2021, the way many unpopular foreign occupations do: in panic and chaos amid a mad scramble to get out and a chorus of pleas to rescue those who helped "us" — translators, drivers, fixers, guards, gardeners, cooks, cleaners. That was the thrust of much media coverage for months in North America and Britain, not of the mess left behind. The real scandal was that we had abandoned a whole nation, especially after promising it the moon.

America's longest-ever war — longer than the First and Second World Wars and the Vietnam War, in fact, all three combined — revealed America as rudderless, incompetent, and incapable of nation-building. Nor even able to win wars decisively and create a stable social order. It only knew how to kill on a mass scale.

When President Hamid Karzai repeatedly condemned the cavalier American bombings of civilians, he was badmouthed as deranged, unstable, unreliable. He might have been all those, but he was on the money in articulating widespread Afghan disgust. On a 2013 visit to Washington, he showed Obama gruesome pictures of an American standing with his boot on an elderly man's severed head. "I asked Obama, 'How can you expect me to be your ally and to go along with such actions when I am the Afghan president and am supposed to protect my people?'" Karzai recalled to Jon Lee Anderson of *The New Yorker*.[5]

Americans and their acolytes said they were setting up democracy, even if by force. Yet they ensured that in 2014 Ashraf Ghani was "elected" president. That election was widely seen to have been stolen from Abdullah Abdullah, who opposed the bilateral security arrangement with the United States. There was skulduggery on both sides, but one was better finagled to the right result. The Americans said they were establishing the rule of law but detained scores of Afghans, tortured many, and kidnapped some to Guantanamo Bay. They promised transparency but bribed murderous warlords under the table with suitcases full of cash.

Most Afghans, meanwhile, remained dirt poor, especially in rural areas where more than two-thirds of the population of 39 million lived and where some of the worst American and NATO atrocities took place. For them, the Taliban were the lesser evil. Living among them, the Taliban knew the feuds

17 Afghanistan and Iraq Wars

and friendships among the tribes — and didn't wage cultural warfare on Islam and Muslims, didn't burn the Qur'an, or draw or defend the Danish cartoons of the Prophet Muhammad.

* * *

Some good was obviously done in Afghanistan. Al Qaeda was scattered, roads were paved, schools and health facilities were constructed. Millions of kids, including girls, went to school. Hundreds of schools got built, even if not all got occupied and some were abandoned, like several other development projects, because of lack of security — an unending circularity of astoundingly expensive stupidity. Women were getting empowered, voting in droves, and running for a fifth of the federal and provincial seats. Civil society was strengthened. Afghans could fly kites and listen to music and sing, albeit only in urban centres.

Most rural areas, however, remained blighted. Far too many Afghans had little or no security. NATO kept comforting itself that most civilian deaths were caused by the Taliban. That was an admission that NATO, including Canada, failed to prevent the massacres, thereby falling short of the most basic duty of an occupying power: to provide security to civilians. Across the country, there was always a humanitarian crisis, with hundreds of thousands of people displaced, many living in squalid camps, and malnutrition among children increasing, while the West kept patting itself on the back for all the splendid things it was doing in Afghanistan.

True to form, the Americans found it hard to swallow their defeat and accept the reality of the Taliban takeover. Rather than give them what they craved most, official recognition in return for a promise of good behaviour — preserving women's rights, protecting religious and ethnic minorities, safeguarding civil society, and controlling the estimated 1,000 or so Al Qaeda/Islamic State jihadists — the Americans imposed a new round of sanctions, thereby starving ordinary Afghans yet again. Worse, Washington froze all Afghan assets in the United States, nearly $7 billion. The sanctions — a revenge, really — aren't likely to be any more successful than the decades-long ones on Cuba or Iran.

Collateral Damage

Pakistan was the main victim of the crises in Afghanistan, both during the 1980–89 Soviet occupation and the 2001–21 U.S. occupation. The Soviet invasion sent nearly five million Afghan refugees into Pakistan, of whom only two million ultimately returned home. The Afghans also brought a drug and Kalashnikov culture to Pakistan. Post-9/11, Bush had given Pakistan an ultimatum: co-operate in Afghanistan or be bombed back to the Stone Age. Pakistan co-operated.

The Afghan conflict kept spilling over into Pakistan. The Pakistani Taliban — some nurtured by Pakistan — and other militant offshoots mounted insurgency after insurgency in Pakistan, some in retaliation for illegal American drone attacks pursuing militants. By 2021, about 70,000 Pakistanis had been killed and one million displaced in the areas along the Afghan border. While the United States gave Pakistan $20 billion in aid, Pakistan estimated its economy lost about $150 billion in disruptions, loss of tourism, and loss of investment.

The 9/11 terrorists murdered nearly 3,000 Americans. The United States presided over the killing of 240,000 in Afghanistan and in neighbouring Pakistan as well as between 186,000 and 209,000 civilians in Iraq. Neither the Afghans and the Pakistanis nor the Iraqis had anything to do with 9/11.

If one adds the nearly one million Iraqis who died slow deaths during the 1990s under American sanctions, including 500,000 children, the total number of Muslims killed under America's watch between 1991 and 2021 stood at close to two million Muslims dead.

There was little or no outrage in the West. Even liberals, guardians of human rights and champions of the rule of law, were mute. In nations where the United States waged its war on terror, overtly and covertly, about 38 million people were displaced. And there was the cultural warfare on Islam and Muslims, the prime victims of which were the estimated 30 million fellow citizens in the West who happened to be Muslims.

Democracy, What Democracy?

George W. Bush et al. said that terrorists hated us for the West's freedoms. So, the best antidote to terrorism was democracy. Yet the United States

17 Afghanistan and Iraq Wars

continued to help crush it in Muslim lands. That pattern dates to 1953 when the CIA organized a coup in Iran to topple an elected prime minister and replace him with the first shah, a piece of skulduggery that played its role in the 1979 revolution and continues to drive the revolutionary regime's deep mistrust of the United States, "the Great Satan."

In Turkey, the United States backed the 1980 military coup: "We admire the way in which law and order has been restored." After another coup in 1997 that toppled a democratically elected government, President Bill Clinton remained suitably silent. Clinton also found the dictatorial Suharto of Indonesia "our kind of guy." In Algeria, the second-largest African nation, the military annulled a 1991 election that the Islamic Salvation Front had won decisively. The junta's rationale was that an Islamic coalition couldn't be trusted with a secular state. France, Algeria's former colonizer, and others in the West winked as the Algerian regime presided over the death of nearly 100,000 of its citizens during the decade. Amnesty International noted: "The international community has turned its back on the Algerian human-rights tragedy. Such indifference in the face of so much horror is an abdication of their responsibility." Or a matter of deliberate policy. In Pakistan, the United States had the closest working relations with all its military dictators: General Mohammad Ayub Khan (1958–66), General Yahya Khan (1969–71), General Muhammad Zia-ul-Haq (1978–88), and General Pervez Musharraf (2001–8).

When Hamas won the election in Gaza in 2006 fair and square, the United States and its allies designated it a terrorist organization and began blockading and starving Gazans, turning the Strip into what has been termed "the world's largest prison." And the West continues to support Palestinian President Mahmoud Abbas, who suspended elections after he won in 2005; he has been Israel's security partner in the military occupation of the West Bank.

The 2011 Arab Spring made the United States and its allies nervous; they feared that the toppling of dictators would open the floodgates to democratic governments that would be more responsive to the popular will than taking orders from Washington, D.C., and other Western capitals. President Barack Obama finally welcomed the Arab Spring but quickly fell in line when Egypt's General Abdel Fattah al-Sisi toppled Mohamed Morsi, the country's first-ever elected leader in its history, and killed more than 1,000 of his supporters. The United States had returned to backing Egypt's dictators: Anwar Sadat, Hosni Mubarak, and General Sisi. As for Canada, Prime Minister Stephen Harper welcomed the Sisi military coup as "a return to stability."

Given this backdrop, it's no surprise that of the only three democracies in the greater Middle East — Israel, Turkey, and Iran — the two Muslim ones have been the most reviled in the West. Turkey and Iran are degraded democracies, all right, but the Muslim states most favoured by the West in that region crush any and every democratic firmament.

What does all this have to do with Canada? Rather than breaking free of America's anti-democratic tendencies, Canada has been complicit in this deeply flawed and dishonest power structure. In the case of Saudi Arabia, Canada has emulated the United States in cashing in with defence contracts of its own, supplying billions of dollars of combat vehicles and other military equipment, some of which was used by Saudi Arabia in its brutal war in Yemen. And in 2021, Canada sold $34 million of military equipment to Algeria.[6]

Sure, Canada has constraints, given our trade with the United States and membership in the Western alliance. But from Lester B. Pearson, to Brian Mulroney, to Lloyd Axworthy, to Jean Chrétien, Canada distinguished itself by pursuing independent foreign policy initiatives. Talking up democracy while actively undermining it is at the heart of the great divide between the West and the world's two billion Muslims. In fact, with Canada's changing demography, a majority Canadian public opinion, too, now sees through Ottawa's hypocrisy. Yet no political leader wants to challenge this Canadian capitulation to American and Israeli interests in the Middle East and take Canada back to its honourable position of being a neutral, honest broker.

18

Cultural Warfare on Muslims

THE WAR ON TERROR WAS TO BE WAGED ON TERRORISTS, NOT MUSLIMS, LET alone Islam. That was what U.S. president George W. Bush and his sidekick, U.K. prime minister Tony Blair, promised. Either they didn't mean it, or they lost control of the narrative to war propagandists and to those whose geopolitical interests were served by a clash of civilizations between the Judeo-Christian world and the world of Muslims.

The war on terror became a cultural war on Muslims and Islam on a scale not seen since the Crusades. It rippled across the United States, Europe, and even Canada. Newer ways were found to insult, humiliate, and demean Muslims:

- Burning the Qur'an.
- Insulting the Prophet Muhammad.
- Firebombing, ransacking, and vandalizing mosques and Muslim institutions.
- Objecting to the building or expanding of mosques, minarets, and even Muslim cemeteries.
- Punching, kicking, shoving, and bullying hijabi women.
- Governments and public institutions, especially across Europe, led mostly by men, ordering women and girls what

to wear or not to, like the ayatollahs and the mullahs in the East.

- Restricting *halal* options in school cafeterias and introducing pork into school menus.
- Doing anything, everything, to jar the religious sensibilities of Muslims and to demean and devalue them.

Islam Bashing

Bush's spiritual adviser, Franklin Graham, son of Billy Graham, called Islam "an evil and wicked religion." Evangelist Pat Robertson insisted the Prophet Muhammad was "an absolute wild-eyed fanatic." Cardinal Ratzinger, who became Pope Benedict XVI, opposed Turkey's entry into Europe on religious grounds: "Turkey should seek its future among Islamic organizations, not in the Christian-rooted Europe." Blair said he was reading the Qur'an to understand terrorism. He didn't say whether he'd consulted the Bible to understand Irish terrorism or the Serb ethnic cleaning of Muslim Bosnians.

In Denmark, where the infamous cartoons of the Prophet Muhammad originated, Queen Margrethe said that there was "something scary" about the "totalitarianism that's part of Islam." French right-wing leader Marine Le Pen compared Muslims praying on a street to Nazi occupation.

Too many liberals turned out to be closet bigots. Cosmopolitan and at ease with other minorities, they said or tolerated things about Muslims and Islam they never would about any other people.

Muslim-bashers included British novelist Martin Amis: "The Muslim community will have to suffer until it gets its house in order.... Not letting them travel. Deportation.... Curtailing of freedoms. Strip-searching people who look like they are from the Middle East or Pakistan.... Discriminatory stuff, until its hurts the whole community and they start getting tough with their children."[1]

Many of the attacks on Muslims were couched in the language of safeguarding secularism, women's liberation, and gay rights. As Justin Trudeau, Liberal Party leader and later prime minister, said: "Cloaking an argument about what women can wear in the language of feminism has to be the most innovative perversion of liberty that conservatives have invented in a while.

It is, of course, not the first time the most illiberal of ends has been packaged in the language of liberation."[2]

Others blamed multiculturalism for letting in too many Muslims in the West or giving them too much freedom to be Muslims. French president Nicolas Sarkozy, British prime minister David Cameron, and German chancellor Angela Merkel all pronounced multiculturalism a failure. So did many conservative Canadian commentators. Even the Tory minister for multiculturalism, Jason Kenney, let his staff know he preferred the term *pluralism*. Anders Breivik, the Norwegian mass murderer, cited multiculturalism for the "Islamization" of Europe.

As French sociologist François Dubet put it, "Talking about secularism has become a way to claim a white Christian France, where everyone shares the same values and traditions, a way to say we don't want Muslims."[3] Evangelical Christians, whose eagerly awaited end of the world wouldn't happen until all Jews returned to the Holy Land and converted to Christianity, joined those whose religious or geopolitical interests were served by demonizing Islam. Many, unfortunately, equated supporting Israel with opposing Arabs and Muslims, even though many Palestinians are Christian and equal participants in resisting the Israeli occupation. Such groups were well funded in the United States, according to the Washington-based Center for American Progress. Its 2011 report, "Fear Inc: Exposing the Islamophobia Network in America," catalogued how seven foundations dispersed $42.6 million between 2001 and 2009 to anti-Muslim groups. The report listed Frank Gaffney's Center for Security Policy, Daniel Pipes's Middle East Forum, Robert Spencer's Jihad Watch, Pamela Geller's Stop Islamization of America, Steve Emerson's Investigative Project on Terrorism, and Brigitte Gabriel's ACT! for America. They all helped poison public discourse and public opinion by successfully setting the agenda for populist politicians and media, including in Canada.[4]

Uri Avnery, long-time Israeli peace activist and a former member of the Knesset, noted that what was being propagated about Muslims were "almost verbatim copies of the diatribes of Joseph Goebbels," the propaganda minister for Adolf Hitler: "The same rabble-rousing slogans. The same base allegations. The same demonization."

Charles Taylor, the Canadian expert on multiculturalism, added: "There's massive Islamophobia in the Western world, and anybody who pretends that's not the case is either a liar or a moron."[5]

As far back as 1997, the Runnymede Trust, the British think tank on race relations, had warned that Islamophobia was more than a phobia, that it was "the dread, hatred, and hostility toward Islam and Muslims perpetrated by a series of closed views that imply and attribute negative and derogatory stereotypes and beliefs" to Muslims. The trust said that Islamophobia was a form of racism, just as anti-Semitism was a form of racism.

Good Versus Evil

For his war on terror, President Bush divided the world into Good Muslims and Bad Muslims. "This could not hide the central message: Unless proved to be 'good,' every Muslim was presumed to be 'bad,'" as Mahmood Mamdani of Columbia University wrote famously in his 2004 book, *Good Muslim, Bad Muslim*.[6]

Wars need propaganda to keep public opinion on side. Wars are waged as much in the media as on the battlefields. Propaganda included outright lies such as the presence of the non-existent weapons of mass destruction in Iraq. And it included soft tactics such as Laura Bush and Cherie Blair becoming the chief cheerleaders of the war in Afghanistan by championing the cause of Afghan women. Afghan women needed liberating, all right, but America didn't invade Afghanistan to liberate them. Yet there was no stopping the *mission civilisatrice* — white folks saving brown women from their cruel fathers, husbands, and brothers.

While waging war on Muslim terrorists in Muslim lands, it wasn't easy to separate out the Muslims over *there* from the Muslims *here*. If Afghans and Arabs were potential terrorists, so could Muslims be everywhere. All Muslims weren't terrorists, but all terrorists were Muslims, so all Muslims had to answer for Muslim terrorists everywhere.

If Afghan and Arab men were misogynists, Muslim men everywhere were likely the same. Therefore, Muslim women in North America and Europe — those who wore hijabs and niqabs, in particular — also had to be rescued from their retrograde menfolk. Women couldn't be wearing the scarves and chadors of their own volition. Therefore, those pieces of cloth had to be banned, and they were in several European nations as well as in Quebec.

Sharia Shrieks

Nearly half the American states took legislative or administrative steps to bar sharia from coming.

"The suggestion that shariah threatens American security is disturbingly reminiscent of the accusation, in 19th-century Europe, that Jewish religious law was seditious," wrote Eliyahu Stern, professor of religious studies at Yale University. "In 1807, Napoleon convened an assembly of rabbinic authorities to address the question of whether Jewish law prevented Jews from being loyal citizens of the republic. (They said that it did not.)"[7]

Canada had its own sharia hysteria in Ontario during 2004–5. At issue was the province's 1991 Arbitration Act. It permitted Christians and Jews to use religious arbitration in business disputes and such family matters as divorce and the distribution of marital assets under the aegis of the churches and Beit Din, the rabbinical court. Such arbitrations had already been in use by Catholics and Mennonites, Orthodox Jews, and one sect of Muslims, the Ismailis. But no sooner had a small group of Sunni Muslims sought permission to do the same than the spectre was raised of Taliban-like justice coming to Canada. It didn't seem to matter that all faith-based arbitration still had to be compatible with Canadian law.

Those opposing included some Muslim women, fearful that their rights would be curtailed. The National Council of Canadian Women, for example, should have known better than lending legitimacy to the Islamophobic hysteria. It should have known that no sharia was coming, no sharia could possibly have come. Canada's rule of law wasn't going to be tossed out. The federal and provincial governments weren't about to become complicit in the hijacking of our entire secular legal framework.

One prominent Muslim who jumped on the anti-sharia bandwagon was a member of the Quebec National Assembly, Liberal backbencher Fatima Houda-Pepin. She reportedly wasn't a practising Muslim, which was her right. She didn't represent Muslims. In fact, she had distanced herself from the community, which was also her right. Yet it was precisely because she was a "Muslim" that she was a useful prop for the Jean Charest government in a symbolic vote in the National Assembly denouncing "sharia" in Ontario. She used scare tactics, invoking Afghanistan, Pakistan, Nigeria, Sudan, Iran, and Saudi Arabia, as though laws from there were being imported here. Houda-Pepin also peddled a conspiracy theory that Islamists were plotting to control Canadian Muslims and use them to sabotage the Charter of Rights and Freedoms.

Ontario premier Dalton McGuinty, shell-shocked by the sharia firestorm, cancelled religious arbitration for all religious groups. He ended up with the right policy for the wrong reasons. It turned out that the sharia panic across North America wasn't a grassroots movement as portrayed, but rather an orchestrated campaign by one man, David Yerushalmi, a lawyer in Brooklyn condemned by the Anti-Defamation League for his "anti-Muslim, anti-immigrant, and anti-black bigotry." He had made it known that the anti-sharia movement was his invention, designed to sow fear and suspicion about Muslims. "The purpose was heuristic — to get people asking this question, 'What is shariah?'," the *New York Times* quoted him in 2011 as saying when it finally got around to exposing him after the damage had been done.

The narrative on sharia didn't have much to do with Muslim women or with logic. It was just another cudgel.

The Real Sharia Creep

One key feature of sharia is capital punishment, which the United States has always had. Other parts of the sharia had been creeping into both the American and Canadian penal systems, courtesy of tough-on-crime conservatives.

The 2001 televised execution of Timothy McVeigh, the Oklahoma bomber, had parallels with a grisly execution carried out by the Taliban following their first takeover of Afghanistan in 1996. In Kabul, the condemned man had been found guilty of murdering a pregnant woman and her three children during a botched robbery. His sentence of death was carried out in the soccer stadium. In Oklahoma, the families of McVeigh's victims, about 300 of them, were given the best seats in the house via closed-circuit TV to watch his last gasps at the federal penitentiary in Terre Haute, Indiana. There, bars and hotels were packed for weeks, and the enterprising peddled souvenir T-shirts, just as vendors sold warm roasted nuts at the Kabul stadium. Closed-circuit TV isn't a packed stadium, but the philosophy driving both events was about the same.

Sharia places great emphasis on the rights of victims. In both the United States and Canada, the trend has been toward empowering victims of crime and their families. They recount their tales of grief, attend trials of the accused, make "impact statements" before sentencing, and pronounce themselves mostly dissatisfied with the lightness of punishment. In the stadium in Kabul, the grieving husband/father was given the right under sharia to forgive the murderer. He chose not to.

The Great Replacement Theory

Sharia fear-mongering went hand in hand with the demographic time-bomb theory — Muslims were outbreeding others and were bound to take over. "Eurabia," "Londonistan," and "New Yorkistan" were on the horizon. The Serbs had fanned just such fears during their ethnic cleansing of Muslims in Bosnia. After 9/11, a scary YouTube video, "Muslim Demographics," with several false assertions, was downloaded millions of times. Anders Breivik, the Norwegian mass murderer, echoed it, saying that that "Islamic demographic warfare" was proceeding at such a clip that "the Europeans" — white Christians — were in danger of becoming "a minority" in their own lands. Breivik quoted many prominent critics of Islam in his 1,500-page anti-Muslim manifesto, including two Canadians: author Mark Steyn and academic Salim Mansur.

Steyn had written that Muslims in the West were "a threat to the survival of the modern world" and that they were destined to take over because "they've calculated that our entire civilization lacks the will to see them off." Responding to Breivik, citing his writings, Steyn offered a unique explanation: since Breivik hadn't killed any Muslims, he, Steyn, or writers of similar ilk couldn't possibly have influenced the killer.[8]

Mansur, a professor at the University of Western Ontario (now Western University), was a frequent critic of fellow Muslims and Islam. He was a member of the academic council of the previously mentioned Gaffney's Center for Security Policy, according to its website. Mansur moved in the same circles as those who admired Israel and criticized Muslims. He also opposed Canada's policy of multiculturalism. In 2006, he was honoured by the American Jewish Congress, along with Salman Rushdie. The occasion was billed as "Profiles in Courage: Voices of Muslim Reformers in the Modern World."

Quebec Pathology

Quebec's Islamophobia began in 2007 when the soccer and tae kwon do federations banned hijabi girls under the excuse of safety. The media were sensationalizing other stories of supposedly outrageous requests for accommodating religious sensitivities such as the Montreal YMCA agreeing to tint its windows to spare young students at a yeshiva next door from being tempted by women in exercise tights.

Premier Jean Charest did what cowardly politicians do — he established a commission, rather than show some leadership to tamp down intolerance against Jews and Muslims, two of the most vulnerable minorities. The commission, co-chaired by eminent academics Gérard Bouchard (a separatist) and Charles Taylor (a federalist), held months of public hearings in which Islamophobes unloaded a lot of bile at Muslims.

A year later, the commission concluded there was no crisis. Muslims and other minorities weren't making unreasonable demands. Opposition to the hijab from both right wingers and leftist feminists was often "irrational."

The commission made several sensible suggestions: Both the public and private sectors should adopt paid leave for religious holidays. Health professionals, teachers, and students should be allowed to wear religious symbols in class such as the hijab, *kippah*, or turban. But the commission made the fatal error of suggesting that officials in positions of authority such as judges, Crown prosecutors, police officers, prison guards, and the president and vice-president of the National Assembly be prohibited from wearing religious symbols.

I took immediate issue with that, perhaps the only one in the media: The provision wasn't anchored in any principle and was a sop to popular prejudices. Worse, it contradicted the commission's own assertion that "the right to freedom of religion includes the right to show it."

Taylor conceded the point in a subsequent conversation, telling me that the recommendation was a political compromise:

> We did struggle over that for weeks. We didn't have any real concern that wearing a religious symbol would make someone an unreliable official. It was never that we mistrusted the judgment of a *kippah*-wearing judge. Rather, we feared that the idea [of rejecting any ban on religious symbols] would run into stiff resistance.
>
> So, we said, "Let's go for this limited recommendation now, and at a later date, when the population feels confident enough with diversity, we can loosen the whole thing." We were recommending it as a prophylactic. It was a scaling down, so that it might provide a way out.

It did the reverse, keeping the issue alive and emboldening the bigoted. Taylor was to acknowledge that, as well, later.

Maryam in Montreal

Maryam was the healthiest of all of us, certainly the most disciplined in eating sensibly and being physically active. She always got her walk in, and biking in the summer. When she couldn't drag husband Ahmed along, she went on her own, often to Parc écologique des Sansonnets, a deciduous forest in her Brossard neighbourhood on the St. Lawrence River across from Montreal. She knew its 14 acres of red oak, maple, hickory, and mayapple, and got irritated when visitors didn't want to know anything more about the surroundings than that the air was refreshing and her company more so.

So it was a shock in the spring of 2008 to get a call from Montreal that she had died suddenly of a heart attack. She had returned from her mid-morning walk and gone upstairs to change. By the time Ahmed downstairs realized what was happening, she was gone.

Yasmeen, Faisal, and I dashed to the Toronto Islands airport. The ticket sales counter had just closed. No, they couldn't make an exception. Maryam's son, Abdul-Basit, however, made it to that flight. We started driving, so did brother Yousuf and family.

We went to the Islamic Centre of Quebec in Ville St-Laurent where Maryam's body had been taken. Yasmeen and Abdul-Basit's wife, Rabab, and her mother, Nasreen, helped bathe Maryam before wrapping her in the white shroud. Maryam and Ahmed had long been associated with the masjid, he as president. The congregation included her students from both the weekend Islamic school and her Brossard high school where she taught biotechnology. She had pioneered that course in Montreal, based on her research at McGill University on the new discipline and her articles in journals.[9]

Although younger than me, Maryam used to berate me back when I was being wayward in college. But she also provided a buffer in dealing with Abba and Amma. After Abba's death, when I became head of the household by default, it made no difference — she wasn't deferential, not then, not

Sister Maryam Ahmed, Montreal.

later. That was her strength, the beauty of her character, combined with a great deal of loving and caring. She didn't take guff from anyone — at home, at college, or at work.

She was the second victim in the family, after Abba, of heart failure. Also, the second younger sister to go, after Syeda. Everyone's time on earth may be fixed, but when your kin departs like that prematurely, it still kills you.

Targeting Muslims

Muslim-bashing returned in 2012 with the election of the separatist Parti Québécois (PQ). The new government introduced a Charter of Quebec Values, proposing to ban all religious attire and symbols from the entire public sector, including teachers and health-care and daycare workers.

The real targets were Muslims. The Pauline Marois PQ government was confident that Montreal Jewish General Hospital and institutions of other faiths would take up its offer of opting out of the charter for five years. That would free the government to ban the hijab from the public sector and fire thousands of hijab-wearing women from daycare centres, schools, and the health sector. PQ strategist and Cabinet minister Jean-François Lisée conceded that much: "We are not dummies. Nobody will be at the doors of Jewish hospitals taking *kippahs* off of doctors' heads. That's not the case." But Jewish General took a principled stand and refused the opt-out option.[10]

One hospital in Ontario chose a cheeky way to entice nursing graduates from Quebec with an ad featuring a hijabi woman and a message: "We don't care what's on your head, we care what's in it." Lakeridge Health in Oshawa ran the ad in the *McGill Daily* university newspaper, aimed at the institution's medical school.

* * *

In the weeks leading up to the election in the spring of 2014, the PQ trotted out a doddering mini-celebrity to warn of the dangers of not just religious symbols but the mere presence of Muslims. Janette Bertrand, 89, garnered much media attention for saying she didn't want to be treated by a hijabi woman because in Islam "women are not given the same care as men, and the elderly are allowed to die sooner." On the contrary, Muslims, including those living in the West, are known for their reluctance to consign their parents to senior citizens' homes but to care for them themselves per a well-known Qur'anic injunction: "Be kind to parents. Whether one or both attain old age, say not to them a word of contempt, nor repel them, but address them in terms of honour" (Qur'an 23).

That commandment makes no distinction between father and mother. But another accords a special place for the mother: "We have commanded people to be good to their parents: their mothers carried them, with strain upon strain, and it takes two years to wean them" (Qur'an 31:14).

And there's the Prophet Muhammad's famous saying, drilled into Muslims: "Paradise lies beneath your mother's feet."

Not only was Janette Bertrand a bigot, so were her admirers, some of whom named their pro-charter group after her — "The Janettes." The PQ lost the election and the charter died. Anti-Muslim sentiments, however, didn't disappear.

The following year, a judge in Montreal refused to hear a routine case unless the defendant, Rania El-Alloul, removed her hijab, which she refused to, saying that it was an integral part of her faith. Quebec's Council of Judges refused to intervene, citing judicial independence. We could reasonably be certain that the council would have had something to say had the judge erred on the side of racism or anti-Semitism.

* * *

Philippe Couillard, the provincial Liberal Party leader who succeeded Marois as premier, made an ill-advised election promise to implement a lighter version of the PQ's Charter of Quebec Values. He did so in two separate bills passed by Quebec's National Assembly in 2017: one banning the niqab for all public sector employees and for anyone receiving a public service, including health care; the other curbing honour killings and forced marriages, found among some Sikhs, Hindus, and Arab Christians, as well, but wrongly assumed to be exclusively Muslim practices.

18 Cultural Warfare on Muslims

The measures, the first of their kind in North America, were described as overkill by Nathalie Des Rosiers, dean of law at University of Ottawa and a former general counsel for the Canadian Civil Liberties Association. "Murder is murder, and laws already exist to take preventive measures for forced marriages," she told me. The Quebec laws were designed to "target one group" — Muslims.

Mosque Massacre

On January 29, 2017, at 7:30 p.m., about 40 people gathered at Centre culturel islamique de Québec in Sainte-Foy, a suburb of Quebec City, for the last of their five daily prayers. A killer entered the prayer hall, and within two minutes, mowed down six congregants dead and injured 19. The killer, André Bissonnette, a former Canadian Army cadet, was an avowed anti-feminist and anti-Muslim admirer of Donald Trump, Marine Le Pen, and the Parti Québécois.

The massacre brought to the fore the need for a Muslim cemetery in or around Quebec City. Five of the dead were repatriated to their homelands and one was interred in the only Muslim-run cemetery in the province in suburban Montreal, a three-hour drive. The Islamic Centre in Quebec City arranged to buy space in a private cemetery in Saint-Apollinaire on the outskirts of Quebec's capital. The project needed a zoning change and was put to a referendum. Objectors said the cemetery could lead to the building of a mosque, and who knows, even the arrival of veiled women. Voters turned down the idea of having even dead Muslims in their precincts.

By this time, Philippe Couillard's government had been replaced by the nationalist Coalition Avenir Québec (CAQ), led by François Legault, a former separatist. The new government banned the hijab for all teachers, daycare workers, police officers, and government lawyers. That prompted Professors Taylor and Bouchard to come out of retirement to warn against the idea. Appearing at a public hearing of a committee of the National Assembly, Taylor repeated what he'd told me a decade earlier — he and Bouchard had made a mistake suggesting the hijab for a limited number of officials. His entreaties made no difference.

My Name Is Not Harry

The government shut out most religious groups from the hearings, including the women who were to be most affected by Bill 21 — hijab-wearing Muslims.

The law was challenged in court. In 2021, the Quebec Superior Court upheld most of it, even while finding that its main provisions trampled on the basic rights of religious minorities. But the government had insulated itself by invoking the Charter of Rights and Freedoms notwithstanding clause that permits both the federal and provincial governments to set aside some rights for a period of five years. Still, the court noted: "The evidence undoubtedly shows that the effects will be felt negatively above all by Muslim women ... by violating their religious freedom and also violating their freedom of expression, because clothing is both expression pure and simple and can also constitute a manifestation of religious belief."

Yet neither the federal Liberal government in Ottawa nor any of the federal opposition parties mounted a substantial critique of the law. They were afraid of being on the wrong side of public opinion in Quebec.

In 2022, Legault won a majority, bigger than his first in 2018, confirming that narrow Quebec nationalism isn't dead. Instead of discriminating against the Jehovah's Witnesses, as in the 1950s, or railing against English Canadians in the 1980s and 1990s, it has found a new enemy: Muslims. In 2023, the Legault government banned prayers in public schools. And the National Assembly unanimously passed a motion — a fatwa of their own — saying that prayers in schools violated the principles of secularism! A similar rationale was at work in the old Communist countries.

* * *

There has been an argument that Quebeckers' hostility toward Muslims doesn't all spring from bigotry but rather from a skewed sense of secularism in Quebec, as in France. Quebec's Quiet Revolution won the Catholic population freedom from the political and social clutches of the Catholic Church. But with increasing immigration of Muslims to Quebec and the visible presence of their religious symbols, old-time Quebeckers, especially women, react viscerally. That might be an explanation for irrationality but not an excuse for state-sanctioned racism and bigotry presented in the shiny foil of secularism.

More Murders

In 2020, Mohamed-Aslim Zafis, 58, was stabbed to death outside a Toronto mosque where he was a caretaker and a volunteer with its food bank, Table of Mercy. The social media accounts of the alleged killer, according to the Canadian Anti-Hate Network, had imagery associated with a neo-Nazi group.

Within a year, four members of a visibly Muslim family out for a walk in their neighbourhood in London, Ontario, were killed. This was rightly called a terrorist act: security forces and the media now seem more ready to acknowledge that terrorism can indeed be perpetrated by non-Muslims.

The murder shook up Canadians in a way neither the Quebec massacre had nor the slaughter at the mosque in Toronto had. The tragedy prompted calls for official acknowledgement of Islamophobia and the appointment of a special representative to tackle it.

Ottawa did both, naming January 30 as the National Day of Action against Islamophobia, and in early 2023, enlisting Amira Elghawaby, a human-rights activist, as Canada's first special representative on combatting Islamophobia, "to serve as a champion, adviser, expert, and representative" to the government, a role similar to that of the special envoy on preserving Holocaust remembrance and combatting anti-Semitism appointed in 2020.

But her appointment raised a firestorm in Quebec. Premier Legault and Bloc Québécois leader Yves-François Blanchet demanded that she resign or be fired. Her crime? She had co-authored a column in 2019 with Bernie Farber, a prominent Jewish-Canadian human-rights activist, that said: "The majority of Quebeckers appear to be swayed not by the rule of law but by anti-Muslim sentiment."[11] That conclusion was drawn from a poll that found two-thirds of Quebeckers, 63 percent, supported the law banning religious symbols, and of those, as many as 88 percent held negative views of Islam. The Farber-Elghawaby opinion was only marginally off the mark — 88 percent of 63 percent makes a majority and does lay bare the bigotry of a swath of the populace. That's the hard truth that touched a raw nerve, presenting the revealing spectacle of two powerful men hectoring a hijabi woman appointed to a job to expose just the sort of bigotry sanctioned in Quebec. "They want to uphold a bigoted law and avoid being described, accurately, as bigots," *Toronto Star* columnist Emma Teitel observed. "Tell me again where Elghawaby got it wrong."[12]

More telling was the failure of Ottawa to call out Legault and Blanchet. Prime Minister Justin Trudeau said initially that Elghawaby would have to explain herself. Ahmed Hussen, minister of diversity and in charge of the file, went to ground and wasn't heard from. Such moments provide insight into a politician's character, and this one didn't show Trudeau and Hussen well, especially the latter.

Elghawaby is a person of integrity. But she needs the full-fledged backing of Ottawa to succeed — presuming the Trudeau government wants her to triumph and not merely be a symbol of a Liberal sop to the Muslim community.

Over the past two decades, Quebec nationalism has been channelled into beating up minorities, especially Muslims. And Ottawa, under Prime Ministers Stephen Harper and Justin Trudeau, has chosen to abandon the most vulnerable for fear of losing votes in the province or rekindling separatism. One pines for a Pierre Trudeau to challenge and wrestle down the bigots who have turned Quebec into a mini-France.

Western Ayatollahs

The Taliban and the ayatollahs tell women what to wear. Too many secularists and feminists in Europe and Canada tell them what not to. The fascist urge to control women is the same. We're left to argue only about the degree of the control and the punishments for disobedience.

The Taliban fire hijab-wearing women from public service jobs and expel girls from schools. In Quebec and many European jurisdictions, hijabi girls are denied public education and women are stripped of their jobs, employment that gives them independence from their menfolk who are ostensibly controlling them and from whose clutches we're trying to pry them free. These are jobs that help such women integrate into society, which we proclaim as our mission.

Stranger still, some Western states, politicians, and media pundits have taken to issuing fatwas on what is, or isn't, Islamic. Jason Kenney, multicultural minister under Stephen Harper, proudly announced that he'd consulted

Shaykh Mohamed Tantawi, Egypt's top Muslim authority, about the niqab. The cleric "clarified for me that people in the West who think this is a religious obligation do not understand Islam [*sic*] law. So, I am not going to second-guess the most pre-eminent Sharia authority in the Sunni world." But Ayatollah Kenney was second-guessing the Supreme Court of Canada, which ruled long ago that a religious practice is what the practitioner sincerely believes it to be. He was ignoring Canada's top court but taking dictation from a mufti in Cairo!

In taking sides in the internal doctrinal issues of Muslims, Kenney and his ilk, especially in France and some other European states, have been behaving like theocratic states, such as Saudi Arabia, that prescribe the brand of Islam that their citizens should practise.

More Absurdities

Osama bin Laden believed he was called by Allah to wage jihad against the United States. George W. Bush said he, too, consulted God before launching his war on Iraq.

The Taliban and bin Laden said Muslims don't belong in the West. Islamophobes in the West have been saying the same.

Just as North America and Europe got into a decade-long tizzy about sharia that couldn't have come, the Swiss voted in a referendum in 2009 to ban the minarets they didn't have — there being only four. None of which broadcast the *azan*, the call to prayers. The Swiss also voted to ban the burka, which virtually nobody wore, and also the niqab, which was worn by about three dozen women. France, Germany, Belgium, the Netherlands, and Denmark imposed similar bans. The European Court of Human Rights, that venerable upholder of basic rights, ruled that those bans were fine, even as the U.N. Human Rights Committee said they violated the human rights of Muslim women and risked "confining them to their homes."

Free of facts and logic was also the 2010 controversy over the so-called Ground Zero Mosque that was neither a mosque nor at the 9/11 site. It was envisaged as a Muslim "Y" with a swimming pool, restaurant, galleries, and an auditorium, open to non-Muslims. It was proposed for a location two blocks north of the World Trade Center and wasn't going to be visible from the site. It had the support of Mayor Michael Bloomberg and the United Jewish

Federation of New York, as well as the project developer, American-born Sharif al-Gamal. He himself had been a victim of 9/11, getting injured while delivering water bottles to emergency crews that fateful day. But opposition to his proposal was based on the premise that nothing associated with Islam should come anywhere near the scarred, secular, but sacred ground of 9/11.

* * *

There's separation of church and state, especially in the United States and France. Yet the Yankee dollar says "In God we trust" and each presidential speech ends with the prayer "God Bless America." In France, *laïcité* supposedly doesn't recognize religious, racial, ethnic, and other identities but does. The French state funds religious schools, churches, and chaplaincy services. Observes Catholic holidays. Ordains that the state funeral for the president be a Mass at Notre-Dame Cathedral. Yet it does little to curb the widespread discrimination against Muslims precisely because of their faith, contrary to the equality promised by *laïcité*. President Emmanuel Macron's government passed a law in 2021 giving the state the power to encroach into the religious affairs of Muslims, control religious associations, and shut down any house of worship.

* * *

Part of the anti-Muslim cultural warfare was also played out in 2011 in Toronto at Canada's largest middle school. Valley Park permitted its Muslim students to say their midday Friday prayers on the premises. There is nothing unique about that. *Jum'ah* prayers are routinely held in thousands of schools, colleges, universities, and businesses across Canada, including some bank towers in downtown Toronto — not surprising, given that the Muslim sabbath falls on a working day, not Saturday or Sunday.

But Hindu Advocacy, a small, openly anti-Muslim and anti-Sikh group, took umbrage, turning up to protest on Fridays and saying that the prayers posed an imminent threat to Canadian secularism. It alleged that the Toronto District School Board was "thoroughly infected with Islamist sympathies."

Of Valley Park's 1,200 students, 80 percent were Muslims. On Fridays, many trekked nearly two kilometres to the nearest mosque. To ease their burden in the fasting month of Ramadan, *jum'ah* was started in the school in 2000. For the rest of the year, however, they were still going to the mosque for two hours. Some weren't coming back at all. So, in 2008, principal Nick Stefanoff regularized the *jum'ah* in the school. It was held after lunch when the cafeteria was vacant. Students and volunteer parents removed the chairs and tables to spread sheets for the 30-minute service, following which they rearranged the furniture. Attendance was voluntary. A third of the Muslim students came. The service didn't cost the school a penny. "It was I who initiated this with the community, not the other way around," Stefanoff told me. "We're doing something that's working. This has provided more instructional time."

The school was only doing what it had to under the law — accommodate different religious practices. Staff members belonging to First Nations, Métis, and Inuit didn't have to get up for "God Save the Queen." Jehovah's Witness students could sit through, or be excused from class during, "O Canada." They were also free not to wear Halloween costumes. Seventh Day Adventists and Jewish students were excused for school-related activities on Saturday. In Jewish neighbourhoods in Toronto, some public schools routinely reschedule tests, assignments, and exams for the Jewish High Holidays.

At Valley Park, Muslim parents also did a great deal of volunteer work, including raising $1.5 million for baseball, soccer, and cricket fields. The local mosque donated $10,000.

It was a good Canadian story all round but not allowed to surface under the dictates of the absurd Islamophobic times.

19

Harper and Muslims

STEPHEN HARPER WAS THE FIRST CONTEMPORARY PRIME MINISTER IN Canada to discriminate against a religious group openly and unapologetically. In his nine years in office (2006–15), he targeted Muslims with a range of legislative and executive measures. In his ugliness toward Muslims, he was well ahead of Donald Trump — and more effective.

He and his ministers incessantly linked Muslim terrorism with Islam. They were forever waging their own jihad against "jihadism," "violent jihadism," "jihadi terrorism," "violent global jihadist movement," "jihadists," "jihadist monsters," et cetera. Harper asserted that the biggest threat to Canada was "Islamicism." That was the vocabulary of those who said they weren't against Islam — no, not at all — but rather "Islamism," "political Islam," "radical Islam," "militant Islam," or "extremist Islam." Terms that lacked precision and could mean whatever one wanted them to mean. Such a formulation was also tailor-made for those who believed that terrorism involving Muslims was "Islamic," whereas the terrorism of Anders Breivik, the Norwegian mass murderer, wasn't Christian; of the Tamil Tigers, not Hindu; of Baruch Goldstein, the Israeli mass murderer, not Jewish.

Harper and his Conservative Party associated mosques with the "Islamist fundamentalist menace" and the "international jihadist movement." And his government promoted its anti-terrorism legislation by posting images of religious-looking Muslims, despite the fact that Harper once conceded, when speaking of radicalized Muslim youth, the following:

> Our experience in Canada has been that their connection to the Muslim community is often extremely tangential. A surprising number of these people have no background in Islam whatsoever. They are individuals who, for whatever reason, drift to these kinds of causes. Even [those with] backgrounds in Islam, they're often people who are not participants in mosques…. They're off on kind of a radical, political fringe. Our security and intelligence people would tell you that a good relationship with our Muslim community has actually really helped to identify a lot of these threats before they become much more serious.

Multiculturalism Minister Jason Kenney, too, made a similar point: "Our security and police agencies will confirm that potentially violent instances have been prevented, radicalization has been diminished, thanks to the proactive co-operation of many in the Canadian Muslim communities."

Yet that didn't stop the Harper government and the ruling Conservative Party from boycotting the one-million-strong Muslim community. Both were dismissive of all mainstream Muslim groups, Sunni and Shia alike, except for two small, tightly knit groups, the Ismailis and Ahmadis, the latter considered by many Muslims to be heretics. His behaviour was in sharp contrast even to those Western leaders who might have been ambivalent toward their Muslim citizenry but still paid lip service to them and their organizations. Harper refused to do what American presidents and British prime ministers had routinely done at the White House and 10 Downing Street, hosting an iftar party for the breaking of the fast during the month of Ramadan. When Harper finally did host one, in 2015, his last year in office, he avoided inviting anyone from well-known Muslim groups.

In keeping with the prevalent post-9/11 Islamophobic practice, Harper patronized only those handful of Muslims who attacked fellow Muslims. He amplified their voices with funding, appointments, and invitations as "expert" witnesses at parliamentary hearings. He paraded them as props at press conferences and events promoting his government's anti-Muslim policies. They, in turn, sang his government's praises, including its hardline pro-Israeli and anti-Iran policies.

One of those groups honoured Kenney for banning the niqab at citizenship ceremonies. At that 2012 event, a woman entered wearing a niqab, only to remove it dramatically in front of the minister, much to his amusement. It was hard to imagine him smirking at a public gathering at which Catholicism was mocked by a woman who came in a nun's habit only to throw it off, or Orthodox Judaism was insulted by a man sporting a fake beard, long locks, and a black hat only to disdainfully cast them off.

Wrote Off Muslim Voters

For election purposes, the Harperites wrote off the Muslim community altogether and courted groups that didn't like Muslims — white nativists, Hindu extremists, and those immigrants who had come to Canada fleeing persecution from Muslim-majority nations, namely, Coptic Christians from Egypt, Bahá'ís from Iran, and Christians and Ahmadis from Pakistan. Those minorities had good reasons to resent their native nations, but the Harper government exploited and fanned their "old-country" fault lines rather than follow the long-standing Canadian tradition of tamping down ancestral conflicts and bringing old warring factions together, even if in an uneasy peace.

It was telling how the Conservatives micro-targeted South Asian Canadians. They are defined by Statistics Canada as those from the Indian subcontinent and from the Indian diaspora in Africa, the Caribbean, the Far East, and Fiji. The Conservative wooing of South Asians was spun to the media as an enlightened outreach to non-white voters. But the truth lay in the details. Harper ignored the Muslims from India, Pakistan, Bangladesh, Sri Lanka, and elsewhere. He sought votes only among Hindus, Sikhs, and Christians. Among the Hindus, he was most solicitous of the more zealous overseas supporters of India's Hindu nationalist Bharatiya Janata Party (BJP). Its leader, Narendra Modi, had been blacklisted by the United States, Canada, and several European countries for his role in the 2002 anti-Muslim pogrom in his state of Gujarat where he was chief minister. The

Harper government was among the first Western governments to sponsor Modi's annual pro-business summits in Gujarat. And when Modi became India's prime minister in 2014, Harper invited him to Canada and escorted him in Ottawa, Toronto, and Vancouver before the mostly Hindu hero-worshippers of Modi.

Looking for Coptic, Ahmadi, and Bahá'í votes, Harper promised during the 2011 federal election to establish an Office of Religious Freedom to monitor the plight of religious minorities worldwide. He unveiled the policy at a Mississauga Coptic church. He announced the position of a new ambassador of religious freedom at the Ahmadiyya mosque in Vaughan, a city just north of Toronto. Once established, the Office of Religious Freedom went to bat mostly for Christian and other minorities in Muslim nations. It did little for the beleaguered Muslim minorities elsewhere, such as the Uighurs in China, the persecuted Rohingyas in Myanmar, or Shia Muslims in Saudi Arabia and Pakistan.

In 2011, Jason Kenney travelled to Pakistan for the funeral of Shahbaz Bhatti, a junior Cabinet minister. Bhatti, a Christian, was murdered for taking up the cause of a Christian woman falsely condemned to death for allegedly defaming Islam. Six weeks earlier, a much more well-known and important Pakistani politician, Salman Taseer, the Muslim governor of Punjab, the most populous province, was shot dead by his own guards for speaking out on behalf of the same Christian woman. Kenney didn't go to that funeral. Nor did Harper send anyone else.

* * *

In sharp contrast to boycotting the Muslim community, Harper assiduously courted the Jewish community and handed a blank cheque to Israel. That was his right. But his political calculus was the same as that of extremist Zionists: equating support for Israel with opposing Muslims.

When Hamas won the 2006 elections, Harper played a leading role in initiating Western revenge on the Gazans for electing the wrong people. After Israel invaded Lebanon, he called the Israeli offensive "measured," even as several G8 leaders thought of it as outrageously disproportionate to the provocations of Hezbollah. During that war, Harper didn't even sound like Canada's leader. He refused to protest the bombing deaths of an unarmed Canadian peacekeeper and a Montreal family of eight.

I asked the Israeli peace activist Uri Avnery what he thought of Harper's being the first government to impose economic sanctions and starve the Gazans. Avnery and I were at a PEN International conference in Berlin. The founder of the Gush Shalom peace group and former member of the Knesset replied: "It is a terrible policy. It is inhumane and it is stupid. No people in the world would react to such a crude outside intervention against a government which they have just now elected in unquestionably democratic elections. Any people, including my own, would react to this by embracing their elected government. Anyone with any modicum of political experience, political wisdom, and political intuition would know this is wrong."

I asked him what Canada's role should be.

"People have this belief that Canadians are better than others, that Canadians are part of the Anglo-Saxon culture but are free from the obvious faults of the U.S. and of the United Kingdom — not so powerful, not so arrogant, maybe a little bit more moral. Whether it is true or not, it is widely believed and I myself believe in it. I do very much hope that Canada could be, or should be, a voice of reason. It's not a question of being pro-Israeli or pro-Palestinian but being pro-peace and pro-reason."

Penalizing Critics of Israel

The Harper government targeted Apartheid Week, a movement against the Israeli occupation of Palestinian lands started in Toronto in 2005 by Arab, Muslim, and Jewish students critical of Israeli policies toward the Palestinians. Minister Jason Kenney, the designated Conservative hitman, called the movement anti-Semitic and attacked universities for not banning it on campuses.

Non-Canadian critics of Israel were also barred by the government from entering Canada, such as British MP George Galloway. Yet it allowed such known anti-Muslim hate-mongers as the Dutch Geert Wilders and the American Pamela Geller to hold rallies in Canada. When Geller came in 2013, the Toronto Board of Rabbis condemned the militant Jewish Defense

League of Canada for hosting her. The board, which represents rabbis from all denominations, said it found both her views as well as the invitation extended to her to be "distasteful" and divisive.

Harper launched a vendetta against Canadians who dared criticize Israel, be they Muslim, Christian, or of any faith. But a majority of those hounded, demonized, and penalized by his government were Muslims.

He cut off federal funding to the Canadian Arab Federation, Palestine House in Toronto, the Christian aid group Kairos, and the United Nations Relief and Works Agency for Palestine Refugees. Harper also destroyed and eventually shut down Montreal-based Rights and Democracy, a human-rights centre that had committed the sin of making small grants to three non-governmental organizations: B'Tselem and two Palestinian groups, critical of Israeli *and* Palestinian human-rights violations, including during the 2009 Israeli war on Gaza.

News coverage of these controversies was sparse, except in the Postmedia group of newspapers, which maligned Rights and Democracy and its staff. As usual, the rest of the Canadian media took a pass on anything controversial about Israel. But the Harper government's machinations weren't all that difficult to unearth.

It had appointed Aurel Braun, a University of Toronto professor long active in B'nai Brith, as chair of Rights and Democracy. He repeatedly clashed with Rémy Beauregard, the highly respected president of the centre. Some directors wrote to Foreign Minister Lawrence Cannon that Braun should be fired. They got no response. At a stormy board meeting, Braun harangued Beauregard. Two directors resigned on the spot and walked out. That night Beauregard died of a heart attack, age 66.

His wife, Suzanne Trépanier, had Braun's name removed from the centre's website messages of condolences, saying: "You don't treat a person like you did with Rémy and then praise his qualities after he is dead. This is hypocrisy."

Ed Broadbent, the former New Democratic Party (NDP) leader and a former chair of the centre, told me: "I don't recall in my long public life such an unwarranted assault on a senior public servant, none. And I don't recall such a total undermining of a PMO [Prime Minister's Office] appointee being treated so shabbily and dying in the middle of it. Without drawing a direct parallel, I can think of only one incident, Herbert Norman, our envoy to Egypt, a friend of Lester B. Pearson, committing suicide in 1957, after having been accused of being a communist sympathizer. That was the McCarthy era."

Forty-five of 47 staff at the centre demanded Braun's resignation. And also of vice-chair Jacques Gauthier and director Elliot Tepper, accusing them of "a pattern of harassment" of Beauregard and others at the centre. The three Harper appointees hired a private investigator. There was a Watergate-style break-in at the centre on the night of Beauregard's funeral, and two laptops were stolen. A gag order was imposed on the staff.

One of the directors who had quit in disgust was Sima Samar, an internationally renowned Afghan women's-rights advocate. She had been made an honorary Canadian the year before. She told me over the phone from Kabul that she found it incongruous that a centre dedicated to human rights had violated the rights of its top employee; that rather than being transparent, it was secretive; and instead of standing up for the victims of human-rights violations, it was siding with the violators.

Harper shut down the centre in 2012. Being vicious to those critical of Israel was more important to him than keeping Canada's long-standing reputation as a defender of human rights. Nor did it matter that the centre had been set up in 1988 by Brian Mulroney, a Conservative prime minister.

Oxygen to Islamophobes

In 2012, Harper axed a section of the Canadian Human Rights Act that prohibited the spreading of hatred or contempt on grounds of race, religion, or ethnic origin. He did so at the behest of anti-Muslim activists demanding their free-speech right to malign Islam and Muslims.

Within a year, though, the Supreme Court of Canada found Section 13 valid. Ruling on an earlier case, it unanimously rejected the argument that unfettered speech helps further public debate. Rather, "hate speech shuts down dialogue by making it difficult or impossible for members of the vulnerable group to respond, thereby stifling discourse." The court went on to define hate as that which "a reasonable person, aware of the context and circumstances, would view the expression as likely to expose a person or persons to detestation and vilification on the basis of a prohibited ground of discrimination. At its core, hate speech is an effort to marginalize individuals based on their membership in a group.... Hate speech seeks to delegitimize group members in the eyes of the majority, reducing their social standing and acceptance within society."

That was precisely what was being done to Muslims.

The court held that the harm done by hate isn't in keeping with the values of equality and multiculturalism contained in other sections of the Charter of Rights and Freedoms.[1]

I asked Max Yalden what he thought of the ruling. The former head of the Canadian Human Rights Commission and a member of the U.N. committee monitoring the International Convention of Civil and Political Rights told me: "It's a wise decision. Canada is not the United States with their absolute emphasis on letting anyone say whatever they want. Nowhere else in the world is that the case. Canadians value free speech but not to the extent that may bring women, gays, Jews, Muslims, or whoever into hatred and contempt. The court has reflected the way Canadians see the issue."[2]

Yet that wasn't the way the Harper government saw it. Or the extensive conservative media across the land. Or the noisy social media, long ago commandeered by bigots. Shamefully, liberal voices remained mostly silent, including, unfortunately, the *Toronto Star*, which by then was part of the misguided campaign to keep expanding the boundaries of free speech no matter the cost to vulnerable groups, and indeed, to our delicately balanced society.

The Harperite stance on free speech, however, ought not to be confused with those who sincerely believe in unhindered free speech. In Canada, the biggest free-speech stalwart was Alan Borovoy, long-time general counsel for the Canadian Civil Liberties Association. He was a liberal's liberal, whom I got to know well when serving on the association's board. I admired and quoted him often and shared dozens of public platforms. But he and I disagreed on his rock-solid commitment to American-style free speech. I used to rib him that he'd spent too much of his impressionable youth in the United States as a student. At least he was consistent in the application of free speech, unlike too many others, liberals and conservatives alike, as I'll argue in the chapters on the media and Salman Rushdie.

19 Harper and Muslims

Between 2018 and 2021, three courts further clarified the Canadian red line against hate. Two anti-Muslim activists, Ron Banerjee and Kevin Johnston of Toronto, were found guilty of defamation.

In a 2018 case, the Ontario Superior Court ruled that Banerjee had defamed Muslim businessman Mohamad Fakih while protesting in front of a restaurant owned by Fakih, saying that anyone patronizing it had to be a "jihadist" who raped his wife. Justice Shaun Nakatsuru wrote:

> We live in a free country where people have as much right to express outrageous and ridiculous opinions as moderate ones. I acknowledge that. But we also live in a country where alleged hateful and defamatory expressions can appropriately be litigated in the judicial system.... This is a case about freedom of expression. But it is also about the limits to that constitutionally protected right. Expressions of hatred and bigotry towards racial, ethnic, religious or other identifiable groups have no value in the public discourse of our nation.

Banerjee issued an abject video apology.[3]

That same year another judge of the same court ordered Johnston to pay $2.5 million in defamation to Fakih. Johnston had been at that 2017 rally with Banerjee, and in a series of videos posted in 2017 and 2018, accused Fakih's restaurant chain of being a "front" that was "up to something nefarious" and said that anyone who entered it must be a "jihadist." The videos also featured an altered photograph of Fakih that depicted him with blood on his hands and face. Justice Jane Ferguson said the case represented "a loathsome example of hate speech at its worst, targeting people solely because of their religion." And when Johnston failed to comply, he was sentenced to 18 months in jail for contempt of court.[4]

In the third case, Walied Soliman, a prominent lawyer in Toronto, won a $500,000 defamation award in 2021 against anti-Muslim agitator Daniel Bordman. The latter had accused Soliman of supporting "extremist, terrorist Islamic organizations such as the Muslim Brotherhood"; of being an anti-Semite; and supporting "the introduction of Sharia law to Canada to supplant or override Canadian law." In summarily dismissing the case, without the need even to go to a trial, Justice Paul Perell of the Ontario Superior Court banned Bordman from making any public comment about Soliman.[5]

These judgments were a clear rejection of the Harper government's, the media's, and the liberal elite's knee-jerk defence of free speech in cases reviling Islam and Muslims.

Aping McCarthyism

The Harperites' penchant for tarring Muslims with the terrorist brush was starkly on display at parliamentary proceedings, especially at the hearings of the Senate committee on national security in the fall of 2014 and spring of 2015. The committee shunned representative Muslim groups. Instead, it preferred anti-Muslim activists such as Ayaan Hirsi Ali, the Somali-born critic of Islam and a favourite of Islamophobes. Using parliamentary immunity, such chosen witnesses hurled unsubstantiated, indeed false, accusations against Canadian Muslims. A Montreal blogger, Marc Lebuis of Point de Bascule (Tipping Point), said that mosques and Muslim organizations in Canada were "controlled and financed, proven, by countries known to harbour the most radical fringes of Muslim, the Wahhabism fringes."

Witnesses who questioned such narratives were harassed by the majority Conservative senators, as illustrated in an exchange with Shahina Siddiqui. The hijab-wearing Siddiqui (no relation) headed the Winnipeg-based Islamic Social Services Association. She'd been honoured for her social justice activism and interfaith work with the YMCA-YWCA Winnipeg Peace Medal, among others. She had worked with federal, provincial, and local security and police forces and also helped produce an anti-radicalization booklet.

She pushed back — "Please do not treat Muslim Canadians as if they are the enemy because we are not…. Don't give in to fear and propaganda, otherwise we will tear each other apart." She was upbraided by Conservative Senator Lynn Beyak, who told her thrice to stop being "thin-skinned." Beyak added that Canadians were "tired of hearing excuses. If 21 Christians were beheaded by Jews, they would be called 'radical extremist Jews.' And if pilots were burned in cages by a Christian, they would be called 'radical violent Christians'.... What would you answer to people who are legitimately concerned?" In Beyak's view, this Muslim from Manitoba had to answer for the atrocities committed by the Islamic State in Syria and Iraq.

Siddiqui told me later that the committee hearing felt "like an inquisition." The Ottawa-based National Council of Canadian Muslims described the committee proceedings as "a witch hunt."

It came as no surprise that in its 2015 report the committee painted a picture of rising "Islamist fundamentalist menace" aided and abetted by Canadian imams. The committee offered no proof. It merely cited the hearsay from some of its favourite witnesses: "The committee heard testimony … that some foreign-trained imams have been spreading extremist religious ideology and messages that are not in keeping with Canadian values. These extreme ideas are *said to be* contributing to radicalization and raise serious concerns *if* they continue to go unchecked" (italics mine). That prompted the *Globe and Mail* to ask editorially: "Would clerics have to wear a crescent symbol on their lapels?"

The committee's work was reminiscent of the 1950s Red Scare tactics of Joseph McCarthy, the American Republican senator who used his committee hearings to ruin the lives of many Americans by falsely accusing them of being communist sympathizers. A more recent comparison was with the 2011 U.S. congressional hearings by the security committee of the U.S. House of Representatives on "homegrown radicalization" of American Muslims. The committee chair, Republican Peter King, claimed without offering proof that "80–85 percent" of America's 1,900 mosques were "controlled by Islamic fundamentalists. This is an enemy living amongst us." Challenged, he couldn't provide any data or cite any government reports.

The Canadian Senate committee's work was, in fact, far more reprehensible, considering that Congress acts independently of the White House, whereas parliamentary committees take orders from the prime minister, especially one commanding a majority, like Harper, who was also known to dictate nearly every aspect of the government's activities.

Vilifying Omar Khadr

Throughout their years in office, the Harperites ran a campaign against Omar Khadr, a Muslim. Taken to Afghanistan by his parents as a child, he was the only child soldier held at Guantanamo Bay. When he was captured in 2002 for allegedly killing an American soldier in a firefight, he was 15. At Gitmo he was interrogated by Canadian intelligence officials after he had been softened up by the Americans who deprived him of sleep by moving him from cell to cell. The Canadian officials then passed on the information they extracted.

Khadr didn't get a trial until 2010 when a military commission said the evidence against him was tainted. Yet the Harper government made no attempt to transfer him to Canada, the only Western country not to ask for repatriation of its citizens. Harper ignored calls by the United Nations Committee Against Torture and numerous human-rights groups.

Even after Khadr was released and returned to Canada following a plea bargain, the government did everything it could to keep him in a federal maximum-security prison; deny media access to him; and oppose his bail until the day he was ordered released by the Alberta Court of Appeal on May 7, 2015, after nearly 13 years of incarceration.

Judges at different levels rejected every one of the Harper government's specious arguments: that Khadr was a danger to public safety when, in fact, he'd been a model prisoner; that freeing him would irreparably harm relations with the United States, even though the U.S. State and Justice Departments had made it abundantly clear that wasn't the case; and that granting him bail would give Canada a bad name for reducing sentences levied abroad.[6]

"Our judicial system is something to be incredibly proud of," said Dennis Edney of Edmonton, Khadr's lawyer. "My view is very clear. Mr. Harper is a bigot. Mr. Harper doesn't like Muslims."

Edney repeated his accusation a week later in Ottawa after the Supreme Court ruled against the government for the third time: "I've come to the conclusion, an honest conclusion felt by many, many Canadians throughout Canada, that Mr. Harper is a bigot, and Mr. Harper doesn't like Muslims, and there's evidence to show that."

I can't recall a contemporary Canadian prime minister being so accused so publicly by a respectable public figure.

Attacking the Niqab

Within a year of taking office, the Harper government tried to strip away the voting rights of niqab-wearing women. That attempt was thwarted by Marc Mayrand, chief electoral officer and one of the principled civil servants who refused to be intimidated by Harper. Mayrand pointed out that about 70,000 voters, including inmates, mailed their federal election ballots without ever being asked to show their face.

The Harperites, however, found another venue to target the niqab. In 2011, Minister Kenney issued a directive barring niqabi women from obtaining their citizenship while covering their faces. A Toronto woman, Zunera Ishaq, took Kenney to court, and in 2015, the Federal Court of Canada ruled the policy to be "unlawful." Judge Keith Boswell said that Kenney was forcing citizenship candidates to "violate or renounce a basic tenet of their religion." That contravened the government's own rules that the oath of citizenship be administered "allowing the greatest possible freedom in the religious solemnization or the solemn affirmation thereof."

Undeterred, the government launched an appeal. Harper said that the niqab was "rooted in a culture that is anti-women.... I think most Canadians believe that it's offensive that someone would hide their identity.... These are not the views only of the overwhelming majority of Canadians, they are the views of the overwhelming majority of moderate Muslims." So, those who agreed with him were moderate, those who didn't were extremists, including the non-Muslims who thought the government had no business telling women what to wear. Would he have obliged if a majority of Canadians believed that gay people be denied their rights?

Immigration Minister Chris Alexander and some other Tories were even more incendiary. The oleaginous Alexander associated the niqab with several nefarious practices: "We are concerned about protecting women from violence, protecting women from human smuggling, protecting women from barbaric practices like polygamy, genital mutilation, honour killings.... We've done a lot in the past year to strengthen the value of Canadian citizenship. People take pride in that. They don't want their co-citizens to be terrorists."

John McCallum, Liberal MP from Toronto, said that it was "obvious that the minister equates terrorism with niqabs." McCallum told the

Commons: "It is the most predictable thing in Canadian politics. Someone says 'Muslim' and a Conservative minister says 'terrorist.'" A less partisan critic, Charles Taylor, the philosopher, told me: "For a highly educated man, Alexander says the most stupid things."

Tory MP Larry Miller told niqab-wearing women to "stay the hell where you came from." He later apologized, but the Conservative Party kept using the government's niqab ban in its fundraising campaign. And Harper, as leader of the Conservatives, signed Miller's nomination papers for the 2015 election.

The Federal Court rejected the government's appeal on the niqab. It said that a candidate's identity could easily be ascertained prior to the ceremony. The government sought leave to appeal the decision to the Supreme Court, but the Appeal Court cleared the way for her to wear the face-covering veil during a scheduled October 9 swearing-in, in time for her to vote in the October 19, 2015, general election.

Before the ceremony, Ishaq showed her face to an official to confirm her identify, as she'd said all along she would. She was sworn in as a citizen, her niqab on. "It was a wonderful moment," her lawyer, Lorne Waldman, told me later. "The judge made a beautiful speech about what it meant to be a Canadian, and especially mentioned democracy and freedom of religion. Then Zunera got her certificate, and we all sang 'O Canada.'"

Throughout the controversy, Ishaq, a former high school teacher from Pakistan, came across as having a better grip on Canadian values than the prime minister and his ministers: "The beautiful part of Canada is that every person here is free to live in a way in which he or she feels is right."

In May 2015, Harper's government proclaimed what it called the Strengthening Canadian Citizenship Act, which weakened citizenship protections for dual citizens. At the discretion of the minister of citizenship and without due process, they could be stripped of citizenship if convicted of terrorism, treason, or spying offences. The government, in fact, moved to take away the citizenship of four Muslims convicted and sentenced for their role in the 2006 "Toronto 18" terror plot to blow up sites in protest against Canada's military mission in Afghanistan. One, in fact, was born in Canada. Where was the government going to deport him? The medieval practice of taking away citizenship had been a favourite of the British, who shipped off convicts to Australia in the 18th century, and from colonial India to Burma in the 19th.

Demonizing Muslim Refugees

During Bashar al-Assad's murderous crackdown on dissent, Harper refused to take refugees from Syria, and the Conservatives raised the spectre of Muslim terrorists coming through. That was what Donald Trump, then a Republican presidential contender, was saying down south: "They could be, listen, they could be ISIS [Islamic State terrorists]."

When Harper finally responded to sustained U.N. pressure by agreeing to take 10,000 refugees, he wouldn't admit Muslims, preferring "persecuted minorities" — Christians, Yazidis, and others. Such groups did experience serious human-rights violations, but Muslims, as the majority community, were the greatest victims by far. Yet the Prime Minister's Office intervened in the refugee-selection process to screen out both Sunnis and Shias. *CTV News* reported: "PMO staff went through the files to ensure that persecuted religious minorities with established communities already in Canada — ones that Harper could court for votes — were being accepted. Insiders say the PMO actively discouraged the department from accepting applications from Shia and Sunni Muslims." Indeed, Minister Kenney had boasted of his friendship with the patriarch of the Chaldean Catholic Church in Iraq, where he'd attended a service for the patriarch in 2013.

During the 2015 election, Joe Daniel, the Conservative candidate in a Toronto riding, said he detected an "agenda" behind the "so-called refugees" — "move as many Muslims into European countries to change these countries in a major way. That's something that I certainly don't want to see happening in Canada."

Barbaric Cultural Practices

In 2014, the Harper government had introduced its ominously named Zero Tolerance for Barbaric Cultural Practices Act, outlawing what was already outlawed — polygamy, family violence, honour killing, and forcing children under 16 to leave Canada for marriages abroad — crimes that in the public mind were associated with Muslims.

The real purpose of the act didn't become clear until a year later. In the middle of the 2015 election, the Conservatives announced with fanfare that they would set up a special RCMP hotline for Canadians to snitch on fellow Canadians who may have committed or were intending to commit "barbaric cultural practices."

Harper's Muslim-baiting gambits were also designed as fundraisers. Hate Omar Khadr? Press 1 to donate. Afraid of jihadists in your neighbourhood? Do stay scared but don't forget to donate. Hate the niqab and the niqabis? Help us fight it and them. The more dollars an issue raked in, the more the Harperites kept it in the news — dragging Khadr and Ishaq through the courts, no matter the legal cost to taxpayers, the likely judicial outcome, or the harm to Canadian values.

Canadians Rebel, Finally

The Harper government's policies left Canadian Muslims bewildered, despondent, angry, and alienated. And incensed the majority of non-Muslims.

The politically docile Muslims organized themselves into a formidable voting bloc. In the 2015 election, 87 percent turned out in key Toronto-area ridings, according to the group Canadian Muslim Vote. Nationally, they voted 65 percent for the Liberals, 10 percent for the NDP, and just 2 percent for the Conservatives, while 19 percent refused to say who they had voted for, according to an Environics survey.

The Harper government was turfed out.

Yet Conservative Muslim-bashing continued long after Harper was gone. Following the 2017 Quebec City massacre, Mississauga Liberal MP Iqra Khalid introduced a motion to acknowledge "the increasing climate of hate and fear" and "condemn Islamophobia and all forms of systemic racism and religious discrimination." The Conservatives questioned whether there was, in fact, a climate of hate; objected to the term *Islamophobia*; whined that Muslims were being given "special treatment"; and posed as free-speech warriors, demanding that Ottawa "reject any call to further restrict free speech." They weren't demanding free speech to have the freedom to be misogynists, anti-Semites, homophobes, et cetera, but rather to say whatever they wanted about Islam and Muslims. All Conservative

19 Harper and Muslims

MPs voted against the motion, with the honourable exception of Michael Chong, a Toronto-area MP.

* * *

In 2019, when a gunman massacred 51 Muslim worshippers and injured 40 at two mosques in Christchurch, New Zealand, Conservative Leader Andrew Scheer couldn't bring himself to use the word *Muslim* in offering condolences. He bemoaned instead that "freedom" had come under attack. Only after a public backlash could he bring himself to find a few right words.[7]

A handful of Conservatives eventually started expressing some regrets. Tim Uppal, the turban-wearing Sikh MP from Alberta who served in the Harper Cabinet, apologized for the years of Muslim-bashing. But neither Scheer nor his successor, Erin O'Toole, ever did. Nor has the party.

Pierre Poilievre, the Conservative Party's leader elected in 2022, had been a staunch supporter of the ban on the niqab for citizenship ceremonies and also the barbaric practices hotline. Reminded of that, he tried to wiggle out by saying, "There was no niqab ban. I'd never support that, nor did Mr. Harper. What Mr. Harper proposed was that a person's face be visible while giving oaths at citizenship ceremonies." Not quite. Harper, in fact, wanted to extend the niqab ban to the public service. It's the courts that stopped him well before he could get there. Harper also wanted to rob niqab-wearing women of their right to vote. And Poilievre's campaign manager for his successful leadership campaign was none other than Jenni Byrne, a close adviser of Harper's and an expert on the dark art of wedge politics.

20

Media and Muslims

An earlier version of this chapter was published as the Inaugural Massey Essay on the Media. Literary Review of Canada, *February 2022 edition.*

MEDIA ORGANIZATIONS SEE THEMSELVES AS CHAMPIONS OF THE UNDERDOG. Yet they're generally deferential to the rich and powerful but careless and cavalier with the poor and vulnerable. Historically, mainstream media have had a poor record of reporting on and portraying Indigenous peoples and new immigrant communities. Where we've improved, we've done so only in keeping with evolving social norms. We've learned to call out overt misogyny, anti-Semitism, and homophobia. But we continue to devalue groups that still suffer racist, religious, and other forms of bigotry in society. When Muslim-bashing became acceptable after 9/11, most media joined right in.

It goes without saying that the media can't be blamed for reporting the anti-Muslim rhetoric that's become an acceptable part of public discourse. Nor for their adversarial and rambunctious nature, a reality that critics, especially Muslim ones, don't always acknowledge. In hundreds of speeches over the years to a wide range of groups, especially minorities in the West, I made it a point to say the following:

- Journalists are not in the business of doing public relations for any group or government.
- We thrive on conflict: "what bleeds, leads." We can be sensationalist and crude, as in a British reporter's shouted query in 1964 at a group of rescued Belgian nuns in war-ravaged Congo disembarking at Stanleyville's airport: "Anyone here been raped and speaks English?"[1]
- We generally follow public opinion, rarely lead it. As a business, we're afraid of getting too far ahead of it. We reflect majority tastes and values, and yes, the prejudices of our time.

Understanding these journalistic practices is essential to appreciating that Muslims aren't the only minority marginalized by the media. Yet that very understanding also lets us see through the myth that the media are equal-opportunity offenders. They aren't.

Studies have shown that more than 75 percent of people in the West rely on the media for their information about Muslims. "What many of us know about Islam, or what we think we know, is filtered primarily through the media," Todd H. Green, an expert on Islamophobia, writes in *The Fear of Islam*. "Without a doubt, the media function as the most powerful and influential conveyor of 'knowledge' of Islam."[2]

As for the ubiquitous social media that have made matters infinitely worse, I've left them out of this analysis. Digital platforms haven't targeted Muslims as disproportionately as have the mainstream media — social media users fulminate against feminists, gays, liberals, Jews, Blacks and Latinos, scientists, experts, everyone. Nor do social media platforms claim to be the balanced and responsible arbiters of truth, guardians of the common good, and the glue that holds democracies together.

Historic Prejudices

Western animosity toward Islam and Muslims has long antecedence, from the Crusades to colonialism, Shakespeare to Orientalists, the last described memorably by Edward Said as the court poets of Western imperialism. There was the Evil Ottomite, the Turbaned Turk, the Wild Wahhabi, the

Bloodthirsty Algerian, and the Mad Mullah. There was the "Islamic nuclear bomb" but not a Christian, Buddhist, Jewish, or Hindu bomb.

A sentiment analysis of print and online headlines in the *New York Times* done in 2015 by 416 Labs, a Toronto-based firm, was instructive. Using computational techniques to gauge the positive, negative, and neutral messages conveyed in them, the study looked at more than 2.6 million examples spanning a quarter-century from 1990 to 2014. It found that the most negative terms appeared in stories about Islam and Muslims — more so than in reports of cocaine and cancer. Of all the headlines associated with Islam and Muslims, 57 percent had a negative connotation, compared with just 8 percent that had a positive one. "We talk a lot about media and Islamophobia, but nobody has done the math," Steven Zhou, one of the analysts, said at the time.[3]

The Islamophobic hysteria since 9/11 has been of a different scale altogether. Scholars in North America, the United Kingdom, and Australia have studiously corroborated the extent of the media's anti-Muslim portrayal. Their findings have been just as studiously ignored by my fellow journalists.

Post-9/11, the problem wasn't necessarily impassioned commentary: drain the terrorist swamps, nuke terrorists' lairs, invade complicit Muslim lands, et cetera. Much of it was over the top, some crossing the line into racism and bloodlust against Muslims. But columnists and cartoonists have traditionally been given wide latitude, a policy I defended as an editor and benefited from as a columnist. Still, those who write commentary and opinion must follow journalistic standards such as adherence to the facts and the test of plausibility. Often that wasn't the case.[4]

The main problem was the news coverage.

Cheerleading Wars

The mainstream media produced more jingoism than journalism. They helped manufacture public consent for the long war on terror. The rah-rah narrative of the Afghan war, especially from those embedded with their nations' armed forces, obscured the reality that after the quick success of toppling the Taliban, the war lost its meaning and was going nowhere. Victory that was ostensibly just around the corner never arrived. No surprise then that the easy-peasy 2021 Taliban takeover was met with utter disbelief among Americans, Canadians, and Europeans.

On Iraq, the American media readily accepted the Bush administration's false assertions about the presence of weapons of mass destruction (WMDs). The *New York Times* and the *Washington Post*, of all the media, led the stampede in quoting copiously from anonymous sources. "Bad intelligence was peddled, circulated, and leaked to the press by a combination of government sources, unreliable Iraqi defectors, and other dubious sources," observed Jill Abramson, former executive editor of the *Times*, in her book *Merchants of Truth*. In particular, "Judith Miller, a longtime Middle East correspondent and investigative reporter for the *Times*, used the specious intelligence from these sources for 'scoops' that were blasted on to the front page. Though other reporters and publications also jumped at the same poisoned bait, Miller's prewar stories were especially egregious and justifiably assailed."[5]

Even the *Washington Post*'s famous investigative reporter Bob Woodward was taken in. Asked on CNN what would happen if the U.S. invaded Iraq and found no WMDs, he said: "The chances of that happening is about zero."

It took more than a year for the *New York Times* and *Post* to apologize about their Iraq coverage, by which time hundreds of thousands of Iraqis were dead and a civilization that was thousands of years old had been smashed to smithereens, including Baghdad, whence my ancestors went to India in the 12th century.

There were no such expressions of regret from Canadian media outlets that acted as trumpeters for the war.

Ignoring Muslim Victims

Once the wars got rolling, the media were more concerned about the victims of terrorism in the West than about the far more numerous Muslim victims. Even allowing for parochial bias, there was no escaping the reality that many media followed the official American script of not counting the Muslim dead. It fell to academics and NGOs to provide estimates, of varying degrees of accuracy, of the mounting death tolls.

As John Pilger, the U.K.-based Australian scholar, noted, "'bad things,' such as America's and Britain's bombing of civilian targets with cluster bombs, and use of napalm and depleted uranium, in Iraq and Afghanistan, are not reported as acts of rapacious conquest but as imperfect liberation.... The principal conveyer of these myths is that amorphous extension of the established order known as 'the media.'"[6]

Most of the media also showed little or no interest in the U.S. Central Intelligence Agency's "extraordinary renditions": cross-border kidnappings of suspects who were forced onto roughly a thousand secret flights. About 3,000 detainees were held worldwide and tortured at so-called black sites. It was the Red Cross, Amnesty International, Human Rights Watch, and others who sounded the first alarms.

Linking Terrorism to Islam

Terrorism by a Muslim was presented as a crime committed by a faith but by a non-Muslim as an individual act. "When a Muslim person mows down innocent victims and terrorizes a community, media and authorities are quick to declare it terrorism," the Poynter Institute, the non-profit journalism school and research organization, observed. "When a white, non-Muslim attacker does the same, he is usually described as a disturbed loner in a freak incident."[7]

The scholar Pavan Kumar Malreddy, who has taught at both York University and the University of Saskatchewan, put it this way: the media routinely labelled non-Muslim killers as crazy lone wolves, nutbars, and mavericks but rarely as homegrown terrorists, "as if 'home' is congenitally incapable of breeding terrorists, let alone the ideological manure required for it. Thus, by definition, a terrorist is always already 'foreign-grown.'"[8]

While terrorism by a Muslim was tied to Islam, terrorism by a Christian wasn't associated with Christianity, nor were a Buddhist's acts to Buddhism, a Jew's to Judaism, a Hindu's to Hinduism, even though some of these perpetrators also invoked their faith or their aggrieved faithful.

Blaming Muslims and Mosques

In too many cases of terrorist incidents, the media's first instinct was to speculate, indeed declare, that the suspect was Muslim. This predated 9/11. In the immediate aftermath of the Oklahoma City bombing in 1995, several outlets confidently pronounced it to have been a jihadist attack. Those initial reports make for amusing reading today — how they got it so horribly wrong with such arrogant certainty and were so shamelessly blasé when it turned out that the culprit, Timothy McVeigh, was a white Christian.

A week after 9/11, letters containing anthrax were sent to two U.S. senators and several news organizations, eventually causing five deaths. The *New York Times* reported that officials were looking into the possibility that "Al Qaeda confederates of the hijackers are behind the incidents," even while noting that investigators "lacked concrete evidence or intelligence to explain who sent the anthrax-contaminated letters." The culprit turned out to be a Catholic microbiologist with the U.S. Army.

Ten years later, when Anders Breivik massacred 77 people in Norway, the *New York Times*, *Washington Post*, and *Wall Street Journal* rushed to call it a Muslim terrorist attack.

* * *

The media besmirched Muslim institutions and ruined individuals by accusing them of having terrorist "links" without ever defining the term, let alone offering any evidence.[9] One frequent journalistic assertion was that mosques in the West were crawling with potential terrorists, incubated by radical imams. The reality was less exotic: some young people were getting radicalized — not so much in mosques and madrasahs but rather online. Periodically, the media found an imam making some outrageous statement, which was then heralded as proof of rampant Muslim militancy and malevolence. There was little or no mention of whether he was representative of the community or a self-appointed imam with no mandate from a mosque or a Muslim organization. That's not to say the media should speak only to authorized representatives of Muslims, but rather that the media often failed to provide context, and more importantly, evidence of institutional complicity.

In fact, imams, mosques, and other institutions were helpful in ferreting out several potential troublemakers. In the United States, a study by the University of South Carolina and Duke University showed that in the 10

20 Media and Muslims

years after 9/11, Muslims tipped off security officials in 48 of the 121 terrorist incidents unearthed.[10] In Canada, as noted in an earlier chapter, Prime Minister Stephen Harper conceded in 2014 that mosques were helpful in warding off radicalization.

Media-Security Nexus

Many of the most damaging stories about mosques and Muslim institutions were planted by intelligence and security agencies in the United States, Britain, and Canada. According to editors Elizabeth Poole and John E. Richardson in *Muslims and the News Media*, there was "a quite frightening degree of complicity between governmental propagandists and the news media in whipping up waves of panic regarding the presence of Muslim terrorists" in Britain. They were citing British sociologist David Miller, co-founder of Spinwatch, which monitors both corporate and government propaganda.[11]

In the United States, such co-operation between security forces and the media extended to editorial and opinion pages. There was "a heavy reliance by editorial writers on official government sources as they constructed their frames," according to Michael Ryan in his essay "Framing the War Against Terrorism."[12]

In Canada, the unholy alliance between the media and the security apparatus was demonstrated in several cases:

- **Maher Arar.** The Syrian Canadian tortured in Syria was repeatedly maligned in the conservative Canadian media without evidence. The stories were clearly planted by unnamed sources in intelligence and security agencies, no doubt to divert attention from their own culpability in framing this innocent Canadian. Skeptical media outlets, such as the CBC and the *Toronto Star*, did little to expose such underhanded tactics. Even after Arar's return to Canada in 2003, the dirty campaign didn't cease, especially in the Canwest group of newspapers, including the *Ottawa Citizen*. The paper ran a story by reporter Juliet

O'Neill based on sources in the security establishment, demonizing Arar as a trained member of an Al Qaeda cell. The Royal Canadian Mounted Police (RCMP) raided O'Neill's house to investigate the leak. The Canadian media establishment was shocked — how dare the RCMP raid a reporter's house? Phil Crawley, publisher of the *Globe and Mail*, thundered: "I woke up and thought, I am in some totalitarian state." Scott Anderson, editor of the *Ottawa Citizen*, complained about the "star chamber-police state attitude that has crept into government and law enforcement post-9/11."

All this was a bit thick coming from people who had long been acting as the echo chamber for Canadian security forces and also the American war machine. The road to the raid on O'Neill's house began in Guantanamo Bay where the rule of law was first set aside brazenly. Due process had since been ignored in many places, against many innocents in the United States, and to a lesser degree, in Canada. "Yesterday, a Mohammad, today an O'Neill," I wrote.

When a judicial commission cleared Arar in 2006 and Ottawa apologized to him, the media never did, except for a few individuals such as Craig Oliver of CTV and Jeff Sallot of the *Globe and Mail*. Arar's response? The media should serve "the weak and the vulnerable, not the powerful."

- **Omar Khadr.** The conservative media fell in line with the Harper government's successful campaign to turn him into a poster child of Ottawa's tough stand against terrorism. Only Michelle Shephard of the *Toronto Star* methodically dismantled the many falsehoods about Khadr. She got his side of the story with 27 trips to Guantanamo Bay, wrote about 250 articles in the paper, and then published a book, *Guantanamo's Child: The Untold Story of Omar Khadr* (2008), later turned into a documentary.[13] When the government was eventually forced by the courts to release him, and later Ottawa apologized to him, the media never offered a mea culpa.

- The media also didn't undertake a post-mortem of their role in the 2003 case of 23 Toronto-area youth, the ostensible "Al Qaeda sleeper cell." They were allegedly plotting to fly planes into the Pickering Nuclear Generating Station and to bomb the CN Tower. The authorities claimed to have gathered "25 boxes of evidence" and 30 computers and "schematics of airplanes." But all the terrorism-related charges turned out to be paranoid fantasies on the part of the authorities and were dropped. An analysis of the news coverage by Felix Odartey-Wellington, a professor of communication at Cape Breton University, showed how the *Globe and Mail* and *National Post* "acted in concert with the Canadian security apparatus in generating a moral panic" and how young Muslims were framed as "folk devils."[14]

- In 2006, police picked up 18 young men in Toronto for planning urban terrorist acts. They were said to have been radicalized at local mosques. In fact, they seemed motivated by Canada's involvement in the war in Afghanistan. John Miller, the former head of journalism at Toronto Metropolitan University, and Cybele Sack, a student in the department, analyzed the coverage in five major newspapers and *Maclean's*. "The media's standards for granting anonymity were violated to an alarming degree," they wrote in the *Canadian Journal of Media Studies*. "Investigators were allowed to violate the accused plotters' presumption of innocence without being held accountable."[15] Many journalists went further by "putting Muslim leaders on the spot to tell Canadians what they were going to do to stop it and encouraging them to pledge allegiance to Canada, as if it were their particular responsibility to do so because they shared a cultural background with the suspects."[16]

Miller and Sack also did a study of opinion pages, examining 225 articles. They found "a significant portion of the published commentary raised unreasonable public alarm, cast suspicion on the followers of a major religion and impugned the religion itself, failed to subject the allegations of our government and security officials to rigorous scrutiny, and predicted guilt before the suspects were able to exercise their democratic rights to a fair trial."[17]

Contributing to Islamophobia

When the Toronto 18 case broke, a mosque in Scarborough held a press conference to plead that the alleged perpetrators weren't representative of the community and that Islam didn't condone terrorism. That they felt compelled to say all this was itself telling of the times. What the *Globe and Mail*'s Christie Blatchford filed after attending the event is worth quoting at length:

> I drove back from yesterday's news conference at the Islamic Foundation of Toronto in the northeastern part of the city, but honestly, I could have just as easily floated home in the sea of horse manure emanating from the building.
>
> So frequent were the bald reassurances that faith and religion had nothing — *nothing*, you understand — to do with the alleged homegrown terrorist plot recently busted open by Canadian police and security forces, that for a few minutes afterward, I wondered if perhaps it was a vile lie of the mainstream press or a fiction of my own demented brain that the 17 accused young men are all, well, Muslims....
>
> Even before I knew for sure that they're all Muslims, I suspected as much from what I saw on the tube.... The accused men are mostly young and mostly bearded in the Taliban fashion. They have first names like Mohamed, middle names like Mohamed and last names like Mohamed. Some of their female relatives at the Brampton courthouse who were there in their support wore black head-to-toe

burkas (now there's a sight to gladden the Canadian female heart: homegrown *burka*-wearers darting about just as they do in Afghanistan), which is not a getup I have ever seen on anyone but Muslim women.[18]

The editors of Canada's self-declared national newspaper featured the column not on opinion pages but rather blared it from A1.

I've done my share of defending columnists, as well as cartoonists, but they normally don't cross certain red lines. In 1997, however, the *Montreal Gazette*'s Aislin depicted an angry dog wearing an Arab headscarf. The headline read, "In the name of Islamic extremism," while a balloon below added, "With our apologies to dogs everywhere." As the American journalist Lawrence Pintak, a Middle East veteran, noted a decade later, "It is difficult to conceive of a North American newspaper running such a cartoon with the headline: 'In the name of Jewish extremism,' or 'In the name of Christian extremism.'"

Six years after Aislin's cartoon appeared, the *Globe and Mail* published one that showed an Arab boy joyously giving his dad a suicide belt for Father's Day. Toronto lawyer Dany Assaf was enraged. As he recounts in his 2021 book *Say Please and Thank You & Stand in Line*, he met with the paper's editorial board and brought with him a picture of his son, Mohamad, and daughter, Danya, then three and two. Sliding the picture across the table, Assaf asked, "Which of my children do you imagine giving me a suicide belt for Father's Day?" The editors offered him "an apology of sorts."

Maclean's Maligns Muslims

European media, in particular, hyped the demographic time-bomb theory: that Muslims were outbreeding others and were bound to take over the continent. "The Muslim-tide hypothesis has no merit," *Globe* columnist Doug Saunders wrote in his book *The Myth of the Muslim Tide*.[19] Yet *Maclean's* ran a 4,800-word excerpt of a Mark Steyn book in 2006. It claimed that Muslims posed a demographic, cultural, and security threat to the West. A group of Muslim students complained to the Canadian Human Rights Commission, as well as to two provincial commissions, on the grounds that the excerpt constituted hate speech. Whether it did or not is a matter of opinion. They had a right to complain. Yet they were vilified by some newspapers as no previous complainants had been.

At times the media made things up.

In Quebec, the Bouchard-Taylor commission on cultural accommodation (2007–8) reviewed publications that had stoked hysteria with stories of outrageous requests for religious accommodation. The commission hired its own reporters and researchers and concluded that the articles they checked bore little or no resemblance to the facts. "The foundations of collective life in Quebec are not in a critical situation," explained the final report.

In Britain, there was the trope of "no-go areas in Britain where sharia law dominates, and non-Muslims cannot enter." A study by the Cardiff School of Journalism, Media and Cultural Studies analyzed 974 stories concerning Muslims between 2000 and 2008. Done for the Channel 4 program *Dispatches*, it concluded that some stories "were pure inventions, others contained a grain of truth but were distorted," according to a booklet, *Muslims Under Siege*, released with the *Dispatches* documentary. Written by Peter Oborne, political columnist, and James Jones, television journalist, it said: "We should all feel a little bit ashamed about the way we treat Muslims in the media, in our politics, and on our streets.… We misrepresent and in certain cases persecute them." Nothing much had changed by 2016 when Oborne bemoaned "a soft apartheid towards Muslims emerging in Britain.… I think anti-Muslim hatred and anti-Muslim bigotry in the media have invented a new kind of concept, called non-violent extremism which is a new kind of word for thought crime."[20]

Not much had changed by 2018. The Centre for Media Monitoring of the Muslim Council of Britain said: "The constant drip feed of misinformation seen in rolling news coverage, particularly concerning suspected 'terror' attacks and the misreporting of Muslim beliefs, actions and ideas … particularly among the right leaning media has the effect of dehumanising Muslims." The centre had surveyed five major broadcasters as well as most mainstream newspapers, including their online versions, 31 online platforms in total. Of the 10,931 articles, a third had misrepresented Muslims, portraying them as anti-Semitic and hostile to non-Muslims. Miqdaad Versi, founder of the centre, told me that the British media had also managed to distort the public perception of British Muslims by fusing Muslim militants anywhere in the world with law-abiding Muslim in Britain.

Writing about Versi's work, Samanth Subramanian of *The Guardian* noted that "no other community in Britain receives such regular torrents of bad press.... Newspapers have, for years now, relentlessly demonized Muslims, setting them up as the implacable enemy of everything that is liberal, British and civilized.[21]"

By 2020, Versi's team had analyzed more than 48,000 online articles and 5,500 broadcast clips. Its report, "British Media's Coverage of Muslims & Islam (2018–2020)," listed 10 case studies of how Muslims had been misrepresented, defamed, and libelled by major publications. It classified almost 60 percent of online media articles and 47 percent of television clips as associating Muslims and Islam with negative aspects or behaviour.[22]

Two prominent editors had this to say about the report:

- Alison Phillips, editor of the *Daily Mirror*: "This shows how much we as journalists must question ourselves, and the work we are producing in relation to reporting of Muslims and Islam."
- Emma Tucker, editor of the *Sunday Times* (now editor-in-chief of the *Wall Street Journal*): "I welcome this report in the full knowledge that it contains criticisms of the press, my own paper included."

Pumping, Deflating

The media exaggerated Muslim terrorism and downplayed terrorism by non-Muslims. "A perpetrator who is not Muslim would have to kill on average about seven more people to receive the same amount of coverage as a perpetrator who is Muslim," according to an academic study published in *Justice Quarterly*. It analyzed 3,541 articles published between 2006 and 2015, including from the *New York Times*, the *Wall Street Journal*, and the *Washington Post*. Attacks by Muslim perpetrators received, on average, 357 percent more coverage than the other attacks. And while Muslims committed just 12.5 percent of the attacks, they received half of the news coverage of 136 terrorist incidents. This imbalance created "a feedback loop of incorrect information fueling prejudice and discrimination."[23]

The January 2017 massacre at the Quebec City mosque didn't make the main headline on the *Globe and Mail's* front page the next day. On television, the CBC's coverage was in "stark contrast to the many hours of live reporting and commentary" it devoted to the London Bridge jihadist attack five months later, as Azeezah Kanji observed in the *Toronto Star*. A legal scholar at the Noor Cultural Centre in Toronto, Kanji also complained to the public broadcaster about a special edition of *The National* prompted by the events in London. Host Peter Mansbridge "focused exclusively on 'jihadist' terrorism" while blithely ignoring the massacre here. The CBC's ombudsperson, Esther Enkin, sent Kanji a six-page reply. In classic bureaucratese, Enkin semi-conceded the lapse but couldn't resist adding that a reporter "did reference Quebec City," as had a panellist in an episode titled "A National Conversation on Terror," as though those passing references mitigated the relative neglect of the deadliest attacks on Canadian Muslims.

Two years later, in 2019, two mass shootings by a single gunman in Christchurch, New Zealand, left 51 Muslims from two mosques dead. Again, the *Globe* failed to give the story prominence on the front page, a point conceded by Sylvia Stead, the paper's public editor. One should avoid second-guessing the placement of news stories unless a pattern emerges, which is what we have here.

The Canadian media kept exemplary vigil for Michael Kovrig and Michael Spavor, who had been unjustly detained for 1,019 days in China, yet hardly bothered about the fate of another Canadian, Huseyin Celil. An activist fighting on behalf of his persecuted people, the Uighurs, he's been in prison since 2006. Unlike the Michaels, he didn't get a single Canadian consular visit. Contact with his mother and sister in China was cut off years ago. We know nothing about his condition. We don't even know if he's alive. A critical difference between Celil's case and that of the two Michaels is that he's not white and is a naturalized Canadian Muslim.

Using Pliant Muslims

While the media have been obsessed with Muslims, they rarely talked to ordinary Muslims. Those they interviewed and quoted copiously tended to be:

- Gun-toting militants and fire-breathing imams.
- "Moderate Muslims," defined as those who attack Islam and tell Muslims to heal themselves but rarely if ever question the received wisdom about the geopolitics that affect Muslims.
- Those who had once been "radical," "fundamentalist," "militant," and "jihadist" but have since seen the error of their ways. No details or proof of their past misdeeds required. The storyline is too good for either party to spoil it by the need for corroboration.
- Ex-Muslims, like the activist Ayaan Hirsi Ali, who confirm every cliché.

The Muslim commentators and pundits most patronized by the media are generally the ones most mistrusted by Muslims. This is true across the West. All of them are entitled to their opinions but not their facts. Many were peddling "alternative facts" long before the Trumpites coined the term to describe misinformation and disinformation. Worse, editors and producers rarely allowed rebuttals, let alone countervailing opinions on a regular basis.

In Britain, for example, "Muslim sources are overwhelmingly only included and only quoted in reporting contexts critical of their actions and critical of their religion," according to Professor John Richardson of Loughborough University. "When Muslim activities are not criticized — or when reported activities are not labelled as *Muslim* actions — Muslim sources are, almost without exception, absent from journalistic texts."[24]

Gendered Islamophobia

Western media organizations have been at the forefront of advocacy for the rights of Muslim women. Paradoxically, many of those same journalists have failed to give Muslim women fair and balanced coverage.

On issues associated with the hijab and niqab, the media provided mostly one-sided views. They shut out even those who personally oppose the hijab or niqab but do respect an individual's choices. It's only since Quebec banned the wearing of religious symbols by public servants in positions of authority in 2019 that some media have come around to providing a semblance of balanced coverage.

The niqab being a powerful symbol of Muslim women's oppression, the media can't resist using the image even when it has little or no relevance to what's being discussed. Reality is thus distorted: an overwhelming majority of Muslim women don't wear the niqab worldwide, and 99 percent of those living in the West don't.

Then there's sharia.

Amid all the hysteria surrounding it, never did the media ask the simplest of reportorial questions: how, exactly, was sharia to come to Canada, the United States, the United Kingdom, or anywhere else in the West? Would the entire Western legal canon be swept aside to permit, say, the chopping off of the hands of thieves?

That the media concern for Muslim women is suspect shows up elsewhere. For years, hate crimes against Muslim women, especially those who wear hijabs and niqabs, have been skyrocketing across Canada, Europe, and the United States. Individuals have been accosted in public spaces, called names, spat on, chased, pushed, shoved, and kicked, and the media, especially in Europe, barely reported the incidents for the longest time.

Reporters and pundits remain oblivious to one of the great ironies of our age: a major concern of the media and the public about Islam has been its treatment of women, yet a major target of Islamophobia and Islamophobic coverage in the West has been Muslim women. As Toronto Metropolitan University's Tariq Amin-Khan observed, this contradiction reflects "a schizophrenic Orientalist attitude."

Domestic Violence

Just as acts of terrorism by Muslims are attributed to their faith, acts of domestic violence are blamed on the perpetrator's faith and culture. Professor Zareena Grewal, an anthropologist at Yale University, explains in her report "Death by Culture? How Not to Talk About Islam and Domestic Violence":

> When white males perpetrate violence, the focus is on the psychological portrait of this individual: family history, childhood, mental health. Yet when a Muslim woman is killed violently by a Muslim man, we are willing to accept culture as an explanation in a way that would never be satisfactory if the perpetrator were white ...[25]

Two tragic cases in Canada helped illustrate the point. In 2009, three Afghan-Canadian girls were killed by their father, Mohammad Shafia, who also killed their mother, his first wife. After a sensational trial that attracted international attention, he was convicted, along with his second wife and his son, on four counts of murder. The girls had been caught between their father's strict rules and their own social mores. Yasmin Jiwani, a communications professor at Concordia University, analyzed the *Globe*'s coverage — some 60 stories over two and a half years. Jiwani said the girls were depicted as "exceptional" or "worthy" victims who were trying to become "like *us*" and "join the dominant society which ... offers them freedom, sexual and otherwise."[26]

Two years earlier, in 2007, Aqsa Parvez, a 16-year-old Pakistani-Canadian girl, was murdered by her father in what was widely characterized as an honour killing triggered by her refusal to don the hijab. But one journalist, Craig Offman of Canwest News Service, found a different narrative. He reported that "the traditional Islamic clothing was *not* a major factor and that other girls in the family did *not* wear the hijab" (italics added). Offman was also told by Aqsa's acquaintances that she herself "was religiously observant but mainly wanted to be more independent."[27] As Wilfrid Laurier University's Jasmin Zine observed in *Studies in Ethnicity and Nationalism*, "any attempt to insert a more normative frame of reference through which to understand Aqsa's death was overshadowed by the barrage of media sensationalism that framed the issue as a 'death by culture.'"[28]

At the time of the tragic Parvez case, I interviewed Vivian Rakoff, the former director of the Clarke Institute of Psychiatry, part of the Centre for Addiction and Mental Health in Toronto. Intergenerational clashes transcend race, religion, and ethnicity, he told me: "It's the story of almost every single immigrant group adhering to the strict values of their past or indeed their present. I've heard this from Greek families, Italian families where the daughter wants to go and be with friends on the Yonge Street strip and the father calls her a whore and kicks her out and she gets beaten up."

Illiberal Liberals

Even the liberal media aren't free of biases when it comes to Muslim women. Rochelle Terman, who teaches at the University of Chicago, analyzed their portrayal in the *New York Times* and *Washington Post* over a 35-year period by looking at 4,531 articles. In 2017, she wrote that coverage was driven by "confirmation bias," which affirmed the papers' pre-existing theories and prejudices.

Journalists placed disproportionate emphasis on inequality in Muslim lands. They ignored egregious violations of women's rights in non-Muslim nations, such as those across much of Africa.

When reporting on non-Muslim women, the papers disproportionately featured those living in societies where their rights were respected. Thus Muslim women were "associated with countries that violate women's rights, whereas non-Muslim women are associated with countries that respect their rights." The two papers also concentrated on Iran and Saudi Arabia rather than, say, Malaysia. Thus, "Muslim women from relatively egalitarian societies are less visible than women in oppressive Muslim countries," further distorting the picture.

But why wouldn't the media concentrate on Saudi Arabia and Iran, given their atrocious records? When I put that question to Terman, she responded, "It may be perfectly reasonable to focus on Iran and Saudi Arabia over Malaysia. But non-Muslim countries that also do horribly on women's rights are not featured in these papers. Also, stories about Muslim women are framed around 'women's rights and gender equality' regardless of the situation on the ground."[29]

20 Media and Muslims

Let me add another example of skewed coverage concerning Muslim women. There's been relentless Western media coverage of the Iranian clerical regime's enforcement of the hijab on women. There's the relative lack of journalistic interest in the Egyptian army's longstanding practice of kettling, groping, and raping women demonstrators as a tool of curbing dissent. The difference is that the mullahs in Tehran are the West's adversaries, whereas the generals in Cairo are allies.

How Muslims View the Media

Regardless of the great diversity of views among them, Muslims are as one in being disappointed, enraged, and estranged from Western media, which they see as anti-Muslim crusaders. The alienated fall into two broad categories: people in the Muslim world and Muslim minorities in the West. The former had the luxury of criticizing from a distance; the latter had to deal with the constant fallout of demonization and the erosion of basic rights.

Muslims generally, and Muslim minorities in the West particularly, don't trust my profession and colleagues. They fear us, especially what they see as our tactics of entrapment. They're petrified that their words will be twisted and distorted if they don't fit the prescribed clichés and stereotypes. "We don't recognize ourselves in your media," I've been told repeatedly over the years across North America, Europe, the Middle East, the Far East, and Africa.

Here are some of their other main concerns:

- The media rarely probe the conflicts of interest or motivations of those whose religious or geopolitical interests are served by demonizing Islam and Muslims: far-right parties across Europe, several evangelical Christian groups in the United States, and those who reportedly had a pecuniary interest in attacking Islam and Muslims. Frank Gaffney, Daniel Pipes, Robert Spencer, Pamela Geller, Steve Emerson, Brigitte Gabriel, and others are people who were often used by the media as experts on Islam and Muslim issues, "but who, in fact, get paid to promote hate," according to Todd H. Green of Luther College, who has studied Islamophobia.[30]

- Media invoke free speech in recycling anti-Islamic content but fall silent when the free speech of Muslims is affected. In 2015, Concordia University culled "controversial" and "inappropriate" books in an office run by the Muslim Students' Association. Three years earlier, the *Toronto Sun* raised a hullabaloo after a visit to an Islamic bookstore in the city's east end rattled the owner into removing a book that referenced beating disobedient wives. Are there not misogynist and other inappropriate materials in the religious texts of most faiths, starting with the Old Testament? Should we be pulling all those from public view, as well?
- Media organizations are usually dismissive of Muslim complaints and don't take Muslims seriously. We saw this attitude in the episode of those infamous Danish cartoons of the Prophet when the editors of *Jyllands-Posten* ignored concerned voices, including a 3,000-strong demonstration in Copenhagen and a petition with 17,000 signatures. Similarly, the editors of *Maclean's* were scornful of a delegation of Muslims upset by author Mark Steyn's tirade about the ostensible Muslim threat. It was only then that the complainants went to the various human-rights commissions.

Even Canada, Eh?

I once thought that Canadian coverage of terrorism would be of a higher standard. Why? Because we're Canadian. I also thought that under multiculturalism our newsrooms had made enough progress to produce more balanced journalism.

Much of the questionable coverage was in the conservative group of newspapers that have come to dominate Canada under owners Conrad Black, then Izzy Asper, and then Postmedia Network. If you lived in Montreal, Ottawa, Regina, Saskatoon, Calgary, Edmonton, or Vancouver, you were subjected to a constant blast of Muslim-bashing, pro-American, pro-Israeli coverage.

20 Media and Muslims

Asper's Canwest, the largest newspaper publisher in Canada, centralized editorial writing in its head office in Winnipeg on subjects that mattered to the Aspers, notably the Israeli-Palestinian dispute. Those corporate editorials had to be carried by all of the chain's major papers. Not only that but independent columnists also had to toe the official line. When Doug Cuthand, columnist for the *Leader-Post* in Regina and the *StarPhoenix* in Saskatoon, compared the plight of Palestinians to that of Indigenous people in Canada, his column was killed. Veteran reporter Bill Marsden of the *Montreal Gazette*, part of the Canwest chain then, now Postmedia, said of his bosses: "They do not want any criticism of Israel. We do not run in our newspaper op-ed pieces that express criticism of Israel and what it's doing."

Such censorship and self-censorship under highly concentrated ownership was the thrust of my 2002 James Minifie Lecture, named after the Canadian journalist, a Saskatchewan native, who served as the CBC's correspondent in Washington, D.C. Covering the event at the University of Regina School of Journalism was Michelle Lang of Regina's *Leader-Post*, a Canwest paper. The story she filed was rewritten to tone down my criticisms of Canwest. In protest, she withdrew her byline. So did her colleagues in solidarity. She and three others were promptly suspended for a week without pay. Six others were handed letters of reprimand. None of this was reported in the newspaper. The residents of Regina heard about it mostly through the CBC, which the Aspers had been lobbying Ottawa to be downsized.

That Minifie Lecture was cited by the National Press Club of Canada and the Canadian Committee for UNESCO, along with my post-9/11 writings, in awarding me their Press Freedom Award. Again, Canwest didn't like what I said on that occasion. In reporting on the award ceremony, the *Ottawa Citizen* had this lead on that story: "An event in Ottawa billed as highlighting the life-and-death perils faced by journalists around the world became the latest stage for a *Toronto Star* columnist's attack on Canwest's alleged censorship ..."

Murdoch Davis, editor-in-chief of Canwest, dismissed my comments at the Ottawa ceremony as "erroneous blather," and my Regina speech as full of "ill-informed views," based on "loopy rumours circulating in journalistic circles." He added: "Who is Haroon Siddiqui? We are not talking about one of the great icons of Canadian journalism. He's just a guy."

I didn't tell him that in 1984 the boss of his bosses, Izzy Asper, founder of Canwest, had written to me from Winnipeg: "There certainly hasn't been a journalist with the same astuteness around here as when you were writing."

In 2010, Canwest got absorbed into Postmedia Network, further increasing concentration. Worse, majority ownership of the chain moved to an American hedge fund. Yet Prime Minister Stephen Harper's government approved the transaction, ignoring a long-standing law that had capped foreign ownership of media at 25 percent. In 2014, Postmedia also acquired the *Sun* group of tabloids, bringing the total number of newspapers it owned to more than 100. It was wall-to-wall anti-Muslim coverage and commentary throughout the land.

They took to peddling what John Cruickshank, then the publisher of the *Toronto Star*, described to me in 2016 as "flat-out racism and bigotry" and "profoundly awful" content.

Governor General Adrienne Clarkson conferring the Order of Canada, the Citadelle, Quebec City, 2002.

Thin-Skinned

Not until I started gathering all the thematic strands of news coverage and commentary did I realize how much and in how many ways the media have demeaned and dehumanized Muslims over more than two decades. In considering the many sins of commission and omission that I've outlined, readers may assess for themselves how various newspapers, magazines, and radio and television outlets stack up. Some might feel that I've overemphasized certain trends and underplayed others. Such is the nature of any subjective exercise.

Democracy dies in darkness, journalists say. It also dies with hateful journalism. Instead of protecting democracy by protecting all citizens, the media have eroded it by their demonstrated animus against the most beleaguered minority since 9/11.

Although journalists are in the business of critiquing everyone, we aren't very gracious when critiqued. If we're indeed central to democracy, we do need a reckoning. We should be summoned to pay heed to our better angels: in the case of the CBC, the *Globe and Mail,* and the *Toronto Star,* by their ombudspersons, and across the profession by the National NewsMedia Council and the Conseil de presse du Québec, as a start. But they all tend to be complaint-driven and have been too absorbed in nitpicking to confront this dark period in our history. Perhaps they can now find the will and the way — in partnership with such groups as News Media Canada, the Canadian Journalism Foundation, the Canadian Association of Journalists, and Canadian Journalists for Free Expression, as well as interested journalism schools — to conduct an honest examination of our post-9/11 record. Should there be such an undertaking, I'd be happy to be proven more wrong than right.

However, in keeping with their state of denial, none had anything to say since the publication of an earlier version of this chapter in the *Literary Review of Canada.* As a letter to the editor in a subsequent edition of that publication by Joel Henderson from Gatineau, Quebec, put it: "In reading it, I felt like I had just landed from Mars and was seeing a period of our history for the first time."

21

Rushdie and Muslims

NO AUTHOR SHOULD BE CONDEMNED TO DEATH OR STABBED FOR HIS OR HER words. There's nothing "Islamic" about it, even if the 1989 fatwa calling for Salman Rushdie's murder was issued by an ayatollah, and the man who stabbed the author in the summer of 2022 is a Muslim. People of different faiths do horrible things in the name of religion.

Yet there's no separating Islam and Muslims from Rushdie and *The Satanic Verses*. The novel vilified the Prophet Muhammad and the Prophet's wives as prostitutes plying their trade in a whorehouse in the holy precincts of the Ka'ba in Mecca. The most patronized was the Prophet's youngest and beloved wife, Ayesha, revered by Muslims as among the most reliable and scholarly witnesses to his Prophethood.

Those and other vulgarities infuriated Muslims worldwide, bestirred Ayatollah Ruhollah Khomeini, forced Rushdie into hiding, got his Japanese translator murdered, his Italian translator attacked, his Norwegian publisher shot, and dozens of protesting Muslims killed in India, where Rushdie was born, and in Pakistan, where his parents had immigrated to and where he himself worked. The book triggered a clash of civilizations long before 9/11.

To the West, the Rushdie affair demonstrated how religion is exploited in the Muslim world and how easily some Muslims are provoked into violence. To Muslims, it proved how incendiary and hypocritical many in the West can be in demonizing Islam and Muslims.

The world remains broadly divided between those for Rushdie and those against — the first group mostly non-Muslim, white, and living in the West; the second mostly Muslim, non-white, and living in the East. Neither side wants to hear the other. It's the global equivalent of dysfunctional America, with half the population deaf to the other.

Another false construct has been the delineation of Muslims into pro-Khomeini or pro-Rushdie. In the real world, most Muslims have been for neither — offended to the core of their beings by the novel but disagreeing wholeheartedly with the ayatollah's edict. The Aga Khan, the most soft-spoken, moderate, and Westernized Muslim leader to be found anywhere, denounced the fatwa but also told me in an interview in 1992: "I don't think there is a practising Muslim who wouldn't have felt offended. This book is something which as a Muslim I find totally unacceptable." In 1993, when 100 leading literary figures from the Muslim world issued a booklet in solidarity, *For Rushdie*, many made it clear that they, too, had been offended by his novel. In 2022, the Muslims who wished Rushdie speedy recovery from the attempted assassination weren't necessarily applauding his depictions of Islam and Muhammad, either.

The most moderate of positions is to condemn violence and not condone the demonization of a religion. The right to religion and the right to be free of constant needling about one's faith is a bedrock principle of secular liberal democracies. So is free speech, with judicially applied limits. Yet the application of an absolutist version of free speech in the Rushdie case has been in sharp contrast to its flexible interpretation and implementation elsewhere, as I'll outline.

Creators often create what they think will get them the widest audience, including catering to the prejudices of their patrons and likely customers. The Rushdie affair is, in my books, less about him than those who have gone to the barricades for him. Just as it is with the army of Western admirers of V.S. Naipaul despite his clearly racist writings.

Crusader Legacy

Rushdie copied the Christian Crusaders (1095–1291) who mocked Muhammad as "Mahound," an Antichrist, a false prophet peddling a fake holy book, the Qur'an, as the Word of God. Dante Alighieri and Francis Bacon called Muhammad the Beast of the Apocalypse, and Islam a world of violence, anarchy, and rage — a framing that's remained a constant in attacks on Islam throughout the ages. Western detractors have also been obsessed with Muhammad's sex life. European colonialists continued the legacy, including in India. In the mid-19th century, British missionary polemicist Sir William Muir published a pamphlet, *The Mohammedan Controversy*, which he later expanded into a book, the four-volume *Life of Mahomet*, portraying the Prophet as a fraud who fabricated revelations "as a means of reaching secular ends," and whose sexual profligacy constituted "a serious movement away from Christianity,"[1] which forbade polygamy.

The Muslim response wasn't to issue a fatwa of death. Rather, the most effective rejoinder was a pamphlet by Shaykh Rahmatullah Kairanvi, a well-regarded scholar from the village of Kairana, where my first family ancestor from Baghdad settled in the 12th century. His widely circulated paper was "a very articulate defence of Islam and an attack on the scriptural inconsistencies and corruptions of the Christian Gospels, based partly on the new findings of German biblical scholars," writes William Dalrymple in *The Last Mughal*.[2]

Similar Script

The Satanic Verses also features Mahound. He's described as "the Devil's synonym," "a drunk in a gutter," a trickster who made up the Qur'an, including the Satanic verses in which he momentarily praised three pagan goddesses of Mecca only to abrogate the verses as the work of Satan. Mahound's dozen wives came with "God's own permission to fuck as many women as he liked." Rushdie located the wives — known to believers as *Ummul-Muminoon*, the "Mothers of Muslims" — in a brothel called The Curtain (Hijab). The clients "curled around the innermost courtyard of the brothel rotating about its centrally positioned Fountain of Love much as pilgrims rotated for other reasons around the ancient pillar of stone," the Ka'ba. Mahound's closest companions were a "bunch of riff-raff, raggle-taggle gang, goons … fucking clowns." One of them, Bilal, the first person of African ancestry to embrace Islam — and whom Muhammad named Islam's first *muezzin*, the one who calls people to prayer — was, in Rushdie's racist terminology, "an enormous black monster, with a voice to match his size."[3]

As Muslims erupted in anger, the publisher, Viking Penguin, said their objections must have sprung from a "misreading of the book." Rushdie said that only fundamentalists and radicals would object to what was a dream sequence in a fictional account. That seemed to contradict his earlier assertion that historical fiction couldn't be excused from critical examination and that *The Satanic Verses* was historical.

When the politically astute Khomeini issued his fatwa, it stirred Muslims worldwide, including those who disagreed vehemently with his call to murder. Such was the clamour for somebody to do something, anything. It didn't matter that the fatwa was illegal under any interpretation of Islamic law. Rushdie hadn't been tried by any sharia court, indeed could not have even been charged because neither Iran nor any Islamic polity anywhere had jurisdiction over him, a British citizen.

Rushdie responded that he wished he'd been more critical of Islam. Then he changed his tune, apologized, even renewed his Islamic faith, disavowed parts of the book, and proposed suspension of the paperback edition. That didn't change the fatwa. He regretted his regret, renounced his repentance — "a mistake," "an embarrassing flirtation with Islam," and "the stupidest thing I ever did" for which "I felt sick with myself."

Most of the West re-embraced him as a principled and brave exemplar of free speech. Most Muslims saw through the bullshitry of a condemned man understandably trying to wiggle out of a conundrum of his own making.

Not everyone defending Rushdie agreed with the contents of the novel, only his right to write what he had. The Muslim response was summarized by Ali Mazrui of the University of Michigan: a Christian equivalent would have been to "portray the Virgin Mary as a prostitute, and Jesus as the son of one of her sexual clients." It would have been interesting to see which leading Western writers would have marched "in a procession in defence of the 'rights' of such a novelist."[4]

In December 1992, Rushdie emerged briefly from his Scotland Yard protection and was reportedly flown in a private jet to Toronto to make a sensational surprise appearance at a PEN Canada gala. The audience of

1,200 went into rapturous applause. The organizers, many my friends, congratulated themselves as victorious soldiers in the war for free speech. I found myself in a minority of one on the *Toronto Star*'s editorial board of eight that I chaired. No one wanted to hear another point of view. The *Star* took one stand, I another in later bylined columns.

Rushdie was taken secretly to Ottawa to meet Foreign Minister Barbara McDougall, who promptly called British foreign secretary Douglas Hurd to tell him: "I just hugged Salman Rushdie, your citizen" — a barb at the cowardly reluctance of the British Conservative government ministers to be seen with the author.

After Iran announced in 1998 that it wouldn't enforce the fatwa, Rushdie moved to the United States — a highly honoured victim-celebrity, a role he revelled in.

* * *

Muslims most lauded in the West are usually the ones most hated by Muslims: the shah of Iran, Anwar Sadat and Hosni Mubarak of Egypt, and to cite a contemporary example, Ayaan Hirsi Ali. An outspoken critic of Islam, she pronounced herself an ex-Muslim in her adopted land, the Netherlands. In 2004, she collaborated with Dutch filmmaker Theo van Gogh for a documentary, *Submission*, the literal meaning of Islam. In it, Qur'anic verses were projected onto women's naked bodies to convey the message that Islam decreed women to be chattels of men. In fact, Islam liberated women in pre-Islamic Arabia where they were inherited by their adult sons after their husbands' deaths. Van Gogh was murdered in Amsterdam by a Dutch Muslim of Moroccan origin. Hirsi Ali was placed under 24-hour police protection. The Dutch adored her until they discovered that her tale as a Somali refugee to Europe was full of holes. She moved to the United States where, like Rushdie, she found a larger and more influential audience.

Rushdie, Hirsi Ali, and other Muslims and ex-Muslims favoured by the West have been key players in the cultural warfare on Muslims. They're the individual equivalents of American client states in the Muslim world. Pliant dictators and oil monarchs are given a free hand to crush democracy in the name of protecting Western interests from the hordes of Muslim terrorists. Writers and other public figures are rewarded for being billboards for Western cultural and moral superiority over Islam and Muslims. The more they vilify Islam and Muslims, the greater the rewards. Islamophobia has been a business model not only for Fox News but also for many media, publishing houses, think tanks, and academic institutions. One is hard-core, the others soft.

Familiar Echoes

Preceding *The Satanic Verses* was the Nobel laureate Naipaul's *Among the Believers: An Islamic Journey*, wherein he expanded his usual disdain for people who looked like him, brown, to include Muslims.

Post-9/11 bestsellers included Samuel P. Huntington's *The Clash of Civilizations and the Remaking of World Order*; academic Bernard Lewis's *What Went Wrong? The Clash Between Islam and Modernity in the Middle East*; Irshad Manji's *The Trouble with Islam Today*; and Hirsi Ali's *Infidel* and *Heretic*. There was also a rise in what the British academic Peter Morey calls "the Muslim misery novel," such as Azar Nafisi's *Reading Lolita in Tehran* and Khaled Hosseini's *The Kite Runner*. "There is a market for the Muslim," writes Morey in *Islamophobia and the Novel*. "Texts that engage with the existing political articulation of 'the Muslim problem' … will be published, circulated, reviewed and critiqued more or less to the extent that they reproduce existing cultural viewpoints."[5]

The Cartoons

The 2005 Danish cartoons of the Prophet, a dozen of them, depicted him as a terrorist with bulging eyes and a bomb-shaped turban with a burning fuse; as a crazed, knife-wielding Bedouin; as the gatekeeper in heaven telling suicide bombers, "Stop. Stop. We have run out of virgins!" When that triggered a boycott of Danish products in the Muslim world, the newspaper *Jyllands-Posten* issued an apology: "We are sorry *if* Muslims have been offended" (italics added). Flemming Rose, the editor who commissioned the cartoons, said he didn't mean to offend anybody. Muslims weren't fooled. He was the same fellow who said of Danish Muslims: "People are no longer willing to pay taxes to help support someone called Ali who comes from a country with a different language and culture that's 5,000 miles away."[6]

In 2022, Muhammad's sex life was raked up in India by three stalwarts of the Hindu nationalist Bharatiya Janata Party (BJP) of Prime Minister Narendra Modi. The government ignored domestic Muslim protests. But in response to an uproar in Saudi Arabia, Kuwait, Qatar, and other states in the Persian Gulf — where about eight million Indian expatriates live and work — the BJP suspended the three officials. But neither Muslims nor secular Hindus were convinced that the BJP was about to change its tactics of goading Muslims to fire up its base.

Naipaul, Rushdie, van Gogh, Hirsi Ali, the Danish cartoonists, and the BJP in India have all followed roughly the same script: demean Islam and Muslims in ways deeply injurious to the Muslim sentiment and psyche.

In 2007, Rushdie was knighted by Queen Elizabeth II. Recently, Sir Salman's admirers have renewed their efforts to have him awarded the Nobel Prize for Literature. Being hostile to Muslims isn't a disqualification for the honour. In 2019, it was bestowed on the Austrian author Peter Handke, who denied the 1995 genocide in Srebrenica where more than 8,000 Bosnian Muslim men and boys were massacred by Bosnian Serb forces. Handke was an admirer of Slobodan Milošević, whom he visited in The Hague tribunal's detention unit during Milošević's trial for war crimes.

Balancing Rights

Most Western democracies maintain anti-hate laws. They may disagree on what constitutes hate but agree on the need for constraints. "Hate speech denies the fundamental premise that underlies all human rights, that of the equal worth and dignity of all human beings and is inconsistent with the human right to be free from incitement to hatred and discrimination," Mark Freiman, former president of the Canadian Jewish Congress and a leading human-rights lawyer, told me.

The International Convention on Civil and Political Rights upholds free speech but also requires states to prohibit "any advocacy of national, racial, or religious hatreds that constitutes incitement to discrimination." Similarly, the European Convention on Human Rights, the Canadian Charter of

Rights and Freedoms, and other human-rights statutes call for just such a balance. So does the charter of PEN International, the free-speech group with nearly 150 centres worldwide. It speaks to the "unhampered transmission of thought" but also calls on members to foster "good understanding and mutual respect among nations to do their utmost to dispel race, class, and national hatreds." Too many PEN members speak of free speech but not its concomitant obligation, something I found myself reminding colleagues of often as president of PEN Canada (2003–5) and as an elected member of the board of PEN International (2007–13).

Something that I was afraid of has happened. The consensus that held that delicate balance is broken. Free speech is shot through with double standards. And self-restraint has been readily and too frequently abandoned, particularly with Islam and Muslims.

What we exercise self-restraint about tells a lot about us. As our values have evolved for the better, we no longer caricature Indigenous peoples as savages. We avoid the n-word. We don't publish racist or offensive cartoons of Chinese, Jews, or others. I rejected some during my time as editorial page editor (1991–98) at the *Toronto Star*.

A similar call was made about the Danish cartoons by most mainstream newspapers and TV stations in the United States and Canada. Edward Greenspon, editor-in-chief of the *Globe and Mail*, Canada's national newspaper, explained: "We came to the conclusion that republishing would be both gratuitous and unnecessarily provocative." In 2015 during a worldwide campaign to reprint the *Charlie Hebdo* cartoons, the *New York Times* rejected the idea, calling the cartoons a "gratuitous insult." So did the *Toronto Star*, with publisher John Cruickshank saying, "Committing blasphemy for reasons of principle seems an oddly childish act."

But many in Europe did reproduce the cartoons, at various times, claiming not only the right to offend Muslims but a duty to do so.

What explains the difference between the West's reaction to the cartoons as opposed to *The Satanic Verses*? The fatwa, obviously, and the West's determined response not to acquiesce to violence. That remains the right response — as long as our aversion to violence isn't selective and self-serving.

Nearly 450 Muslims were killed in India, Pakistan, Afghanistan, Nigeria, Somalia, Libya, and elsewhere protesting *The Satanic Verses*, the Muhammad cartoons, a 2012 short video on Muhammad made by a Coptic Christian in California, and various incidents of Qur'an burnings. Ironically, some were shot dead by local police protecting Western embassies where the demonstrators were headed. Yet in the West, few tears were shed. The largely unsaid assumption was that the victims had brought it on themselves.

The dead weren't princes, sultans, and oil shaykhs, but rather ordinary people. Yet there were no efforts to replenish the daily bread of the poor widows and orphaned children from the soaring revenues of *The Satanic Verses* and other anti-Islam products.

Third World blood is cheap. About 900,000 Muslims have been killed and an estimated 37 million people displaced in the largely illegal American-led war on terror waged overtly and covertly in more than 80 countries, according to Brown University's Cost of War Project.[7] That's more people killed than in the Rwandan genocide. Such catastrophic levels of state violence, death, destruction, and displacement aren't irrelevant to the Rushdie affair. The victims have been Muslims. Those doing the victimizing have been from the lands where Rushdie has been domiciled and hailed a hero. His supporters, who have been in the forefront of lecturing Muslims about the evils of extraterritorial violence, have largely been silent about these killing fields, including the extrajudicial assassinations of America's enemies on the basis of fatwas issued in Washington, London, and other Western capitals.

We can't pronounce fidelity to universal values, such as no truck or trade with violence, only when it appeals to our prejudices and suits our agenda.

Free-Speech Fraud

The principle of free speech has been discredited. It's been invoked too often to rationalize Islamophobia, "the most dominant mode of prejudice in contemporary Western societies."[8] There's no shortage of examples of how the implementation of free speech has been brazenly selective and highly political:

My Name Is Not Harry

- There was the absurdity in 2001 of Secretary of State Colin Powell hectoring the emir of Qatar to rein in the free-wheeling Al Jazeera television network. Long the only free voice in the oppressive Arab world, Al Jazeera was also providing extensive and balanced coverage of the American war on terror. Shaykh Hamad smiled at the secretary and said he was taking the request as "advice," which he then proceeded to ignore.
- While the Western media and media organizations have shown admirable solidarity with imperilled journalists and media institutions worldwide, their reaction to Al Jazeera was instructive. They barely raised a peep when American forces bombed Al Jazeera's offices in Kabul in 2001, and in Baghdad in 2003, as well as raided the Al Jazeera bureau in Ramadi where they detained 21 staffers. The Pentagon claimed that the Kabul bombing was an accident. Al Jazeera called it an implausible explanation, given that the network had conveyed its coordinates to the Americans. It was only much later that General Tommy Franks, commander of U.S. operations in Afghanistan, admitted that the attack in Kabul had indeed been deliberate. But claimed that the building was "a known al-Qaeda facility."

  And free-speech advocates didn't go to bat for Al Jazeera when its entry into North America and Europe was blocked for years, either for reasons of anti-Arab prejudice or to avoid competition. The *Toronto Star*'s was long the lone voice in the Canadian media in support of the network being aired in Canada.
- Three years prior to publishing the Muhammad cartoons, *Jyllands-Posten* had rejected caricatures of Christ, saying they were offensive and "will provoke an outcry." Insulting Christ bad, insulting Muhammad good. Muslim sentiment was captured in a cartoon in *Al-Quds al-Arabi*, the pan-Arab daily from London, showing an artist at work

21 Rushdie and Muslims

at *Jyllands-Posten*. In the first panel, he rejects a grotesque drawing of a black person: "This is racism." He rejects the second, which equates the Star of David with the swastika: "This is anti- Semitism." He keeps the longer third panel of the Prophet's cartoons, saying: "This is freedom of speech."

- In 2006, notorious British historian David Irving was sentenced to three years for denying the Holocaust, while radical British Muslim cleric Abu Hamza al Masri was jailed for, among other things, inciting hatred. It was about time. There were few or no protests against the curtailment of the freedom of speech of Irving or Masri.
- In 2012, there was an uproar when major league baseballer Yunel Escobar took to the field wearing eye black with the word *maricon*, "faggot," and outfielder Kevin Pillar yelled "Faggot" at a pitcher. Both were upbraided by the media for their homophobia. Free-speech advocates didn't go to bat for the right of free speech of either.
- In 2015, two Muslims calling themselves "defenders of the Prophet Muhammad" massacred a dozen people at *Charlie Hebdo*. Another Muslim killed four people at a kosher deli and threatened to kill several hostages unless the two murderers at the *Charlie Hebdo* office were freed. All three killers were gunned down by police. President François Hollande led a solidarity march of about one million people in Paris under the banner JE SUIS CHARLIE, I AM CHARLIE. About 40 world leaders participated, including such stalwarts of free speech as Vladimir Putin's hand-picked foreign minister, Sergey Lavrov, Palestinian leader Mahmoud Abbas, and Israeli prime minister Benjamin Netanyahu. While they marched, police were busy charging nearly 100 people for refusing to stand in silence in solidarity with the *Charlie Hebdo* victims. No free speech for them.
- In the wake of the *Charlie Hebdo* murders, the British government enacted laws to suppress extremist activity,

My Name Is Not Harry

including a clause to clamp down "vocal opposition to British values." Whatever they may be, the values were deemed too fragile to be subjected to the travails of free speech.

- That same year, 2015, PEN American Center bestowed its Freedom of Expression Courage prize on *Charlie Hebdo*. Suzanne Nossel, executive director, lauded the magazine for "ensuring that nothing was above comment or debate." Would her PEN centre have similarly honoured a magazine that had published overtly racist, misogynist, anti-Semitic, or anti-LGBT cartoons, and drawn widespread condemnation and death threats? More than 200 PEN members protested the award, including Canadian author Michael Ondaatje, saying in an open letter: "There is a critical difference between staunchly supporting expression that violates the acceptable, and enthusiastically rewarding such expression." Among those attending the gala was Rushdie, pooh-poohing the critics, in keeping with his proclivity to pour scorn on those who don't line up with him.

- In 2020, when French high school teacher Samuel Paty was beheaded by a Muslim after he showed the Muhammad cartoons to his class, police interviewed four 10-year-olds for hours on suspicion of "apology of terrorism." The kids' crime? Objecting to the showing of the cartoons in the class. Amnesty International said: "Being opposed to the cartoons does not make one a 'separatist,' 'a bigot,' or an 'Islamist.'" It noted that several people were convicted every year for a crime known as "contempt of public officials" and that two citizens had been convicted of burning an effigy of President Emmanuel Macron. Amnesty added: "It is hard to square this with the French authorities' vigorous defence of the right to depict the Prophet Muhammad in cartoons. Freedom of expression means nothing unless it applies to everyone."[9]

21 Rushdie and Muslims

Paty was rightly seen as a martyr to free speech. Still, Erna Paris, Canadian author and a historian of the Holocaust, who had studied at the Sorbonne, didn't find him all that innocent. Writing in the *Globe and Mail*, Canada's national daily, in 2020, she said: "Let us imagine Berlin in 1934. Hitler is in power, but Jewish children still attend school. In the name of free speech, the teacher pulls out examples of Julius Streicher's caricatures of Jews and suggests that anyone who might be offended leave the room. Such scenes risk toxic consequences."[10]

Paris wasn't justifying the murder, but rather providing context, as only she could.

- Free speech is routinely curtailed in universities and other institutions. Speakers are disinvited, academics and administrators fired or demoted for making ill-advised comments or inappropriate jokes. Or for not being sufficiently sensitive to student demands for "safe spaces" and "trigger warnings" about potentially disturbing content. Usually, it's the conservatives who get exercised over "political correctness" and "cancel culture," while liberals are generally supportive in the name of sensitivity to minorities and oppressed groups. One is entitled to either position, but it's ideology, not the principle of free speech, that's been driving the responses.

- Too many free-speech crusaders are complicit in stifling criticism of Israel, labelling it hate speech. Even if it is, it's odd to be suppressing it while waving the free-speech flag for other forms of hate speech. Those who don't want Rushdie silenced are mostly silent when Palestinian and Jewish human-rights agencies in Israel and the occupied territories are shut down; human-rights activists are hounded; and North American and European journalists, academics, and activists critical of Israeli policies toward the Palestinians are dubbed anti-Semites and harassed and penalized. No free speech for them. Either Rushdie and his supporters agree with what Israeli governments have been doing, or they're afraid to speak up, notwithstanding their self-image as courageous warriors for free speech.

- There's the censorship of social media shaming. People are silenced or fired or hounded out of jobs or public office or as candidates in elections for what they had said at some point somewhere. Free-speech absolutists haven't exactly been standing up to the lynch mobs enforcing the latest political and social fashions.

- Social media owners, such as Facebook, once routinely cited free speech in refusing to monitor, let alone stop transmitting, content that was anti-Semitic, racist, misogynistic, homophobic, Islamophobic, xenophobic, white nationalistic, et cetera. Mark Zuckerberg argued that "we are not in the censorship business. In America, we have the First Amendment guaranteeing freedom of speech." He wouldn't even ban Holocaust deniers, saying they may not "be intentionally getting it wrong." But he and other social media titans have since changed tack in response to public outcry and government strictures, especially from the European Union. They've instituted rules for content and political advertising; added filters, fact checkers, and moderators; and shut out Donald Trump and others, temporarily or permanently. We're left only to argue what should or shouldn't be censored and by whom, not that nothing should be. The holy grail of free speech turns out to be elastic, after all.

* * *

Double standards are facts of life. We're all full of contradictions in varying degrees. Muslims aren't the only ones impacted by such inconsistencies, only more extensively and more often.

Prime Minister Justin Trudeau has said: "We would always defend freedom of expression, but freedom of expression is not without limits. We owe it to ourselves to act with respect for others and to seek not to arbitrarily or unnecessarily injure those with whom we are sharing a society and a planet."

The First Amendment to the U.S. Constitution — barring Congress from making any laws abridging free speech — has evolved into what's been dubbed the "First-ness of the First Amendment," undermining the right to life, equality, and inclusiveness that was also an American ideal. This imbalance has only worsened since the catastrophic 2010 U.S. Supreme Court ruling granting corporations their ostensible free-speech right to spend unlimited amounts for a cause, candidate, or party. Free-speech absolutism works well for the rich, powerful, and organized, not the weak and vulnerable, the very people most in need of protection. It works for groups who already have public opinion on their side or who have the resources, connections, and organizational and lobbying skills to mould public opinion to their values and viewpoints. It doesn't work well for those who must challenge racism and bigotry with few or no resources, except to take to the streets, as have Indigenous peoples and organizers of the Black Lives Matter movement. Nor does it work for those who find themselves on the wrong side of prevailing dogma. This perpetuates the existing echo chamber, as in the Rushdie case.

The Heresy

Group think on Rushdie took on religious certainty long ago. Avowed champions of tolerance, his supporters have been remarkably intolerant of majority Muslim sentiment. The only Muslim voices they want to listen to have been those who want Rushdie murdered or those who agree wholeheartedly with him. Muslim objections and protests — fundamental forms of free speech — are discredited and dismissed:

- It's repeated ad nauseum that Khomeini and those protesting *The Satanic Verses* hadn't even read it. Have all its defenders? Do voters read the detailed election policy platforms of political parties before casting their ballots?
- Muslims who burned a copy of *The Satanic Verses* in Bradford, England, in 1989 were compared to the Nazis burning books in 1933. Yet burning the American flag in

protest has been held up by the U.S. Supreme Court as a free-speech right. And the 1992 burning of the iconic National Library of Sarajevo by the Serbs is now barely mentioned in the West — the "culturecide" that destroyed three million books and rare manuscripts with the aim of obliterating the multicultural, mostly Muslim cultural identity of the place.

- When India became the first country to ban *The Satanic Verses* in 1989, Prime Minister Rajiv Gandhi, a secular Hindu, was upbraided as an unprincipled leader assuaging the Muslim minority there. One of his key advisers was the erudite intellectual Mani Shankar Aiyar, a self-described "fundamentalist secular Hindu." He was still exercised 25 years later when I met him at a dinner in 2014 in Delhi: "Rushdie, that sod — he deliberately insulted and provoked Muslims but in the guise of literature. Everyone in a democracy has the right to freedom of expression and everyone also has the right to be outraged. To be absolutist about the freedom to offend is absolutism, not democracy."

Aiyar wasn't the only prominent non-Muslim to take issue with Rushdie. In varying degrees, so did:

- The Vatican newspaper *L'Osservatore Romano*, reflecting the semi-official views of Pope John Paul II.
- Robert Runcie, the archbishop of Canterbury.
- Immanuel Jakobovits, the chief rabbi in Great Britain.
- Rabbi Wolfe Kelman, chair of the American section of the World Jewish Congress.
- John Cardinal O'Connor, archbishop of New York.
- Former U.S. president Jimmy Carter.
- Authors John le Carré and Germaine Greer, among others.

Their opinions have long been forgotten, especially in the wake of the fatwa, but they did augment the Muslim argument, and still do.

Love of Muhammad

Still, why do Muslims overreact? Haven't other prophets been lampooned? Wasn't there the novel *The Last Temptation of Christ* by Nikos Kazantzakis? Aren't other sacred cows gored?

Yes. But with Muslims, there is, to start, the legacy of Christian churches and European institutions and leaders rationalizing massacres, plunder, and colonialization by positing Islam, Muhammad, and Muslims as the greatest enemies of Christianity and Western civilization. In our own ostensibly cosmopolitan age, no other faith has been attacked as persistently as Islam and its sacred figures. After all, we aren't arguing over whether Mary really was a virgin, or Moses did part the Red Sea, or Lord Ganesh had that elephant head. Believers have a right to sincerely held beliefs as long as those beliefs don't contravene the laws of our lands.

The relationship of Muslims to Muhammad — literally, "the praise-worthy" — is central to their faith: "There is no God but Allah, and Muhammad is his messenger." While they don't worship him, for he was human, they do revere him. They invoke his name dozens of times per day, rarely without saying, *"Sallallah-o-Alaihi Wassallam,"* "Peace be upon him." There are more people called Muhammad in the world than by any other name. The love of the Prophet "runs like blood in the veins of his community," in the famous phrase of the great Indian philosopher, poet, and politician Sir Muhammad Iqbal (1877–1938).

Besmirching Muhammad is tantamount to shouting "Fire" in a crowded theatre.

All this is known. Those doing the provoking do want to get the Muslims' goat. That's the idea. It's a bonus that the exercise garners publicity, praise, fame, funds, and profits, which speaks to the seemingly insatiable market for it in the West.

As American academic Asma Barlas has written:

> It should be possible to condemn violence by Muslims without giving a free pass to those who defame and vilify their religion, their prophet and their scripture. Yet, this

rarely happens. Instead, the Muslim-baiting intelligentsia relies on precisely its own vilifications to incite the violence which it then feigns to be horrified and surprised by. I say feigns because ... provocateurs require such a response to anathematize all Muslims as a threat to European identities and values.[11]

Muhammad's Sex Life

How old was Ayesha when Muhammad married her? Accounts vary, from age 9 to 15. There are also differing accounts of when she was betrothed and when she went from her parents' house to his. The prevailing custom at that time was for girls to be married at 13. It remains the norm in sub-Saharan Africa and the Indian subcontinent. Mahatma Gandhi married Kasturba when she was 13. Nobel laureate Rabindranath Tagore married Mrinalini Devi when she was 10. Jhansi ki Rani, queen of a princely state in western India lionized for her valiant battlefield leadership against the British in the Great Mutiny of 1857 was married when she was 10. Loretta Lynn, the American country singer, was married at 15. Juliet of Shakespeare's *Romeo and Juliet*, a play written 900 years after the Prophet, was 13.

How many wives did Muhammad have? Thirteen. He wasn't the first patriarch to be polygamous — Abraham, Jacob, Moses, Hosea, Saul, David, and Solomon had multiple wives or concubines. David was said to have had 100 and Solomon 1,000. Muhammad often married outside his tribe, mostly to consolidate his expanding domain, a much-used modus operandi of many rulers of the time and since, including in Europe. Two of Muhammad's wives were Jews, one a Coptic Christian. Fostering political alliances, however, wasn't his sole motive. He was a human being who was attracted to women. All his relationships were open. He had no closet affairs that came to light later. No secret mistresses or children born out of wedlock materialized at his funeral, as with French president François Mitterrand and former Canadian prime minister Pierre Elliot Trudeau. We know of Rushdie's five wives and what some said about him. But for those who care, we know very little about his "fairly frequent infidelities and betrayals."[12]

The Muslim Malaise

Contributing to Muslim unrest and violence is the internal state of much of the Muslim world. Most Muslims live in post-colonial societies, highly tuned to Western attacks on their faith and Prophet. The poor in Asia and Africa, sustained by faith, feel the hurt more acutely. The Muslims of the Middle East live under mostly undemocratic, oppressive, and suffocatingly censorious regimes, including the most populous, Egypt, and the oil-rich Gulf States, especially Saudi Arabia and the United Arab Emirates. All are supported by the United States and its allies. Iran was also in this American-led orbit until the shah was overthrown in 1979. The Islamic Republic has since become as oppressive as others in the region. One tactic common to all is to keep their populations focused on foreign enemies, including those who attack Islam and belittle Muhammad. Diverting attention abroad is easier than addressing demands for democratic and social reforms at home.

This is partly responsible for the culture of intolerance toward non-Muslims and Muslims alike, as well as harsher interpretations of Islam, which suits the rulers just fine. They're in the business of staying in power, not looking after the state of the *ummah* (the Muslim collective) to which they pay lip service. The richer states throw around money for building mosques and the free distribution of Qur'ans, but on issues affecting Islam and Muslims globally, they avoid punitive measures against other states for fear of interference in their own domestic affairs. They rely instead on the 57-member Organisation of Islamic Cooperation (OIC) that represents the interests of the 1.6 billion Muslims worldwide. The Jeddah-based, mostly Saudi-funded group responded to the Rushdie and cartoon affairs by asking the U.N. Human Rights Committee to act against defamation of religion. We at PEN International opposed it, naturally. What the OIC, indeed most Muslims, forget is that free speech is an Islamic principle: "Read in the name of the Lord who created you from a cell…. Read in the name of the Lord who taught you by the pen" (Qur'an 96:1).

That was the very first injunction from God to the believers, according to Muslim tradition. Significantly, it wasn't about the omnipotence and omniscience of God, nor about the greatness of Muhammad or Islam, but rather a simple yet profound exhortation to read and write, acquire and spread knowledge. Yet there's neither the full freedom to read nor write in too many Muslim nations. There is in the West, with constraints.

The OIC erred in calling for an international anti-blasphemy law. In advocating a sharia solution that wasn't going to fly, anyway, the OIC made it easier for the West to dismiss Muslim grievances that should have been, and still ought to be, addressed within the liberal democratic framework — equality of and respect for all faiths, as long as they function within the law; equal application of and protection for all citizens, regardless of faith; and free speech balanced with freedom from hate.

The West erred in not extending to fellow citizens who happened to be Muslims, about 30 million, the same courtesies as offered to other groups within the broad canopy of free speech. It missed an opportunity to showcase, especially to Muslims the world over, the moderating checks and balances of democracy. Indeed, it has discredited democracy. That was the inevitable outcome of allowing anti-Islam and anti-Muslim discourse to be one of our last acceptable forms of racism and bigotry. The late Edward Said's dictum that Arabs could be maligned with impunity has been extended to Muslims. It's in this milieu that Rushdie and the Rushdie affair have thrived.

The Bottom Line

Should Rushdie not have written what he did? Should his publisher have refused to publish it? The answers lie in other questions. Would he have written a novel that risked being seen as racist, misogynistic, homophobic, anti-Semitic? If he indeed had, would his publishers have published it? This isn't hypothetical whataboutism. Many publishers, media outlets, TV networks, and streaming services refuse books and articles and cancel shows that might offend Indigenous or Black people and other BIPOC groups. They either believe that it's the principled thing to do or they dread a backlash they'd rather not tackle. Either way, the current zeitgeist should have prompted a rethink of *The Satanic Verses*. It hasn't.

Who's been using whom? Has Rushdie been exploiting Western prejudices, benefiting especially from the fact that he was born a Muslim? Or has

21 Rushdie and Muslims

the West been using him as a shield for its own prejudices? Or is this a case of mutual convenience?

An honest debate is long overdue as we absorb the shock of Salman's loss of his left eye and the full use of his left arm, and pray for his physical recovery and the return of his feisty spirit. *Inshallah*, God willing.

22

An Incurably Optimistic Canadian

MORE THAN WE USUALLY ACKNOWLEDGE, SUCCESS DEPENDS ON LUCK. I'VE had more than my share.

I was lucky to have grown up in an era where, despite the horrors of the 1947 Partition, India's millennia-old multicultural ethos prevailed. Lucky to have had teachers, mostly Hindus, who guided me.

Lucky to have landed in Canada.

Lucky to have had good mentors. Lucky to have been encouraged to go to Brandon, Manitoba, where I went reluctantly but stayed 10 years. There I learned what I wouldn't have in Toronto, the centre of the universe.

So lucky to have worked at Canada's largest newspaper. And covered and commented on geopolitical developments in parts of the world and on topics I happened to know something about. Lucky also to have had a say in the multicultural evolution of Canada. Lucky to have lived through a time when the industry was flush with cash and resources. Lucky to have been given the freedom to write what I wanted. A writer is a nobody without a platform and without ample protection.

And one obvious point — to benefit from all this luck I had to stay alive. So, yes, I have been lucky in doctors and a free medical system that saved my life more than once.

My Name Is Not Harry

* * *

Canada and Canadians didn't violate the core of my being. They let me be me — in my faith, my culture, my language, my cricket, my many quirks.

I don't drink, I don't do drugs, and only vaguely know what marijuana smells like. I stopped smoking cigarettes and cigars in 1995 after bypass surgery.

I haven't been to a McDonald's or any other burger joint for more than 40 years, except once to get a salad. Nor have I had a Coke or Pepsi or any pop except once on a doctor's say-so.

I don't tweet, don't have a Facebook page, don't do social media.

After 9/11, I switched off Fox News, then CNN and others. I didn't miss much. Saved time, kept my blood pressure down. Regained my Canadian perspective. I never did find out how Tucker Carlson huffed and puffed.

I haven't watched TV for years, haven't seen a single reality show. Nor *Schitt's Creek, Degrassi, Kim's Convenience, Seinfeld, The Sopranos,* or *Housewives*, desperate or otherwise.

I don't wear clothes with logos, refusing to be a human billboard. I'm averse to celebrities: not curious about Madonna's belly button, Rihanna's butt, Bieber's tattoos. It wasn't all that long ago that Dennis Rodman of the Chicago Bulls was thought to be a weirdo for his tattoos.

I care even less about those who are famous for being famous — Paris Hilton or the Kardashians. I don't want to know their ideas on subjects they know little or nothing about. I don't want to be influenced by influencers.

I don't like dogs, even less their owners who let them urinate in public spaces, brush against people who don't want to be brushed against, crowd sidewalks, and clutter parks clearly marked as off limits to canines. If the Indigenous, Black, or any other minority broke the law so brazenly and so regularly, neighbours and the police would be on their cases.

I don't own a cottage, don't want to. Traffic jams and mosquitos are all yours. I don't golf. I've not taken to baseball. Or the NBA. Or the AFL or the CFL. I'm happy with my cricket and tennis.

I don't advertise my idiosyncrasies, nor do I apologize for them. They're there — my personal choices that don't affect others.

Canada allowed me to evolve in my way into an incurably optimistic Canadian. I doubt if that would have been possible anywhere else without paying a price.

Love at 35,000 Feet

I must have gone back to India 50 times since 1967. On one of those return trips in the early years, I happened to have a window seat as the plane flew over Gaspé. The breathtaking view of the forests and rivers below evoked an unexpected emotion — all this majestic expanse of Canada belonged to me. This was my Canada, too. It was a moment of lasting bonding.

I've always preferred aisle seats on long flights, still do. But from that day on, I try to take window seats on return flights to Canada. Also when flying across the country, especially over the Lake of the Woods or the Rockies. One of my achievements with sons Fahad and Faisal has been to get them to two of the coasts, and I hope they'll get to the third themselves.

If I were prime minister, I'd subsidize every Canadian to travel the country — details to be determined.

Canadian Firsts

I'm a sucker for Canadian firsts. They're a barometer of Canada's ongoing demographic evolvement:

- Jean Chrétien, the first francophone federal finance minister (1977).
- Gurbax Singh Malhi of the Toronto suburb of Malton, the first turbaned Sikh MP in the Western world (1993).
- Sergio Marchi of Toronto, the first immigrant immigration minister (1994).
- Adrienne Clarkson, the first refugee and Chinese-Canadian governor general (1999).
- Michaëlle Jean, the first Black governor general (2005).
- Tim Uppal, the first turbaned and bearded Sikh federal Cabinet minister (2011).

- Justin Trudeau, the first prime minister in the Western world to name a gender-equal Cabinet (2015).
- Maryam Monsef, the first Muslim federal Cabinet minister, a refugee from Afghanistan (2015).
- Ahmed Hussen, the first Somali-born Cabinet minister (2017).
- Mary Simon, the first Indigenous governor general (2022).
- Aliya Mawani, Canada's first Muslim woman ambassador, posted to Kuwait (2022).

And in the provinces and cities:

- Joe Ghiz of Prince Edward Island, the first Arab Canadian premier (1986).
- Ujjal Dosanjh of British Columbia, the first Sikh premier (2000).
- Naheed Nenshi, the first Muslim mayor of a large North American city, Calgary (2010).
- Kathleen Wynne, the first woman premier of Ontario and also the first openly gay premier in Canada (2013).
- Ausma Malik, the first hijab-wearing elected councillor in Toronto, indeed Canada (2022).

This record, to which you no doubt can add your own list of firsts, is unmatched in the Western world. It speaks to the remarkable integration of immigrants and minorities into the highest echelons of Canadian government.

* * *

In 2002, when Adrienne Clarkson visited Canadian frigates patrolling the Persian Gulf as part of Canada's military mission in Afghanistan, she went to Abu Dhabi, the capital of the United Arab Emirates. It had to declare her an honorary man for President Sheikh Zayed bin Sultan al-Nahyan to see her.

22 An Incurably Optimistic Canadian

When her successor, Michaëlle Jean, visited South Africa in 2006, President Thabo Mbeki, usually aloof, came alive when he realized that the Right Honourable from Canada was a Haitian-born immigrant. He was so inspired that he suggested European nations should make similar appointments.

Three years later, Jean bonded with Barack Obama the moment he came down from Air Force One at Ottawa's airport. She said something and he lit up. The two spent several animated moments together on the tarmac while the VIPs waited. The priceless moment was triggered by her comment that it was hard to believe that the two were there — the first Black people in their respective roles.

The Obama visit provided another great Canadian moment — the interview that CBC-TV news anchor Peter Mansbridge did at the White House on the eve of that presidential visit. Peter was the antithesis of showboating American anchors. He didn't preen. He didn't say a word more than he had to. He went prepared, in his head, not with notes on a clipboard. In 11 minutes, he led the president through a list of issues: NAFTA, energy, oil sands and the environment, Afghanistan, and finally, Obama's "sense of Canada," noting, "You carry Canada on your belt. That BlackBerry is a Canadian invention."

I took to telling colleagues and journalism students to watch that video to learn how to do a high-profile interview with low-key Canadian professionalism.

*   *   *

In my own little world, Reza Baraheni, the famous Iranian writer and dissident, "the Solzhenitsyn of Iran" who came to Canada as a refugee in 1997, produced two firsts for Canada. Within four years of his arrival as a refugee, he was elected president of PEN Canada, the prestigious writers' free-speech group. In no other country would a new immigrant, even of Baraheni's stature, have been embraced and elevated to the presidency so quickly.

And then singlehandedly he had the wording of the charter of PEN International changed to make it more universal. Its first words used to be: "Literature, national though it may be in origin, knows no frontiers and must remain common currency among people in spite of political or international upheavals." He proposed deleting the words "national though it may be in origin." That simple yet profound wordsmithery was approved in 2003, the first change to the document since it was agreed to in 1948. The revised charter now reads simply: "Literature knows no frontiers ..."

Other Canadian Contributions

A major first for Canada was the election of John Ralston Saul as president of PEN International, which has 146 centres in 104 countries and an office in London. I'd been elected to its international board in 2007 and immediately thought of getting John to help fix the nearly dysfunctional organization. He was a rare combination of a novelist, essayist, and public intellectual who also had managerial experience and financial acumen.

Helping me to convince John was Émile Martel, the president of PEN Quebec. A former Canadian diplomat, poet, and award-winning translator, he happily came to be known late in his distinguished life as the father of Yann Martel, author of *Life of Pi*.

John's fame had preceded him in PEN circles. Still, a campaign had to be waged and won. The trilingual Émile — French, English, and Spanish — lobbied delegates from Latin America, Spain, and parts of Europe. I, with English, Urdu, Hindi, and a sprinkling of Arabic and Persian, talked to those from the United States, the Middle East, Asia, and Africa. John won handily. Three years later, in 2012, he was elected to his second three-year term. He was tireless in going from continent to continent wherever writers were in danger, travelling more than any PEN president in its nearly 100-year history.

Along with Margaret Atwood as an honorary vice-president, and Marian Botsford Fraser as chair of the Writers and Prison Committee, Canadians played an outsized role in PEN International for many years. We found that people generally listened to us, principally because we were Canadians. In 2011, we were in Belgrade for PEN's annual international conference. When the Serbian PEN bid to host it, John said the Serbs could do so on the condition they invited the smaller, newly formed PEN centres from Bosnia, Kosovo,

22 An Incurably Optimistic Canadian

and Macedonia. They did, and we were particularly chuffed at pulling off that mini-reconciliation between people who had been at war a few years earlier.

John and I usually raised eyebrows — he carrying his fresh ginger to breakfast, and I my own tea bags everywhere. We also left some hosts puzzled by insisting that rooms and convention centres for PEN meetings had to have windows for fresh air.

In 2015, Canada hosted PEN International's annual congress, John's last as president. Among the delegates in Quebec City was Djibril Ly from Mauritania. A writer, playwright, and poet, he'd been jailed for his defence of the many Mauritanian languages. He had proposed a PEN centre in Mauritania, which was to be voted on at the congress. But no sooner had he arrived than he got sick and was rushed to the Hôtel-Dieu hospital where John and Émile Martel kept a vigil at his bedside. When his condition didn't improve, he asked for the Qur'an to be read to him. John called me from the hospital. Unfortunately, I was fast asleep. John had the hospital contact the Quebec Islamic Centre, the same place where two years later six worshippers were gunned down. The centre sent over an imam to read the Qur'an in Djibril's ears during the last hours of his journey from this life to the afterlife.

John Ralston Saul.

Over the next few days, in the middle of the congress, John worked with the mayor of the city and the Quebec government to have Djibril's body flown home to Mauritania for burial. John's poignant letter to the family was read at the funeral:

> I realize how difficult this has been for his family and friends, who have been obliged to follow this tragedy from a distance. I can only assure you that he was never alone. At all moments through to the end, the warmth of our friendship was with him.
>
> Know that around the world, the writers of PEN are with you in your sadness. For us his legacy must first be that of an admired writer. But there is also the legacy of his example, his ethical standards, his unflinching courage.
>
> And then there is the legacy of his creation — PEN Mauritania, which was unanimously voted into official existence by the General Assembly of PEN, each one of us conscious that not far away, Djibril lay in his hospital bed.

That was John's Canadian way.

Canadian Moments

When Kathleen Wynne ran for the Ontario Liberal Party leadership in 2013, she addressed the not-so-hidden but largely unspoken issue of her being a lesbian: "I want to put something on the table. Is Ontario ready for a gay premier? You've all heard that question." It was one of the most electrifying moments at a political convention in contemporary Canada. Not everyone applauding was necessarily approving of her personal choice but rather of her candour and courage. The moment she said her piece, the contest was over — she had it won.

Another very Canadian thing happened at that convention. One of her rivals was Harinder Takhar, a Sikh immigrant to Canada. He told the delegates how traumatized he was after cutting his hair in the 1970s to get a job: "I ended up losing a part of myself forever, which I've regretted every day of my entire life." It was a measure of his maturity, and Canada's, that he could say so from a very public platform, just as Wynne could talk about being gay.

Wynne represented the mid-Toronto riding of Valley West (40 percent visible minorities). Some of her biggest supporters there were Muslims in the Thorncliffe Park area, most of them observant and conservative. Her sexuality made little difference, even when both the Conservative and New Democratic Parties ran Muslim candidates against her.

Such is the cosmopolitan alchemy of Canada.

Europe, on the other hand, lacks the confidence to let such democratic processes play themselves out. As Will Kymlicka of Queen's University, a leading expert on multiculturalism, wrote in 2007:

> In much of Europe, this confidence is completely lacking, particularly in relation to Muslim immigrants.... If we believe that the liberal expectancy is holding, then we do not need to continuously test or provoke minorities, as is the fashion these days in Europe, whether in the form of the Muhammad cartoons in Denmark or the veil law in France. This sort of provocation is self-defeating. If we tell immigrants that we do not trust them, and that we are monitoring their every word and reaction for hints of disloyalty or illiberalism, they will not feel that their political participation is welcomed and their political integration will be delayed, if not derailed entirely.[1]

We can see Kymlicka's wise counsel in how Muslims have progressed, or not, across the West.

Love Us or Hate Us

What doesn't kill you makes you stronger. Much like other immigrant groups that were persecuted but survived and became an integral part of the Canadian mainstream, Muslims are on their way, as well.

Canada's 1.8 million Muslims have emerged with their identity intact, indeed strengthened. As they become more Muslim, they become more Canadian.

That's true, in varying degrees, of the 30 million Muslims across parts of the Western world. More Muslim, more American, for example. This is one of the most significant yet least appreciated developments in the Muslim diaspora.

After 9/11, some Muslims became defensive, even apologetic: "I am a Muslim but not a fundamentalist Muslim, not a bin Laden Muslim, not a Wahhabi Muslim." But rather, "I am a moderate Muslim," "modern Muslim," or "a Sufi Muslim." Not that many knew who or what a Sufi was.

But the more Islam and Muslims were reviled, the more they turned to their religion. This followed a historic pattern. Whenever Europeans, especially colonizers, tried to make Muslims less Muslim, they ended up making them more so.

In Canada, demonized minorities such as people of Japanese, Germanic, and Italian origins hid or downplayed their identities during and after the Second World War. Mennonites in Southern Ontario temporarily disappeared from the Canadian census. Yet Muslims have remained Muslim — Muhammad is still the most popular name for male babies, and there's no evidence of Muslims avoiding the decennial census question on religion in 2011 and 2021.

Mosques and mosque-based institutions have become stronger with increasing membership. Politicians were the first to sniff that out and begin trolling for votes there. On the Friday sabbath, most mosques hold two or three services and are overflowing. In Ramadan, the late-evening prayers when the entire Qur'an is recited in the month, congregations spill over into corridors, classrooms, gyms, all available spaces in an orderly Canadian manner. They no longer need to import *huffaz*, plural of *hafiz*, those who have memorized the Qur'an, from overseas. There are plenty of graduates of Canadian Qur'an academies. So many youngsters of such high quality that American mosques have started recruiting them as guest imams for Ramadan.

Any rise in faith activity spooks some people, especially those who consider religion as evil or think of it as incompatible with a secular society. On the contrary, secularism guarantees freedom of religion. Any violation of that fundamental principle, especially against non-Christians, is discrimination. As long as a religious activity is within the law, we have no reason to panic. Indeed, it should be welcome if it leads to ethical behaviour and a more humane society. Sikh gurdwaras, for example, serve Sikhs and non-Sikhs alike at their *langar*, free mass feeding, including from mobile kitchens, as during Covid.

An unprecedented number of women in Canada, the United States, Britain, and parts of Europe took to the hijab as a marker of identity. Most of them were born or raised in the West and were the first in their families to do so, often defying their parents. By proudly and fearlessly wearing their religion on their heads, they put themselves in the front lines of confronting both religious and gender discrimination.

As Islamophobia intensified, the varied theological, ethnic, linguistic, racial, cultural, and nationalist affiliations of Muslims began to take a back seat to their pan-Islamic identity. Or, in the case of the religiously non-observant, pan-Muslim identity. Now only 48 percent of Canadian Muslims consider their ethnic or cultural identity as very important, but 84 percent cite being Muslim and 81 percent cite being Canadian as their primary identity.[2]

Muslim and Canadian.

This is a remarkably swift evolution for a relatively recent immigrant group, both in terms of internal ecumenism as well as integration into the larger society.

Besides co-operating across denominational lines, Muslims engaged in outreach to peoples of other faiths. They raised funds for their neighbourhood schools and hospitals. Their food banks served people of all faiths and no faith.

As they learned to stand on their own, Muslims found and funded their voices within the democratic framework. That disabused them of the notion that Muslim states "back home," or at least the influential ones, would somehow come to their rescue. Or that the Organisation of Islamic Cooperation would.

Greater independence led to a greater awareness of the differing interpretations of Islam. What is permissible in India and Malaysia isn't in Saudi

Arabia. In Canada, everything is permissible, as long as it's not against the law. That speaks to the range of Islamic thought within the broad framework of the faith. But it also points to a greater truth, one that was enunciated in 1930s India by the rector of my father's madrasah in Deoband, whom I quoted in chapter 4.

Shaykh Husain Ahmed Madani had said that given the racial, ethnic, linguistic, cultural, and crucially doctrinal diversity of Muslims, there was unlikely to be consensus on the nature of an Islamic polity. Only an authoritarian state could define and enforce the Islamic conformity it opted for. Therefore, the best protection for peoples of faith was a democratic state that stayed neutral between faiths and advanced mutual respect. He was making the case for Muslims in the democratic framework of post-colonial India. Yet his prescience is proving itself in the West. This is good news for both Muslims and the democracies that treat all faiths equally.

Muslims have traditionally divided the world in *Dar al-Islam* and *Dar al-Harb*, the dominion of Islam and the dominion that didn't permit the free practice of Islam. Canadian Muslims speak of Canada as *Dar al-Amn*, an abode of peace. I, for one, have argued that Canada is a *muslim* nation with a lowercase *m*. It has incorporated key Islamic principles, as it has from other religions.

The Charter of Rights and Freedoms, in guaranteeing freedom of religion, echoes the Qur'an, which urges no coercion in religion: "Whoever will, let him believe, and whoever will, let him disbelieve" (18:29). In outlawing racism, the charter follows a Qur'anic precept: "We have made you into nations and tribes that you may know one another" (49:13).

The charter also reflects the message of the Prophet Muhammad's famous last *hajj* sermon delivered in 632 CE about the equality of human beings: "An Arab has no superiority over a non-Arab nor a non-Arab has any superiority over an Arab; a white has no superiority over a black, nor a black has any superiority over a white — except by piety and good deeds." A precursor of Sections 15 and 27 of the charter.

Muhammad's edict about the treatment of enslaved people was similarly pioneering: "If a black slave is appointed your emir [leader], listen to him, and obey him." The Prophet also spoke of the sanctity of human life and the need to end tribal savagery. "The blood revenges of pre-Islamic days are over." An early version of Section 7's right to life, liberty, and security of person.

About women, Muhammad said: "O People, you have certain rights over your women and your women have certain rights over you…. My dictum to you is that you treat women well and be kind to them, for they are your partners." The words, patronizing to today's ears, were revolutionary for the times.

Sadly, many of Muhammad's injunctions are now routinely violated by Islamic nations, which tolerate, indeed in some cases foster, racism and bigotry toward their Black or non-Arab residents. And they mistreat women. These thoughts on my faith and my faith in Canada I finished writing in a cramped Quebec City hotel room with Yasmeen and teenagers Fahad and Faisal. "Echoes of Our Charter in Muhammad's Message" appeared in the *Toronto Star* the next morning, February 24, 2002. That day, Governor General Adrienne Clarkson presided over an Order of Canada ceremony at the Citadelle. I hadn't planned the column to coincide with my award, but the timing proved propitious.

Muslim Successes

"There is an astonishing disconnect between the reality of Muslims making successful inroads in the media, as writers and as elected representatives and businesspeople all over Europe and North America, and the continuation of a media narrative of Muslim unwillingness to 'integrate,'" Jytte Klausen, a Brandeis University professor and the author of *The Cartoons That Shook the World*, told me.[3]

Muslim advocacy groups got stronger, learned the lingo of effective intervention in the democratic process, and helped increase Muslim participation in elections as both voters and candidates. In the 2021 Canadian federal election, 28 Muslim candidates ran and 12 won. Two hold senior Cabinet portfolios: Omar Alghabra and Ahmed Hussen. In Britain, which has been slower in integrating minorities into the political process, there were 55 Muslim candidates in the 2019 general election and 19 were elected. Two became prominent Conservative Cabinet ministers — Sajid Javid and Nadhim Zahawi. The mayor of London since 2016 has been Sadiq Khan. In Scotland, Humza Yousaf became first minister in 2023, the first Muslim to lead a major U.K. party, and at 37, the youngest. In fact, he's the first Muslim to lead a democratic Western European nation. His wife, Nadia El Nakla, is a councillor in the City of Dundee, the first member of any minority elected there.

Javid, Khan, and Yousaf demonstrate how Muslims, like any other people, practise their faith differently or not at all. And how defensive or proud they are about their religion.

Javid: "I do not practise any religion. My wife is a practising Christian and the only religion practised in my house is Christianity." And: "There's a special, unique burden on the Muslim community" to do something about terrorism. He attacked the Muslim Council of Britain as not being representative of British Muslims.

Khan, a practising Muslim, headed the legal-affairs committee of the Muslim Council of Britain. As a Labour MP, he voted against Tony Blair's draconian anti-terrorism legislation in 2005. In 2009, he was sworn in as a member of the Privy Council at Buckingham Palace on the Qur'an. Upon discovering that the palace had none, he left his copy there.

When Yousaf first entered Parliament in 2011, he, too, took his oath on the Qur'an. When he was sworn in as first minister, he wore the traditional Pakistani outfit of long shirt and pantaloon. Watching him were his proud parents, including his hijab-wearing mother, Shaaista Bhutta.

Even in the United States, the hotbed of Islamophobia, 57 Muslims were elected in the 2020 national and state elections. We're already familiar with Keith Ellison, the first Muslim elected to the House of Representatives. He took his oath of office in 2007 on a copy of the Qur'an owned by President Thomas Jefferson who, unlike contemporary American politicians, had bought an English translation of the Qur'an out of a "desire to understand Islam on its own terms, looking directly to its most sacred source."[4] Two other Muslims have followed Ellison: Representatives Ilhan Omar and Rashida Tlaib.

We're also acquainted with entertainers Hasan Minhaj, Mahershala Ali, and Aziz Ansari; the writers Fareed Zakaria, Reza Aslan, and Ayad Akhtar, president of PEN America; the painter Salman Toor; and singer Ali Sethi, whose song "Pasoori," Punjabi for "conflict," has exceeded 500 million views at the time of this writing and was the most searched song in the world in 2022, according to Google Trends.

Less known is that American Muslims are a highly educated and successful minority. They're disproportionately represented in professions such as medicine, pharmacy, and engineering. Muslim women, as well, are more likely to have college degrees than American women overall, and they're the second-most educated group after Jewish women.

Contrast all of the above with Europe where governments have tried to curb religious expression through discriminatory laws and practices while doing little to tackle entrenched discrimination. Unfortunately, this is the path Quebec is following.

Cultural Paradise

When I came to Canada in 1967, I couldn't find yogurt — or much of any provisions for an Indian palate. Now we have cuisines from everywhere. Within this short period, Canada has also become the welcoming locale of all the world's cultures.

The first Ravi Shankar concert I attended wasn't in India but rather in Stratford, Ontario, in 1968. The greatest classical music vocalists and instrumentalists from India and Pakistan have since come by regularly, as well as Sufi mystics with their chants, and the best cricketers from either side of the border.

There was also world music aplenty: the greatest rai singers from the Maghreb, Cheikha Rimitti, Cheb Khaled, and Cheb Mami; the twangy guitar desert blues of Tinariwen; Tuareg musicians from Mali, whence also came Toumani Diabaté and Baaba Maal; and the unique *mbalax* pop of Youssou N'Dour from Senegal.

And then there was the Iranian goddess, Googoosh, whose songs I used to hear on tapes in taxis and hotel rooms when visiting Iran in the 1970s, and surreptitiously, in the Islamic Republic in the 1980s. I only had the vaguest notion of what she was crooning about. But it didn't matter, as with any great voice and melody. Following the 1979 Islamic Revolution, when women were banned from singing, she fell silent for two decades until the progressive president, Mohammad Khatami, lifted the ban. She left Iran, and a year later in 2000, gave her first comeback concert — in Toronto. When she made her grand entrance, the mostly Iranian audience rose as one, clapped, cheered, and cried tears of joy.

At the 2015 Christmas concert of Ottawa French public schools, a choir of 200 grade four to six students sang "Tala' al-Badru Alayna." That's the Arabic poem that the people of Medina welcomed the Prophet Muhammad with when he arrived there in 622 CE, seeking refuge from persecution in

Okay bowling action, wrong clothes on the *Toronto Star* team in the annual Toronto Mayor's Cricket Trophy.

Mecca. Muslims in every culture have sung it throughout the ages. And here was Canadian Robert Filion, choral director at Ottawa's École secondaire publique De La Salle, leading the choir of Canadian kids as part of his annual attempt at reflecting different traditions. No sooner was the video posted on YouTube than it went viral — people the world over confessing to getting goosebumps and crying at this rendition by Canadian Muslim and non-Muslim kids, including children of recently arrived Syrian refugees.[5]

An earlier, much bigger example of Canada's soft power was the CBC sitcom *Little Mosque on the Prairie* about a small Muslim community in the West. When it premiered in 2007 in the middle of the then-burgeoning paranoia about Muslims, the show drew a record audience of 2.1 million. That itself said something about Canadians.

Created by Zarqa Nawaz, an immigrant who grew up in Brampton, Ontario, and moved to Regina in 1997 after marrying a psychiatrist based there, the show remained a sensation for six seasons, was sold in 60 foreign markets, and has since been studied at universities for its social and political significance in the post-9/11 world. "The show could not have been made in any other country," Nawaz said. "I have benefited by being Canadian."

The flip side of its success was also instructive — the failure of a Fox TV copycat in Canada. Sun TV was a collaboration of two corporations hated by Muslim Canadians: the *Sun* chain of newspapers and Quebecor's TVA network. Started in 2011, it folded within four years, having failed to draw sufficient audiences.

Immigrant integration is too often spoken of as a one-way street, *they* adjusting to *our* ways. But inevitably, we all benefit from each other's cultures. Mother tongue being a central part of our identity, it's gratifying that most languages of the world are spoken in Canada — 120 in Toronto-area schools — and that great literature and political treaties are published in Canada in languages other than English and French. Think of the Czech writers Josef Škvorecký and his wife, Zdena Salivarová, who came to Canada after the 1968 Soviet invasion of Czechoslovakia. The couple founded 68 Publishers, which produced banned Czech and Slovak books, including ones by such dissidents as Václav Havel and Milan Kundera, and smuggled them back to their home countries.

My language is Urdu, and its speakers have been able to create an Urdu literary scene in Canada, as have other linguistic communities. Urdu is written, like Persian and Arabic, from right to left. But being Indo-Aryan, its vocabulary has much in common with Hindi, the main language of India, so that speakers from either language can understand one another. Urdu is now the language of about 100 million people in India, Pakistan, Bangladesh, and their diaspora overseas. In Canada, it's the second-most spoken language in Mississauga, the largest of Toronto's suburbs.

It was in Canada that I heard the most iconic Urdu poets from India, Pakistan, and elsewhere.

* * *

It was in Canada that I saw the original of a photo taken in 1893 in Hyderabad of Archduke Ferdinand, heir to the Austro-Hungarian Empire. His host, the nizam, engaged him in a friendly shooting competition. As an attendant tossed a silver rupee coin into the air, the archduke went first and missed. Then the nizam, a crack shot, hit the rupee. The image capturing the two was brought to Toronto by the Royal Ontario Museum in 2013 as part of an exhibition of rare photographs taken by Raja Deen Dayal (1844–1905). He was the legendary photographer of colonial India and Indian royalty. Dayal was a rajah without a kingdom, having been given the title of *Raja Mussavir*, "King of Photography." Dayal was a Hindu whose chief patron was the Muslim nizam. Dayal shot nearly 30,000 images, showing the English and the Indians working and playing together, as well as Hindus, Zoroastrians, Jews, Armenians, and Sunni and Shia Muslims.

The New Canada

In 1999, Canadian historian Desmond Morton of the University of Toronto and later director of the McGill Institute for the Study of Canada, wrote: "We started out as a country for the white trash of Europe but look where we have ended up! People from all over the world want to come here. We have a lot that works, and what doesn't, can be fixed, unlike in many other places."[6] That is truer now than when Morton wrote it in the introduction to a remarkable book, *Who Speaks for Canada?*, an anthology of the speeches and writings of prominent Canadians over two centuries, showing the many ways of being Canadian.

Historic assumptions have since been challenged and mostly dismantled — principally that Canada was a white Christian nation where peoples of other faiths and colour were expected to, and often did, assume second-class status. Canadians of long-established ancestry have had to make, and have made, the difficult psychological journey toward accepting all Canadians as equal.

Canada isn't quite nirvana on Earth, but it's closer than most. There remain undeniable tensions: How best to come to terms with our geno-cidal treatment of Indigenous peoples. How to tackle persistent racism to-ward BIPOC communities, especially two-tier policing. There's our double standard in the selection of refugees, as clearly demonstrated by the ready preference shown those from Ukraine as opposed to those fleeing wars and persecution in Myanmar, Afghanistan, and parts of Africa and the Middle East. But such issues now weigh heavily on the national conscience, signalling that we may be ready to try to tackle them without tearing one another apart.

Canada is now the only Western nation with an overwhelming national consensus in favour of immigration — that is, in favour of more non-whites joining the Canadian family. No overtly anti-immigrant, let alone racist, party or politician can find much success here. Those who have tried have failed. This is remarkable at a time when skin colour has become a major fault line of the West. The democratic liberal order is in disarray across the West, but not in Canada.

Our unique history and contemporary multiculturalism, constitutional as well as a lived reality, have provided a ballast against the racial divisions of both the United States and most of Europe.

In making Marshall McLuhan's global village a reality at home, ours has been the most successful heterogeneous experiment in human history. Everything is always up for discussion. Nothing is frozen in time. Canadians don't have the conceit of a fixed culture. Canadian culture is a living, breathing entity that evolves every day. We keep reworking, reshaping, and improving our home and native and adopted land.

Acknowledgements

WRITING IS HARD WORK. IT IS FOR ME. HAS REMAINED SO EVEN AFTER TWO million published words over six decades. This book has been particularly difficult.

I only wanted to write about how Canada has evolved so wondrously so quickly. But India was tugging at me. "Write about your origins," encouraged Patsy Aldana, founder of Groundwood Books. "We bring complicated histories to Canada — that's how we enrich our collective sense of self."

A memoir, however, is an alien genre for me after a lifetime of focusing on issues. Besides, how does one write about oneself without boasting?

Ron Graham, one of our most elegant writers and astute commentators, said, "Write about yourself as though you were reporting on someone else."

Ram Guha, the great biographer of Mahatma Gandhi, warned, "Remember, you are not writing the history of India or your family's but your story." In the context of the people and circumstances encountered.

But how does regurgitating the big issues of our time add value for readers? A unique perspective? Sober second thoughts? A re-reading of contexts?

All those, said Ian Urquhart, former managing editor of the *Toronto Star*, whose knowledge of contemporary Canada is encyclopedic.

Friends and family read and critiqued various chapters. Patsy, Ron, Ram, Ian, of course. And Adrienne Clarkson, former governor general. Author, philosopher, public intellectual John Ralston Saul. Veteran CBC and Al Jazeera editor Tony Burman. Former *Toronto Star* columnist Carol Goar and foreign editor Mike Pieri. Professors Anver Emon and Jim Reilly of the University of Toronto. MD-turned-human rights advocate Michael Dan. News Media Canada's former president John Hinds. Editor Jane Springer. Brothers Suleman and Yousuf.

Joanne Madden, former *Toronto Star* librarian, mined several archives. Mariam Palmer and Keiran Pace, during their university breaks, helped sort through boxes and boxes of clippings and tens of thousands of responses from *Star* readers.

Ace agent and lawyer Michael Levine has been a good adviser and friend.

At Dundurn Press, associate publisher Kathryn Lane and editors Russell Smith, Elena Radic, and Michael Carroll kept me focused on the task.

It goes without saying that the shortcomings and mistakes here have all been mine.

Notes

2 Ram and Rumi

1 Ebrahim Moosa, *What Is a Madrasa?* (Chapel Hill, NC: University of North Carolina Press, 2015), 53.

2 Rumi, *The Masnavi*, trans. Jawid Mojaddedi (London: Oxford University Press, 2008), x, xxiv, book 2.

3 Rumi, *The Masnavi*, trans. Jawid Mojaddedi, xixv, Book 2.

4 Rumi, *The Masnavi*, trans. E.H. Whinfield (Santa Cruz, CA: Evinity Publishing, 2009), sacred-texts.com. First published in 1898.

5 Rumi, *The Essential Rumi*, trans. Coleman Barks (New York: HarperOne, 2004), 290.

3 The Milieu That Made Me

1 W.A. Shaheen, "Aziz Ahmad," *The Canadian Encyclopedia*, thecanadianencyclopedia.ca/en/article/aziz-ahmad.

2 Moosa, *What Is a Madrasa?*, 103.

3 Pankaj Mishra, *The Ruins of Empire* (Toronto: Doubleday Canada, 2012), 38.

4 William Dalrymple, *The Last Mughal* (London: Bloomsbury, 2006), 463.

5 Gail Minault, "Sayyid Mumtaz Ali and 'Huquq un-Niswan': An Advocate of Women's Rights in Islam in the Late Nineteenth Century," *Modern Asian Studies* 24, no. 1 (February 1990): 147–72.

6 Barbara Metcalf, *Perfecting Women: Maulana Ashraf 'Ali Thanawi's Bihishti Zewar* (Berkeley, CA: University of California Press, 1990), vii.

7 Metcalf, *Perfecting Women*, 10.

8 Metcalf, *Perfecting Women*, 8.

9 Metcalf, *Perfecting Women*, 10.

10 Metcalf, *Perfecting Women*, 9.

11 Emre Aytekin, "Imam Recites in NZ Parliament in Wake of Terror Attacks," *Anadolu Agency*, March 19, 2019, aa.com.tr/en/world/imam -recites-in-nz-parliament-in-wake-of-terror-attacks/1422611.

12 Yoginder Sikand, *Bastions of the Believers: Madrasas and Islamic Education in India* (New Delhi: Penguin Books India, 2005), 65.

13 E.M. Forster, *A Passage to India* (Delhi, India: Pearson Longman, 2006), 223.

14 Shaharyar M. Khan, *The Begums of Bhopal: A History of the Princely State of Bhopal* (London: I.B. Tauris, 2000), 55, 75, 86, 148.

15 Mohammed Mian Siddiqui Kandhlavi, *Tazkira-e Maulana Mohammed Idris Kandhlavi* (Lahore, Pakistan: Maktaba-e-Osmania, 1977), 37–38.

16 Mohammed Mian Siddiqui Kandhlavi, *Tazkira-e Maulana Mohammed Idris Kandhlavi*, 38.

17 Aziz Ahmad, *An Intellectual History of Islam in India* (Edinburgh: Edinburgh University Press, 1969), 138.

18 Damon Galgut, "EM Forster: 'But for Masood, I Might Never Have Gone to India,'" *Guardian*, August 8, 2014, theguardian.com/books/2014/aug /08/em-forster-passage-to-india-rereading.

4 The End of Colonialism

1 Asghar Ali Engineer, ed., *Role of Minorities in Freedom Struggle* (Delhi: Ajanta Publications, 1986), 13.

2 Engineer, ed., *Role of Minorities in Freedom Struggle*, 10.

3 Barbara Metcalf, *Husain Ahmad Madani: The Jihad for Islam and India's Freedom* (Oxford, UK: Oneworld Publications, 2009), 2.

4 Metcalf, *Husain Ahmad Madani*, 147.

5 Metcalf, *Husain Ahmad Madani*, 8.

6 Maulana Abul Hasan Ali Nadvi, *Mashaekh-e-Kandhla* (The Shaykhs of Kandhla) (Karachi: Mahad Al-Khaleel al-Islami, 1963), 176–79.

7 Yoginder Sikand, *Bastions of the Believers: Madrasas and Islamic Education in India* (New Delhi: Penguin India, 2005), 261.

8 Dietrich Reetz, "The Deoband Universe: What Makes a Transcultural and Transnational Educational Movement of Islam?" *Comparative Studies of South Asia, Africa, and the Middle East* 27, no. 1: 139–59.

5 The Fall of Hyderabad

1 D.F. Karaka, *Fabulous Mughal: Nizam VII of Hyderabad* (London: Derek Verschoyle, 1955), 110.

2 Karaka, *Fabulous Mughal*, 112–13.

Notes

3 Karaka, *Fabulous Mughal*, 112.
4 Karaka, *Fabulous Mughal*, 113.
5 Karaka, *Fabulous Mughal*, 123.
6 A.G. Noorani, *The Destruction of Hyderabad* (New Delhi: Tulika Books, 2021), 237–38.
7 Metcalf, *Husain Ahmad Madani*, 153.
8 Samuel P. Huntington, *The Clash of Civilizations and the Remaking of World Order* (New York: Simon & Schuster, 2011).

6 Happy Childhood

1 See Victoria Lautman, "The Stepwell of Chand Baori," *AramcoWorld* 71, no. 1 (January-February 2020); "India's Stepwells Are Relics of a Nuanced History," *Economist*, July 13, 2019, economist.com/books-and-arts /2019/07/13/indias-magnificent-stepwells-are-relics-of-a-nuanced -history.

7 The Making of a Journalist

1 Ashis Nandy, "Enlightened Scholar," *Hindu*, March 31, 2022.
2 "*Times*' Allen Bradford, 64, Dies," *Washington Times*, June 8, 2002, washingtontimes.com/news/2002/jun/8/20020608-031225-7414r.
3 "Paradesi Synagogue," britannica.com/topic/Paradesi-Synagogue.

8 End of the Good Life

1 Hafiz Syed Sarwar Hussain, *Kalaam-e-Sarwar* (Sarwar's Poems) (Hyderabad, India, 2018).
2 Vasant K. Bawa, *The Last Nizam: The Life and Times of Mir Osman Ali Khan* (New York: Viking, 1992), xiv.
3 See "Full Mir Barkat Ali Khan Mukarram Jah Asaf Jah VIIIs Coronation Gaddi Nashini Ceremony (Complete)," YouTube video, 29:47, youtube .com/watch?v=xy06xW218t4.

9 An "Indian" on the Prairies

1 Howard Pawley, *Keep True* (Winnipeg: University of Manitoba Press, 2011), 5.
2 Chris Wood, "The Newest Boat People," *Maclean's*, July 27, 1987.
3 Mohammed Mian Siddiqui Kandhlavi, *Tazkira-e Maulana Mohammed Idris Kandhlavi*.
4 Charles Gordon, "A Publisher Out of Sync with the Times," *Maclean's*, September 30, 1996, 410.

10 Good to Go at a Moment's Notice

1 Haroon Siddiqui, "Inside Khomeini's Lair: Ragtag Centre of Power,'"
Toronto Star, November 27, 1979.

11 In the Trenches

1 Olivia Ward, "It's Not Overt — but Blacks Still Find Prejudice," part of
seven-part "A Minority Report" series, *Toronto Star*, November 3, 1985.

12 The Browning of Canada

1 Roy McMurtry, *Memoirs and Reflections* (Toronto: Osgood Society for
Canadian Legal History, 2013), 343.

2 Chris Wood, "The Newest Boat People," *Maclean's*, July 27, 1987.

3 Ali Kazimi, *Undesirables: White Canada and the Komagata Maru*
(Vancouver: Douglas & McIntyre, 2012).

4 "Air India Flight 182 Memorial Sundial," sunposition.com/air_india
_sundial/air_india_memorial_sundial.html; Anthony Reinhart, "PM Issues
Apology to Relatives of Air India Victims," *Globe and Mail*, June 23, 2010,
theglobeandmail.com/news/national/pm-issues-apology-to-relatives-of-air
-india-victims/article4322762.

5 Shawna Richer, "Sikh Refugees Revisit N.S. Coast 17 Years Later," *Globe
and Mail*, July 14, 2004, theglobeandmail.com/news/national/sikh
-refugees-revisit-ns-coast-17-years-later/article18268597.

6 Jan Raska, "Canada's Refugee Determination System," Canadian Museum
of Immigration at Pier 21, August 21, 2020, pier21.ca/research/immigration
-history/canada-s-refugee-determination-system.

7 "Meet the Young Somali Canadian Playwright Taking the Story of
Toronto's Dixon Road to the Stage," *CBC News*, December 30, 2021,
cbc.ca/news/canada/toronto/fatuma-adar-dixon-road-somali-canadians
-toronto-1.6295223.

8 Mahmood Mamdani, "The Asian Question," *London Review of Books* 44,
no.19 (October 6, 2022), lrb.co.uk/the-paper/v44/n19/mahmood-mamdani
/the-asian-question.

13 The Editorial Perch

1 Christopher Ondaatje, *Sindh Revisited: A Journey in the Footsteps of Captain
Sir Richard Burton: 1842–1849, the India Years* (Toronto: HarperCollins,
1996), 141–43.

2 Haroon Siddiqui, "Let Kosovo Become Independent," *Toronto Star*,
January 21, 1999.

Notes

14 Multicultiphobia

1 Douglas Fisher, "Respect at Last for Immigration Critic," *Toronto Sun*, November 19, 1994.

2 Daniel Stoffman, "Why Canada Must Reassess Its Wide-Open Immigration Policy," *Toronto Star*, September 20, 1992, immigrationwatchcanada .org/dainel-stoffman-articles. Stoffman was the fourth annual winner of the Atkinson Fellowship in Public Policy.

3 Richard Gwyn, *Nationalism Without Walls: The Unbearable Lightness of Being Canadian* (Toronto: McClelland & Stewart, 1996), 2.

4 Richard Gwyn, "Is Multiculturalism Becoming Multinationalism," *Toronto Star*, February 28, 1993, and "Canadian Society Owes a Debt to Vanishing WASPS," *Toronto Star*, March 7, 1993.

5 Gwyn, *Nationalism Without Walls*, 113.

6 Gwyn, *Nationalism Without Walls*, 8.

7 Neil Bissoondath, *Selling Illusions: The Cult of Multiculturalism in Canada* (Toronto: Penguin Canada, 1994), 21, 133.

8 J.L. Granatstein, *Who Killed Canadian History?* (Toronto: HarperCollins Canada, 1998).

9 Desmond Morton and Morton Weinfeld, eds., *Who Speaks for Canada? Words That Shape a Country* (Toronto: McClelland & Stewart, 1998), Introduction.

10 John Porter, *The Vertical Mosaic: An Analysis of Social Class and Power in Canada* (Toronto: University of Toronto Press, 1965), 71. A 50th anniversary edition of this book was released by the same publisher in 2015.

11 Phil Ryan, *Multicultiphobia* (Toronto: University of Toronto Press, 2018).

12 Charles Rusnell, "Minorities in the Media, Three-Part Series, Part 1: Why Are the Newsrooms of the Nation White Enclaves?" *Ottawa Citizen*, August 25, 1990.

13 Carol Tator, Frances Henry, and Winston Mattis, *Challenging Racism in the Arts: Case Studies of Controversy and Conflict* (Toronto: University of Toronto Press, 1998), 198.

14 Frances Henry and Carol Tator, *The Colour of Democracy* (Toronto: Nelson, 2009), 231.

15 Henry and Tator, *The Colour of Democracy*, 2.

16 Henry and Tator, *The Colour of Democracy*, 1.

17 John Miller, "White Newsrooms: History Repeats Itself," *New Canadian Media*, November 25, 2021, newcanadianmedia.ca/white-newsrooms -history-repeats-itself.

15 Becoming a Columnist

1 Anna Politkovskaya, *A Dirty War: A Russian Reporter in Chechnya* (London: Harvill Press, 2001).

2 Kishore Mahbubani, *Can Asians Think?* (Toronto: Key Porter, 2001).

3 Robert Fulford, "Blame Canada," *Toronto Life*, June 2001.

4 Fulford, "Blame Canada."

16 Post-9/11 Canada

1 Brown University, "Costs of War," Watson Institute for International and Public Affairs, watson.brown.edu/costsofwar.

2 Rasha Mourtada, "Haroon and the Sea of Opinions," *Review of Journalism* (Spring 2002), rrj.ca/haroon-and-the-sea-of-opinions.

3 Mourtada, "Haroon and the Sea of Opinions."

4 Mourtada, "Haroon and the Sea of Opinions."

5 Haroon Siddiqui, "Tutu Berates Bellicose Bush," *Toronto Star*, September 26, 2002.

6 Amnesty International, "The Maher Arar Case," March 6, 2017.

7 Haroon Siddiqui, "Scandal Bigger Than Prison Abuse," *Toronto Star*, May 5, 2004.

8 Jameel Jaffer, *Administration of Torture: A Documentary Record from Washington to Abu Ghraib and Beyond* (New York: Columbia University Press, 2007).

17 Afghanistan and Iraq Wars

1 Reza Baraheni, "Two Soldiers and a Tank," *Toronto Star*, April 22, 2003.

2 All Lakdhar Brahimi quotations from Haroon Siddiqui, "Expert Advice on Afghanistan," *Toronto Star*, September 14, 2006.

3 Haroon Siddiqui, "On the 'Wild West' Afghan-Pakistan Frontier," *Toronto Star*, February 18, 2007, A15; Siddiqui, "Baluchistan an 'Administrative Nightmare,'" *Toronto Star*, February 22, 2007, A19; Siddiqui, "Pakistan Fed Up with U.S. and Allies on Afghanistan," *Toronto Star*, February 25, 2007, A15.

4 Bill Graham, *The Call of the World: A Political Memoir* (Vancouver: On Point Press, 2016), 35.

5 Jon Lee Anderson, "The Taliban Confront the Realities of Power," *New Yorker*, February 21, 2022, newyorker.com/magazine/2022/02/28/the-taliban-confront-the-realities-of-power-afghanistan.

Notes

6   Steven Chase, "Saudi Arabia Top Export Destination for Canadian Arms After United States in 2021," *Globe and Mail*, May 31, 2022, theglobeandmail.com/politics/article-saudi-arabia-top-export-destination-for -canadian-arms-after-united.

18 Cultural Warfare on Muslims

1   Ginny Dougary, "The Voice of Experience: Martin Amis," *Times Online*, September 9, 2006, ginnydougary.co.uk/the-voice-of-experience.

2   Aaron Wherry, "For the Record: Justin Trudeau on Liberty and the Niqab," *Maclean's*, March 10, 2015, macleans.ca/politics/for-the-record -justin-trudeau-on-liberty-and-the-niqab.

3   Angelique Chrisafis, "Pork or Nothing: How School Dinners Are Dividing France," *Guardian*, October 13, 2015, theguardian.com/world/2015/oct/13 /pork-school-dinners-france-secularism-children-religious-intolerance.

4   Matthew Duss et al., "Fear, Inc. 2.0: The Islamophobia Network's Efforts to Manufacture Hate in America," *Center for American Progress*, February 11, 2015, americanprogress.org/article/fear-inc-2-0.

5   Frédérik-Xavier Duhamel and Eric Andrew-Gee, "Quebeckers Voice Support for Anti-Islamophobia Representative," *Globe and Mail*, February 3, 2023.

6   Mahmood Mamdani, *Good Muslim, Bad Muslim: America, the Cold War, and the Roots of Terror* (New York: Pantheon, 2004).

7   Eliyahu Stern, "Don't Fear Islamic Law in America," *New York Times*, September 2, 2011, nytimes.com/2011/09/03/opinion/dont-fear-islamic -law-in-america.html.

8   Mark Steyn, "Islamophobia and Mass Murder," *National Review*, July 25, 2011, nationalreview.com/corner/islamophobia-and-mass-murder-mark-steyn.

9   For example, see Maryam Ahmed, "Biotechnology in the High School Classroom," *American Biology Teacher* 58, no. 3 (March 1996): 178–80, jstor.org/stable/4450111?seq=1&cid=pdf-reference#references_tab_contents.

10   Terence McKenna, "The Political Strategy Behind Quebec's Values Charter," *CBC News*, November 7, 2013, cbc.ca/news/canada/the-political -strategy-behind-quebec-s-values-charter-1.2418405.

11   Bernie Farber and Amira Elghawaby, "Quebec's Bill 21 Shows Why We Fear the Tyranny of the Majority," *Ottawa Citizen*, July 11, 2019, ottawacitizen.com/opinion/columnists/elghawaby-and-farber-quebecs-bill -21-shows-why-we-fear-the-tyranny-of-the-majority.

12   Emma Teitel, "Tell Me Again Where Elghawaby Got It Wrong," *Toronto Star*, February 11, 2023.

19 Harper and Muslims

1 Julian Walker, "Hate Speech and Freedom of Expression: Legal Boundaries in Canada," Library of Parliament, Parliament of Canada, June 29, 2018, lop .parl.ca/sites/PublicWebsite/default/en_CA/ResearchPublications/201825E.

2 Haroon Siddiqui, "Free Speech, Yes, but Not Hate Speech," *Toronto Star*, March 17, 2013.

3 Jennifer Yang, "Videotaped Apology Hailed as Victory in Struggle Against Hate Speech," *Toronto Star*, December 17, 2018, thestar.com/news /gta/2018/12/17/videotaped-apology-hailed-as-victory-in-struggle-against -hate-speech.html; Jennifer Yang, "Anti-Muslim Agitator Gives Video Apology to Owner of Paramount Foods over 'Jihadist' Comments," *Toronto Star*, December 17, 2018, thestar.com/news/gta/2018/12/17/anti -muslim-agitator-gives-video-apology-to-owner-of-paramount-fine-foods -over-jihadist-comments.html.

4 Shanifa Nasser, "Kevin Johnston Ordered to Pay $2.5M for 'Hateful, Islamophobic' Remarks Against Restaurant Chain Owner," *CBC News*, May 13, 2019, cbc.ca/news/canada/toronto/kevin-johnston-paramount -2-5-million-mohamad-fakih-1.5134227; Canadian Anti-Hate Network, "'Untruthful, Hateful, and Harmful,'" October 4, 2021, antihate.ca/kevin _johnston_sentenced_18_months_prison_six_counts_contempt.

5 Annabel Oromoni, "Muslim Lawyer Walied Soliman Wins $500,000 Damages in Libel Lawsuit for Terrorism Accusations," *Law Times*, October 25, 2012, lawtimesnews.com/practice-areas/litigation/muslim-lawyer-walied -soliman-wins-500000-damages-in-libel-lawsuit-for-terrorism-accusations /361073.

6 Colin Perkel, "Transfer to Canada," *Encyclopaedia Britannica*, britannica.com /event/Omar-Khadr-case/Transfer-to-Canada.

7 Alex Boutilier, "Scheer Issues Second Statement on New Zealand Attack After Backlash," *Toronto Star*, March 15, 2019, thestar.com/news/canada/2019/03/15/ scheer-issues-second-statement-on-christchurch-after-backlash.html.

20 Media and Muslims

1 Edward Behr, *Anyone Here Been Raped & Speaks English?* (London: Hodder & Stoughton, 1985).

2 Todd H. Green, *The Fear of Islam: An Introduction to Islamophobia in the West* (Minneapolis, MN: Fortress Press, 2015), 233.

3 Dorgham Abusalim, "Study: 'NYT' Portrays Islam More Negatively Than Alcohol, Cancer, and Cocaine," *Mondoweiss*, March 5, 2016, mondoweiss

Notes

.net/2016/03/study-nyt-portrays-islam-more-negatively-than-alcohol
-cancer-and-cocaine.

4   Davide Mastracci, "Remembering Canadian Media's Post-9/11 Bloodlust," *Maple*, September 8, 2021.

5   Jill Abramson, *Merchants of Truth: The Business of News and the Fight for Facts* (New York: Simon & Schuster, 2019), 79.

6   John Pilger, "Foreword" in *Guardians of Power: The Myth of the Liberal Media*. David Edwards and David Cromwell (New York: Pluto Press, 2006).

7   Indira A.R. Lakshmanan, "'Lone Wolf' or 'Terrorist'? How Bias Can Shape News Coverage," Poynter Institute, October 2, 2017 poynter.org /ethics-trust/2017/lone-wolf-or-terrorist-how-bias-can-shape-news-coverage.

8   Malreddy Pavan Kumar, "Introduction: Orientalism(s) After 9/11," *Journal of Postcolonial Writing* 48, no. 3 (June 1, 2012): 233–40, tandfonline.com /doi/abs/10.1080/17449855.2012.678707.

9   Muslim Advocates, "Losing Liberty: The State of Freedom Ten Years After the Patriot Act," October 2011, muslimadvocates.org/wp-content /uploads/2019/06/Losing_Liberty_The_State_of_Freedom_10_Years_After _the_PATRIOT_Act.pdf.

10 Charles Kurzman, "Terrorism Since 9/11: An Accounting," Duke University and University of North Carolina, February 2, 2011, kurzman .unc.edu/wp-content/uploads/sites/1410/2011/06/Kurzman_Muslim -American_Terrorism_Since_911_An_Accounting.pdf.

11 Elizabeth Poole and John E. Richardson, eds., *Muslims and the News Media* (London: I.B. Tauris, 2006), 3–4.

12 Michael Ryan, "Framing the War Against Terrorism: U.S. Newspaper Editorials and Military Action in Afghanistan," *International Communication Gazette* 66, no. 5 (2004): 363–82.

13 Michelle Shephard, *Guantanamo's Child: The Untold Story of Omar Khadr* (Mississauga, ON: John Wiley & Sons, 2008).

14 Felix Odartey-Wellington, "Racial Profiling and Moral Panic: Operation Thread and the Al-Qaeda Sleeper Cell That Never Was," *Global Media Journal* 2, no. 2 (December 2009): 25–40.

15 John Miller and Cybele Sack, "Terrorism and Anonymous Sources: The Toronto 18 Case," *Canadian Journal of Media Studies* 8 (2010): 1–24.

16 Miller and Sack, "Terrorism and Anonymous Sources."

17 John Miller and Cybele Sack, "The Toronto 18 Terror Case: Trial by Media? How Newspaper Opinion Framed Canada's Biggest Terrorism

Case," *International Journal of Diversity in Organizations, Communities, and Nations: Annual Review* 10, no. 1 (August 7, 2010): 279–96.

18 Christie Blatchford, "Ignoring the Biggest Elephant in the Room," *Globe and Mail*, June 5, 2006, theglobeandmail.com/news/national/ignoring -the-biggest-elephant-in-the-room/article1100051.

19 Doug Saunders, *The Myth of the Muslim Tide: Do Immigrants Threaten the West?* (Toronto: Alfred A. Knopf Canada, 2012), 37.

20 Kerry Moore, Paul Mason, and Justin Lewis, "Images of Islam in the UK: The Representation of British Muslims in the National Print News Media 2000–2008," Cardiff School of Journalism, Media and Cultural Studies, July 7, 2008, orca.cardiff.ac.uk/id/eprint/53005/; Peter Oborne and James Jones, "Muslims Under Siege: Alternating Vulnerable Communities," *Channel 4 Dispatches*, July 2008, channel4.com/news/media/pdfs /Muslims_under_siege_LR.pdf; YouTube, "A Soft Apartheid Towards Muslims Is Emerging in Britain: Owen Jones Meets Peter Oborne," youtube.com/watch?v=PXkKbFQRHcs.

21 Samanth Subramanian, "One Man's (Very Polite) Fight Against Media Islamophobia," *Guardian*, October 18, 2018, theguardian.com/news/2018 /oct/18/miqdaad-versi-very-polite-fight-against-british-media-islamophobia.

22 Centre for Media Monitoring, "British Media's Coverage of Muslims & Islam (2018–2020)," November 2021, cfmm.org.uk/wp-content/uploads /2021/11/CfMM-Annual-Report-2018-2020-digital.pdf.

23 Erin M. Kearns, Allison E. Betus, and Anthony F. Lemieux, "Why Do Some Terrorist Attacks Receive More Media Attention Than Others?" *Justice Quarterly* 36, no. 6 (January 25, 2019): 985–1022.

24 John E. Richardson, "Who Gets to Speak? A Study of Sources in the Broadsheet Press," in *Muslims and the News Media*, eds. Elizabeth Poole and John E. Richardson (London: I.B. Tauris, 2006), 115.

25 Zareena Grewal, "Death by Culture? How Not to Talk About Islam and Domestic Violence," Institute for Social Policy and Understanding, July 1, 2009, ispu.org/death-by-culture-how-not-to-talk-about-islam-and -domestic-violence.

26 Yasmin Jiwani, "Posthumous Rescue: The Shafia Young Women as Worthy Victims," *Girlhood Studies* 7, no. 1 (2014): 27–45.

27 Craig Offman, "Aqsa Parvez Mourned Slain Teen Wanted 'To Get More Out of Life,' Friends Say," *Edmonton Journal*, December 16, 2007.

28 Jasmin Zine, "Unsettling the Nation: Gender, Race, and Muslim Cultural

Politics in Canada," *Studies in Ethnicity and Nationalism* 9, no. 1 (2009), academia.edu/34530643/Unsettling_the_Nation_Gender_Race_and _Muslim_Cultural_Politics_in_Canada.

29 Rochelle Terman, "Islamophobia and Media Portrayals of Muslim Women: A Computational Text Analysis of U.S. News Coverage," *International Studies Quarterly* 61, no. 3 (September 2017): 489–502, doi.org/10.1093 /isq/sqx051.

30 Green, *The Fear of Islam*, 329.

21 Rushdie and Muslims

1 Jabal Buaben, *Images of the Prophet Muhammad in the West: A Study of Muir, Margoliouth and Watt* (Leicester, UK: Islamic Foundation, 1996), 34.

2 Dalrymple, *The Last Mughal*, 70.

3 Salman Rushdie, *The Satanic Verses* (New York: Viking, 1988), 381–88.

4 Ali A. Mazrui "The Satanic Verses or a Satanic Novel? Moral Dilemmas of the Rushdie Affair," *Alternatives: Global, Local, Political* 15, no. 1 (1990): 97–121.

5 Peter Morey, *Islamophobia and the Novel* (New York: Columbia University Press, 2018), 6.

6 Dan Bilefsky, "Cartoon Dispute Prompts Identity Crisis for Liberal Denmark," *New York Times*, February 12, 2006.

7 See watson.brown.edu/costsofwar.

8 Morey, *Islamophobia and the Novel*, 1.

9 Amnesty International, "France Is Not the Free-Speech Champion It Says It Is," November 12, 2020, amnesty.org/en/latest/news/2020/11/france -is-not-the-free-speech-champion-it-says-it-is.

10 Erna Paris, "A Rigid Belief in Freedom Is Driving France and the U.S. to Tragedy," *Globe and Mail*, November 16, 2020, theglobeandmail.com /opinion/article-a-rigid-belief-in-freedom-is-driving-france-and-the-us-to -tragedy.

11 Asma Barlas, "Reprinting the Charlie Hebdo Cartoons Is Not About Free Speech," *Al Jazeera*, September 10, 2020, aljazeera.com/opinions /2020/9/10/reprinting-the-charlie-hebdo-cartoons-is-not-about-free-speech.

12 Zoe Heller, "The Salman Rushdie Case," *New York Review of Books*, December 20, 2012, nybooks.com/articles/2012/12/20/salman-rushdie-case.

22 An Incurably Optimistic Canadian

1   Will Kymlicka, "Disentangling the Debate," in *Uneasy Partners: Multiculturalism and Rights in Canada* (Waterloo, ON: Wilfrid Laurier University Press, 2007), 152–53.

2   Statistics Canada, "The Canadian Census: A Rich Portrait of the Country's Religious and Ethnocultural Diversity," October 26, 2022, www150.statcan.gc.ca/n1/daily-quotidien/221026/dq221026b-eng.htm.

3   Jytte Klausen, *The Cartoons That Shook the World* (New Haven, CT: Yale University Press, 2009).

4   Denise A. Spellberg, *Thomas Jefferson's Qur'an* (New York: Alfred A. Knopf, 2013), 84.

5   See "Alhamdoulillah — Tala 'Ala Al Badru Alayna — French Canadian Choir with Lyrics," December 11, 2015, YouTube video, 3:56, youtube .com/watch?v=K3qYC3X25nk.

6   Morton and Weinfeld, eds., *Who Speaks for Canada?*, xii.

Image Credits

All other images courtesy of the author.

xiv   Patrick Corrigan/*Toronto Star.*

37   Shaharyar M. Khan, *The Begums of Bhopal: A History of the Princely State of Bhopal* (London: I.B. Tauris, 2000).

78–81   Miriam Palmer.

92   *Hindu.*

95   *Hindu.*

128   *Brandon Sun.*

208   Sir Christopher Ondaatje.

214   Terry Mosher, aka Aislin, *Toronto Star.*

237   Ken Faught/*Toronto Star* via Getty.

256   Steve Russell/*Toronto Star* via Getty.

262   Mike Slaughter/*Toronto Star* via Getty.

356   Rideau Hall.

396   David Cooper/*Toronto Star* via Getty.

Index

Locators in italics refer to images.

A Passage to India (Forster), 35, 41
Abbas, Mahmoud, 295, 369
Abdul Majid Khan II, 122
Abdul-Basit (author's nephew), 120, 306
Abella, Irving, 210, 226
Abramson, Jill, 338
Abu Ghraib, 19, 269–70, 271
access to information, 235–36
Administration of Torture (Jaffer and Singh), 271
Afghanistan
    abandoned by West, 292
    government, Karzai, 292
    loya jirga and government, 283
    Pakistan border, 285–87, 288–89
    refugees from, 245
    Soviet incursions, 49
    Soviet invasion, 162–69
    war on terror and, 263
Afghanistan, war in
    Al Jazeera bombing, 368
    atrocities, 292–93
    Canadian involvement and mistakes, 282–84
    death toll, 294
    detainees, 270

effects of in Canada, 343
effects on Pakistan, 294
failures and end of American presence, 290–92
failures and end of Canadian mission, 289
Khadr, detention of, 328
media's role in support for, 337–38
positive and negative impacts, 293
women's rights as propaganda, 300–301
aftermath of 9/11
    blame of Islamic groups, 47
    Canadian government and Islamophobia, 318–19
    erosion of journalistic integrity, 357
    literary, 364
    media portrayals and discussion of Muslims, 337
    media purge, 382
    military actions, 49
    moderate Muslim identity, 390
    narrative and counter-narratives, 263–65
    police powers, 342
    public reactions to, 260–62

Aga Khan, 196–97, 360
Ahmadis, 320
Ahmadiyya mosque, 320
Air India Bombing, 186–87, 190
Aislin (Terry Mosher), 345
Aiyar, Mani Shankar, 374
Akhavan, Payam, 217
Al Jazeera, 368
Al Qaeda, 293
    alleged Toronto sleeper cell, 343
    anthrax letters, blamed for, 340
    media associations with Arar, 342
    prisoners and, 276
Alboim, Naomi, 225
Albright, Madeleine, 244
Alexander, Chris, 329–30
Algeria, 259, 295, 296
Ali, Tariq, 132, 268
Aligarh Muslim University, 41, 48
Alighieri, Dante, 360–61
All India Radio, 108
Almalki, Abdullah, 272
Al-Quds al-Arabi, 368–69
American Jewish Congress, 304
Amin, Idi, 193, 196
Amin-Khan, Tariq, 350
Amis, Martin, 298
Amnesty International, 154, 295, 370
Among the Believers: An Islamic Journey
    (Naipaul), 364
Amtul Baseer (Amma - author's mother)
    care for children, 6, 20
    children's education, 91
    children's weddings, 86, 124, *135*
    death of Abbi, 126
    death of husband, 115, 116
    flight from Warangal, 53, 54–55
    food preferences, 72

    grandchildren and, 120
    as *hafiza*, 17
    health troubles, 57, 134–35
    help with *taraweeh* prayers, 69
    husband's heart attack, 113
    marriage, 42
    pictures of, 87–88, 119
    politics and poetry, 46–47
    protecting community, 82
    travel with family, 43
    views of, 120
Anand, Dev, 105
Anderson, Scott, 342
Andhra Pradesh, 248
Anglican Church, 149, 374
anthrax letters, 340
anti-colonial struggles, 29–31, 38, 44–47
Anti-Defamation League, 302
anti-immigrant sentiments, 185–86,
    187–88, 193, 206, 219–23, 226–27
anti-Iranian sentiments, 160
anti-Muslim activists and groups,
    299–300, 325–26
anti-Muslim sentiments. *See also*
    Muslims, cultural warfare on;
    Muslims and Western media
    9/11, impact of, 257–58
    American, 242–43
    attempts to deny, 333
    Canadian politicians and, 177
    Canadian rallies, 321–22
    defamation charges, 325–26
    dichotomies and, 300–301
    discussed by author, 279
    effects of, 378
    Great Replacement Theory, 303–4
    Islamic fundamentalism and,
        266–68

Index

opposition to cemetery, 309

post 9/11, 263–65

public figures and organizations, promotion by, 298–300

Quebec and, 311

secularism and, 310

terrorist "links" discussed in media, 340–41

use in Sharia law discussions, 302

in Western media, 335–37

anti-Semitism. *See also* Islamophobia; MS St. Louis

as accusation against Muslims, 325–26, 346–47

accusations of, 371–72

Canadian politics and, 137–39

efforts to combat, 311

Holocaust denial, 369

political use of accusations, 321

in Quebec, 304

Quebec and referendum, 206

views of, 260

anti-Sikh sentiments, 187–89

apartheid, 210, 229

Apartheid Week, 321

Arar, Maher, 268–69, 270, 341–42

Arberry, A.J, 26–27

Arbitration Act (1991), 301–2

Armenia, 211

Arts of the Sikh Kingdoms (exhibit), 191

Asper, Izzy, 137, 138, 139, 354, 355, 356

Asper family, 355

al-Assad, Bashar, 331

Assaf, Dany, 345

Atkins, Jimmy, *237*

Atkinson, Joseph, 182–83, 184, 240–41

Atkinson Foundation, awards and principles, 183, 221, 240–41

Atwood, Margaret, 386

Augustine, Jean, 227

Avnery, Uri, 299, 321

Axworthy, Lloyd, 216, 244, 296

Ayatollah Sadegh Khalkhali, 173–74

Ayesha (wife of Prophet Muhammad), 359, 376

Azerbaijan, 211

Azmi, Kaifi, 105–7

Azmi, Shabana, 105–6, 107

Azmi, Shaukat, 107

Bacon, Francis, 360–61

Baghdad Museum, 280–81

Bahá'ís, 319, 320

Baig, Mumtaz Ali, 70, 73

Bains, George, 179

Bains, Navdeep, 190

Baker, James, 277

Baksh, Abdul Hasan, 30

Baksh, Mahmud (Maulana Shah), 13

Baksh, Muhammad Ilahi, 24, 25–26, 27, 29, 31, 35

Bamiyan Buddhas, 252–53

Baraheni, Reza, 280–81, 385–86

Barks, Coleman, 26–27

Barlas, Asma, 375–76

Bassett, John, 180

Bata Nagar, 88

Bawa Muhaiyaddeen, Muhammad, 27

Bazargan, Mehdi, 174

Beauregard, Rémy, 322

Behest-e-Zahra Cemetery, 156

Behishti Zewar (Heavenly Ornaments - BZ), 33–34

Bell, Carole, 195

Benaud, Ritchie, 89

Berton, Pierre, 179

Bertrand, Janette, 307–8

Beyak, Lynn, 326–27

Bhatti, Shahbaz, 320

Bhopal, 35–40, 57

Biden, Joe, 291

Bilal, 361–62

bin Laden, Osama

    Afghanistan, invasion of, 275

    assassination of, 290

    beliefs and calling, 266, 313

    CIA and, 259

    failure to capture, 245

    first attacks by, 243

    North American ties, 282

Bissonnette, André, 309

Bissoondath, Neil, 222–23, 224

Black, Conrad, 354

Black Canadians, 231–32, 233–34,
    235–36, 384, 385

Black Lives Matter, 373

Blair, Bill, 236

Blair, Tony, 279, 297, 298, 394

Blanchet, Yves-François, 311, 312

Blatchford, Christie, 344

Bloomberg, Michael, 313–14

Bly, Robert, 26–27

B'nai Brith, 255, 322

Bollywood, 105–6, 144

book burning, Sarajevo Library and
    Bradford 373–74

Borden, Robert, 189

Bordman, Daniel, 325–26

Borovoy, Alan, 324

Bosnia, 387–88

Bosnia and Herzegovina, 212

Boswell, Keith, 329

Bouchard, Gérard, 304, 309

Bouchard, Lucien, 206

Bouchard-Taylor commission, 346

Bourassa, Robert, 203, 227

Bradford, Allen, 99–100, 101

Brahimi, Lakdhar, 283–84, 289

Brandon Sun

    author's time at, 8–11, 125

    columns, 276

    fair coverage and journalist security,
        131–32

    foreign coverage, 146

    Lew Whitehead and, 127–29

    liberal politics of, 126

    managing editors, 140, 149

Brandon University, 125, 126, 133

Braun, Aurel, 322

Breivik, Anders, 299, 303, 317, 340

Bremer, Paul, 281

British Broadcasting Corporation (BBC),
    121, 168

British colonialism, 15, 104, 152, 231–32

British India

    abandonment of Hyderabad, 57–60

    chaos and massacres, 54

    early struggle for independence, 29

    education within, 34

    end of rule, 44–47

    Gandhi and, 38–39

    Little London, 104

    Muslims and, 32, 34–36

    the Mutiny, 30–31

    remnants of, 82

Broadbent, Ed, 322–23

Brzezinski, Zbigniew, 169

B'Tselem, 322

burkas, 36, 313

Burney, Shehla, 105–6, 124, 125, 148

Burney, Siddiq, 5

Burton, Richard, 206–7, 209

Index

Bush, George H. W., 212, 243, 278
Bush, George W.
  beliefs and calling, 313
  criticisms of, 258, 271
  loss of Iraqi support, 281
  response to torture accusations, 271
  responses to 9/11, 259, 294
  views of war on terror, 266
  war on terror and, 251, 297
Byrne, Jenni, 333

Cairns, Alan, 223
The Call of the World (Graham), 287–88
Callaghan, Bill, 148
Cameron, David, 299
Camp, Dalton, 137, 276
Canada. *See also* immigration to Canada
  1982 Constitution, 203–4
  Afghanistan, end of presence in, 289
  Air India Bombing, 186–87, 190
  anti-Semitism in, 137–39
  Arar and security services, 268–69
  Arar commission of inquiry, 271
  beauty of, 383
  Canadian flight shot down by Iran, 195–96
  demographics, 383–84
  embassy and Islamic Revolution, 161
  foreign policies, 287–88, 296, 320–21
  free trade and, 183–84
  historic mistreatment of minorities, 390
  immigration, changing perspectives, 195–96
  immigration, increase in, 194
  immigration and identity, 398–99
  India and, 188, 246

  international news, interest in, 210–11
  Iraq, war in, 211
  multiculturalism and, 180–83, 236–38, 381
  prayers in school, 314–15
  racism and denialism, 232–34
  racism in, 125–26, 224–26
  religious accommodations, 315
  Rushdie and, 362–63
  separatism, 205–6
  Sharia law, connections to, 189, 302–3
  support of dictators, 296
  views of, 3
Canadian Advertising Foundation, 228–29
Canadian Arab Federation, 255, 322
Canadian Armed Forces (CAF), 189, 270, 276, 282–83, 285, 290
Canadian Asian Artists' Association, 227
Canadian Association of Journalists, 236, 357
Canadian Broadcasting Corporation (CBC)
  Arar, failure to expose media's role in detention, 341
  colonialism and language, 7
  criticisms and, 357
  Little Mosque on the Prairie (TV Show), 397
  Obama interview, 385
  TV shows, 184, 229
Canadian Club, 270
Canadian Committee for UNESCO, 355
Canadian Council of Churches, 245, 255
Canadian Daily Newspaper Publishers Association (CDNPA), 128, 228, 229

Canadian Human Rights Act, 323–26
Canadian Human Rights Commission,
  324, 345–46
Canadian Jewish Congress, 155, 365
Canadian Journal of Media Studies, 343
Canadian Managing Editors Conference,
  11
Canadian media, 127–29, 210–12, 354–
  56. *See also* individual organizations
  and journalists
Canadian Muslim Vote, 332
Canadian Security Intelligence Service
  (CSIS), 268
Canadian Sikh Centennial Foundation,
  191
Cannon, Lawrence, 322
Canwest, 341–42, 355–56
capital punishment, 302–3
Cardiff School of Journalism, Media and
  Cultural Studies, 346
Cardus, Neville, 93, 96
career, author's
  Air India Bombing, 186–87
  Brandon Sun, 8–11, 125, 140
  Burton and Ondaatje, 206–9
  Clinton trip, 245–51
  college journalism, 3–4, 90–91
  as columnist, 239–42, 254–55,
    258–63, 279
  covering cricket, 107–8
  diversity in media, 213
  early rejections, 5, 8
  editorial page editor, 199
  editorial policies, 337
  foreign reporting, Afghanistan,
    162–69
  foreign reporting, general, 143–45
  foreign reporting, India, 145–47,

  163, 169–70, 176
  foreign reporting, Iran, 153–62
  foreign reporting, Iran-Iraq, 172–74,
    175–76
  Hindu, 102–3
  Israeli-Palestinian conflict, 210
  Macdonald Commission report,
    183–84
  move to Toronto, 148–49
  Osmania Courier, 98–99
  post 9/11, 1, 257–65
  PTI, 103–8
  Sadat's death, 171–72
  Shaykh Sabah al Salem al Sabah
    interview, 109–11
  Simpsons department store, 5–6
  Tamil refugee reporting, 191–92
  Toronto Star, 98, 151–53, 172,
    176–78
  writing challenges, 198–99
Carter, Jimmy, 155, 169
Catholic Church, 130, 138, 182–83,
  224, 301, 374
Cechnya, 211–12
Celil, Huseyin, 348
Center for American Progress, 299
Central Intelligence Agency (CIA), 14,
  19, 154, 259, 290, 339
Centre culturel islamique de Québec,
  309, 332
Centre for Media Monitoring (Muslim
  Council of Britain), 346–47
Chabad House, 104
Chacha Ayub (author's uncle), 88
Chamberlain, Neville, 212
Charest, Jean, 302, 304
Charlie Hebdo, 366, 369–70
Charter of Quebec Values, 307, 308

Index

Charter of Rights and Freedoms
conspiracy theories and, 302
defence of, 241
free speech and, 365–66
freedom of religion, 392–93
hijab bans and, 310
multicultural rights and, 219–24, 324
Chattopadhya, Aghorenath, 93
Chechen wars, 210, 244
China, 348
Chinese head tax, 190
Chinese Canadians, 195, 222, 229, 236–37, 255, 383
Chong, Michael, 33
Chrétien, Jean
1993 election, 220
Canadian first, 383
Iraq, invasion of, 277, 278–79
Ismailis, admiration for, 196
Serbian conflict (1995), 216
Christchurch shooting, 34, 333, 348
Christian fundamentalism, 266–67
Christian right, denunciations of Islam, 298
Churchill, Winston, 7
Citizens' Forum on Canada's Future, 219–220
citizenship, 186–87, 210, 223, 319, 329–31
Clancy, Lou, 204–5
Clark, Joe, 210, 211
Clarkson, Adrienne, *356*, 383, 384, 393
Clinton, Bill, 216, 245–48, 249–50, 295
Coalition Avenir Québec (CAQ), 309–10
Coffin, William, 160
Cohn, Martin, 200
The Colour of Democracy: Racism in

Canadian Society (Henry and Tator), 232–33
Concordia University, 354
Conservative Party of Canada (CPC)
anti-Muslim policies and free speech, 323–33
anti-Muslim sentiments and funding, 330
Manitoba, provincial party, 11, 137, 138
Muslim votes and, 332
Coptic Christians, 319, 320, 376
Cost of War Project, 367
cottage culture, 77, 382
Couillard, Philippe, 308
Crane, David, 183–84
Crawley, Phil, 342
Crimea, 253–54
criticisms of author, 254–55, 260, 355
Croatia, 212
Cruickshank, John, 356, 366
Crusades, 360
Cuthand, Doug, 355
Czechoslovakia, 193

Dadi (author's grandmother), 44
Dairat ul-Ma'arif (House of Wisdom), 41
Dalai Lama, 93
Dalrymple, William, 361
Daniel, Joe, 331
Danish cartoons, 354, 364–65, 389
Davey, Clark, 5, 8, 11, 125
David, Tirone, 202
Davis, Bill, 185, 204
Davis, Murdoch, 355
Davis, Walter, 193
Davloor, Ram, 148
Dayal, Raja Deen, 398

democracy, 145–47, 294–96, 320–21, 329–31, 357

denialism, 232–34

Deoband
  accounts of, 21
  Darul Uloom, 32–33, 38, 42, 44, 46, 49–51
  education in, 34
  elders of, 32, 33
  end of British rule, 44–47
  Siddiquis and, 42

Desai, Morarji, 146–47

Diefenbaker, John (Dief), 7, 136–37, 276

Dimant, Frank, 210

Dinsdale, Walter, 131, 132, 147, 148

diversity
  in advertising, 228–29
  in journalism, 236
  in media, 212–16, 227–28, 229–30
  within Muslims, 392

diversity and media, work in
  advertising, 228–29
  as columnist, 241–42
  early days, 227–28

domestic violence, 351–52

Dorval International Airport, 70

Dosanjh, Ujjal, 384

Douglas, Tommy, 136–37

Dow, Alastair, 179

Doyle, Richard, 11

Dr. Aziz (*A Passage to India*), 35, 41

Dr. Radhakrishnan, 121–22

Dubet, François, 299

Dubin, Charles, 205

Dubuc, Alain, 205

Duke University, 340–41

Durand Line, 285

Dzhemilev, Mustafa, 253–54

East India Company, 29–30, 34

Easter, Wayne, 268

Economic Council of Canada, 220

Edney, Dennis, 328

education, author's
  discipline, 69
  Hyderabad and Tayabba, 61–62
  journalism, 100–101
  path to journalism, 90, 94–96
  Qur'an, memorization of, 64
  secular, 83–85
  shift in interests, 94–96

Egypt, 171–72, 259, 295–96, 353, 377

Eid, 18, 73

El Maati, Ahmad, 272

El Nakla, Nadia, 394

El-Alloul, Raina, 308

Elghawaby, Amira, 311–12

Ellison, Keith, 394

Ellora Caves, 41

Emerson, Steve, 299, 353

Emperor Bahadur Shah Zafar, 29, 31, 72

Emperor Jalal-ud-din Muhammad Akbar, 23

employment equity act, 213–14

Eng, Susan, 227

Enkin, Esther, 348

Equality Now, 228

Escobar, Yunel, 369

Estonia, 211

European Convention on Human Rights, 365–66

European Court of Human Rights, 313

Evangelical Christians, 299

Eves, Ernie, 278–79

ex-Muslims, 349, 363–64

Expo 67, 1, 4

Index

Fabulous Mogul: Nizam VII of Hyderabad
(Karaka), 58
Fahad (author's son), 76, 83, 242, 383,
393
Faisal (author's son), 83, 242, 306, 383,
393
Fakih, Mohamad, 325
family business
challenges of, 123–24
founding of, 42
resumption of, 61
takeover by author, 113–14, 116–18
Warangal and, 93
Faruqis, 15
fatwas, 29–30, 38, 362, 363, 366
Federal Court of Canada, 329, 330
federalism, 203–4
Ferguson, Jane, 325
Filion, Robert, 397
First Gulf War, 210
Fisher, Doug, 221
food
author's favourites, 63
bananas, 104
as bribe, 57
cultural connections, 6, 132, 165
family and, 72–74
fast food, 111, 382
gajar halwa, 14
gardening, 77
halal, 10, 89, 298
immigrant experiences and, 133, 272
Kuwaiti, 111
mangoes, 73, 74–76, 81, 88
Manitoba rallies and, 140
memories of, 44
picnics, 82–83
poisoning, 169

South Indian cuisine, 101
tea, 75, 387
travel and, 43–44
vegetarianism, 63, 67, 84, 93, 133,
213
yogurt, 10, 101, 159, 395
forced marriages, 308
Foreign Affairs Committee, 244–45
Forrest, A.C., 131
Forster, E.M., 35, 41, 94
Foster, Cecil, 227
France, 237, 295, 313, 314, 389
Franks, Tommy, 275, 368
Fraser, Marian Botsford, 386
freedom of information, 271
freedom of speech, 323–26, 332–33,
359–60, 367–73, 377–78
freedom of the press, 145–47, 163–67,
235–36
Freiman, Mark, 365
Fulford, Robert, 254–55

G8, 320–21
Gabriel, Brigitte, 299, 353
Gaddafi, Muammar, 282
Gaffney, Frank, 299, 304, 353
Galloway, David, 246
al-Gamal, Sharif, 314
Gandhi, Indira
1977 election and loss, 146–47
assassination of, 176, 186
Emergency Rule, 145–46
return to power, 163
Satya Sai Baba and, 101
Sikh terrorism and, 187
Gandhi, Kasturba, 376
Gandhi, Mahatma
assassination of, 48

Churchill and, 7
international influence of, 126, 247
Kasturba and, 376
Pandit marriage intervention, 100
as a student, 133
support of and from Darul Uloom,
38–39
vision and goals, 45, 60, 147
Gandhi, Rajiv, 186, 188, 374
Gandhi, Sanjay, 145–46
Garvey, Bruce, 179
Gates, Bill, 249
Gauthier, Jacques, 323
Gavaskar, Sunil, 97
Gaza, 295
Gee, Marcus, 260
Geller, Pamela, 299, 321–22, 353
Geneva Conventions, 263, 276
Germany, 193, 237, 313
Ghaffar, Qazi Abdul, 59
Ghani, Ashraf, 292
Ghani, Owais Ahmad, 285
Ghiz, Joe, 384
Ghotbzadeh, Sadegh, 160, 174
Globe and Mail
    author and, 5, 11, 148
    Christchurch shooting, lack of
        coverage, 348
    criticisms and, 357
    Danish cartoons and, 366
    diversity, lack of, 228
    foreign coverage, 146
    free speech and Paty, 371
    honour killings, coverage of, 351
    Islamophobia, contributions to, 327,
        344–45
    letters to the editor, 213
    post 9/11, 258, 260

Quebec City mosque massacre
    (2017), 348
    reaction to RCMP raid, 342
    security forces and, 343
    Thomsons, 180
Goar, Carol, 177, 200
Goenka, Ramnath, 145–46
van Gogh, Theo, 363, 365
Goldbloom, Michael 227
Goldbloom, Victor, 227
Goldfarb, Martin, 181
Goldstein, Baruch, 258, 317
Golpayegani, Mohammed Reza, 159
Good Muslim, Bad Muslim (Mamdani),
    300
Googoosh, 395–96
Gordon, Charles (Charlie), 129, 131,
    140, 149
Gordon, J. King, 129
Govindarajan, S.A. (SAG), 95, *95*, 101,
    102–3
Graham, Bill, 244, 287, 288
Graham, Billy, 298
Graham, Franklin, 298
Granatstein, J.L., 223
Great Replacement Theory, 221, 303–4,
    345–46
Greek Canadians, 217
Green, Todd H., 336, 353
Greenspon, Edward, 366
Grewal, Zareena, 351
Griffith, Andrew, 190
Grossman, Larry, 137
Ground Zero Mosque, 313–14
Guantanamo Bay, 19, 271, 290, 328,
    342. *See also* war on terror
Guha, Ram, 98
Gujral, Inder, 277

Index

Gulf War (1991), 213, 278
Gumbleton, Thomas, 160
Gupte, Subash, 90
Gwyn, Richard, 179, 221–22, 223

Hadith, 32, 41
hafiz, 17, 44, 134
Hafiz Mohammad Ismail (Dada), 14, 27, 35–38, 42, 44, 60
Hall, Wesley, 94
Hamas, 295, 320
Hamid, Mohammed, 86
Handke, Peter, 365
Haroon, Hamid, 207–8
Harper, Stephen
    Afghanistan, war in, 283, 289
    Aga Khan museum opening, 197
    Air India tragedy and, 190
    anti-Muslim figures, support of, 330
    anti-Muslim sentiment and fundraising, 332
    attempt to remove hate speech bans, 323–24
    Bhatti and Taseer, funerals of, 320
    immigrants and voting, 189
    Iraq, war in, 277
    Israel, support for, 320–21, 322
    Khadr, incarceration of, 328
    media and, 356
    mosques and the prevention of radicalization, 341
    Muslim refugees and, 331
    niqab and citizenship, 329, 333
    Rights and Democracy Centre, 323
    Strengthening Canadian Citizenship Act (2015), 330
    support of Modi, 319–20

targeting of Muslims, 317–19
    treatment of veterans, 290
Harper government
    anti-Muslim discourse, lending platform to, 326–27
    anti-Muslim policies, 318–20
    Canadian Human Rights Act, 323–26
    Israeli-Palestinian policies, 320–23
    niqab campaigns, 329–31
    Strengthening Canadian Citizenship Act (2015), 330–31
    Syrian refugees, rejection of, 331
    vilification of Khadr, 328
    Zero Tolerance for Barbaric Cultural Practices Act (2014), 331–32
Harris, Mike, 214, 216
Hasan, Ghulam Ali, 127
Hasan, Nurul, 27
hate speech, 323–26, 365–73
Head, Wilson, 228–29
Henry, Frances, 225, 227, 232–34
Henry, Jeff, 232
Hepburn, Bob, 177, 200
Hezbollah, 320–21
hijabs
    attacks on hijabi women, 297, 311, 350
    bans of, 304, 307–8, 309–10
    education and, 312
    honour killings, association with, 351–52
    increase in adoption, 391
    Iranian enforcement of, 353
    opposition to, 33
    risk of bans, 313
    The Satanic Verses and, 361
    symbolism of, 250

U.S. propaganda and, 300–301
Western media portrayal, 350
Hillier, Rick, 282–83
Hindu (Madras), 95, 102–3
Hindu Advocacy, 314–15
Hindu Canadians, 190
Hinduism
British colonialism, ties to, 29
clothing, 18
holy texts, 41
prayers and rituals, 44, 61, 91
Rumi and, 24
temples, 13–14, 41
tilak, 84
women and, 32, 224
Hindu-Muslim relations. *See* Muslim-Hindu relations
Hindus
British India and, 39
customs of, 83–84
Darul Uloom and, 51
massacres of, colonial, 54
resistance to British India, 44
The Satanic Verses and, 374
Hines, Janice, 191
Hiro, Dilip, 154
Hirsi Ali, Ayaan, 326, 349, 363, 364, 365
HMC *Rainbow*, 189
Holbrooke, Richard, 216
Hollande, François, 369
Holocaust, 194, 371
Holocaust denial, 369, 372
Honderich, Beland (Bee)
1992 media strike, 202–3
Atkinson Foundation, trustee of, 183
free trade, 184
influence of, 273–74
media prejudice against non-white

immigrants, 181
pictures of, *273*
politicians and, 178–80
Honderich, Florence, 180
Honderich, John
accommodation of Quebec in *Star*, 204
author and, 199, 263
Dubuc and, 205
employee relations, 239, 240
Order of Canada, 273
pictures of, *237*
Hong Kong, 193–94, 226
honour killings, 308, 351–52
Hosseini, Khaled, 364
Houda-Pepin, Fatima, 301–2
Hungary, 193
Hunter, Eileen, 213
Huquq-e-Niswan (Rights of Women), 33
Hurd, Douglas, 363
Husain Ahmad Madani: The Jihad for Islam and India's Freedom (Metcalf), 45–46, 47
Husaini, Syed Ahmed, 118–19
Husayn, Sharif, 39
Hussain, M.F., 103–4
Hussain, Syed Sarwar (Chote Tayabba)
advice from, 148
author's education and, 61–63, 69, 91
death of Abba, 115–16
food preferences, 72
as *hafiz*, 68
Hyderabad City, 40
Islam, knowledge of, 118
Pandit marriage and, 100
pictures of, *87*
poetry of, 119–20
record keeping, 64

Index

relationship to author, 38
remembered, 70
Siddiquis, support of, 57
views of, 96, 120
Warangal, 53, 55–56, 65
weddings and, 86, 124, *142*, 174–75
Hussein, Saddam
chemical weapons, 173
fall of, 280
invasion of Iraq, 277
invasion of Kuwait, 210, 211
trial and execution, 282
Hussen, Ahmed, 312, 384, 393
Hutterites, 126, 152, 224
Hyder, Syed Sajjad, 3–4, 99–100, 103,
105, 107, 121, *230*
Hyder Senior, 109
Hyderabad
Clinton visit, 248–49
death of nizam, 121–22
food of, 132
history of, 35–36
Indian control, 57–60
invasion of, 53
Siddiquis and, 41–42
survival of Muslim families, 63–64
technology and, 248–49
Hyderabad House, 246–47

Iacobucci, Frank, 272
Ikhtetam-e-Masnavi (Masnavi Completed
- Baksh), 26
immigration
challenges of faith, 10
cultural differences, food, 6
cultural differences, social, 6, 7
economic impact, 226
familiarities in Canada, 7
family and cultural challenges, 352
identity and, 181, 221–24
job experience, limitations on, 5
multiculturalism and, 180–83
opposition to, 185–86
pressure to assimilate, 2–3
records and, 64, 195
social contracts and, 220
immigration, author's experience
arrival, 1, 4–5, 195–96
career challenges, 141
identity retention and expansion,
395–98
impact of, 381–83
leaving India, 124
immigration and faith, 10, 19
immigration and identity
benefits to Canada, 398–99
Canadian contributions, literary,
386–88
Canadian firsts, 383–84
Canadian firsts, global impact, 385
challenges of immigration, 389–93
evolving perspectives, 7–8
identity retention and expansion,
395–98
preservation of identity, 381–83
pride in identity, 388–89
successes, 393–95
Immigration and Refugee Board, 194
India
American views of, 99–100
Bombay, 104
British colonialism and, 60–62, 82
bureaucracy, 109, 114, 117
Burton, 207
Canada, relations with, 188, 246
Clinton visit, 246–50

Dalai Lama and, 93
death of nizam, 121–22
divisions with Pakistan, 120
early independence movements,
29–30
elections, 163
Emergency Rule, 145–47
food, 43–44
Golden Temple and Indira Gandhi,
176
hikmat, 27–28
Hyderabad, invasion of, 53, 57–60,
63–64
Indo-Pakistani war, 114
Iraq, opposition to war in, 277–78
multiculturalism and, 102–3, 104,
180–81
Muslims, discrimination against, 117
Muslims in, 48
Pakistan, relations with, 86, 87–88,
136, 246
Partition, 44–45
post-Partition, 60–62
Rumi and, 23, 26
The Satanic Verses and, 374
Soviet Union and, 100, 253
summers, 77
U.S., relations with, 271
Indian nationalism, 45
Indigenous Peoples of Canada
Canadian firsts, 384
education, 134
journalists, 236
language and, 125–26
media portrayals, 335, 355
presence at government ceremonies,
152
rights of, 315

Indonesia, 295
Indo-Pakistani conflicts, 114, 136, 163
InterCultural Media Committee, 227
International Convention on Civil and
Political Rights, 324, 365
International Criminal Tribunal -
Yugoslavia, 217–18
International Security Assistance Force,
285
Into the Heart of Africa (exhibit), 231–32
Inuit, 315
Iqbal, Asif, 93
Iqbal, Sir Muhammad, 44, 46, 375
Iran
Canadian flight, shooting down of,
195–96
censorship and, 377
democracy and, 296
diaspora, 195
hijab enforcement, 353
Iraq, war with, 172–74, 175–76, 281
Islamic Revolution, 153–62, 172,
395–96
refugees and war, 193
refugees from, 280, 385
White Revolution, 145
Iran-Iraq war, 172–74, 175–76
Iraq
American invasion, 211
economic sanctions and impact,
244–45
immigration from, 15
Iran, war with, 172–74, 175–76
Kenney and, 331
religious class, power of, 281–82
war on terror and, 263
weapons of mass destruction, 338
Iraq, war in

Index

call from God, 313
Canadian support, 278–79
death toll, 294
end of, 291
international resistance to, 277–78
oil, 280–81
U.S. displays of violence, 282
weapons of mass destruction and,
   300
weapons of mass destruction in
   media, 338
Irving, David, 369
Irvings, 180
Ishaq, Zunera, 329, 330, 332
ISIS, 331
Islam
   British colonialism, ties to, 29–30
   call to prayer, 19, 61, 68, 286
   in Canada, 10, 392
   conversion, 41
   death rituals, 115–16, 218, 306
   domestic violence and, 351–52
   Eid, 18, 73
   halal, 10, 70, 89
   increased faith activity, 390–91
   interpretations of, 391–92
   Islamic Revolution and, 154–55
   Jum'ah prayers, 314–15
   literary depictions of, 360–63
   marriage traditions and celebrations,
     17, 87
   modesty and, 19, 21
   Ottoman Caliphate and, 39
   poetry and, 22–27
   polygamy, 33
   prayers, performance of, 44
   the Prophet, relationship with,
     375–76

Qur'anic interpretation, 24
Sufism, 26, 30
ulama, 15–16
views of terrorism, 243
women, protection of, 32
women and, 69–70, 224, 269,
   312–13, 329, 393
Islam, cultural warfare on. *See also* Sharia
   law
   about, 297–98
   denunciations of Islam by public
     figures, 298–300
   extremists and Islamophobes, 313
   hypocrisy of, 314
   links to terrorism, 317–18, 339–41
   misrepresentation of faith, 307–8
   prayer bans, 310, 314–15
   Taliban and Afghanistan and,
     292–93
   Zero Tolerance for Barbaric Cultural
     Practices Act (2014), 331–32
Islam, Faizul, 14–15, 17–18, 21, 48–49,
   145
Islam, Riazul, 48–49
Islam, Ziaul, 48
Islamic Centre (Quebec), 309
Islamic Culture, 41
Islamic fundamentalism
   Bamiyan Buddhas, 252–53
   as boogeyman, 244, 266–68
   views of, 260
   as weapon against Canadian
     Muslims, 317–18, 326–27
   Western media and, 250
Islamic Revolution (1979), 153–62, 172,
   395–96
Islamic Salvation Front (Algeria), 295
Islamic scholarship, 16–17. *See also*

Qur'an; Rumi, Jalal al-Din
author's, 61–63, 64
in Canada, 390–91
importance of, 20–21
madrasahs, 21, 22, 29
preservation of knowledge, 32–35
Qur'an, interpretation of, 24
Qur'anic commentaries, 42
Sharia, discussions of, 36–37
shayk-as-tafseer, 38
Siddiqui women and, 16–17
Sufi Nakshbandi Order, 24
Islamophobia. *See also* anti-Semitism
American, 394
condemnation, rejection of, 332–33
corruption of women's rights as,
350–52
free speech and, 367–73
hijabi women, attacks on, 350
intensification of, 391
liberals and, 352–53
media and, 304–5, 336
Muslim reactions to, 353–54
Runnymede Trust and, 300
Sharia law and, 313
violence and, 311
Western media and, 344–45
Ismaili Muslims, 195, 196–97, 301
Israel, 210, 296, 321–23
Israeli-Palestinian conflict
Canadian politics and, 321–23
Christian anti-Muslim movements
and, 299
coverage of, 210
election interference, 295
even-handed coverage, 131
free speech and media, 371
Harper and Palestinian elections,

320–21
media portrayals, 355
U.S. and, 259

Jaffer, Jameel, 270–71
Jah, Mukarram, 121–22
Jaisimha, M.L., 93, 94
Jakobovits, Immanuel (chief rabbi in
Great Britain), 374
Jama Masjid, 36
James, Royson, 200, 236
James Minifie Lecture, 355
Jami Masjid, 37
Janata Party (People's Party of India),
146
Japanese Canadians, 194
Jasper, Ernest, 96
Javid, Sajid, 393, 394
Jean, Michaëlle, 383, 385
Jefferson, Thomas, 394
Jethalal, Bhiku, 202
Jewish Defence League, 321–22
Jews, 102, 210, 307, 320–21
Jhansi ki Rani, 376
jingoism, 337–38
Jinnah, Muhammad Ali, 44, 46
Jiwani, Yasmin, 351
Jones, James, 346
Judaism, 104, 224, 301, 315, 374, 376
Junagarh, 57
Jung, Basit, 55, 63–64
Jyllands-Posten, 354, 364, 368–69

Ka'ba, 359, 361
Kairanvi, Rahmatullah (Shaykh), 361
Kairos, 322
Kandhla, 13–15, 17, 18, 19, 20
Kanhai, Rohan, 94

Index

Kanji, Azeezah, 348

Kaplan, Robert, 177

Karadžić, Radovan, 217

Karaka, D.F., 58

Karanth, Shivaram, 180–81

Karbala, 280

Karzai, Hamid, 283, 292

Kashmir, 57, 246

Kasturi, Gopalan, 102

Kazimi, Ali, 189

Kelly, Cathal, 290

Kelman, Wolfe (rabbi), 374

Kenney, Jason

    Apartheid Week, opposition to, 321

    Bhatti and Taseer, funerals of, 320

    defence of *Komagata Maru* apology,
       190

    Islamic law, views on, 312–13

    multiculturalism *vs.* pluralism, 299

    niqabi women and citizenship, 329

    targeting of Muslims, 318, 319

    ties to Chaldean Catholic Church,
       331

Kenya, 243

Khadr, Omar, 328, 332, 342–43

Khalid, Iqra, 332

Khalifa bin Hamad al-Thani, 144

Khan, Khan Abdul Ghaffar (Frontier
    Gandhi), 167–68

Khan, Khusro Yar, 174, 248

Khan, Mohammad Ayub, 295

Khan, Nader, 174–75

Khan, Nusrat Fateh Ali, 209

Khan, Sadiq, 393, 394

Khan, Siddiq Ahmed, 59, 118–19, 124,
    126, 127

Khan, Sir Syed Ahmed, 34–35, 41, 68,
    155

Khan, Yahya, 295

Khanna, Bharat Chand, 108

Khatami, Mohammad, 395

Khomeini, Ruhollah (Imam)

    dealing with opposition, 173–74

    mockery of, 160

    political evolution of, 281

    Rushdie fatwa, 359, 360, 362

    Shia and Sunni relations and, 155

    Tabriz and, 159

King, Peter, 327

King Charles III, 203

King George V, 36, 104

Kipling, Rudyard, 96, 104, 192

Kissinger, Henry, 251

Klausen, Jytte, 393

Klein, Ralph, 204

Knesset, 299, 321

Komagata Maru, 189, 190, 194

Kosovar Canadians, 216

Kosovo, 212, 387–88

Kovrig, Michael, 348

Kruse, Hans, 118

Kumar, S.K., 94

Kuwait, 109–11, 144, 210–11, 365

Kymlicka, Will, 223, 389

La Presse, 203–4

La Salle, Roch, 177

Lakhnavaram Forest, 82

Lal, Jawahar, 67

Lal, Kanhayya, 67

Lal, Kishan, 67

Lambie, Kerry, 227

Lamer, Antonio, 219

Lang, Michelle, 355

Laurence, Margaret, 138

Laurie, Nate, 184, 200, 260

Lavrov, Sergey, 369

Laxmi Narayana Mandir, 13

Le Pen, Marine, 237, 298, 309

Lebuis, Marc, 326

Lee, Angela, 232

Legault, François, 309, 310, 311, 312

letters to the editor, 213, 260–62, 279

Lévesque, René, 139, 177, 203

Levine, Michael, 161

Lewis, Bernard, 364

Lewis, David, 136–37

Liberal Party of Canada
  Islamophobia, motion against,
    332–33
  Muslim votes and, 332
  provincial party, Manitoba, 137,
    147–48
  provincial party, Ontario, 388–89
  provincial party, Quebec, 308
  Sikh-Canadians and, 188

life in India, author's
  Bombay and the PTI, 103–8
  education, 62–63
  food and family, 72–76
  as head of household, 118–20
  homes, 76–77, *78–81*, 81, 82
  Hyderabad, flight from, 53–57
  leaving India, 124
  photographs, 87–88
  picnics, 82–83
  play, 71–72
  Warangal, 67–70
  weddings, 86–87

Lindwall, Ray, 89

Lisée, Jean-François, 307

Little Mosque on the Prairie (TV Show),
  397

Lok Sabha, 51

London Bridge jihadist attack, 348

London Central Mosque, 41

London subway bombing, 267

Long, Tom, 215

Lord Mountbatten, 58

Los Angeles Times, 213

Lothian, Arthur, 58

The Loyal Mohammedans of India (Syed),
  34–35

Lucy, Roger, 161

Lutyens, Edwin, 246–47

Ly, Djibril, 387–88

Lyon, Sterling, 11, 138, 181

Macdonald, Donald, 183

Macedonia, 212, 217, 387–88

Machel, Graça, 237

Maclean's (magazine), 188, 343, 345–47,
  354

Macron, Emmanuel, 314, 370

Madani, Husain Ahmed (Shaykh), 44,
  45–46, 47, 48–49, 60, 392

Madari, Ayatollah Kazem Shariat,
  158–59, 174

madrasahs
  Darul Uloom, 32, 38, 41, 44–47,
    49–51
  family, 14
  Jami Masjid, 37
  Madrasa-e-Rahimiyahh, 29
  Rumi and, 22
  travelogue, 21
  western views of, 49–50

Madrid train bombing, 267

Maharajah Fateh Singh Roa Gaekwad, 207

Mahbubani, Kishore, 245

Mahound (*The Satanic Verses*), 360,
  361–62

Index

Major, John, 187, 212

Makka Masjid, 121

Makki, Imadullah, 30–31, 32

Malhi, Gurbax Singh, 383

Malik, Ausma, 384

Malreddy, Pavan Kumar, 339

Mamdani, Mahmood, 300

Mandela, Nelson, 229, *237*

mangoes, 73, 74–76, 81, 88

Manley, John, 289

Manning, Preston, 220, 236–37

Manningham-Buller, Elizabeth, 267

Mansbridge, Peter, 348, 385

Mansur, Salim, 303–4

Marchi, Sergio, 383

Marsden, Bill, 355

Martel, Émile, 386, 387

Martin, Paul, 282–83

Marx, Karl, 94, 211

Mashaekh-e-Kandhla (The Shaykhs of
   Kandhla), 15–16

Masnavi ye-Ma'navi (The Spiritual
   Couplets - Rumi), 22, 23, 24, 25,
   30, 31

Masood, Ross, 41, 68

Massey, Lionel, 152

Mawani, Aliya, 384

Mayrand, Marc, 329

Mazigh, Monia, 268–69

Mazrui, Ali, 362

Mbeki, Thabo, 385

McCallum, John, 329–30

McCarthyism, 327

McDonough, Alexa, 268–69, 271

McDougall, Barbara, 363

McGill Daily, 307

McGill University, 88

McGunity, Dalton, 302

McKenzie, Bob, 177

McLuhan, Marshall, 237, 399

McMurtry, Roy, 185, 187, 188

McNaughton, Andrew, 58

McVeigh, Timothy, 302–3, 340

Mecca

   control of, 39

   holy pilgrimage, 206

   literary portrayals of, 36

   nizam of Hyderabad and, 41

   in poetry, 396–97

   Ramadan and, 10

   as refuge, 31

   The Satanic Verses and, 359, 361

   women and, 19

media, right wing, 277

media and minorities, 232–35

media and politicians

   boundaries between, 147, 178

   close connections, 177

   early relationships, 130

   informal relationships, 139–40

   long term connections, 288

   Mulroney and *Star*, 204–5

   Pierre Trudeau, death of, 251–52

   undue pressure, 131

media in Canada. *See also* Muslims and
      Western media

   anti-immigrant sentiments in,
      185–86, 221–23

   anti-Muslim sentiments, coverage of,
      335–37

   Canadian experience of, 141

   columnists, 98, 239–42

   diversity and, 227–28, 212–16,
      229–30

   free speech and, 145–47, 163–67,
      324, 365–66

435

representation in, 157–58, 236, 354–56

role of, 357

technological limitations, 161–62, 168

Toronto Star, influence of, 199

views of, 240

women and, 229–30

Medina, 10, 39, 41

Mendelson, Joe, 264, 287

Mennonites, 178, 183, 224, 245, 301, 390

Merkel, Angela, 299

Metcalf, Barbara, 33, 34, 45–46, 47, 50

Methodists, 130, 183

Métis, 315

Metro Toronto Police Services Board, 227

Mevlavi Sufi Order, 22

Mian, Mohammed, 37, 86–87, 114, 116, 124

Michener, Roland, 4

Middle East Forum, 299

Miller, David, 341

Miller, John, 179, 230–31, 343–44

Miller, Judith, 338

Miller, Larry, 330

Milošević, Slobodan, 217, 365

Minault, Gail, 33

Mitterrand, François, 212, 376

Mladić, Ratko "Butcher of Bosnia," 217

Modi, Narendra, 190, 319–20

Mohammed, Lal, 73, 74–75, 113, 115–16

Mohammed, Wazir, 73, 74–75, 82, 113, 115–16

Mohammed Ayub (author's great-uncle), 44, 60

Mohammed Idris (Bade Tayabba - author's uncle)

Abbi's wedding, 86–87

anti-colonial struggle and, 44

death of, 141

family relations, 38

leaves for Pakistan, 60

moves to Deoband, 42

work, 40, 41, 46, 141–42

Mohammed Moosa (Abba - author's father)

anti-British leanings, 46

birth of, 38

care for wife, 57

children at school, 84, 85, 91

children's marriages and, 118–19

construction business, 21, 61, 93, 114

construction business handed over to children, 140

death of, 115

family flight from Warangal, 53, 54–55, 56

food preferences, 72, 73, 74–75

generosity, 103, 116

as *hafiz*, 68–69, 70

heart attack and health issues, 4, 113

influence of, 94–95, 117–18, 170

life in Hyderabad, 40

loss of family lands, 60

marriage of, 42

picnics, 82–83

pictures of, *20*, 87

religious views, 47

sayings of, 127

views, 75–76, 92

views of journalism, 124

women and, 82

Mojaddedi, Jawid, 22, 24

monarchism, 7, 9–10, 181. *See also* republicanism

Index

Monsebraaten, Laurie, 200
Monsef, Maryam, 384
Montenegro, 212
Montreal, 70, 88, 305
Montreal Gazette, 345, 355
Moosa, Ebrahim, 21
Morey, Peter, 364
Morgan, Bill, 131
Morrison, Denise, 202
Morton, Desmond, 223, 398–99
Moses, 137–38
MS *St. Louis*, 194. *See also*
   anti-Semitism
Mubarak, Hosni, 296, 363
Mufti Ilahi Baksh Academy, 27
Muir, William, 361
Mukherjee, Bharati, 185
Mulroney, Brian
   1982 constitutional conflict with
      Quebec, 203
   Air India Bombing, 186
   Arab equalization payment plan, 211
   break-up of Yugoslavia, 212
   Citizens' Forum on Canada's Future,
      219–20
   conflict with media, 204–5
   foreign policies, effects of, 296
   free trade and, 184
   immigration policies and efforts, 189,
      193, 194
   intelligence-sharing with India, 188
   Rights and Democracy centre, 323
   U.S. invasion of Iraq, 278
Multicultiphobia (Ryan), 224, 238
multiculturalism
   art and, 196–97
   attacks on Muslims and, 299
   in Canada, 180–83, 236–38, 398–99

Canadian Charter of Rights and
   Freedoms, 219–24
   criticisms of, 221–23
   development of, 381
   in education, 91–94
   in Europe, 389
   failures of, Quebec and referendum,
      206
   faith and, 224–26
   history of, 223
   in India, 102–3, 104, 122, 180–81
   in journalism, 129
   minister of, 190
   opposition to, 219–21, 304
   Pierre Trudeau and, 251
   political advocates for, 129
   in the Prairies, 125–26
Multiculturalism Act, 219, 220
multi-faith ceremonies, 122
multi-faith co-operation, 102–3
multi-lingualism, 129. *See also* Official
   Languages Act (1969)
multi-nationalism, 223
Mumtaz Ali, Sayyid, 32–33
Musharraf, Pervez, 250, 251, 284, 288, 295
music, 208–9, 395–97
Muslim Brotherhood, 325–26
Muslim Canadians, 332–33, 344,
   353–54, 390
   as voters, 319–20
Muslim Council of Britain, 346–47, 394
Muslim Students' Association
   (Concordia), 354
Muslim-Hindu relations, 13–15, 41,
   44–45, 48, 56, 67–70
Muslims
   advocacy groups, 393–94
   anti-colonial struggles, 31

association with women's rights
violations, 352–53
British India and, 39
Canadian firsts, 384
Chechnya and Soviet Union, 211–12
dichotomies of, 300–301, 360,
363–64
discrimination against, 117
dismissal of, 373–75
diversity within, 392
domestic violence and, 351–52
entertainers, 394–95
immigration and identity, 389–93
massacres of, 54, 59, 365
in media, 335–37
the Mutiny and expulsion, 30–31
narratives and challenges, 241
"pliant Muslims," 349
the Prophet, relationship with,
375–76
radicalization and, 267–68
resistance to British India, 44
role in fighting radicalization and
terrorism, 340–41
Tatars, 253–54
ties to British India, 34–36
verbal attacks on, 325–26
violence against, 309, 311
Wynne and, 389
Muslims, cultural warfare on. *See also*
anti-Muslim sentiments; Sharia law
about, 297–98
Charter of Quebec Values, 307, 308
defamation of individuals, 325–26
free speech arguments, 332–33
Harper and, 317–19
Harper Senate hearings and, 326–27
hijab bans, 304, 307–8, 309–10

public attacks on Muslims, 298
Quebec ban on religious symbols,
304–5
Steyn and Mansur, 303–4
women as victims of right and left,
312–13
Muslims, Rushdie, and free speech
about, 359–60
author's views on, 378–79
context, treatment of Muslims,
377–78
Danish cartoons, 364–65
early influences and associated texts,
364
free speech as hate speech
justification, 367–73
historic depictions of Muslims,
360–61
Muslim voices dismissed, 373–75
portrayal of Islam in *The Satanic
Verses*, 361–63
the Prophet, relationship with,
375–76
right to free speech, balance of,
365–67
Western definitions of free speech, 373
Muslims and the News Media (Poole and
Richardson), 341
Muslims and Western media. *See also*
anti-Muslim sentiments
Al Jazeera and, 368
author's observations of, 357
Canadian media, 354–56
co-operation with security forces,
341–44
corruption of women's rights
discussions, 350–53
Danish cartoons, 364–65

Index

depictions of, 347

imbalance in coverage, 347–48

interview choices and portrayals, 349

Islamophobia, contributions to,
344–45

Islamophobia in liberal media,
352–53

lack of empathy and victims' stories,
338–39

links to terrorism, 339–41

Muslim views of, 353–54

role in legitimizing hate speech and
myths, 345–47

role in public understandings,
335–37

myths

diversity quotas, 229

population (Great Replacement
Theory), 221, 303–4, 345–46

quota laws, 215

Sharia law and "no-go" zones, 346

unwillingness to integrate, 393

Nadella, Satya, 94

Nadvi, Abul Hasan Ali, 16

al-Nahyan, Zayed bin Sultan (President
Sheikh), 384

Naidu, Chandra Babu, 248–49

Naidu, Sarojini, 93

Naipaul, V.S., 222–23, 360, 364, 365

Najaf, 280

Nakatsuru, Shaun, 325

Nandy, Ashis, 98

Narasimhan, Gopalan, 102

National Day of Action against
Islamophobia, 311

National Newspaper Award, 192, 212

National Post, 234, 258, 343

National Press Club of Canada, 355

Nawab Mohammad Mansoor Ali Khan
Pataudi, 108

Nawaz, Zarqa, 397

Nehru, Jawaharlal, 7, 18, 59, 87, 146

Nenshi, Naheed, 384

Netanyahu, Benjamin, 369

Netherlands, the, 237, 313, 363–64

New Democratic Party (NDP), 9, 126,
129–30, 268–69, 271, 332

New York Times

anthrax letters, 340

anti-Muslim bias, 337

Charlie Hebdo cartoons, 366

letters to the editor, 213

Norway massacre, 340

portrayal of Muslim women, 352

portrayal of Muslims, 347–48

weapons of mass destruction and,
338

New Zealand, 333, 348

Newfoundland and Labrador, 11, 191,
193

Nicol, Eric, 240

Nigeria, 367

niqabs, 308, 312–13, 319, 329–31, 350

Nixon, Richard, 157, 251

Nizam College, 93

nizam of Hyderabad

about, 40–41

death of, 121

economic blockades, 58

Osmania University art college
building, 96

pictures of, *39*

shooting competition with Archduke
Ferdinand, 398

support of British, 46

439

Nobel Prize for Literature, 365

Norman, Herbert, 323

North Atlantic Treaty Organization (NATO), 49, 212, 216–17, 285

Norway massacre, 340

Nossel, Suzanne, 370

Nova Scotia, 191

Novaya Gazeta (Russia), 244

Nureddin, Muayyed, 272

Nutan (actress), 105

Obama, Barack, 290, 291, 292, 295–96, 385

Oborne, Peter, 346

O'Connor, John Cardinal (archbishop of New York), 374

Odartey-Wellington, Felix, 343

Office of Religious Freedom, 320

Official Languages Act (1969), 131

Offman, Craig, 351

Oklahoma City bombing, 339–40

Oliver, Craig, 342

Oman, 144

Omar, Ilhan, 394

Omidvar, Ratna, 225

Ondaatje, Michael, 370

Ondaatje, Sir Christopher, 206, 207–8

O'Neill, Juliet, 341–42

Ontario Superior Court, 325

Orange Order, 182

Order of Canada, 149, 273

Order of Ontario, 256

Organisation of Islamic Cooperation (OIC), 377, 378, 391

Orientalism, 26–27, 157, 336–37, 350, 360–61, 364

Ornstein, Michael, 252

Osman Ali. *See* nizam of Hyderabad

Osmania University, 41, 88, *97,* 99

O'Sullivan, Brian, 200–201

O'Toole, Erin, 333

Ottawa Citizen, 140, 228, 341–42

Ottoman caliphate, 39

Padma Vibhushan, 60

Pakistan

Afghanistan, effects of war in, 294

Afghanistan border, 285–87, 288–89

CIA and, 14

Clinton visit, 249–51

Darul Uloom and, 49

food of, 132

governments, 250

Hindu in, 48

Indian relations, 86, 87–88, 120, 136, 246

Indo-Pakistani war, 114

Kenney travels to, 320

partition, 44–45, 57

refugees from, 60

Siddiqui family archives, 38

Taliban and, 284–87

U.S. support of dictators, 295

U.S. torture sites, 270

Palestine, 210, 211, 295, 320–21

Palestine House (Toronto), 322

Palestine Liberation Organization, 210

Palin, Sarah, 290

Pandit, Vijaya Lakshmi, 100

Paris, Erna, 370

Parizeau, Jacques, 204, 206

Parti Québécois (PQ), 307–8

Participation of Visible Minorities in Canadian Society (committee), 227–28

Partition (1947), 15, 44–45, 47–48, 57

Index

Parvez, Aqsa, 351
Pashtuns, 162, 164, 167, 285, 286
Patriot Act, 270
Paty, Samuel, 370
Pawley, Adele (née Schreyer), 130
Pawley, Howard, 130
Pearson, Lester B., 296, 323
PEN American Center, 370
PEN Canada, 280, 362–63, 366, 385
PEN International, 321, 366, 377, 385–88
PEN Mauritania, 387–88
PEN Serbia, 386–87
People's Republican Party (Iran), 159
Perell, Paul, 326
Petherbridge, Steve, 178
Petrich, Ernie, 137
Philip, Nourbese, 232
Phillips, Alison, 347
Pickthall, Marmaduke, 41
Picton, John, 192
Pieri, Mike
    care for staff, 169
    community pages (*Star*), 234–35
    as foreign editor, 153, 162, 163
    foreign respondent challenges, 168
    warning to foreign correspondents, 167
Pilger, John, 338–39
Pillar, Kevin, 369
Pintak, Lawrence, 345
Pipes, Daniel, 299, 353
pluralism, 197, 299
Polanyi, John, 216–17
police and minorities in Canada, 235–36
police violence, 59
Polievre, Pierre, 333
Politkovskaya, Anna, 244

polygamy, 33
Poole, Elizabeth, 341
Pope Benedict XVI, 298
Pope John Paul II, 374
population and immigration, 226–27
Porter, John, 223
Postmedia Network, 322, 354, 356
Powell, Colin, 368
Powers, Gary, 251
Poynter Institute, 339
Prasad, Rajendra, 60
prejudice and stereotypes, 137–39, 181–82, 227, 232, 308, 336–37
Press Trust of India (PTI), 103–8, 109, 121
Prince Azam Jah, 40
Prince Moazzam Jah, 40
Prince Mukarram Jah, 99, *123*
Prince Philip, 9
Princess Durru Shehvar, 122
Pritchard, Tim, 227
Progressive Conservatives, 138
Prophet Muhammad
    cartoons of, other, 370
    Danish cartoons, 293, 298, 354, 364–65, 368–69
    depiction in *The Satanic Verses*, 359
    insults to, 297, 298
    literary depictions of, 360–61
    marriages of, 376–77
    Muslim relationship with, 375–76
    Qur'an and Hadith, 32
    sermons and sayings, 72, 308, 392–93
    "Tala' al-Badru Alayna," 396–97
    women and, 19
Putin, Vladimir, 244, 253, 254, 369

Qatar, 144, 211, 365
Quebec
   1982 Constitution, 203–4
   anti-Sharia movement, 301–2
   Charter of Quebec Values, 307, 308
   Constitution, 219–20
   corruption and influence peddling, 177
   institutionalized Islamophobia,
      304–5
   nationalism and, 312
   resistance to wars, 46
   separatism, 205–6, 223
Quebec City mosque massacre (2017),
   348
Quebec Islamic Centre, 387
Queen Elizabeth II, 7, 9, 203, 365
Queen Margrethe (Denmark), 298
Queen Victoria, 34, 36
Queen's University, 148, 225
Qur'an. *See also* Islamic scholarship
   hafiz, 134
   hfiz, 17, 64, 69
   memorization of, 42, 62, 64
   readings of, 34, 387–88
   recitations, 68, 69
   rituals and, 122, 218
   Rumi and, 22, 24
   as symbol in cultural warfare, 297
   use in art, 363
   western associations with terrorism,
      298

racial profiling, 235–36
racism, 1–2, 125–26, 185–86, 224–26,
   231–34, 369
Radhakrishnan, S., 90, 102–3
radicalization, 49–50, 267–68, 318, 340,
   343, 349

Rajya Sabha, 51
Rakoff, Vivian, 352
Ram, Jagjivan, 146–47
Ramadan
   generosity during, 74
   iftar, 70
   as immigrant, 10
   increased faith activity and, 390
   politics and, 47, 318
   prayers during, 68
   schools and, 315
Raman, C.V., 102–3
Ramanujan, Srinivasa, 102–3, 133
Rankin, Jim, 235–36
Reform Party of Canada, 225, 236–37
Rehman, Nasir, 286, 287
Rennie, Jim, 179
Republican Party, 157
republicanism, 203. *See also* monarchism
Richardson, John, 349
Richardson, John E., 341
Rideau Hall, 152
Rights and Democracy (human rights
   centre), 322–23
Risalo (Bhitai), 208–9
Robbins, John, 132
Robertson, Pat, 298
Rohingyas, 320
Rose, Flemming, 364–65
Des Rosiers, Nathalie, 309
Royal Canadian Mounted Police
   (RCMP), 186–87, 194, 268, 342
Royal Ontario Museum (ROM), 191,
   209, 231–32, 398
Rumi, Jalal al-Din, 22, 23–25, 26–27,
   208. *See also* Islamic scholarship
Rumsfeld, Donald, 282, 284, 290
Runcie, Robert (archbishop of

Index

Canterbury), 374

Rushdie, Salman

American Jewish Congress, honoured
by, 304

analysis of work and intention,
378–79

conflicting views of, 367

depiction of Prophet Muhammad,
360–61

effects of depiction of Muslims, 365

influence as victim-celebrity of Islam,
363–64

marriages and affairs, 376

PEN award attendance, 370

The Satanic Verses, response to,
361–63

The Satanic Verses and the fatwa,
359–60

supporters and detractors, 371–72,
373

Russell, Bertrand, 90

Russia, 244, 253–54

Ryan, Michael, 341

Ryan, Phil, 224, 238

Ryerson. *See* Toronto Metropolitan
University

Sadat, Anwar, 171–72, 296, 363

Saddam, Qusay, 282

Saddam, Uday, 282

Sadr, Abol Hasan Bani, 174

Safdie, Moshe, 4

Said, Edward, 148, 336, 378

Sajjan, Harjit, 190

Salivarová, Zdena, 397

Sallot, Jeff, 342

Samar, Sima, 323

Samuels, Mike, 140

Sara (author's niece), 201

Sarajevo, 374

Sarkozy, Nicolas, 299

The Satanic Verses, 359, 361–63, 364,
367, 373–74, 378–79

Saudi Arabia, 144, 211, 243, 296, 365,
377

Saul, John Ralston, 160, 386–88, *387*

Saunders, Doug, 345

Scheer, Andrew, 333

Schiller, Bill, 192

Schreyer, Ed, 9, 11, 129–30, 137, 138,
139–40, 152

Schreyer, Lily, 152–53

Scotland Yard, 362

Sellar, Don, 199

Serbia, 212, 216–17

Shah Abdul Aziz, 29–30, 31

Shah Abdul Latif Bhitai, 207–8

Shah of Iran, 154, 156–57, 363, 377

Shah Waliuallah, 29, 31, 58

Shankar, Ravi, 395

Sharia law. *See also* Islam, cultural
warfare on; Muslims, cultural
warfare on

anti-Muslim activists, views of,
325–26

connections to western laws, 302–3

disagreements and scholarly
discussion, 36–37

government bans on, 301–2

hijabs, niqabs and, 313

"no-go" zones myth, 346

Sufism and, 50

Western media and, 350

Sharif of Mecca, 36

Shaykh Sabah al Saleh al Sabah, 109–11,
144

Shaykh Zaki Ahmed Yamani, 144
Shephard, Michelle, 342
Shia Muslims, 103
    imams, 155
    massacres of, 282
    mourning, 156
    persecution of, 320
    post-invasion, 280
    refugees, 331
Show Boat (musical), 232
Siddiq, Abu-Bakr, 15, 154
Siddiqui, Haroon
    cartoons of, *xiv*
    cricket pictures, *396*
    family pictures, *54, 201*
    professional pictures, *208, 256, 262, 356*
Siddiqui, Shahina, 326–27
Siddiqui, Yousuf (Shaykh), 47
Siddiquis, history of
    archives, 38
    Deoband and, 42
    early history, 15–18
    fall of British India and divided loyalties, 47
    family business, 61
    flight from Hyderabad, 53–56, 57
    food, 44
    Hyderabad and, 41–42
    recovery from fall of British India, 60–62
    resistance to bribery and wealth, 21–22
    Rumi and, 24–27
    settlement in Hyderabad, 41
    staying in Kandhla, 48–49
    women and, 19–20
Sikand, Yoginder, 49

Sikhs
    British colonialism, ties to, 29
    British India, resistance to, 44
    in Canada, 186–89, 190–91
    Canadian politics and, 333, 383
    clothing, 18
    Golden Temple and Indira Gandhi, 176
    hair, importance of, 388–89
    journalists, 212–13
    massacres of, 54, 176, 246
    RCMP and, 194
    service, 391
    Sikh Centennial Foundation, 255
Simon, Mary, 384
Simpsons department store, 5–6
Sinclair, Gordon, 157–58
Sindh Revisted (Ondaatje), 207, 209
Sing Tao Daily (Hong Kong), 235
Singh, Charan, 145
Singh, Jagmeet, 190
Singh, Manmohan, 246, 271
Singh, Ranjit (Maharaja), 191
al-Sisi, Abdel Fattah, 296
Sistani, Syed Ali (Grand Ayatollah), 281
Škvorecky, Josef, 397
Smith, Wilfred Cantwell, 41, 59
Sobers, Garfield, 8
social conservatism, 131–32
social media, 336, 372, 382
Soliman, Walied, 325–26
Solzhenitsyn, Alexander, 211
Somalia, 194, 367
South Africa, 210, 229, 385
Southams, 180
Soviet Union
    Afghanistan, challenges to occupation, 14

Index

Afghanistan, influence in, 49

Afghanistan, invasion of, 162–69

American rivalry, 100

Chechen War, 211–12

collapse of, 210, 211

India and, 100, 253

Spavor, Michael, 348

Speirs, Rosemary, 177

Spencer, Robert, 299, 353

Spicer, Keith, 219–20

Spivak, Sidney, 137–39

Srebrenica, 365

Stalin, Joseph, 211, 253

Stanfield, Robert, 131, 137, 276

Stead, Sylvia, 348

Stefanoff, Nick, 315

stereotypes. *See* prejudice and stereotypes

Stern, Eliyahu, 301

Steyn, Mark, 303, 345–46, 354

Stoffman, Daniel, 221

Streicher, Julius, 371

Strengthening Canadian Citizenship Act
(2015), 330–31

Strong, Maurice, 147–48

Subramanian, Samanth, 347

Sufi Muslims

accusations of distortion, 50

Baghdad and, 281

birthplace of Sufism, 15

Chisti Order, 30

ilham (celestial guidance), 26

lifestyle, 141

Masnavi, 22, 23

Mevlavi Sufi Order, 22

poetry, 208–9

saints, 24, 50, 72, 91

scholarship and, 16

shrines, 207

Sufi Nakshbandi Order, 24

Suharto (Indonesian dictator), 295

Sultan, Shaukat, 284

Sultan Jahan Begum, 36–37, *37*

Sultana Nilofar Hanim, 40

Sultanate of Delhi, 21

Sunderlal, Pandit, 59

Sunni Muslims, 7, 38, 154, 301, 331

Supreme Court of Canada, 272, 313,
323–24, 328, 330

Switzerland, 313

Syria, 272, 331, 341–42, 397

Tablighi Jamaat, 47

Tagore, Rabindranath, 92, 376

Takhar, Harinder, 388–389

Taliban

Afghanistan, end of western war in,
291–92

Bamiyan Buddhas, 252–53

border crossings, 286

Canadian mission against, 282–84

economic sanctions and, 245

fall of, 280

media portrayals, 337–38

Pakistan and, 284–87

recruitment and madrasahs, 49

treatment of enemies, 282

views of, 292–93

women and, 312

Tamils, 191–92, 193, 194

Tantawi, Mohamed (Shaykh), 313

Taseer, Salman, 320

Tatars, 253–54

Tator, Carol, 225, 227, 232–33

Tayabba. *See* Hussain, Syed Sarwar
(Chote Tayabba)

Taylor, Charles, 186, 225, 300, 304, 305,

309, 330
Taylor, Ken, 161
Teitel, Emma, 311–12
Telegram (Toronto), 8, 180
Tepper, Elliot, 323
Terman, Rochelle, 352–53
terrorism
  Air India Bombing, 186–87, 190
  Al Qaeda sleeper cell, 343
  coverage of, 354–56
  fear of refugees and, 331
  Harper and, 317
  linked to Islam, 317–18
  portrayed in Western media, 339–41
  Sikh, 176
  Sikh massacres, 246
  in Toronto, 343
  victim dichotomies, 338–39
  views of, 243, 258
Thanvi, Ashraf Ali, 33, 34, 38
Thanvi, Ehtisham Haq, 34
Thanvi, Musharraf, 38
Thanvi, Nizam ul-Haq, 34
Thanvi, Sadiqa, 38
Thomson Newspapers, 149, 180, 228
Timson, Ray
  hires author, 11, 151, 152
  Islamic Revolution, coverage of, 153
  praise for author, 176
  Tamil refugee coverage, 192
Tlaib, Rashida, 394
tokenism, 230
Tomb of Humayun, 31, 32
Toronto 18 (group), 330–31, 343,
  344–45
Toronto Board of Rabbis, 321–22
Toronto District School Board, 314–15
Toronto Metropolitan University, 179,

225, 230
Toronto Star
  1982 Constitution, 203–4
  amalgamation, 215–16
  anti-immigration sentiments, 221–22
  Arar, failure to expose media's role in
    issue, 341
  author, early career, 151–53
  Charlie Hebdo cartoons, 366
  Chechen war, 211–12
  columnists, 239–42
  criticisms and, 357
  deadlines and process, 171–72
  editorial board, 199
  editorial page, 276
  editorial page editors, 199
  Honderich era, 178–80
  immigrant issues, coverage of,
    185–86
  influence of, 199
  Islamophobia, commentary on,
    311–12
  letters to the editor, 213–15, 260–62,
    279
  Macdonald Commission report,
    183–84
  monarchy and, 203
  police and Black Canadians, 235–36
  portrayals of Kadr, 342
  post 9/11, 258
  prejudice, efforts against, 181–82
  referendum letters, 205
  Rushdie, free speech, and, 363
  Serbian conflict, 216–17
  Show Boat, support of, 232
  special sections, 234–35
  staff diversity, 212–16
  staffing, 11

Index

strike, 202–3

Tamil refugee coverage, 191–92

Toronto Sun, 234, 258, 354, 397

Torstar, 246, 272

torture, 19, 269–71, 272, 290, 339

Tory, John, 236

Trépanier, Suzanne, 322

Trudeau, Justin

comments on anti-Muslim activities/ language, 298–99

father's eulogy, 251

fears of losing votes, 312

freedom of expression, statements on, 372–73

gender-equal Cabinet, 384

Komagata Maru apology, 190

reaction to Elghawaby's findings, 312

response to PS752, 195–96

St. Louis apology, 194

Trudeau, Margaret, 147, 179

Trudeau, Pierre Elliott. *See also* War Measures Act (1970)

death of, 251–52

election of, 7

family travels, 147

immigrants and, 223

Ismaili refugees, 196

marriage, 179

Meech Lake Accord opposition, 203–4

multiculturalism and, 180, 181

War Measures Act, 139

Trump, Donald, 291–92, 309, 317, 372

Tucker, Emma, 347

Tully, Mark, 168

Turkey, 22, 259, 295, 296, 298

Turner, John, 178

Tutu, Desmond (Bishop), 266–67

Uganda, 193, 196

Uighurs, 320, 348

Ukraine, 193, 211

ulama (Islamic scholars), 15–16

ul-Islam, Zubair (uncle of author), 57

Umair (author's cousin), 116

Umrigar, Polly, 90

United Arab Emirates (UAE), 144, 211, 377, 384

United Church, 126, 129

United Jewish Federation of New York, 313–14

United Kingdom, 277–78, 282, 363, 393–94

United Nations (UN), 58, 212, 216, 245, 331

United Nations Human Rights Committee, 313, 377

United States

9/11, early reactions, 259

Afghanistan, war in, 279–81, 284, 290–92

Al Jazeera and, 368

anti-Muslim attitudes, 242–43, 244–45

bin Laden, assassination of, 290

Checen war, 212

Church and State, failure to separate, 314

democracy, ideals *vs.* reality, 294–96

First Amendment, 373

free speech, views and influence, 324

India and, 99–100, 246–50, 271

influence of, 111

Iran, scapegoating am, 281

Iraq, war and displays of violence, 282

Iraq, war in, 211, 277–78, 291

Islamic Revolution, media and, 154

447

Islamic Revolution and diplomats,
153, 155, 156, 160–62, 172
Islamophobia and, 394
Patriot Act, 270
Sharia law, connections to, 302–3
Soviet rivalry, 100
torture, 269–71
war on terror, death toll, 294
United States Supreme Court, 373, 374
University of South Carolina, 340–41
Uppal, Tim, 333, 383
Urquhart, Ian, 179, 184, 199, 204
Utting, Gerry, 166–67

Vaidyanathan, Indira, 93, 98
Vaidyanathan, T.G. (TGV), 91–93, *92*,
94, 95, 96–98, 102–3
Vajpayee, Atal Bihari, 246
Valad, Baha al-Din, 22
Versi, Miqdaad, 346–47
Vietnam War, 131, 156
Vietnamese Canadians, 233–34
Vincennes (warship), 243

Waldman, Lorne, 330
Waliuallah. *See* Shah Waliuallah
war on terror. *See also* Guantanamo Bay
actual prevention of terrorism, 284
death tolls, 294, 367
democracy and, 292, 294–96
failures of, 289
international resistance, 277–78
Islam, demonization of, 266–68
media and jingoism, 337–38
motivations, 284
Patriot Act, 270
security certificates, 272
torture and, 272, 290

Warangal, 56, 76–77, *78–81*, 82
Warangal Club, 120–21
Ward, Olivia, 212
Warr, John, 89
Washington Post, 338, 340, 347, 352
Weir, Walter, 138
Wente, Margaret, 260
Westell, Tony, 228
Weston, Hilary, *256*
Whinfield, E.H., 26
Whitehead, Lewis D. (Lew)
Brandon Sun, 127–29
defence of journalists, 131, 132
monarchism of, 9
pictures of, *128*
promoting author, 140–41
staff encouragement, 143, 148
tribute to, 149
Wilders, Geert, 237, 321
Wilton, Bill, 131
women
abuse of, 82
attire as political, 312–13
Aurat (poem), 106, 107
begums of Bhopal, 36–40
birth of girls, 20
Clarkson declared honorary man,
384
cultural war on Islam and, 297–99
education and, 33
equal rights, fight for, 32–33
hijabis, attacks on, 350
Islam and, 32, 42, 69–70, 269,
307–8
in media, 229–30
niqab and, 329–31
Pakistani ID cards, 286
Prophet and, 393

Index

religious identity and, 224–26

The Satanic Verses and, 361

scholarship, 16–17

traditional roles and families, 18–19, 20, 44

U.S. propaganda and, 300

violence against, 220

war in Afghanistan and, 293

Woodward, Bob, 338

World Trade Center, 313

writing, post 9/11, 258–63, 275–76, 279, 290–91, 342, 355

Wynne, Kathleen, 236, 384, 388, 389

Yalden, Max, 225–26, 324

Yasmeen (author's wife)

caring for Syeda, 201

death of Maryam, 306

experiences with author, 216, 393

meeting and wedding, 174–75

pictures of, *175, 201, 242*

Yeltsin, Boris, 212

Yerushalmi, David, 302

yogurt, 6, 10, 101, 159, 395

Yoo, John, 271

Yousaf, Humza, 393–94

Yugoslavia, 210, 212

Zafis, Mohamed-Aslim, 311

Zahawi, Nadhim, 393

Zaheeruddin, Mohammed, 48

Zakariyya, Muhammad, 21–22, 47

Zero Tolerance for Barbaric Cultural Practices Act (2014), 331–32

Zia-ul-Huq, Muhammad, 295

Zine, Jasmin, 351–52

Zink, Lubor, 129

Zuckerberg, Mark, 372

About the Author

HAROON SIDDIQUI IS EDITORIAL PAGE EDITOR emeritus of the *Toronto Star*, Canada's largest newspaper, and a senior fellow at Massey College, University of Toronto. He has covered or supervised news coverage of Canada for 48 years through nine prime ministers, and also reported from 50 nations. He lives in Toronto.

In 2001, he received the Order of Canada, the nation's highest civilian honour, for being "an advocate for fairness and equality of opportunity, for challenging stereotypical thinking about minorities ... and promoting a broader role for Canada in the global village."

He was awarded the Order of Ontario in 2000 for helping to create a "broader definition of the Canadian identity."

York University granted him an honorary doctor of letters for continuing in the tradition of Canadian author Bruce Hutchison, who in his 1944 book *The Unknown Country* "described this country and its people as few Canadians knew it. Mr. Siddiqui is giving voice and substance to what we sense around us yet need to know far more immediately. His work helps in the creation and sustaining of a contemporary Canada in which individuals can truly recognize and speak to each other across their differences of religion, race and culture.... He is an exemplary citizen."

The National Press Club's UNESCO Award was given to him in 2002 for "working against the dangers of group think. He challenged the orthodoxy that the only proper response to the 9/11 tragedy was silence and no questioning of American foreign policy, and no probing of the root causes of anti-Americanism around the world."

In 2013, he received the Canadian Civil Liberties Association Award "for explaining and re-explaining diversity and equality, for denouncing racism and stupidity, for challenging Islamophobia, for doing so wittingly and irreverently, and with unshattered confidence and hope in democracy."

He has received three citations of the National Newspaper Award, and in 2023, the Lifetime Achievement Award from the Canadian Journalism Foundation "in recognition of his decades-long ground-breaking career in Canadian journalism and his commitment to diversity, journalistic integrity, and social justice; championing free speech balanced with freedom from hate; and confronting racism, anti-Semitism, and Islamophobia."

Siddiqui started at the Press Trust of India news agency in Mumbai (1963–65); worked at the *Brandon Sun* in Manitoba as reporter, city editor, and managing editor (1968–78); at the *Toronto Star* as copy editor, news editor, national editor, editorial page editor, and columnist (1978–2015); and as distinguished visiting professor at Toronto Metropolitan University (2016–18).